STM32 Arm Programming for Embedded Systems

Using C Language with STM32F4 Arm

Muhammad Ali Mazidi

Shujen Chen

Eshragh Ghaemi

Copyright © 2014-2018 Mazidi and Naimi

Visit our website for tutorials, source codes, PowerPoints, and other support materials.

https://www.NicerLand.com

ISBN-13: 978-1-970054-15-6

ISBN-10: 1-970054-15-8

"Regard man as a mine rich in gems of inestimable value. Education can, alone, cause it to reveal its treasures, and enable mankind to benefit therefrom."

Baha'u'llah

Dedication

To the faculty, staff, and students of BIHE university for their dedication and steadfastness.

Preface

Since the early 2000s, hundreds of companies have licensed the Arm CPU and the number of licensees is growing very rapidly. While the licensee must follow the Arm CPU architecture and instruction set, they are free to implement peripherals such as I/O ports, ADCs, Timers, DACs, SPIs, I2Cs and UARTs as they please. In other words, while one can write an Assembly language program for the Arm chip, and it will run on any Arm chip, a program written for the I/O ports of an Arm chip for company *A* will not run on an Arm chip from company *B*. This is due to the fact that special function registers and their physical address locations to access the I/O ports are not standardized and every licensee implements it differently. We have dedicated the first volume in this series to the Arm Assembly language programming and architecture since the Assembly language is standard and runs on any Arm chip regardless of who makes them. Our Arm Assembly book is called *"Arm Cortex-M Assembly Programming for Embedded Programmers"* and is available from Amazon. See the following link:

https://www.NicerLand.com/

For the peripheral programming of the Arm, we had no choice but to dedicate a separate volume to each vendor. This volume covers the peripheral programming of the STM32 Arm chip. Throughout the book, we use C language to access the special function registers and program the STM32F4xx peripherals. We have provided an Assembly language programs for I/O ports in Chapter 2 for those who want to experiment with Assembly language in accessing the I/O ports and their special function registers. The Assembly language programs also help to see the contrast between the C and Assembly versions of the same program in Arm.

Two approaches in programming the Arm chips

When you program an Arm chip, you have two choices:

1. Use the functions written by the vendor to access the peripherals. The vast majority of the vendors/companies making the Arm chip provide a proprietary device library of functions allowing access to their peripherals. These device library functions are copyrighted and cannot be used with another vendor's Arm chip. For students and developers, the problem with this approach is you have no control over the functions and it is very hard to customize them for your project.

2. The second approach is to access the peripheral's special function registers directly using C language and create your own custom library since you have total control over each function. Much of these functions can be modified and used with another vendor if you decide to change the Arm chip vendor. In this book, we have taken the second approach since our primary goal is to teach how to program the peripherals of an Arm chip. We know this approach is difficult and tedious, but the rewards are great.

Compilers and IDE Tools

For programming the Arm chip, you can use any of the widely available compilers from Keil (www.keil.com), IAR (www.IAR.COM) or any other one. For this book, we have used the Keil Arm compiler IDE to write and test the programs. See our web site for the tutorials.

STM (STMicroelectronics) Arm Trainer

The STM has many inexpensive trainers for the Arm STM32F4xx series. Among them is STM32F446 Nucleo board. Although we used the STM32F446 board to test the programs, the programs can run on other STM32F4xx chips with small or no modifications.

Chapters Overview

In Chapter 1, we examine the C language data types for 32-bit systems. We also explore the new ISO C99 data types since they are widely used in IDE compilers for the embedded systems.

Chapter 2 examines the simple I/O port programming and shows sample programs on how to access the special function registers associated with the general purpose I/O (GPIO) ports.

Chapter 3 shows the interfacing of the Arm chip with the real-world devices: LCD and keypad. It provides sample programs for the devices.

In Chapter 4, the interfacing and programming of serial UART ports are examined.

Chapter 5 is dedicated to the timers in Arm. It also shows how to use timers as an event counter.

The Interrupt programming of the Arm is discussed in Chapter 6.

Chapter 7 examines the ADC and DAC concepts and shows how to program them with the Arm chip. It also examines the sensor interfacing and signal conditioning.

Chapter 8 covers the SPI protocol and interfacing with sample programs in Arm.

The I2C bus protocol and interfacing of an I2C based RTC is discussed in Chapter 9.

Chapter 10 explores the relay and stepper motor interfacing with Arm.

The DC motor and PWM are examined in Chapter 11.

The Graphics LCD concepts and programming are discussed in Chapter 12.

Chapter 13 examines the concept of DMA and shows how to program it.

- Appendix A provides an introduction to IC chip technology and IC interfacing along with the system design issues and failure analysis using MTBF. See our website for this appendix.
- Appendix B provides a single source for STM32F446 microcontroller alternate pin functions.
- The CPU clock source is examined in Appendix C.

Online support for this book

All the programs in this book and other support materials such as PowerPoints and tutorials are available on our website:

https://www.NicerLand.com/

Many of the interfacing programs such as LCD can be tested using the STM32 Arm Nucleo or Discovery boards connected to an LCD on a breadboard. However, many courses use a system approach to the embedded course by using an interface trainer. For this reason, we have modified the programs for the EduPad interface trainer using STM32F446 Nucleo board. See the following for the sample programs:

http://www.MicroDigitalEd.com/Arm/STM_Arm_books.html

Where to buy STM32 Arm Evaluation kit?

See our web site for STM32 evaluation kits and datasheet.

Contact us

Please contact the authors if use this book for a university course.

mdebooks@yahoo.com

Arm Trademarks

"From 1 August 2017, Arm has a new look and feel. The business has a new corporate logo and it is now using the Arm word in sentence case instead of the ARM word in uppercase in text. We ask all of Arm's customers, partners, licensees and any other third parties to use the Arm word in sentence case in text in all relevant materials. The only exception to this rule will be when using the ARM word in any circumstances, where all of the surrounding words also appear in uppercase, e.g. headings."

https://www.arm.com/company/policies/trademarks

Table of Content

Chapter 1: C for Embedded Systems

In reading this book we assume you already have some understanding of how to program in C language. In this chapter, we will examine some important concepts widely used in embedded system design that you may not be familiar with due to the fact that many generic C programming books do not cover them. In section 1.1, we examine the C data types for 32-bit systems. The bit-wise operators are covered in section 1.2.

Section 1.1: C Data types for Embedded Systems

In general C programming textbooks, we see *char*, *short*, *int*, *long*, *float*, and *double* data types. We need to examine the size of C data types in the light of 32-bit processors such as Arm. The C standards do not specify the size of data types. The compiler designers are free to decide the size for each data type. The *float* and *double* data types are standardized by the IEEE754 and covered in Volume 1 of this book series and are often followed by all the compilers. The sizes of char and short are often set at 1 byte and 2 bytes. The size of int is often depending on the data size of the CPU but rarely go below 16 or above 32. The sizes of long and long long are implemented the same way everywhere.

If you think this is confusing, there are three methods that may help you to find out the exact sizes of the data types.

1. Read the manuals of the compiler. Because the data sizes are not standardized, the compile user's manuals usually specify them.

2. Use pseudo function sizeof(). C compilers supports a pseudo function sizeof(), which returns the size of the parameter in the number of byte(s). The parameter may be a data type or a variable. For example, sizeof(int) returns the number of bytes in an int variable.

3. Use C99 data types. Realized the confusion of lack of standard for data size, the C standard committee developed a new set of well-defined data type with standard sizes. We will cover them later in this chapter.

For now, we will discuss the data types defined by Keil MDK-Arm first.

char

The *char* data type is a byte size data whose bits are designated as D7-D0. It can be *signed* or *unsigned*. In the signed format the D7 bit is used for the + or - sign and takes values between -128 to +127. In the *unsigned char* we have values between 0x00 to 0xFF in hex or 0 to 255 in decimal since there is no sign and the entire 8 bits are used for the magnitude. (See Chapter 5 of Volume 1.)

short int

The *short int* (or usually referring as *short*) data type is a 2-byte size data whose bits are designated as D15-D0. It can be *signed* or *unsigned*. In the signed format, the D15 bit is used for the + or - sign and takes values between -32,768 to +32,767. In the *unsigned short int* we have values between 0x0000 to

0xFFFF in hex or 0 to 65,535 in decimal since there is no sign and the entire 16 bits are used for the magnitude. See Chapter 5 of Volume 1 (the Arm assembly book).

A 32-bit processor such as the Arm architecture with 32-bit data bus reads the memory with a minimum of 32 bits on the 4-byte boundary (address ending in 0, 4, 8, and C in hex). If a short int variable is allocated straddling the 4-byte boundary, access to that variable is called an *unaligned access*. Not all the Arm processors support unaligned access. Those devices (including the MSP432 used in the MSP432 LaunchPad) supporting unaligned access pay a performance penalty by having to read/write the memory twice to gain access to one variable (see Example 1-1). Unaligned access can be avoided by either padding the variables with unused bytes (Keil) or rearranging the sequence of the variables (CCS) in allocation. The compilers usually generate aligned variable allocation.

Example 1-1

Show how memory is assigned to the following variables in aligned and unaligned allocation. Begin from memory location 0x20000000.
unsigned char a;
unsigned short int b;
unsigned short int c;

Solution:
Unaligned allocation of variable c

a	b	b	c
20000000	20000001	20000002	20000003
c			
20000004			
	20000005	20000006	20000007

Aligned allocation of variables by padding one byte between variable a and b

a		b	b
20000000	20000001	20000002	20000003
c	c		
20000004	20000005		

Aligned allocation of variables by rearranging the variable sequence

b	b	c	c
20000000	20000001	20000002	20000003
a			
20000004	20000005	20000006	20000007

---

int

The *int* data type usually represents for the native data size of the processor. For example, it is a 2-byte size data for a 16-bit processor and a 4-byte size data for a 32-bit processor. This may cause confusion and portability issue. The C99 standard addressed the issue by creating a new set of integer variable types that will be discussed later. For now, we will stick to the conventional data types.

The *int* data type of the Arm processors is 4-byte size and identical to *long int* data type described below.

long int

The long int (or *long*) data type is a 4-byte size data whose bits are designated as D31-D0. It can be signed or unsigned. In the signed format the D31 bit is used for the + or - sign and takes values between -2^{31} to $+2^{31}-1$. In the unsigned long we have values between 0x00000000 to 0xFFFFFFFF in hex. See Chapter 5 of Volume 1. In the 32-bit microcontroller when we declare a long variable, the compiler sets aside 4 bytes of storage in SRAM. But it also makes sure they are aligned, meaning it places the data in locations with addresses ending with 0, 4, 8 and C in hex. This avoids unaligned data access performance penalty covered in Volume 1. The unsigned long is widely used in Arm for defining addresses since Arm address size is 32-bit long.

Example 1-2

Show how memory is assigned to the following variables in aligned and unaligned allocation. Begin from memory location 0x20000000.

unsigned char a;
unsigned short int b;
unsigned short int c;
unsigned int d;

Solution:

Unaligned allocation of variable c

a	b	b	c
20000000	20000001	20000002	20000003
c	**d**	**d**	**d**
20000004	20000005	20000006	20000007
d			
20000008	20000009	2000000A	2000000B

Aligned allocation of variables by padding byte(s) between variable a and b

a		b	b
20000000	20000001	20000002	20000003
c	**c**		
20000004	20000005	20000006	20000007
d	**d**	**d**	**d**
20000008	20000009	2000000A	2000000B

Aligned allocation of variables by rearranging the variable sequence

d	d	d	d
20000000	20000001	20000002	20000003
b	**b**	**c**	**c**
20000004	20000005	20000006	20000007
a			
20000008	20000009	2000000A	2000000B

long long

The *long long* data type is an 8-byte size data whose bits are designated as D63-D0. It can be signed or unsigned. In the signed format the D63 bit is used for the + or - sign and takes values between -2^{63} to $+2^{63}-1$. In the *unsigned long long* we have values between 0x0000000000000000 to 0xFFFFFFFFFFFFFFFF in hex. In the 32-bit microcontroller, when we declare a long long variable, the compiler sets aside 8 bytes of storage in SRAM and it makes sure they are aligned, meaning it places the data in locations with addresses ending with 0 and 8. This avoids unaligned data access performance penalty.

Why should I care about which data type to use?

There are three major reasons why a programmer should care about data type, performance, overflow, and coercion.

Performance

It must be noted that while in the 8-bit microcontrollers we need to use the proper data type for the variables to improve the performance, this is less of problem in 32-bit CPUs such as Arm. For example, for the number of days working in a month (or number of hours in a day) we use unsigned char since it is less than 255. Using unsigned char in 8-bit microcontroller is important since it saves RAM space, memory access time, and computation clock cycles. If we use int instead, the compiler allocates 2 bytes in RAM and that is a waste of RAM resource. The CPU will have to access the additional byte and perform additional arithmetic instructions with it even if the byte contains zero and has no effect on the result. This is a problem that we should avoid since an 8-bit microcontroller usually has few RAM bytes with slower clock speed for bus and CPU. In the case of 32-bit systems such as Arm, 1, 2, or 4 bytes of data will result in the same memory access time and computation time. Most of the 32-bit systems also have more generous amount of RAM to alleviate the concern of memory usage and allow padding for aligned access.

Data type	Size	Range
char	1 byte	-128 to 127
unsigned char	1 byte	0 to 255
short int	2 bytes	-32,768 to 32,767
unsigned short int	2 bytes	0 to 65,535
int	4 bytes	-2,147,483,648 to 2,147,483,647
unsigned int	4 bytes	0 to 4,294,967,295
long	4 bytes	-2,147,483,648 to 2,147,483,647
unsigned long	4 bytes	0 to 4,294,967,295
long long	8 bytes	-9,223,372,036,854,775,808 to 9,223,372,036,854,775,807
unsigned long long	8 bytes	0 to 18,446,744,073,709,551,615

Table 1-1: ANSI C (ISO C89) integer data types and their ranges

Notes

1. By default variables are considered as *signed* unless the *unsigned* keyword is used. As a result, *signed long* is the same as *long*; the *long long* is the same as *signed long long*, and so on with the exception of *char*. Whether *char* is signed or unsigned by default varies from compiler to compiler. In some compilers, including Keil, there is an option to choose if the char variable should be considered as *signed char* or *unsigned char* by default. (To choose this in Keil, go to *Project* menu and select *Options*. Then, in the *C/C++* tab, check or uncheck the choice *Plain char is signed*, as you desire.) It is a good practice to write out the *signed* keyword explicitly, when you want to define a variable as *signed char*.

2. In some compilers (including Keil and IAR) the *int* type is considered as long int while in some other compilers (including AVR and PIC compilers) it is considered as *short int*. In other words, the *int* type is commonly defined so that the processor can handle it easily. As we will see next, we can use int16_t and int32_t instead of short and long in order to prevent any kind of ambiguity and make the code portable between different processors and compilers.

Overflow

Unlike assembly language programming, high level program languages do not provide indications when an overflow occurs and the program just fails silently. For example, if you use a short int to hold the number of seconds of a day, 9 hours 6 minutes and 7 seconds into the day, the second count will overflow from 32,767 to -32,768. Even if your program handles negative second count, the time will jump back to the day before.

With 32-bit int in a 32-bit Arm processor, overflow is a much less frequent problem because a 32-bit int will hold a number up to 2,147,483,647 but it does not eliminate the potential of the problem. One of the critical overflow problem waiting to happen is the Unix Millennium Bug. Unix keeps track of time using a 32-bit int for the number of seconds since January 1st 1970. This variable is going to overflow comes January 19, 2038. Because of the popularity of Unix, not only Unix systems are extensively used, many other systems use the same or similar format to keep track of time. So far, there is no universal solution to mitigate this problem yet.

Coercion

In C language, the data types of the operands must be identical for binary operations (the operator with two operands such as A + B). If you write a statement with different operand data types for a binary operation, the compiler will convert the smaller data type to the bigger data type. If it is an assignment operator (A = B), the right hand side operand is converted to the left hand side data type before the assignment. These implicit data type conversion is called *coercion*. The compiler may or may not give you warning when coercion occurs.

In two conditions, coercion may result in undesirable result. If the variable is signed and the data sized is increased, the new bits are filled with the sign bit (most significant bit) of the original value. For example, if an 8-bit number 0b10010010 is coerced into a 16-bit signed number, the result will be 0b1111111110010010. This may work just fine in most cases, but there are few occasions that will became an issue.

The other problem is when you assign a larger data type to a smaller data type variable, the higher order bits will be truncated. For example, in the statement "A = B;" if A is 8-bit and B is 16-bit, the upper 8 bits of B is discarded before the assignment.

There is not a simple solution for the data type size issues. As a programmer, you have to be cognizant about them all the time.

Data types in ISO C99 standard

While every C programmer has used ANSI C (ISO C89) data types, many C programmers are not familiar with the ISO C99 standard. In C standards, the sizes of integer data types were not defined and are up to the compilers to decide.

In ISO C99 standard, a set of data types were defined with number of bits and sign clearly defined in the data type names. See Table 1-2. The C99 standard is used extensively by embedded system programmer for RTOS (real time operating system) and system design. It is also supported by most of C compilers. Notice the range is the same as ANSI C standard except it uses explicitly descriptive syntax.

These integer data types are defined in a header file called *stdint.h*. You need to include this header file in order to use these data types.

Data type	Size	Range
int8_t	1 byte	-128 to 127
uint8_t	1 byte	0 to 255
int16_t	2 bytes	-32,768 to 32,767
uint16_t	2 bytes	0 to 65,535
int32_t	4 bytes	-2,147,483,648 to 2,147,483,647
uint32_t	4 bytes	0 to 4,294,967,295
int64_t	8 bytes	-9,223,372,036,854,775,808 to 9,223,372,036,854,775,807
uint64_t	8 bytes	0 to 18,446,744,073,709,551,615

Table 1-2: ISO C99 integer data types and their ranges

Review Questions

1. In an 8-bit system we use (char, unsigned char) for the number of months in a year.
2. For a system with 16-bit address, bus we use (int, unsigned int) for address definition.
3. For an Arm system the address is _____bit wide and we use _____data type for it.
4. True or false. In C programming of Arm, compiler makes sure data are aligned.

Section 1.2: Bit-wise Operations in C

One of the most important and powerful features of the C language is its ability to perform bit manipulations. Because many books on C do not cover this important topic, it is appropriate to discuss it in this section. This section describes the action of bit-wise logic operators and provides some examples of how they are used.

Bit-wise operators in C

While every C programmer is familiar with the logical operators AND (&&), OR (||), and NOT (!), many C programmers are less familiar with the bitwise operators AND (&), OR (|), EX-OR (^), invert (~), right shift (>>), and left shift (<<). These bit-wise operators are widely used in software engineering for embedded systems and control; consequently, their understanding and mastery are critical in microprocessor-based system design and interfacing. See Table 1-3.

A	B	AND (A & B)	OR (A | B)	EX-OR (A ^ B)	Invert ~B
0	0	0	0	0	1
0	1	0	1	1	0
1	0	0	1	1	1
1	1	1	1	0	0

Table 1-3: Bit-wise Logic Operators for C

The following shows some examples using the C bit-wise operators:

```
0x35 & 0x0F results in 0x05      /* ANDing */
0x04 | 0x68 results in 0x6C      /* ORing:  */
0x54 ^ 0x78 results in 0x2C      /* XORing */
~0x55 results in 0xAA            /* Inverting 0x55 */
```

Examples 1-3 and 1-4 show how the bit-wise operators are used in C. Run the following programs on your simulator and examine the results.

Example 1-3

Run the following program on your simulator and examine the results.
```
int main(void) {
    volatile unsigned char temp;   /* declare volatile otherwise the optimizer will remove it. */
    temp = 0x35 & 0x0F;      /* ANDing    : 0x35 & 0x0F = 0x05 */
    temp = 0x04 | 0x68;      /* ORing     : 0x04 | 0x68 = 0x6C */
```

```
    temp = 0x54 ^ 0x78;      /* XORing    : 0x54 ^ 0x78 = 0x2C */
    temp = ~0x55;            /* Inverting : ~0x55 = 0xAA */
    while (1);
    return 0;
}
```

Setting and Clearing (masking) bits

As discussed in Volume 1 of the series, OR can be used to set a bit or bits, and AND can be used to clear a bit or bits. If you examine Table 1-3 closely, you will see that:

- Anything ORed with a 1 results in a 1; anything ORed with a 0 results in no change.

- Anything ANDed with a 1 results in no change; anything ANDed with a 0 results in a zero.

- Anything EX-ORed with a 1 results in the complement; anything EX-ORed with a 0 results in no change.

See Example 1-4.

Example 1-4

The following program toggles only bit 4 of var1 repetitively without disturbing the rest of the bits.

```
int main(void)
{
    unsigned char var1;
    while(1)
    {
        var1 = var1 | 0x10;      /* Set bit 4 (5th bit) of var1 */
        var1 = var1 & 0xEF;      /* Clear bit 4 (5th bit) of var1 */
    }
}
```

Notice that we can also toggle the bit using EX-OR as shown below:
```
var1 = var1 ^ 0x10;
```

Testing bit with bit-wise operators in C

In many cases of system programming and hardware interfacing, it is necessary to test a given bit to see if it is high or low. For example, many devices send a high signal to signify that they are ready for an action or to indicate that they have data available. How can the bit (or bits) be tested? In such cases the unused bits are masked and then the remaining data is tested. See Example 1-5.

Example 1-5

Write a C program to monitor bit 5 of var1. If it is HIGH, change value of var2 to 0x55; otherwise, change value of var2 to 0xAA.

Solution:

```
...
  while(1)
  {
    if (var1 & 0x20)      /* check bit 5 (6th bit) of var1 */
       var2 = 0x55;       /* this statement is executed if bit 5 is a 1 */
    else
       var2 = 0xAA;       /* this statement is executed if bit 5 is a 0 */
  }
...
```

Bit-wise shift operation in C

There are two bit-wise shift operators in C. See Table 1-4.

Operation	Symbol	Format of Shift Operation
Shift Right	>>	data >> number of bit-positions to be shifted right
Shift Left	<<	data << number of bit-positions to be shifted left

Table 1-4: Bit-wise Shift Operators for C

The following shows some examples of shift operators in C:

1. 0b00010000 >> 3   /* it equals 00000010. Shifting right 3 times */
2. 0b00010000 << 3   /* it equals 10000000. Shifting left 3 times */
3. 1 << 3   /* it equals 00001000. Shifting left 3 times */

Compound Operators

In C language, whenever the left-hand-side of the assignment operator (=) and the first operand on the right-hand-side are identical we can avoid repeating the operand by using the compound operators. As shown in Table 1-5, in compound operators, one of the operands is written just on the left-hand-side of the equal sign.

Instruction	Its equivalent using compound operators
a = a + 6;	a += 6;
a = a − 23;	a −= 23;
y = y * z;	y *= z;
z = z / 25;	z /= 25;
w = w	0x20;	w |= 0x20;
v = v & mask;	v &= mask;
m = m ^ togBits;	m ^= togBits;

Table 1-5: Some Compound Operator Examples

Review Questions

1. What is result of 0x2F & 0x27?
2. What is result of 0x2F | 0x27?
3. What is result of 0x2F ^ 0x27?
4. What is result of 0x2F >> 3?
5. What is result of 0x27 << 4?
6. In Example 1-5 what is stored in var2 if the value of var1 is 0x03?

Bit-wise operations using compound operators

The majority of hardware access level code involves setting a bit or bits in a register, clearing a bit or bits in a register, toggling a bit or bits in a register, and monitoring the status bits. For the first three cases, the operations read the content of the register, modify a bit of bits then write it back to the same register. The compound operators are very suitable for these operations.

To set bit(s) in a register,

register |= MASK;
where MASK is a number that has '1' at the bit(s) to be set.

register |= 0x08;
The number 0x08 has a '1' at bit 3, therefore the statement sets bit 3 of the register.

register |= 0x42;
The number 0x42 has a '1' at bit 6 and bit 1, therefore the statement sets bit 6 and bit 1 of the register.

To clear bit(s) in a register,

register &= ~MASK;
where MASK is a number that has '1' at the bit(s) to be cleared.

register &= ~0x20;
The number 0x20 has a '1' at bit 5, therefore the statement clears bit 5 of the register.

register &= ~0x12;
The number 0x12 has a '1' at bit 4 and bit 1, therefore the statement clears bit 4 and bit 1 of the register. Notice the mask for clearing the bits is the same as the mask for setting the bits, where the bits to be modified are '1' and the rest of the bits are '0' except that in clearing the bits, the mask is complemented in the statements.

To toggle bit(s) in a register,

register ^= MASK;
The examples are similar to setting bits so we will skip them here.

Using shift operator to generate mask

With the statements above, one challenge may be to generate the mask with the correct bit(s) set to 1 depending on how proficient you are with converting binary numbers to hexadecimal. Some compilers allow you to write a literal binary number in the format of 0b00000000 but since it is not in the C standards, many compilers do not accept this notation.

One way to ease the generation of the mask is to use the left shift operator. To generate a mask with bit n set to 1, use the expression:

1 << n

If more bits are to be set in the mask, they can be "or" together. To generate a mask with bit n and bit m set to 1, use the expression:

(1 << n) | (1 << m)

Now to set bit 3 of the register, we can rewrite the statement

register |= 0x08;

as

register |= 1 << 3;

And to set bit 6 and bit 1 of the register, we can rewrite the statement

register |= 0x42;

as

register |= (1 << 6) | (1 << 1);

The same goes for clearing bit 5 of the register, we can use the statement

register &= ~(1 << 5);

And to clear bit 4 and bit 1 of the register

register &= ~((1 << 4) | (1 << 1));

Notice that regardless of setting or clearing bits, the mask always has 1s at the bit locations for the bits to be modified and when multiple bits are used in the mask, they are always ORed together. We will leave the toggling of the bits for the readers.

Setting the value in a multi-bit field

Some of the bits in a register form a field with meaningful values. For example, if register bits 30-28 determine the divisor value to divide the clock and we would like to set the divisor to 5. One way of doing so is to set or clear the bits one by one.

register |= 1 << 30;
register &= ~(1 << 29);
register |= 1 << 28;

Although this method will achieve the desired result, the divisor value 5 is not apparent from reading the code. An alternative way is to clear the field first then set the value.

```
register &= ~(7 << 28);
register |= 5 << 28;
```

The first statement clears bit 30-28 and the second statement set the value 5 in the field. With this method, the divisor 5 is visible in the second statement.

These two statements may be combined into a single statement:

```
register = (register & ~(7 << 28)) | (5 << 28);
```

Reading of the articles by Michael Barr on embedded.com is strongly recommended:

http://www.embedded.com/user/Michael.Barr

Answer to Review Questions

Section 1.1: C Data types for Embedded Systems

1. unsigned char
2. unsigned int
3. 32 – unsigned long (or uint32_t)
4. True

Section 1.2: Bitwise Operations in C

1. 0x27
2. 0x2F
3. 0x08
4. 0x05
5. 0x70
6. 0xAA

Chapter 2: STM Arm I/O Programming

In a microcontroller, we use the general-purpose input output (GPIO) pins to interface with LED, switch (SW), LCD, keypad, and so on. This chapter covers the programming of GPIO using LED, switches, and seven segment LEDs as examples. This is a very important chapter since the vast majority of embedded products have some kind of I/O. More importantly, this chapter sets the stage for the understanding of peripheral I/O addresses and how they are accessed and used in Arm processors. Because some of the core materials covered in this chapter are used in subsequent chapters, we urge you to study this chapter thoroughly before moving on to other chapters. Section 2.1 examines the memory and I/O map of the STMicroelectronics (from now on STM) Arm chip. Section 2.2 shows how to access the special function registers associated with the GPIO of STM Arm. In Section 2.2, we also use simple LEDs and switches to show the programming of GPIO. Section 2.3 examines the 7-segment LED connection to Arm and how to program it. Section 2.4 shows how to program I/O ports of the STM Arm chip in Assembly language.

Section 2.1: STM32 Microcontroller

The STM32 is MCUs built on Arm® Cortex™M processor core. The STM32 microcontrollers can cover Arm® Cortex™ M0, M0+, M3, M4 and M7 cores. They can have few K bytes to few M bytes of on-chip Flash memory for code. Their on-chip SRAM can vary depending on the chip. They all have a large number of on-chip peripherals. See Figure 2-1. In this book, we focus on STM32F446 chips. The STM32F4xx is based on Cortex-M4 while STM32F0 uses Cortex-M0+. We use STM32 Nucleo trainer board which uses STM32F446RE chip to test the programs in this book. This board is Arduino Nano Compatible. See Figures 2-1 to 2-6.

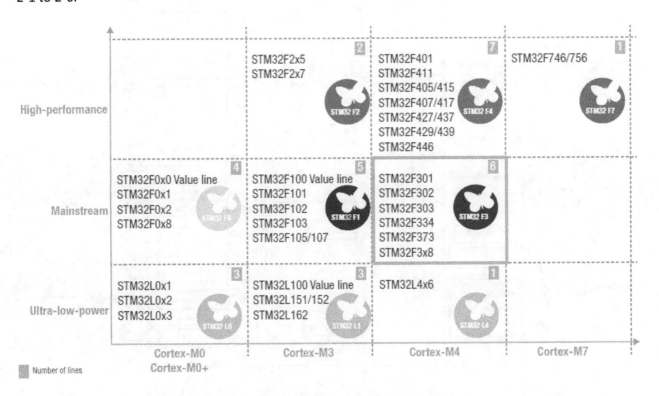

Figure 2 – 1: STM32 Arm Cortex Portfolio

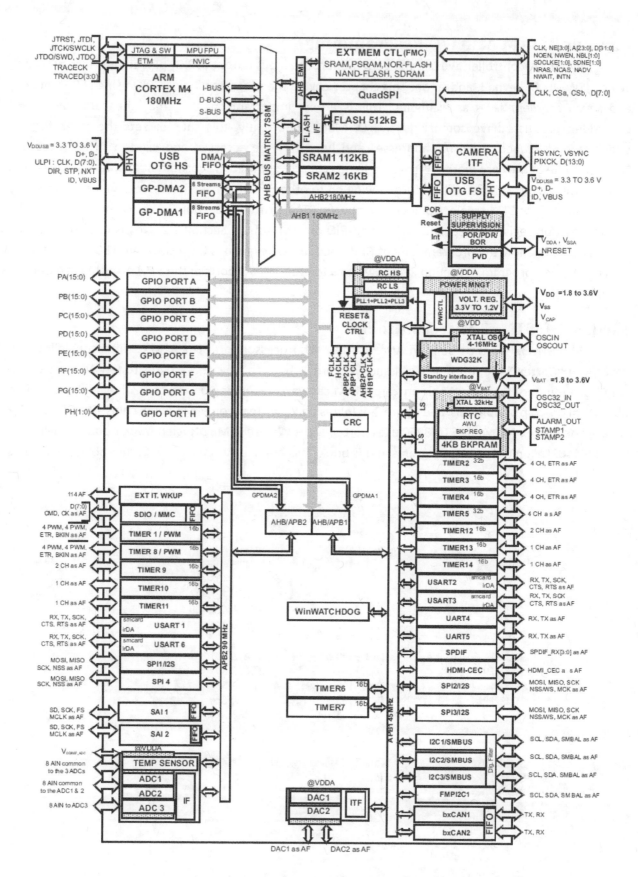

Figure 2 - 2: STM32F446RE Arm Microcontroller Block Diagram

24

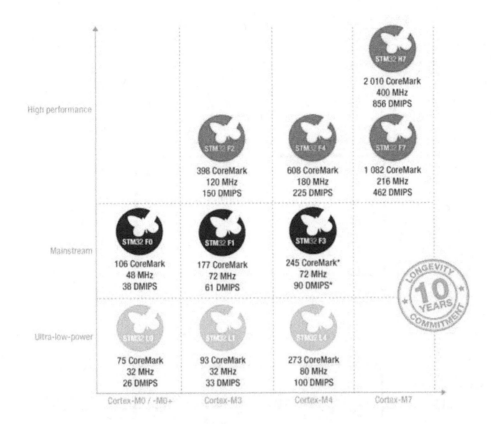

Figure 2 – 3: STM32 Arm Cortex Portfolio

Figure 2 - 4: STM32F446RE Nucleo Board

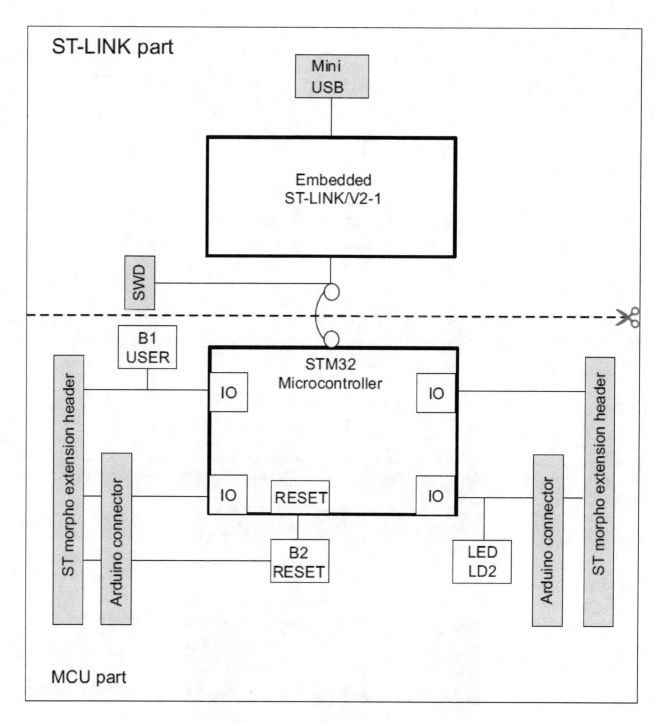

Figure 2 - 5: STM32F446RE Nucleo Block Diagram

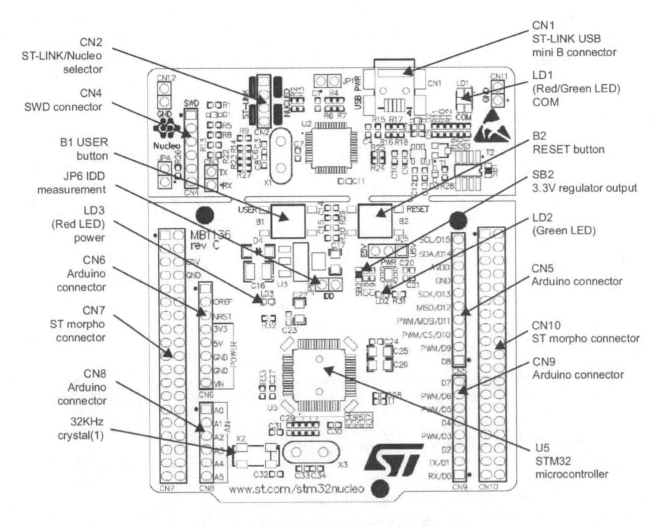

CN2
ST-LINK/Nucleo
selector

CN4
SWD connector

B1 USER
button

JP6 IDD
measurement

LD3
(Red LED)
power

CN6
Arduino
connector

CN7
ST morpho
connector

CN8
Arduino
connector

32KHz
crystal(1)

CN1
ST-LINK USB
mini B connector

LD1
(Red/Green LED)
COM

B2
RESET button

SB2
3.3V regulator output

LD2
(Green LED)

CN5
Arduino connector

CN10
ST morpho connector

CN9
Arduino connector

U5
STM32
microcontroller

Figure 2 - 6: STM32F446RE Nucleo board top layout

Note

For more information about the STM32 series see the following websites:

http://www.st.com/content/st_com/en/products/microcontrollers/stm32-32-bit-Arm-cortex-mcus.html?querycriteria=productId=SC1169

http://www.st.com

The tutorials for Keil using STM32 Nucleo and other trainer boards can be found on our website:

http://www.microdigitaled.com/ARM/STM_ARM_books.html

The above site also has source code programs used in this book in addition to PowerPoints

STM32F4xx Memory Map

As we stated in Volume 1, the Arm has 4GB (Giga bytes) of memory address space. It also uses memory mapped I/O, meaning the I/O peripheral registers are mapped into the 4GB memory space. See Table 2-1 for memory map of STM32F446 chip. It must be noted that the upper limit address varies among the chips depending on the size of on-chip Flash, SRAM, and peripherals. Check the memory map of your STM Arm in device datasheet.

	Memory sizes	Address range
Flash	512KB	0x00000000-0x0007FFFF
SRAM	128KB	0x20000000-0x20001FFFF
I/O	All the peripherals	0x40000000-0x4xxxxxxx

Table 2-1: Memory Map of STMF446RE

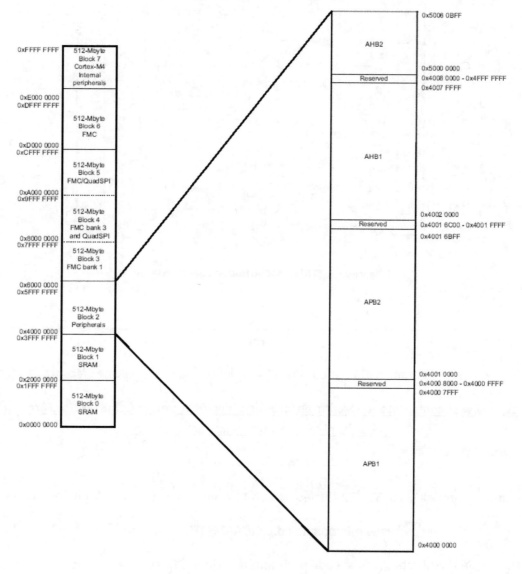

Figure 2 - 7: Memory map for STM32F446RE

Regarding of Figure 2 - 7, the following points must be noted:

1) The Flash memory is used for program code. One can also store in Flash ROM constant (fixed) data such as look-up table if needed. The Flash memory is organized in n-byte paged. Each block can be independently erased and written to. Various Arm chips have different block page size depending on the on-chip Flash size.

2) The SRAM is for variables, scratch pad, and stack. It starts at address 0x20000000. Address aliases can be used for a portion of SRAM to allow individual bit-access. This is called *bit-banding* and is discussed in Volume 1.

3) The peripherals such as GPIO, Timers, ADCs are mapped to addresses starting at 0x40000000. The upper limit address can vary among the family members of Arm chips depending on the number of peripherals the chip supports.

STM32's naming convention

STM32 part numbers have the following format:

STM32 F 4xx P FFF T 6

Table 2-2 lists the possible values for each field in the part number (not all combinations are valid):

Field	Description	Some Valid Values
STM32	Product Family	Arm® based 32-bit microcontroller
F	Product Type	
4xx L4	Device subfamily	407: STM32F4xx , 446: STM32F4xx, L4: STM32L4xx, and so on.
P	Pin count	K = 32 pins R = 64 pins J = 72 pins M = 81 pins O = 90 pins V = 100 pins Q = 132 pins Z = 144 pins
FFF	Flash Memory size	B = 128 KB C = 256 KB E = 512 KB G = 1 MB
T	Packaging	LQFP
6		temperature

Table 2 - 2: STM32 Arm Naming

For example, STM32F446_Nucleo board uses the STM32F446RE chip. From Table 2-2 we see that the chip has 64 pins and comes with 512KB of on-chip Flash memory.

In Figure 2-8, the STM Arm Families and their features are shown.

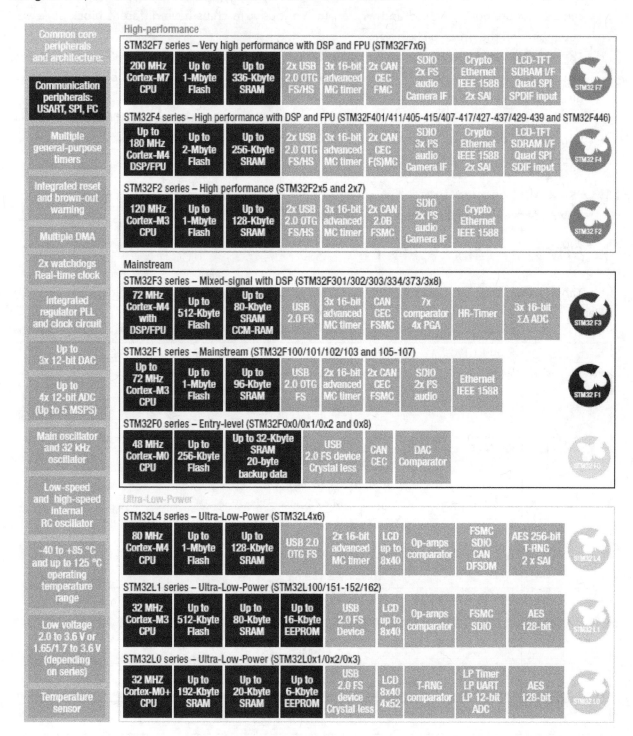

Figure 2 - 8: STM32 Cortex-M Portfolio

Review Questions

1. STM32F446RE has _____KB of on-chip Flash memory.
2. STM32F446RE has _____KB of on-chip SRAM memory.
3. The Flash memory is used mainly for (program code, data).
4. The SRAM memory is used for (program code, data).
5. Give the starting address of the Flash memory of STM32F446RE.
6. Give the meaning of RE in STM32F446RE.

Section 2.2: GPIO (General Purpose I/O) Programming and Interfacing

While memory holds code and data for the CPU to process, the I/O ports are used by the CPU to access input and output devices. In the microcontroller, we have two types of I/O. They are:

a. **General Purpose I/O (GPIO):** The GPIO ports are used for interfacing devices such as LEDs, switches, LCD, keypad, and so on.
b. **Special purpose I/O:** These I/O ports have designated function such as ADC (Analog-to-Digital), Timer, UART (universal asynchronous receiver transmitter), and so on.

We have dedicated many chapters to these special purpose I/O ports. In this chapter, we examine the GPIO and its interfacing to LEDs, switches, and 7-segment LEDs and show how to access them with C programs.

I/O Pins on Nucleo board

In STM Arm chips, general purpose I/O ports are named with alphabets A, B, C, D, E, F, G, and H. Each port can have up to 16 pins and they are designated as PA0-PA15, PB0-PB15, and so on. It must be noted that not all 16 pins of each port are implemented in every chip. The Arm chip used in STM Nucleo-F446RE board is from the STM32F446 chip series. See Figures 2-9 and 2-10.

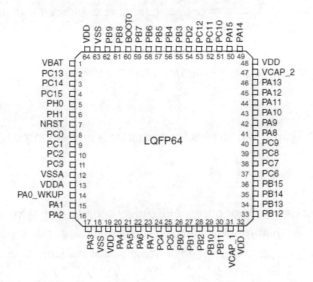

Figure 2 – 9: STM32F4xx LQFP 64 pinout used in Nucleo-F446RE board

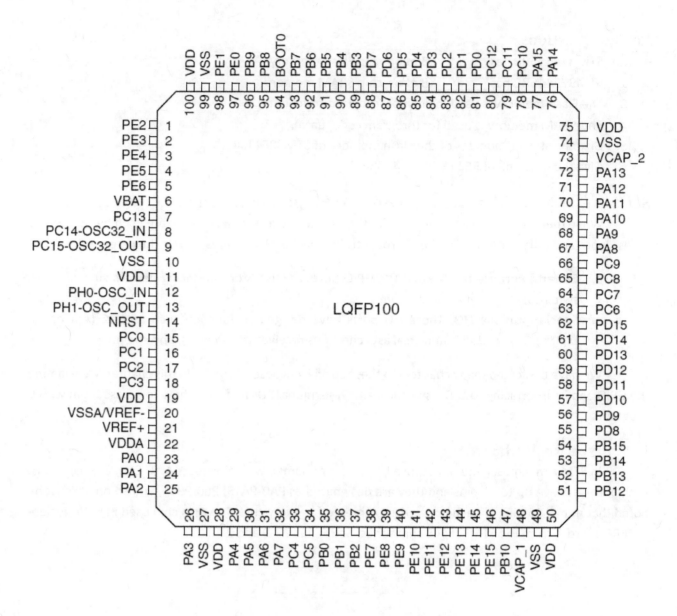

Figure 2 – 10: STM32F4xx LQFP 100 pinout

Notice from about figures, not all pins for each port is implemented. For example, only two pins of Port H are implemented.

GPIO Registers Address

The Arm chips have two types of buses: APB (Advanced Peripheral Bus) and AHB (Advanced High-Performance Bus). The AHB is a high-performance bus designed to interface memory and fast I/Os directly to the CPU. The APB is designed for lower speed and low power consumption memory and peripherals.

Bus	Boundary address	Peripheral
AHB1	0x4002 2000 - 0x4002 23FF	GPIOI
	0x4002 1C00 - 0x4002 1FFF	GPIOH
	0x4002 1800 - 0x4002 1BFF	GPIOG
	0x4002 1400 - 0x4002 17FF	GPIOF
	0x4002 1000 - 0x4002 13FF	GPIOE
	0x4002 0C00 - 0x4002 0FFF	GPIOD
	0x4002 0800 - 0x4002 0BFF	GPIOC
	0x4002 0400 - 0x4002 07FF	GPIOB
	0x4002 0000 - 0x4002 03FF	GPIOA
	0x4001 5800 - 0x4001 FFFF	Reserved
APB2	0x4001 4C00 - 0x4001 57FF	Reserved
	0x4001 4800 - 0x4001 4BFF	TIM11
	0x4001 4400 - 0x4001 47FF	TIM10
	0x4001 4000 - 0x4001 43FF	TIM9
	0x4001 3C00 - 0x4001 3FFF	EXTI
	0x4001 3800 - 0x4001 3BFF	SYSCFG
	0x4001 3400 - 0x4001 37FF	Reserved
	0x4001 3000 - 0x4001 33FF	SPI1
	0x4001 2C00 - 0x4001 2FFF	SDIO
	0x4001 2400 - 0x4001 2BFF	Reserved
	0x4001 2000 - 0x4001 23FF	ADC1 - ADC2 - ADC3
	0x4001 1800 - 0x4001 1FFF	Reserved
	0x4001 1400 - 0x4001 17FF	USART6
	0x4001 1000 - 0x4001 13FF	USART1
	0x4001 0800 - 0x4001 0FFF	Reserved
	0x4001 0400 - 0x4001 07FF	TIM8
	0x4001 0000 - 0x4001 03FF	TIM1
	0x4000 7800 - 0x4000 FFFF	Reserved

Bus	Boundary address	Peripheral
APB1	0x4000 7800 - 0x4000 7FFF	Reserved
	0x4000 7400 - 0x4000 77FF	DAC
	0x4000 7000 - 0x4000 73FF	PWR
	0x4000 6C00 - 0x4000 6FFF	Reserved
	0x4000 6800 - 0x4000 6BFF	CAN2
	0x4000 6400 - 0x4000 67FF	CAN1
	0x4000 6000 - 0x4000 63FF	Reserved
	0x4000 5C00 - 0x4000 5FFF	I2C3
	0x4000 5800 - 0x4000 5BFF	I2C2
	0x4000 5400 - 0x4000 57FF	I2C1
	0x4000 5000 - 0x4000 53FF	UART5
	0x4000 4C00 - 0x4000 4FFF	UART4
	0x4000 4800 - 0x4000 4BFF	USART3
	0x4000 4400 - 0x4000 47FF	USART2
	0x4000 4000 - 0x4000 43FF	I2S3ext
	0x4000 3C00 - 0x4000 3FFF	SPI3 / I2S3
	0x4000 3800 - 0x4000 3BFF	SPI2 / I2S2
	0x4000 3400 - 0x4000 37FF	I2S2ext
	0x4000 3000 - 0x4000 33FF	IWDG
	0x4000 2C00 - 0x4000 2FFF	WWDG
	0x4000 2800 - 0x4000 2BFF	RTC & BKP Registers
	0x4000 2400 - 0x4000 27FF	Reserved
	0x4000 2000 - 0x4000 23FF	TIM14
	0x4000 1C00 - 0x4000 1FFF	TIM13
	0x4000 1800 - 0x4000 1BFF	TIM12
	0x4000 1400 - 0x4000 17FF	TIM7
	0x4000 1000 - 0x4000 13FF	TIM6
	0x4000 0C00 - 0x4000 0FFF	TIM5
	0x4000 0800 - 0x4000 0BFF	TIM4
	0x4000 0400 - 0x4000 07FF	TIM3
	0x4000 0000 - 0x4000 03FF	TIM2

Table 2 - 3: Partial listing of Peripheral address map for STM32F446

The AHB bus is much faster than APB. The AHB allows one clock cycle access to the memory and fast peripherals without any wait state. The APB is slower and its access time is a minimum of 2 clock cycles. In many cases, there are multiple AHB-APB bridges to connect AHB to the APB busses. Each APB bus connects to certain peripherals and each peripheral is allocated certain address space. In the STM32 Arm, the GPIO ports are connected to AHB bus via AHB/APB1 and AHP/APB2 bridges. The AHB and memories are connected to CPU via what is called Bus Matrix. See Figures 2-11 and 2-2.

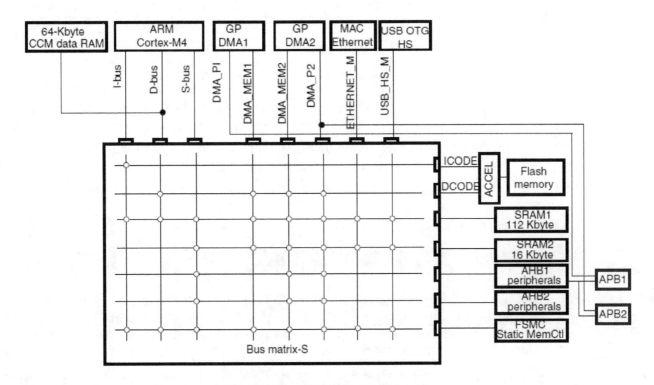

Figure 2-11: STM Arm Bus Matrix

Each peripheral such as GPIO, Timer, and ADC are assigned a set of addresses. The first address is called the base address. Each peripheral has multiple special function registers. Each register has an address. The register address is an offset address from the base address, as we will see soon. The following shows the address ranges assigned to Ports of STM32F4xx chip.

- GPIO Port A: 0x4002 0000 - 0x4002 03FF
- GPIO Port B: 0x4002 0400 - 0x4002 07FF
- GPIO Port C: 0x4002 0800 - 0x4002 0BFF
- GPIO Port D: 0x4002 0C00 - 0x4002 0FFF
- GPIO Port E: 0x4002 1000 - 0x4002 13FF
- GPIO Port F: 0x4002 1400 - 0x4002 17FF
- GPIO Port G: 0x4002 1800 - 0x4002 1BFF
- GPIO Port H: 0x4002 1C00 - 0x4002 1FFF
- GPIO Port I: 0x4002 2000 - 0x4002 23FF

Table 2 - 4 shows some of the registers associated with each GPIO ports.

Address (Offset)	Name	Description	Type
0x00	GPIOx_MODER	GPIOx Port Mode(Direction) Register	R/W
0x04	GPIOx_OTYPER	Output Type Register	R/W
0x08	GPIOx_OSPEEDR	Output Speed Register	R/W
0x0C	GPIOx_PUDR	Pull-Up / Down Register	R/W
0x10	GPIOx_IDR	Port Input Data Register	R/W
0x14	GPIOx_ODR	Port Output Data Register	R/W
0x18	GPIOx_BSRR	Bit Set / Reset Register	R/W
Where x=A, B, C, ... for ports			

Table 2 – 4: Some of the GPIO Registers in STM32F4xx Arm

Generally, every microcontroller has a minimum of two registers associated with each of I/O port. They are *Data Register* and *Direction Register*. The Direction register is used to make the pin either input or output. After the Direction register is properly configured, then we use the Data register to actually write to the pin or read data from the pin. It is the Direction register (when configured as an output) that allows the information written to the Data register to be driven to the pins of the device. See Figure 2-12.

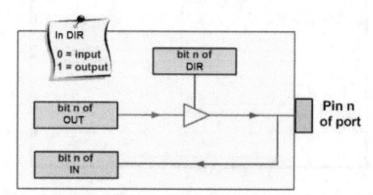

Figure 2 - 12: The Data and Direction Registers and a Simplified View of an I/O pin

Port Output Register

The output register in STM Arm is called GPIO port output data register (GPIOx_ODR) in which x can be A, B, C and so on depending on the number of ports implemented in a given chip. They are located at the offset address of 0x14 from the Base address of that port. This is shown below.

31	30	29	28	27	26	25	24	23	22	21	20	19	18	17	16
Res.	Res.	Res.	Res.	Res.	Res.	Res.	Res.	Res.	Res.	Res.	Res.	Res.	Res.	Res.	Res.

15	14	13	12	11	10	9	8	7	6	5	4	3	2	1	0
ODR15	ODR14	ODR13	ODR12	ODR11	ODR10	ODR9	ODR8	ODR7	ODR6	ODR5	ODR4	ODR3	ODR2	ODR1	ODR0
rw	rw	rw	rw	rw	rw	rw	rw	rw	rw	rw	rw	rw	rw	rw	rw

Bits 31:16 Reserved, must be kept at reset value.

Bits 15:0 **ODRy**: Port output data (y = 0..15)

These bits can be read and written by software.

Figure 2 - 13: GPIOx_ODR Output Data Register (x=A, B,C, ..)

36

Direction Register

In STM Arm the direction register is part of the GPIOx_MODER which stands for GPIO Mode Register. For each GPIO pin, there are two corresponding bits in the MODER register. These two bits need to be a 00 to configure the port pin as input and a 01 as output. This register is also used to set the alternative function mode for each pin, in addition to deciding if it is used for analog or digital I/O.

31	30	29	28	27	26	25	24	23	22	21	20	19	18	17	16
MODER15[1:0]		MODER14[1:0]		MODER13[1:0]		MODER12[1:0]		MODER11[1:0]		MODER10[1:0]		MODER9[1:0]		MODER8[1:0]	
rw	rw	rw	rw	rw	rw	rw	rw	rw	rw	rw	rw	rw	rw	rw	rw
15	14	13	12	11	10	9	8	7	6	5	4	3	2	1	0
MODER7[1:0]		MODER6[1:0]		MODER5[1:0]		MODER4[1:0]		MODER3[1:0]		MODER2[1:0]		MODER1[1:0]		MODER0[1:0]	
rw	rw	rw	rw	rw	rw	rw	rw	rw	rw	rw	rw	rw	rw	rw	rw

Bits 2y:2y+1 **MODERy[1:0]:** Port x configuration bits (y = 0..15)

These bits are written by software to configure the I/O direction mode.

00: Input (reset state)
01: General purpose output mode
10: Alternate function mode
11: Analog mode (reset state)

Figure 2 - 14: GPIOx_MODER (GPIO Mode) for Direction Register (x=A, B, C, …)

For example, by writing 0x05 (0000 0101 in binary) into the GPIOA_MODER register, pins 0 and 1 of PORT A become outputs while the other pins become inputs.

See Example 2-1.

Example 2-1

In a gives circuit board, an LED is connected to PA5. Find the value we need to write to the direction register.

Solution:

Since LEDs is an output, we need to write 0x0400 to the Mode register. Notice the pins are designated as PA15-PA0. The binary and hex numbers are as follow:
0000 0100 0000 0000 = 0x0400.

The Clock Enable of the Peripheral Registers

Before accessing the peripheral registers, we need to examine the clock enable registers. Most of the digital electronic circuits these days are built with CMOS technology because at quiescent state, a CMOS circuit consumes almost no power at all. To conserve power, Arm microcontrollers have ways of either slowing down the peripheral circuit clock or stopping the clock altogether.

By default, the GPIO modules of the STM32 Arm microcontrollers have the clock disabled coming out of power-on reset. So the programmers have to enable the clock to a given I/O port or peripheral before using it. This is done with a group of registers belonging to RCC (Reset and Clock Control) registers. For the STM32F446 chips, the GPIO clock enable is controlled by lower bits of RCC_AHB1ENR (AHB1 Enable Register) register as seen in Figure 2 - 15. Notice this is not standard across all STM Arm family members.

31	30	29	28	27	26	25	24	23	22	21	20	19	18	17	16
Res	OTGHS ULPIEN	OTGHS EN	Res	Res	Res	Res	Res	Res	DMA2 EN	DMA1 EN	Res	Res	BKP SRAMEN	Res	Res
	rw	rw							rw	rw			rw		

15	14	13	12	11	10	9	8	7	6	5	4	3	2	1	0
Res	Res	Res	CRC EN	Res	Res	Res	Res	GPIOH EN	GPIOG EN	GPIOF EN	GPIOE EN	GPIOD EN	GPIOC EN	GPIOB EN	GPIOA EN
			rw					rw	rw	rw	rw	rw	rw	rw	rw

Bit 7 **GPIOHEN:** IO port H clock enable
This bit is set and cleared by software.
0: IO port H clock disabled
1: IO port H clock enabled

Bit 6 **GPIOGEN:** IO port G clock enable
This bit is set and cleared by software.
0: IO port G clock disabled
1: IO port G clock enabled

Bit 5 **GPIOFEN:** IO port F clock enable
This bit is set and cleared by software.
0: IO port F clock disabled
1: IO port F clock enabled

Bit 4 **GPIOEEN:** IO port E clock enable
This bit is set and cleared by software.
0: IO port E clock disabled
1: IO port E clock enabled

Bit 3 **GPIODEN:** IO port D clock enable
This bit is set and cleared by software.
0: IO port D clock disabled
1: IO port D clock enabled

Bit 2 **GPIOCEN:** IO port C clock enable
This bit is set and cleared by software.
0: IO port C clock disabled
1: IO port C clock enabled

Bit 1 **GPIOBEN:** IO port B clock enable
This bit is set and cleared by software.
0: IO port B clock disabled
1: IO port B clock enabled

Bit 0 **GPIOAEN:** IO port A clock enable
This bit is set and cleared by software.
0: IO port A clock disabled
1: IO port A clock enabled

Figure 2 - 15: RCC_AHB1ENR register bits to enable clock to I/O ports

It must be noted that the clocks for the serial communication modules, timers and other peripheral are not enabled upon reset. There are several registers belonging to RCC_AHBxENR group of registers such as RCC_AHB1ENR and RCC_AHB2ENR depending on which family of STM32 you are using. There are also RCC_APBxENR group of registers used to enable the clock to various peripherals. They have slower speed than the RCC_AHBx option. We will discuss the configuration of their clocks in their respective chapters.

LED connection in Nucleo boards

Many of the STM32 Nucleo and Discovery trainer boards have a single or multiple user LEDs. By user LED we mean the LED connected to GPIO pins and can be programmed directly. In an STM32F4 Nucleo board, the user LED is active HIGH meaning when the I/O is HIGH value, the LED is on and when the I/O is LOW, the LED is off. There are other LEDs on the board such as serial link and Power LEDs. Check your trainer board user manual. In STM32F446RE Nucleo board, there is a single user LED. It is designated as LD2. The user LED is connected to PA5 pin of Port A, as shown in Figure 2-16. Again, this is not consistent across all the STM boards. You need to check the user manual and schematic for your board. On STM Arm boards, there are other LEDs such as COM which provides information about ST-LINK communication status. The PWR LED indicates that the STM32 part is powered and power is available.

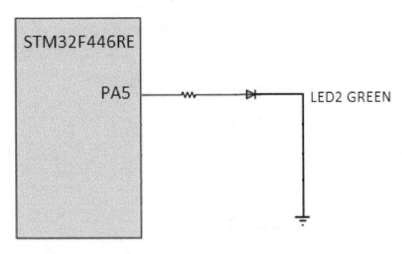

Figure 2 - 16: User LED connection for STM32F446RE Nucleo board

Toggling LED in Software

To toggle the user LD2 (green) of the Nucleo board, the following steps must be followed.

1) Set the Mode register bits for PA5 as output,
2) write HIGH to PA5 in data OUT register,
3) call a delay function,
4) write LOW to PA5 in data OUT register,
5) call a delay function,
6) repeat steps 2 to 5.

Program 2-1 implements the algorithm to toggle the LED continuously. The device header file for STM32F446 in Keil MDK-Arm v5 is "stm32F446xx.h". But if you include "stm32F4xx.h", it will select the header file to match the device of choice for the project. The one-millisecond delay was achieved by using 16MHz default frequency for SYSCLK. See Appendix C for more on STM32 clock frequency.

Program 2-1: Toggling an LED in C

```
/* p2_1.c Toggle Green LED (LD2) on STM32F446RE Nucleo64 board at 1 Hz
 *
 * This program toggles LD2 for 0.5 second ON and 0.5 second OFF
 * by writing 0 or 1 to bit 5 of the Port A Output Data Register.
 * The green LED (LD2) is connected to PA5.
 * The LED is high active (a '1' turns on the LED).
```

```
 * The default system clock is running at 16 MHz.
 *
 * This program was tested with Keil uVision v5.24a with DFP v2.11.0
 */

#include "stm32f4xx.h"

void delayMs(int n);

int main(void) {
    RCC->AHB1ENR |= 1;              /* enable GPIOA clock */

    GPIOA->MODER &= ~0x00000C00;    /* clear pin mode */
    GPIOA->MODER |=  0x00000400;    /* set pin to output mode */

    while(1) {
        GPIOA->ODR |=  0x00000020;  /* turn on LED */
        delayMs(500);
        GPIOA->ODR &= ~0x00000020;  /* turn off LED */
        delayMs(500);
    }
}

/* 16 MHz SYSCLK */
void delayMs(int n) {
    int i;
    for (; n > 0; n--)
        for (i = 0; i < 3195; i++) ;
}
```

The Register Naming Convention

Keil MDK-Arm uses the syntax to define registers to be compliant with CMSIS (Cortex Microcontrollers Software Interface Standard). In this syntax, each port is defined as a pointer to a struct with the register as the members of struct. For example, the GPIO Port D MODE Register is referred to as GPIOD->MODER and the Out Data Register for Port D is referred to as GPIOD->ODR. There are several ways of declaring a name in C for a register. We will discuss more in details in Section 2.4. Another reason we use the naming convention above is that they are supplied by the device manufacturer. The program starts with a statement of `#include "stm32F4xx.h"`, which in term includes the appropriate header files based on the device used for the project (stm32f446xx.h). The file that contains the definitions of the port registers for Keil MDK-Arm is at:

C:\Keil\Arm\PACK\Keil\STM32F4xx_DFP\2.11.0\Drivers\CMSIS\Device\ST\STM32F4xx\Include\

Bit Set/Reset Register

In the program above, the register bits are modified using "|=" operator to set the bit and "&=" to clear the bit. These read-modify-write (RMW) operations, meaning the value of the port register is read into the CPU register, the selected bit is set or cleared then the value is written back to the port register. There are few potential issues with an RMW operation. One is that it takes three steps to change the selected bit(s). In a multithreaded environment, there is a chance that one RMW operation is interrupted by the other. After the first operation is completed, the second write will wipe out the modification done by the first one.

The STM32 Family GPIO ports have an additional register that make turning a pin (or more) on and off easier. This register allows the program to set or reset a bit or bits of the register by a single write instruction. See the GPIOx_BSRR (GPIO bit set/reset register). Writing to the register only affects the pin(s) that the corresponding bit(s) in the value written is (are) '1'. This makes it easier to turn on or off a single pin or a few pins without affecting the other pins. The lower 16 bits (D15-D0) of GPIOx_BSRR register turns on (set) a bit and the upper 16 bits (D31-D16) turns off (reset) a bit. For example, writing a value 0x00000020 to GPIOA_BSRR will turn on bit PA5 of that port without modifying any other pins. These registers make the program more readable, faster to run and since a write to these registers are a single instruction execution and will not to be interrupted. See Figure 2 - 17.

31	30	29	28	27	26	25	24	23	22	21	20	19	18	17	16
BR15	BR14	BR13	BR12	BR11	BR10	BR9	BR8	BR7	BR6	BR5	BR4	BR3	BR2	BR1	BR0
w	w	w	w	w	w	w	w	w	w	w	w	w	w	w	w

15	14	13	12	11	10	9	8	7	6	5	4	3	2	1	0
BS15	BS14	BS13	BS12	BS11	BS10	BS9	BS8	BS7	BS6	BS5	BS4	BS3	BS2	BS1	BS0
w	w	w	w	w	w	w	w	w	w	w	w	w	w	w	w

Bits 31:16 **BRy:** Port x reset bit y (y = 0..15)

These bits are write-only. A read to these bits returns the value 0x0000.

0: No action on the corresponding ODRx bit

1: Resets the corresponding ODRx bit

Note: If both BSx and BRx are set, BSx has priority.

Bits 15:0 **BSy:** Port x set bit y (y= 0..15)

These bits are write-only. A read to these bits returns the value 0x0000.

0: No action on the corresponding ODRx bit

1: Sets the corresponding ODRx bit

Figure 2 - 17: GPIOx_BSRR (GPIO Bit Set Reset) Register

Program 2-2 performs the same function as Program 2-1 but uses the GPIOx_BSRR register to control Mode register and toggle the green LED (LD2).

Program 2-2: Toggling an LED using the alternative registers

```
/* p2_2.c Toggle Green LED (LD2) on STM32F446RE Nucleo64 board at 1 Hz
 *
 * This program toggles LD2 for 0.5 second ON and 0.5 second OFF
 * by writing a '1' to bit 5 or bit 21 of the Bit Set/Reset
 * Register (BSRR). The lower 16 bits of BSRR turns on the pins
 * and the upper 16 bits of BSRR turns off the pins.
 * Writing a '1' to bit 5 turns on pin 5. Writing a '1' to
 * bit 21 (5 + 16) turns off pin 5.
 * The green LED (LD2) is connected to PA5.
 * The LED is high active (a '1' turns on the LED).
 * The default system clock is running at 16 MHz.
 *
```

```
 * This program was tested with Keil uVision v5.24a with DFP v2.11.0
 */

#include "stm32f4xx.h"

void delayMs(int n);

int main(void) {
    RCC->AHB1ENR |=  1;                /* enable GPIOA clock */

    GPIOA->MODER &= ~0x00000C00;       /* clear pin mode */
    GPIOA->MODER |=  0x00000400;       /* set pin to output mode */

    while(1) {
        GPIOA->BSRR = 0x00000020;      /* turn on LED */
        delayMs(500);
        GPIOA->BSRR = 0x00200000;      /* turn off LED */
        delayMs(500);
    }
}

/* 16 MHz SYSCLK */
void delayMs(int n) {
    int i;
    for (; n > 0; n--)
        for (i = 0; i < 3195; i++) ;
}
```

CPU clock frequency and time delay

Many microcontrollers have at least three clock sources that may be used to drive the CPU.

1) The on-chip oscillator circuit. This is the least precise clock source for the CPU. But it does not require additional external devices and is always available regardless of the circuit design of the system.

2) The externally connected crystal (XTAL) oscillator. It offers the most precise clock but at high frequency, such as above 100MHz, crystals are expensive. Also, the frequency is fixed by the crystal.

3) PLL (phase locked loop). A compromise between precision, flexibility, and economy is to use a crystal oscillator along with the on-chip PLL circuitry to generate a high-frequency clock source for the CPU. This option is often used for systems with CPU frequency of 20MHz and higher. Another added benefit of using the PLL is that the clock frequency is programmable. You may run high clock frequency for CPU intensive tasks and slow down the clock at other times to conserve energy.

For more about the clock generation see Appendix C.

Measuring time delay in a C program loop

One simple way of creating a time delay is using a "for loop" in C language. The length of time delay loop for a given system is a function of two factors: the CPU frequency and the compiler. It must be noted that a time delay C loop measured using a given compiler (e.g. Keil) may not give the same result if a different compiler such as IAR is used. Another factor that complicates the delay time is the use of cache, which is available on an STM32F446 device.

Regardless of clock source to CPU and the C compiler used, always use an oscilloscope to measure the duration of the time delay loop for a given system with a given compiler and compiler option setting.

Input Data

Reading the GPIOx_IDR (GPIO input data) register will return the status of the port pins. If the pin is high, it returns a '1' and if the pin is low, it returns a '0'. See Figure 2-18.

31	30	29	28	27	26	25	24	23	22	21	20	19	18	17	16
Res	Res	Res	Res	Res	Res	Res	Res	Res	Res	Res	Res	Res	Res	Res	Res

15	14	13	12	11	10	9	8	7	6	5	4	3	2	1	0
IDR15	IDR14	IDR13	IDR12	IDR11	IDR10	IDR9	IDR8	IDR7	IDR6	IDR5	IDR4	IDR3	IDR2	IDR1	IDR0
r	r	r	r	r	r	r	r	r	r	r	r	r	r	r	r

Bits 31:16 Reserved, must be kept at reset value.

Bits 15:0 **IDRy**: Port input data (y = 0..15)

These bits are read-only and can be accessed in word mode only. They contain the input value of the corresponding I/O port.

Figure 2 - 18: GPIOx_IDR (Input Data) Register

Reading a switch in STM Arm

The NUCLEO-F446RE board comes with a single user push-button switch (B1). This switch is connected to PC13 pin of the Port C in STM32F446 chip. See Figure 2-19. Notice that there is also a reset switch called B2. The B2 push-button is connected to NRST, and it is used to reset the STM32F466RE chip.

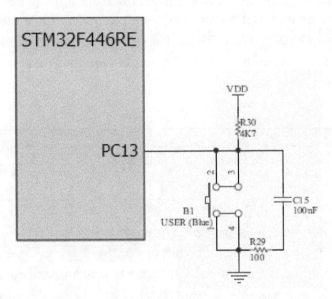

Figure 2 - 19: Switch connection to STM32F4-NUCLEO board

You can also connect an external switch to the board and experiment with the concept of inputting data via a port. Depending on how the external switch is connected, you need to enable the internal pull-up or pull-down resistor for the pin. If the switch is connected to the ground, the internal pull-up resistor is enabled. If the switch is connected to the power, the internal pull-down resistor is enabled (See Figure 2 - 20).

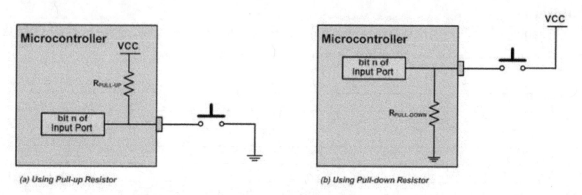

(a) Using Pull-up Resistor   *(b) Using Pull-down Resistor*

Figure 2 - 20: Connecting external switches to the microcontroller

---

Note

Each of the GPIO ports has four 32-bit memory-mapped control registers (GPIOx_MODER, GPIOx_OTYPER, GPIOx_OSPEEDR, GPIOx_PUPDR) to configure up to 16 I/Os. The GPIOx_MODER register is used to select the I/O mode (input, output, AF, analog). The GPIOx_OTYPER and GPIOx_OSPEEDR registers are used to select the output type (push-pull or open-drain) and speed. The GPIOx_PUPDR register is used to select the pull-up/pull-down whatever the I/O direction.

It was mentioned earlier that the MODE register is used to change the data direction of the corresponding pin. In addition to the MODE register, there are three more registers associated with the GPIO function. They are GPIOx_OTYPER (GPIO Output Type Register), GPIOx_OSPEEDR (GPIO Output Speed Register), and GPIOx_PUPDR (GPIO Pull-up/Pull-down Register). The GPIOx_OTYPER and GPIOx_OSPEEDR registers are used to select the output type (push-pull or open-drain) and speed. The GPIOx_PUPDR register is used to select the pull-up/pull-down whatever the I/O direction. See Figures 2-21, 2-22, and 2-23.

31	30	29	28	27	26	25	24	23	22	21	20	19	18	17	16
Res.	Res.	Res.	Res.	Res.	Res.	Res.	Res.	Res.	Res.	Res.	Res.	Res.	Res.	Res.	Res.

15	14	13	12	11	10	9	8	7	6	5	4	3	2	1	0
OT15	OT14	OT13	OT12	OT11	OT10	OT9	OT8	OT7	OT6	OT5	OT4	OT3	OT2	OT1	OT0
rw	rw	rw	rw	rw	rw	rw	rw	rw	rw	rw	rw	rw	rw	rw	rw

Bits 31:16 Reserved, must be kept at reset value.

Bits 15:0 **OTy**: Port x configuration bits (y = 0..15)

These bits are written by software to configure the output type of the I/O port.

0: Output push-pull (reset state)

1: Output open-drain

Figure 2 - 21: GPIOx_OTYPER Register

31	30	29	28	27	26	25	24	23	22	21	20	19	18	17	16
OSPEEDR15 [1:0]		OSPEEDR14 [1:0]		OSPEEDR13 [1:0]		OSPEEDR12 [1:0]		OSPEEDR11 [1:0]		OSPEEDR10 [1:0]		OSPEEDR9 [1:0]		OSPEEDR8 [1:0]	
rw	rw	rw	rw	rw	rw	rw	rw	rw	rw	rw	rw	rw	rw	rw	rw
15	14	13	12	11	10	9	8	7	6	5	4	3	2	1	0
OSPEEDR7 [1:0]		OSPEEDR6 [1:0]		OSPEEDR5 [1:0]		OSPEEDR4 [1:0]		OSPEEDR3[1:0]		OSPEEDR2 [1:0]		OSPEEDR1 [1:0]		OSPEEDR0 1:0]	
rw	rw	rw	rw	rw	rw	rw	rw	rw	rw	rw	rw	rw	rw	rw	rw

Bits 2y:2y+1 **OSPEEDRy[1:0]:** Port x configuration bits (y = 0..15)

These bits are written by software to configure the I/O output speed.

00: Low speed

01: Medium speed

10: Fast speed

11: High speed

Figure 2 - 22: GPIOx_OSPEEDR Register

31	30	29	28	27	26	25	24	23	22	21	20	19	18	17	16
PUPDR15[1:0]		PUPDR14[1:0]		PUPDR13[1:0]		PUPDR12[1:0]		PUPDR11[1:0]		PUPDR10[1:0]		PUPDR9[1:0]		PUPDR8[1:0]	
rw	rw	rw	rw	rw	rw	rw	rw	rw	rw	rw	rw	rw	rw	rw	rw
15	14	13	12	11	10	9	8	7	6	5	4	3	2	1	0
PUPDR7[1:0]		PUPDR6[1:0]		PUPDR5[1:0]		PUPDR4[1:0]		PUPDR3[1:0]		PUPDR2[1:0]		PUPDR1[1:0]		PUPDR0[1:0]	
rw	rw	rw	rw	rw	rw	rw	rw	rw	rw	rw	rw	rw	rw	rw	rw

Bits 2y:2y+1 **PUPDRy[1:0]:** Port x configuration bits (y = 0..15)

These bits are written by software to configure the I/O pull-up or pull-down

00: No pull-up, pull-down

01: Pull-up

10: Pull-down

11: Reserved

Figure 2 - 23: GPIOx_PUPDR Register

Example 2-4

Write the statements to configure Port A0 as an input pin with pull-up resistor.

Solution:

GPIOA->MODER &= ~0x00000003;   /* clear pin mode bits to input mode for PA0 */

GPIOA->PUPDR &= ~0x00000003;   /* clear pull-up/pull-down bits for PA0 */

GPIOA->PUPDR |= 0x00000001;   /* set pull-up for PA0 */

To read a switch and display it on an LED, the following steps must be taken.

1) Make pin PA5 as output in MODER register for the LD2,
2) configure PC13 as input,
3) read switch from PC13,
4) if PC13 is high, set PA5 high to turn on the LED,
5) else clear PA5 low to turn off the LED
6) Repeat steps 3 to 5.

See Programs 2-3.

Program 2-3: Reading a switch and displaying it on an LED

```c
/* p2_3.c Turn on or off LED by a switch
 *
 * This program turns on the green LED (LD2) by pressing the user
 * button B1 of the Nucleo board.
 * The user button is connected to PC13. It has a pull-up resitor
 * so PC13 stays high when the button is not pressed.
 * When the button is pressed, PC13 becomes low.
 * The green LED (LD2) is connected to PA5.
 * A high on PA5 turns on the LED.
 *
 * This program was tested with Keil uVision v5.24a with DFP v2.11.0
 */

#include "stm32f4xx.h"

int main(void) {
    RCC->AHB1ENR |=  4;                  /* enable GPIOC clock */
    RCC->AHB1ENR |=  1;                  /* enable GPIOA clock */

    GPIOA->MODER &= ~0x00000C00;         /* clear pin mode */
    GPIOA->MODER |=  0x00000400;         /* set pin to output mode */

    GPIOC->MODER &= ~0x0C000000;         /* clear pin mode to input mode */

    while(1) {
        if (GPIOC->IDR & 0x2000)         /* if PC13 is high */
            GPIOA->BSRR = 0x00200000;    /* turn off green LED */
        else
            GPIOA->BSRR = 0x00000020;    /* turn on green LED */
    }
}
```

Alternate pin functions of the GPIO

The STM Arm microcontrollers, like other Arm core microcontrollers, have a rich set of peripheral modules. If each peripheral has its own I/O pins, a microcontroller will need several hundred pins to support all of its on-chip features. In order to reduce the cost of the devices, the peripheral modules share the I/O pins. Using a single pin for multiple functions is called pin multiplexing. Pin multiplexing allows several peripheral modules or core functions to use the same pin but only one at the time similar to a multiplexer circuit (see Figure 2 - 24).

In STM Arm chips, the default function of a pin is digital input mode upon reset. To use any other alternate function, we must modify GPIOx_MODER register first. The alternate function registers are called GPIOx_AFLR (GPIOx Alternate Function Low) and GPIOx_AFHR (GPIOx Alternate Function High). In Keil MDK-Arm, they are named GPIOx->AFR[0] and GPIOx->AFR[1] respectively. Notice for pins 0 to 7 we use GPIOx_AFLR and for pins 8 to 15 we use GPIOxAFHR registers. We will see their use in future chapters.

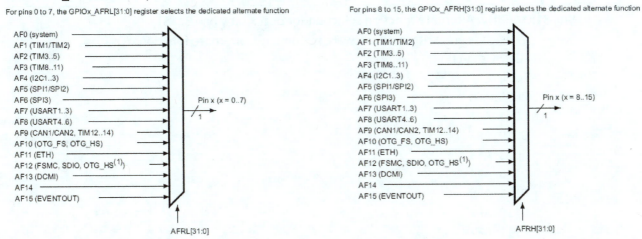

Figure 2 - 24: STM32 Arm Pin Multiplexing of Alternate Functions

When GPIOx_MODER bits are set to 10, the pin is used by one of the alternate functions. The actual alternate function for the pin is selected by GPIOx_AFLR and GPIOx_AFHR registers only after GPIOx_MODER is configured. The four bits of GPIOxAFLR and GPIOxAFHR registers are allocated for each pin. See Figures 2-25A, 2-25B and Table 2-5.

31	30	29	28	27	26	25	24	23	22	21	20	19	18	17	16
AFRL7[3:0]				AFRL6[3:0]				AFRL5[3:0]				AFRL4[3:0]			
rw	rw	rw	rw	rw	rw	rw	rw	rw	rw	rw	rw	rw	rw	rw	rw

15	14	13	12	11	10	9	8	7	6	5	4	3	2	1	0
AFRL3[3:0]				AFRL2[3:0]				AFRL1[3:0]				AFRL0[3:0]			
rw	rw	rw	rw	rw	rw	rw	rw	rw	rw	rw	rw	rw	rw	rw	rw

Bits 31:0 **AFRLy:** Alternate function selection for port x bit y (y = 0..7)

These bits are written by software to configure alternate function I/Os

AFRLy selection:

0000: AF0   1000: AF8
0001: AF1   1001: AF9
0010: AF2   1010: AF10
0011: AF3   1011: AF11
0100: AF4   1100: AF12
0101: AF5   1101: AF13
0110: AF6   1110: AF14
0111: AF7   1111: AF15

Figure 2 - 25A: GPIOx_AFRL (GPIOx Alternate Function Low) register to select alternate pin functions

31	30	29	28	27	26	25	24	23	22	21	20	19	18	17	16
AFRH15[3:0]				AFRH14[3:0]				AFRH13[3:0]				AFRH12[3:0]			
rw	rw	rw	rw	rw	rw	rw	rw	rw	rw	rw	rw	rw	rw	rw	rw
15	14	13	12	11	10	9	8	7	6	5	4	3	2	1	0
AFRH11[3:0]				AFRH10[3:0]				AFRH9[3:0]				AFRH8[3:0]			
rw	rw	rw	rw	rw	rw	rw	rw	rw	rw	rw	rw	rw	rw	rw	rw

Bits 31:0 **AFRHy:** Alternate function selection for port x bit y (y = 8..15)

These bits are written by software to configure alternate function I/Os

AFRHy selection:

0000: AF0
0001: AF1
0010: AF2
0011: AF3
0100: AF4
0101: AF5
0110: AF6
0111: AF7
1000: AF8
1001: AF9
1010: AF10
1011: AF11
1100: AF12
1101: AF13
1110: AF14
1111: AF15

Figure 2 - 25B: GPIOx_AFRH (GPIOx Alternate Function High) register to select alternate pin functions

Since each pin uses four bits in GPIOx_AF registers, it requires 64 bits (16 x 4 bits = 64bits) to select alternate functions for 16 pins of a GPIO port. For this reason we need two 32-bit registers of GPIOxAFLR and GPIOx_AFHR to cover all the options. The alternate functions available for each pin of STM32F446RE are listed in Table 2 - 5. For the detailed mapping of the alternate function I/O pins in your STM Arm chip, please refer to the "Alternate function mapping" table in the device datasheet. We will discuss how to select the alternate functions in the future chapters when the peripherals are introduced.

Port	SYS (AF0)	TIM1/2 (AF1)	TIM3/4/5 (AF2)	TIM8/9/10/11/CEC (AF3)	I2C1/2/3/4/CEC (AF4)	SPI1/2/3/4 (AF5)	SPI2/3/4/SAI1 (AF6)	SPI2/3/USART1/2/3/UART4/5/SPDIFRX (AF7)	SAI/USART6/UART4/5/6/SPDIFRX (AF8)	CAN1/2 QUADSPI TIM12/13/14/QUADSPI (AF9)	SAI2/OTG2_HS/OTG1_FS (AF10)	OTG1_FS (AF11)	FMC/SDIO/OTG2_FS (AF12)	DCMI (AF13)	- (AF14)	SYS (AF15)
PA15	JTDI	TIM2_CH1/TIM2_ETR	-	-	HDMI_CEC	SPI1_NSS/I2S1_WS	SPI3_NSS/I2S3_WS	-	UART4_RTS	-	-	-	-	-	-	EVENTOUT
PA14	JTCK-SWCLK	-	-	-	-	-	-	-	-	-	-	-	-	-	-	EVENTOUT
PA13	JTMS-SWDIO	-	-	-	-	-	-	-	-	-	-	-	-	-	-	EVENTOUT
PA12	-	TIM1_ETR	-	-	-	-	-	USART1_RTS	SAI2_FS_B	CAN1_TX	OTG_FS_DP	-	-	-	-	EVENTOUT
PA11	-	TIM1_CH4	-	-	-	-	-	USART1_CTS	-	CAN1_RX	OTG_FS_DM	-	-	-	-	EVENTOUT
PA10	-	TIM1_CH3	-	-	-	-	-	USART1_RX	-	-	OTG_FS_ID	-	-	DCMI_D1	-	EVENTOUT
PA9	-	TIM1_CH2	-	-	I2C3_SMBA	SPI2_SCK/I2S2_CK	-	USART1_TX	-	-	-	-	-	DCMI_D0	-	EVENTOUT
PA8	MCO1	TIM1_CH1	-	-	I2C3_SCL	-	-	USART1_CK	-	-	OTG_FS_SOF	-	FMC_SDNWE	-	-	EVENTOUT
PA7	-	TIM1_CH1N	TIM3_CH2	TIM8_CH1N	-	SPI1_MOSI/I2S1_SD	-	-	-	TIM14_CH1	-	-	-	-	-	EVENTOUT
PA6	-	TIM1_BKIN	TIM3_CH1	TIM8_BKIN	-	SPI1_MISO	I2S2_MCK	-	-	TIM13_CH1	-	-	-	DCMI_PIXCLK	-	EVENTOUT
PA5	-	TIM2_CH1/TIM2_ETR	-	TIM8_CH1N	-	SPI1_SCK/I2S1_CK	SAI1_SD_B	-	-	-	OTG_HS_ULPI_CK	-	-	-	-	EVENTOUT
PA4	-	-	-	-	-	SPI1_NSS/I2S1_WS	SPI3_NSS/I2S3_WS	USART2_CK	SAI1_FS_A	-	-	-	OTG_HS_SOF	DCMI_HSYNC	-	EVENTOUT
PA3	-	TIM2_CH4	TIM5_CH4	TIM9_CH2	-	-	-	USART2_RX	-	-	OTG_HS_ULPI_D0	-	-	-	-	EVENTOUT
PA2	-	TIM2_CH3	TIM5_CH3	TIM9_CH1	-	-	-	USART2_TX	SAI2_SCK_B	-	-	-	-	-	-	EVENTOUT
PA1	-	TIM2_CH2	TIM5_CH2	-	-	-	-	USART2_RTS	UART4_RX	QUADSPI_BK1_IO3	-	-	-	-	-	EVENTOUT
PA0	-	TIM2_CH1/TIM2_ETR	TIM5_CH1	TIM8_ETR	-	-	-	USART2_CTS	UART4_TX	-	SAI2_MCLK_B	-	-	-	-	EVENTOUT

Table 2 - 5: STM32F446RE Alternative Functions (AF0-AF15) Pin Selection (Partial listing, see Appendix B for full listing)

Review Questions

1. STM STM32F446RE chip has _____ GPIO ports.
2. True or false. Every Arm microcontroller must have minimum of 3 memory spaces of Flash (for code), SRAM (for data), and I/O (peripherals).
3. Port A in STMicro Arm can have maximum of _____ pins.
4. STM32F446RE Nucleo board comes with ....user on-board LED for simple I/O.
5. STM32F446RE Nucleo board comes with a ......user on-board switch for simple I/O.

Section 2.3: Seven-segment LED interfacing and programming

A popular numeric display is a seven-segment LED. The 7-seg LED can have a common anode or a common cathode. With common anode, the anode of the LED is driven by the positive supply voltage and the microcontroller sinks the individual cathodes LOW for current to flow through LEDs to light up. In this configuration, the sink current capability of the microcontroller is critical. With common cathode, the cathode of the LED is connected to the ground and microcontroller drives the individual anodes HIGH to light up the LED. In this configuration, the microcontroller pins must provide sufficient source current for each LED segment. In either configuration, if the microcontroller does not have sufficient drive or sink current capacity, we must add a buffer between the 7-seg LED and the microcontroller. The buffer for the 7-seg LED can be an IC chip or transistors.

The seven segments of LED are designated as a, b, c, d, e, f, and g. See Figure 2-26.

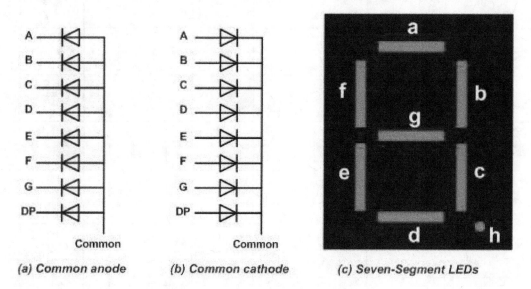

(a) Common anode   (b) Common cathode   (c) Seven-Segment LEDs

Figure 2 - 26: Seven-segment Display

A byte of data should be sufficient to drive all of the segments. In the example below, segment a is assigned to bit D0, segment b is assigned to bit D1, and so on as shown below:

D7	D6	D5	D4	D3	D2	D1	D0
.	g	F	e	d	c	b	a

Table 2 – 6: Assignments of port pins to each segments of a 7-seg LED

The D7 bit is assigned to the decimal point. One can create the following patterns for numbers 0 to 9 for the common cathode configuration:

Num	D7	D6	D5	D4	D3	D2	D1	D0	Hex value
	.	g	f	e	d	c	b	a	
0	0	0	1	1	1	1	1	1	0x3F
1	0	0	0	0	0	1	1	0	0x06
2	0	1	0	1	1	0	1	1	0x5B
3	0	1	0	0	1	1	1	1	0x4F
4	0	1	1	0	0	1	1	0	0x66
5	0	1	1	0	1	1	0	1	0x6D
6	0	1	1	1	1	1	0	1	0x7D
7	0	0	0	0	0	1	1	1	0x07
8	0	1	1	1	1	1	1	1	0x7F
9	0	1	1	0	1	1	1	1	0x6F

Table 2 - 7: Segment patterns for the 10 decimal digits for a common cathode 7-seg LED

In Figures 2-27 and 2-28 the connection for 2-digit 7-seg LED and the microcontroller is shown. The Program 2-5 shows the code.

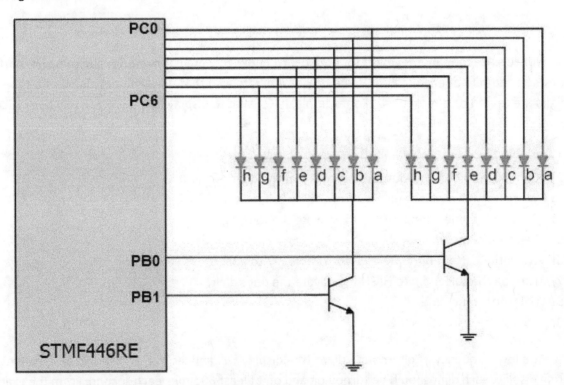

Figure 2 - 27: Connections between microcontroller and a two-digit 7-segment LED

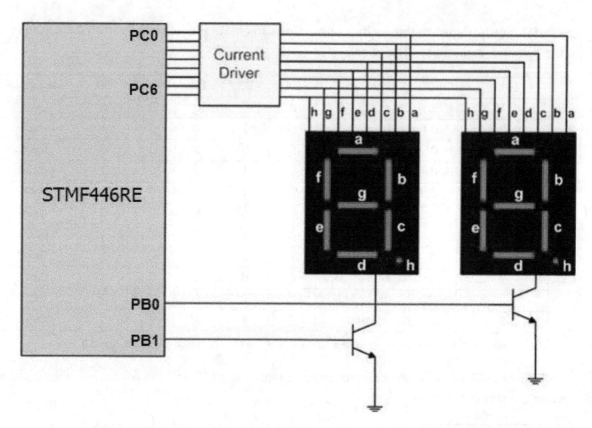

Figure 2 - 28: Connections between microcontroller and 7-segment LED with drivers

Notice since the same segment for both digit 1 and digit 2 are connected to the same I/O port pin, the common cathode of each digit must be driven separately so that only one digit is on at a time. The two digits are turned on alternatively. For example, if we want to display number 75 on the 7-seg LED, the following steps should be used:

1) Configure Port C as output port to drive the segments,
2) Configure PortB0-1 as output port to select the digits,
3) Write the pattern of numeral 7 from Table 2-7 to Port C,
4) Turn on the select pin to HIGH to activate the tens digit,
5) Delay for some time,
6) Write the pattern of numeral 5 from Table 2-7 to Port C,
7) Turn on the select pin to HIGH to activate the ones digit,
8) Delay for some time,
9) Repeat from step 3 to 8.

At a low frequency of alternating digits, the display will appear to be flickering. To eliminate the flickering display, each digit should be turned on and off at least 60 times each second. From the example above, the delay for steps 6 and 9 should be 8 milliseconds or less.

$$1 \text{ second} / 60 / 2 = 8 \text{ millisecond}$$

See Program 2-4.

Program 2-4: Displaying "75" on 2-digit 7-segment LED display

```c
/* p2_4.c Display number 75 on a 2-digit 7-segment common cathode LED.
 *
 * The segments are driven by Port C0-C6.
 * The digit selects are driven by PB0 and PB1.
 *
 * This program was tested with Keil uVision v5.24a with DFP v2.11.0
 */

#include "stm32f4xx.h"

void delayMs(int n);

int main(void) {
    RCC->AHB1ENR |=  2;             /* enable GPIOB clock */
    RCC->AHB1ENR |=  4;             /* enable GPIOC clock */

    GPIOC->MODER &= ~0x0000FFFF;    /* clear pin mode */
    GPIOC->MODER |=  0x00005555;    /* set pins to output mode */
    GPIOB->MODER &= ~0x0000000F;    /* clear pin mode */
    GPIOB->MODER |=  0x00000005;    /* set pins to output mode */

    for(;;)
    {
        GPIOC->ODR = 0x0007;            /* display tens digit */
        GPIOB->BSRR = 0x00010000;       /* deselect ones digit */
        GPIOB->BSRR = 0x00000002;       /* select tens digit */
        delayMs(8);
        GPIOC->ODR = 0x006D;            /* display ones digit */
        GPIOB->BSRR = 0x00020000;       /* deselect tens digit */
        GPIOB->BSRR = 0x00000001;       /* select ones digit */
        delayMs(8);
    }
}

/* 16 MHz SYSCLK */
void delayMs(int n) {
    int i;
    for (; n > 0; n--)
        for (i = 0; i < 3195; i++) ;
}
```

Notice in Figure 2-28, a single pin is used to select each digit. That means if we want 4 digits we must use a total of 12 pins. That is 8 pins for the segments a through g, decimal point, and 4 pins to select each digit. This might not be feasible in applications in which we have a limited number of microcontroller pins to spare. One solution is to use a decoder for the digit selection. For example, a 74LS138 decoder can be used for up to 8-digit 7-seg LED system with three select pins. Another approach is to use a 7-segment LED driver chip such as MAX 7221, which only uses two interface pins. An additional advantage of MAX7221 is that the refreshing of the segments is handled by the driver chip itself so the microcontroller does not have to spend time refreshing the display and can concentrate on other important tasks. The MAX7221 is an I^2C device and the vast majority of microcontrollers come with on-chip I^2C serial communication feature, which we will discuss in a separate chapter.

53

Review Questions

1. In a common cathode 7-seg LED connection, to turn on a segment the microcontroller drives it (high, low).
2. True or false. In connecting the 7-seg LED directly to microcontroller, the refreshing of digits is done by microcontroller itself.
3. What is the disadvantage of letting microcontroller do the refreshing of 7-seg LEDs?
4. List two advantages of using an IC chip such as MAX7221 chip?
5. In an application, we need 8 digits of 7-seg LED. (a) How many pins of microcontroller will be used if we connect microcontroller to 7-seg directly? (b) How about if we use 3-8 decoder for digit selection?

Section 2.4: I/O Port Programming with Assembly Language

In Program 2-2, we let the header file to define the physical address of the special function registers belonging to the I/O ports. *Often the manufacturer of the device will provide these definitions* in a C header file. In program 2-5, we define the physical addresses of special function registers. Since this is tedious and prone to error, we avoid using this method. This is given simply as an example for learning purpose.

Program 2-5: Toggling LED in C (using special function registers by their addresses)

```
/* p2_5.c Toggle Green LED (LD2) on STM32F446RE Nucleo64 board at 1 Hz
 *
 * This program toggles LD2 for 0.5 second ON and 0.5 second OFF.
 * It is identical to Program 2-2 but was written without using
 * the header file. The registers are defined locally in the file.
 *
 * This program was tested with Keil uVision v5.24a with DFP v2.11.0
 */

#define RCC_AHB1ENR (*((volatile unsigned int*)0x40023830))
#define GPIOA_MODER (*((volatile unsigned int*)0x40020000))
#define GPIOA_BSRR  (*((volatile unsigned int*)0x40020018))

void delayMs(int n);

int main(void) {
    RCC_AHB1ENR |= 1;              /* enable GPIOA clock */

    GPIOA_MODER &= ~0x00000C00;    /* clear pin mode */
    GPIOA_MODER |= 0x00000400;     /* set pin to output mode */

    while(1) {
        GPIOA_BSRR = 0x00000020;   /* turn on LED */
        delayMs(500);
        GPIOA_BSRR = 0x00200000;   /* turn off LED */
        delayMs(500);
    }
}

/* 16 MHz SYSCLK */
void delayMs(int n) {
    int i;
    for (; n > 0; n--)
```

```
        for (i = 0; i < 3195; i++) ;
}
```

Program 2-6 shows the assembly version of the Program 2-5 using Keil Arm assembler.

Program 2-6: Toggling LED in assembly language (Keil)

```
; p2_6.s
; Assembly program to toggle the green LED (LD2)
;   on STM32F446RE Nucleo64 board at 1 Hz
;
            EXPORT    __Vectors
            EXPORT    Reset_Handler
            AREA      vectors, CODE, READONLY

__Vectors   DCD       0x10010000  ; 0x20008000     ; Top of Stack
            DCD       Reset_Handler                ; Reset Handler

RCC_AHB1ENR equ 0x40023830
GPIOA_MODER equ 0x40020000
GPIOA_BSRR  equ 0x40020018


            AREA      PROG, CODE, READONLY
Reset_Handler
            ldr       r4, =RCC_AHB1ENR    ; enable GPIOA clock
            ldr       r5, [r4]
            orr       r5, #1
            str       r5, [r4]

            ldr       r4, =GPIOA_MODER    ; set pin to output mode
            ldr       r5, [r4]
            bic       r5, #0x00000C00
            orr       r5, #0x00000400
            str       r5, [r4]

L1          ldr       r4, =GPIOA_BSRR
            ldr       r5, =0x00000020    ; turn on LED
            str       r5, [r4]
            mov       r0, #500
            bl        delay

            ldr       r4, =GPIOA_BSRR
            ldr       r5, =0x00200000    ; turn off LED
            str       r5, [r4]
            mov       r0, #500
            bl        delay
            b         L1                 ; loop forever

; delay milliseconds in R0
delay       ldr       r1, =5325
DL1         subs      r1, r1, #1
            bne       DL1
            subs      r0, r0, #1
            bne       delay
            bx        lr

            end
```

Answer to Review Questions

Section 2-1
1. 512KB
2. 128KB
3. Program code
4. Data
5. 0x0000 0000 to 0x0007 FFFF
6. R is for 64-pin and E is for 512 KB of Flash memory

Section 2-2
1. 3 (A, B, and C). It also has part of port H.
2. True
3. 16
4. 1
5. 1

Section 2-3
1. High
2. True
3. It takes time and pins of microcontroller to scan the 7-segments.
4. (1) It refreshes the 7-segment displays, (2) it is connected to the microcontroller using I^{2}C which uses just 2 pins of the microcontroller.
5. (a) 8 pins for data and 8 pins for selector; (b) 8 pins for data and 3 pins for selector.

Chapter 3: LCD and Keyboard Interfacing

In this chapter, we show interfacing to two real-world devices: LCD and Keyboard. They are widely used in different embedded systems.

Section 3.1: Interfacing to an LCD

This section describes the operation modes of the LCDs, then describes how to program and interface an LCD to the STM Arm board.

LCD operation

In recent years the LCD is replacing LEDs (seven-segment LEDs or other multi-segment LEDs). This is due to the following reasons:

1. The declining prices of LCDs.
2. The ability to display numbers, characters, and graphics. This is in contrast to LEDs, which are limited to numbers and a few characters. (The new OLED panels are relatively much more expensive except the very small ones. But their prices are dropping. The interface and programming to OLED are similar to graphic LCD.)
3. Incorporation of the refreshing controller into the LCD itself, thereby relieving the CPU of the task of refreshing the LCD.
4. Ease of programming for both characters and graphics.
5. The extremely low power consumption of LCD (when backlight is not used).

LCD module pin descriptions

For many years, the use of Hitachi HD44780 LCD controller dominated the character LCD modules. Even today, most of the character LCD modules still use HD44780 or a variation of it. The HD44780 controller has a 14 pin interface for the microprocessor. We will discuss this 14 pin interface in this section. The function of each pin is given in Table 3-1. Figure 3-1 shows the pin positions for various LCD modules.

Pin	Symbol	I/O	Description
1	VSS	--	Ground
2	VCC	--	+5V power supply
3	VEE	--	Power supply to control contrast
4	RS	I	RS = 0 to select command register, RS = 1 to select data register
5	R/W	I	R/W = 0 for write, R/W = 1 for read
6	E	I	Enable
7	DB0	I/O	The 8-bit data bus
8	DB1	I/O	The 8-bit data bus
9	DB2	I/O	The 8-bit data bus
10	DB3	I/O	The 8-bit data bus
11	DB4	I/O	The 4/8-bit data bus
12	DB5	I/O	The 4/8-bit data bus

13	DB6	I/O	The 4/8-bit data bus
14	DB7	I/O	The 4/8-bit data bus

Table 3-1: Pin Descriptions for LCD

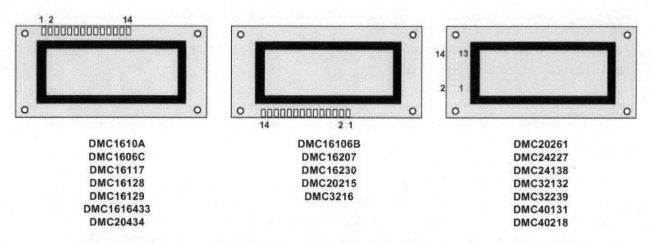

DMC1610A	DMC16106B	DMC20261
DMC1606C	DMC16207	DMC24227
DMC16117	DMC16230	DMC24138
DMC16128	DMC20215	DMC32132
DMC16129	DMC3216	DMC32239
DMC1616433		DMC40131
DMC20434		DMC40218

Figure 3-1: Pin Positions for Various LCDs from Optrex

VCC, VSS, and VEE: While VCC and VSS provide +5V power supply and ground, respectively, VEE is used for controlling the LCD contrast.

RS, register select: There are two registers inside the LCD and the RS pin is used for their selection as follows. If RS = 0, the instruction command code register is selected, allowing the user to send a command such as clear display, cursor at home, and so on (or query the busy status bit of the controller). If RS = 1, the data register is selected, allowing the user to send data to be displayed on the LCD (or to retrieve data from the LCD controller).

R/W, read/write: R/W input allows the user to write information into the LCD controller or read information from it. R/W = 1 when reading and R/W = 0 when writing.

E, enable: The enable pin is used by the LCD to latch information presented to its data pins. When data is supplied to data pins, a pulse (Low-to-High-to-Low) must be applied to this pin in order for the LCD to latch in the data present at the data pins. This pulse must be a minimum of 230 ns wide, according to Hitachi datasheet.

D0–D7: The 8-bit data pins are used to send information to the LCD or read the contents of the LCD's internal registers. The LCD controller is capable of operating with 4-bit data and only D4-D7 are used. We will discuss this in more details later.

To display letters and numbers, we send ASCII codes for the letters A–Z, a–z, numbers 0–9, and the punctuation marks to these pins while making RS = 1.

There are also instruction command codes that can be sent to the LCD in order to clear the display, force the cursor to the home position, or blink the cursor. Table 3-2 lists some commonly used command codes. For detailed command codes, see Table 3-4.

Code (Hex)	Command to LCD Instruction Register
1	Clear display screen
2	Return cursor home
6	Increment cursor (shift cursor to right)
F	Display on, cursor blinking
80	Force cursor to beginning of 1st line
C0	Force cursor to beginning of 2nd line
38	2 lines and 5x7 character (8-bit data, D0 to D7)
28	2 lines and 5x7 character (4-bit data, D4 to D7)

Table 3-2: Some commonly used LCD Command Codes

Sending commands to LCDs

To send any of the commands to the LCD, make pins RS = 0, R/W = 0, and send a pulse (L-to-H-to-L) on the E pin to enable the internal latch of the LCD. The connection of an LCD to the microcontroller is shown in Figure 3-2.

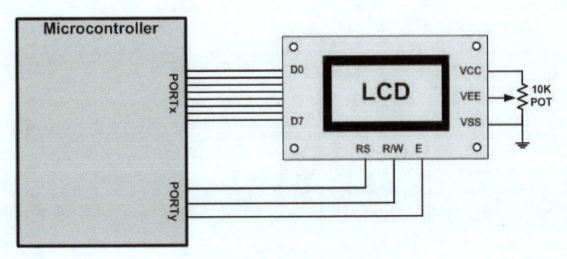

Figure 3-2: LCD Connection to Microcontroller

Notice the following for the connection in Figure 3-2:

1. The LCD's data pins are connected to PORTD of the microcontroller.
2. The LCD's RS pin is connected to Pin 2 of PORTA of the microcontroller.
3. The LCD's R/W pin is connected to Pin 4 of PORTA of the microcontroller.
4. The LCD's E pin is connected to Pin 5 of PORTA of the microcontroller.
5. Both Ports D and A are configured as output ports.

Sending data to the LCD

In order to send data to the LCD to be displayed, we must set pins RS = 1, R/W = 0, and also send a pulse (L-to-H-to-L) to the E pin to enable the internal latch of the LCD.

Because of the extremely low power feature of the LCD controller, it runs much slower than the microcontroller. The first two commands in Table 3-2 take up to 1.64 ms to execute and all the other commands and data take up to 40 us. (At the highest clock speed, MKL25Z4 can execute more than 1,000 instructions in 40 us.) After one command or data is written to the LCD controller, one must wait until the LCD controller is ready before issuing the next command/data otherwise the second command/data will be ignored. An easy way (not as efficient though) is to delay the microcontroller for the maximal time it may take for the previous command. We will use this method in the following examples. All the examples in this chapter use much more relaxed timing than the original HD44780 datasheet (See Table 3-4) to accommodate the variations of different LCD modules. You may want adjust the delay time for the LCD module you use.

Program 3-1: This program displays a message on the LCD using 8-bit mode and delay.

```c
/* p3_1.c: Initialize and display "hello" on the LCD using 8-bit data mode.
 *
 * Initialize LCD controller and flash hello on the LCD.
 * This program does not poll the status of the LCD.
 * It uses delay to wait out the time LCD controller is busy.
 * For simplicity, all delay below 1 ms uses 1 ms. You may
 * want to adjust the amount of delay for your LCD controller
 * to enhance the performance.
 *
 * The LCD controller is connected to the Nucleo-F446RE
 * board as follows:
 *
 * PC0-PC7 for LCD D0-D7, respectively.
 * PB5 for LCD R/S
 * PB6 for LCD R/W
 * PB7 for LCD EN
 *
 * This program was tested with Keil uVision v5.24a with DFP v2.11.0
 */

#include "stm32f4xx.h"

#define RS 0x20    /* PB5 mask for reg select */
#define RW 0x40    /* PB6 mask for read/write */
#define EN 0x80    /* PB7 mask for enable */

void delayMs(int n);
void LCD_command(unsigned char command);
void LCD_data(char data);
void LCD_init(void);
void PORTS_init(void);

int main(void) {
    /* initialize LCD controller */
    LCD_init();

    while(1) {
        /* Write "hello" on LCD */
        LCD_data('h');
        LCD_data('e');
        LCD_data('l');
```

```
        LCD_data('l');
        LCD_data('o');
        delayMs(1000);

        /* clear LCD display */
        LCD_command(1);
        delayMs(500);
    }
}

/* initialize port pins then initialize LCD controller */
void LCD_init(void) {
    PORTS_init();

    delayMs(30);                /* initialization sequence */
    LCD_command(0x30);
    delayMs(10);
    LCD_command(0x30);
    delayMs(1);
    LCD_command(0x30);

    LCD_command(0x38);          /* set 8-bit data, 2-line, 5x7 font */
    LCD_command(0x06);          /* move cursor right after each char */
    LCD_command(0x01);          /* clear screen, move cursor to home */
    LCD_command(0x0F);          /* turn on display, cursor blinking */
}

void PORTS_init(void) {
    RCC->AHB1ENR |=  0x06;          /* enable GPIOB/C clock */

    /* PB5 for LCD R/S */
    /* PB6 for LCD R/W */
    /* PB7 for LCD EN */
    GPIOB->MODER &= ~0x0000FC00;    /* clear pin mode */
    GPIOB->MODER |=  0x00005400;    /* set pin output mode */
    GPIOB->BSRR = 0x00C00000;       /* turn off EN and R/W */

    /* PC0-PC7 for LCD D0-D7, respectively. */
    GPIOC->MODER &= ~0x0000FFFF;    /* clear pin mode */
    GPIOC->MODER |=  0x00005555;    /* set pin output mode */
}

void LCD_command(unsigned char command) {
    GPIOB->BSRR = (RS | RW) << 16;  /* RS = 0, R/W = 0 */
    GPIOC->ODR = command;           /* put command on data bus */
    GPIOB->BSRR = EN;               /* pulse E high */
    delayMs(0);
    GPIOB->BSRR = EN << 16;         /* clear E */

    if (command < 4)
        delayMs(2);         /* command 1 and 2 needs up to 1.64ms */
    else
        delayMs(1);         /* all others 40 us */
}

void LCD_data(char data) {
    GPIOB->BSRR = RS;                   /* RS = 1 */
    GPIOB->BSRR = RW << 16;             /* R/W = 0 */
    GPIOC->ODR = data;                  /* put data on data bus */
```

```
    GPIOB->BSRR = EN;                 /* pulse E high */
    delayMs(0);
    GPIOB->BSRR = EN << 16;           /* clear E */

    delayMs(1);
}

/* delay n milliseconds (16 MHz CPU clock) */
void delayMs(int n) {
    int i;
    for (; n > 0; n--)
        for (i = 0; i < 3195; i++) ;
}
```

Checking LCD busy flag

The above programs used a time delay before issuing the next data or command. This allows the LCD a sufficient amount of time to get ready to accept the next data. However, the LCD has a busy flag. We can monitor the busy flag and issue data when it is ready. This will speed up the process. To check the busy flag, we must read the command register (R/W = 1, RS = 0). The busy flag is the D7 bit of that register. Therefore, if R/W = 1, RS = 0. When D7 = 1 (busy flag = 1), the LCD is busy taking care of internal operations and will not accept any new information. When D7 = 0, the LCD is ready to receive new information.

Doing so requires switching the direction of the port connected to the data bus to input mode when polling the status register then switch the port direction back to output mode to send the next command. If the port direction is incorrect, it may damage the microcontroller or the LCD module. The next program example uses polling of the busy bit in the status register.

Program 3-2: This program displays a message on the LCD using 8-bit mode and polling of the status register

```
/* p3_2.c:  Initialize and display "Hello" on the LCD using 8-bit data mode.
 *
 * Data pins use Port C; control pins use Port B.
 * Polling of the busy bit of the LCD status register is used for timing.
 *
 * The LCD controller is connected to the Nucleo-F446RE
 * board as follows:
 *
 * PC0-PC7 for LCD D0-D7, respectively.
 * PB5 for LCD R/S
 * PB6 for LCD R/W
 * PB7 for LCD EN
 *
 * This program was tested with Keil uVision v5.24a with DFP v2.11.0
 */

#include "stm32f4xx.h"

#define RS 0x20     /* PB5 mask for reg select */
#define RW 0x40     /* PB6 mask for read/write */
#define EN 0x80     /* PB7 mask for enable */

void delayMs(int n);
```

```c
void LCD_command(unsigned char command);
void LCD_command_noPoll(unsigned char command);
void LCD_data(char data);
void LCD_init(void);
void LCD_ready(void);
void PORTS_init(void);

int main(void) {
    /* initialize LCD controller */
    LCD_init();

    while(1) {
        /* Write "Hello" on LCD */
        LCD_data('H');
        LCD_data('e');
        LCD_data('l');
        LCD_data('l');
        LCD_data('o');
        delayMs(500);

        /* clear LCD display */
        LCD_command(1);
        delayMs(500);
    }
}

/* Initialize port pins then initialize LCD controller */
void LCD_init(void) {
    PORTS_init();

    delayMs(30);                    /* initialization sequence */
    LCD_command_noPoll(0x30);       /* LCD does not respond to status poll yet */
    delayMs(10);
    LCD_command_noPoll(0x30);
    delayMs(1);
    LCD_command_noPoll(0x30);       /* busy flag cannot be polled before this */

    LCD_command(0x38);        /* set 8-bit data, 2-line, 5x7 font */
    LCD_command(0x06);        /* move cursor right after each char */
    LCD_command(0x01);        /* clear screen, move cursor to home */
    LCD_command(0x0F);        /* turn on display, cursor blinking */
}

void PORTS_init(void) {
    RCC->AHB1ENR |= 0x06;            /* enable GPIOB/C clock */

    /* PB5 for LCD R/S */
    /* PB6 for LCD R/W */
    /* PB7 for LCD EN */
    GPIOB->MODER &= ~0x0000FC00;    /* clear pin mode */
    GPIOB->MODER |= 0x00005400;     /* set pin output mode */
    GPIOB->BSRR = 0x00C00000;       /* turn off EN and R/W */

    /* PC0-PC7 for LCD D0-D7, respectively. */
    GPIOC->MODER &= ~0x0000FFFF;    /* clear pin mode */
    GPIOC->MODER |= 0x00005555;     /* set pin output mode */
}

/* This function waits until LCD controller is ready to
```

```
 * accept a new command/data before returns.
 * It polls the busy bit of the status register of LCD controller.
 * In order to read the status register, the data port of the
 * microcontroller has to change to an input port before reading
 * the LCD. The data port of the microcontroller is return to
 * output port before the end of this function.
 */
void LCD_ready(void) {
    char status;

    /* change to read configuration to poll the status register */
    GPIOC->MODER &= ~0x0000FFFF;    /* clear pin mode */
    GPIOB->BSRR = RS << 16;         /* RS = 0 for status register */
    GPIOB->BSRR = RW;               /* R/W = 1 for read */

    do {    /* stay in the loop until it is not busy */
        GPIOB->BSRR = EN;           /* pulse E high */
        delayMs(0);
        status = GPIOC->IDR;        /* read status register */
        GPIOB->BSRR = EN << 16;     /* clear E */
        delayMs(0);
    } while (status & 0x80);         /* check busy bit */

    /* return to default write configuration */
    GPIOB->BSRR = RW << 16;         /* R/W = 0, LCD input */
    GPIOC->MODER |= 0x00005555;     /* Port C as output */
}


void LCD_command(unsigned char command) {
    LCD_ready();                    /* wait for LCD controller ready */
    GPIOB->BSRR = (RS | RW) << 16;  /* RS = 0, R/W = 0 */
    GPIOC->ODR = command;           /* put command on data bus */
    GPIOB->BSRR = EN;               /* pulse E high */
    delayMs(0);
    GPIOB->BSRR = EN << 16;         /* clear E */
}

/* This function is used at the beginning of the initialization
 * when the busy bit of the status register is not readable.
 */
void LCD_command_noPoll(unsigned char command) {
    GPIOB->BSRR = (RS | RW) << 16;  /* RS = 0, R/W = 0 */
    GPIOC->ODR = command;           /* put command on data bus */
    GPIOB->BSRR = EN;               /* pulse E high */
    delayMs(0);
    GPIOB->BSRR = EN << 16;         /* clear E */
}

void LCD_data(char data) {
    LCD_ready();                    /* wait for LCD controller ready */
    GPIOB->BSRR = RS;               /* RS = 1 */
    GPIOB->BSRR = RW << 16;         /* R/W = 0 */
    GPIOC->ODR = data;              /* put data on data bus */
    GPIOB->BSRR = EN;               /* pulse E high */
    delayMs(0);
    GPIOB->BSRR = EN << 16;         /* clear E */
}

/* delay n milliseconds (16 MHz CPU clock) */
```

```
void delayMs(int n) {
    int i;
    for (; n > 0; n--)
        for (i = 0; i < 3195; i++) ;
}
```

LCD 4-bit Option

To save the number of microcontroller pins used by LCD interfacing, we can use the 4-bit data option instead of 8-bit. In the 4-bit data option, we only need to connect D7-D4 to microcontroller. Together with the three control lines, the interface between the microcontroller and the LCD module will fit in a single 8-bit port. See Figure 3-3.

With 4-bit data option, the microcontroller needs to issue commands to put the LCD controller in 4-bit mode during initialization. This is done with command 0x20 in Program 3-3. After that, every command or data needs to be broken down to two 4-bit operations, upper nibble first. In Program 3-3, the upper nibble is extracted using **command & 0xF0** and the lower nibble is shifted into place by **command << 4**.

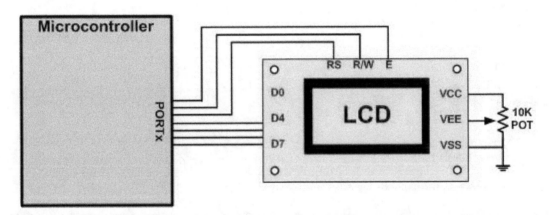

Figure 3-3: LCD Connection for 4-bit Data

Program 3-3: This program uses the 4-bit data option to show a message on the LCD.

```
/* p3_3.c: Initialize and display "HELLO" on the LCD using 4-bit data mode.
 *
 * Because of 4-bit data mode, every byte of command or data is
 * transmitted twice, one for the upper nibble and one for lower nibble.
 * This program does not poll the status of the LCD.
 * It uses delay to wait out the time LCD controller is busy.
 * For simplicity, all delay below 1 ms uses 1 ms. You may
 * want to adjust the amount of delay for your LCD controller
 * to enhance the performance.
 *
 * The LCD controller is connected to the Nucleo-F446RE
 * board as follows:
 *
 * PC4-PC7 for LCD D0-D7, respectively.
 * PB5 for LCD R/S
 * LCD R/W is tied to ground
 * PB7 for LCD EN
 *
```

```c
 * This program was tested with Keil uVision v5.24a with DFP v2.11.0
 */

#include "stm32f4xx.h"

#define RS 0x20    /* PB5 mask for reg select */
#define EN 0x80    /* PB7 mask for enable */

void delayMs(int n);
void LCD_nibble_write(char data, unsigned char control);
void LCD_command(unsigned char command);
void LCD_data(char data);
void LCD_init(void);
void PORTS_init(void);


int main(void) {
    /* initialize LCD controller */
    LCD_init();

    while(1) {
        /* Write "HELLO" on LCD */
        LCD_data('H');
        LCD_data('E');
        LCD_data('L');
        LCD_data('L');
        LCD_data('O');
        delayMs(1000);

        /* clear LCD display */
        LCD_command(1);
        delayMs(1000);
    }
}

/* initialize GPIOB/C then initialize LCD controller */
void LCD_init(void) {
    PORTS_init();

    delayMs(20);                    /* LCD controller reset sequence */
    LCD_nibble_write(0x30, 0);
    delayMs(5);
    LCD_nibble_write(0x30, 0);
    delayMs(1);
    LCD_nibble_write(0x30, 0);
    delayMs(1);

    LCD_nibble_write(0x20, 0);  /* use 4-bit data mode */
    delayMs(1);
    LCD_command(0x28);              /* set 4-bit data, 2-line, 5x7 font */
    LCD_command(0x06);              /* move cursor right */
    LCD_command(0x01);              /* clear screen, move cursor to home */
    LCD_command(0x0F);              /* turn on display, cursor blinking */
}

void PORTS_init(void) {
    RCC->AHB1ENR |=  0x06;          /* enable GPIOB/C clock */

    /* PORTB 5 for LCD R/S */
```

```
    /* PORTB 7 for LCD EN */
    GPIOB->MODER &= ~0x0000CC00;      /* clear pin mode */
    GPIOB->MODER |=  0x00004400;      /* set pin output mode */
    GPIOB->BSRR = 0x00800000;         /* turn off EN */

    /* PC4-PC7 for LCD D4-D7, respectively. */
    GPIOC->MODER &= ~0x0000FF00;      /* clear pin mode */
    GPIOC->MODER |=  0x00005500;      /* set pin output mode */
}

void LCD_nibble_write(char data, unsigned char control) {
    /* populate data bits */
    GPIOC->BSRR = 0x00F00000;         /* clear data bits */
    GPIOC->BSRR = data & 0xF0;        /* set data bits */

    /* set R/S bit */
    if (control & RS)
        GPIOB->BSRR = RS;
    else
        GPIOB->BSRR = RS << 16;

    /* pulse E */
    GPIOB->BSRR = EN;
    delayMs(0);
    GPIOB->BSRR = EN << 16;
}

void LCD_command(unsigned char command) {
    LCD_nibble_write(command & 0xF0, 0);    /* upper nibble first */
    LCD_nibble_write(command << 4, 0);      /* then lower nibble */

    if (command < 4)
        delayMs(2);             /* command 1 and 2 needs up to 1.64ms */
    else
        delayMs(1);             /* all others 40 us */
}

void LCD_data(char data) {
    LCD_nibble_write(data & 0xF0, RS);      /* upper nibble first */
    LCD_nibble_write(data << 4, RS);        /* then lower nibble */

    delayMs(1);
}

/* delay n milliseconds (16 MHz CPU clock) */
void delayMs(int n) {
    int i;
    for (; n > 0; n--)
        for (i = 0; i < 3195; i++) ;
}
```

LCD cursor position

In the LCD, one can move the cursor to any location in the display by issuing an address command. The next character sent will appear at the cursor position. For the two-line LCD, the address command for the first location of line 1 is 0x80, and for line 2 it is 0xC0. The following shows address locations and how they are accessed:

RS	R/W	DB7	DB6	DB5	DB4	DB3	DB2	DB1	DB0
0	0	1	A6	A5	A4	A3	A2	A1	A0

where $A_6A_5A_4A_3A_2A_1A_0$= 0000000 to 0100111 for line 1 and $A_6A_5A_4A_3A_2A_1A_0$ = 1000000 to 1100111 for line 2. See Table 3-3.

Table 3-3: LCD Addressing Commands

	DB7	DB6	DB5	DB4	DB3	DB2	DB1	DB0
Line 1 (min)	1	0	0	0	0	0	0	0
Line 1 (max)	1	0	1	0	0	1	1	1
Line 2 (min)	1	1	0	0	0	0	0	0
Line 2 (max)	1	1	1	0	0	1	1	1

The upper address range can go as high as 0100111 for the 40-character-wide LCD while for the 20-character-wide LCD the address of the visible positions goes up to 010011 (19 decimal = 10011 binary). Notice that the upper range 0100111 (binary) = 39 decimal, which corresponds to locations 0 to 39 for the LCDs of 40 × 2 size. Figure 3-4 shows the addresses of cursor positions for various sizes of LCDs. All the addresses are in hex. Notice the starting addresses for four line LCD are not in sequential order.

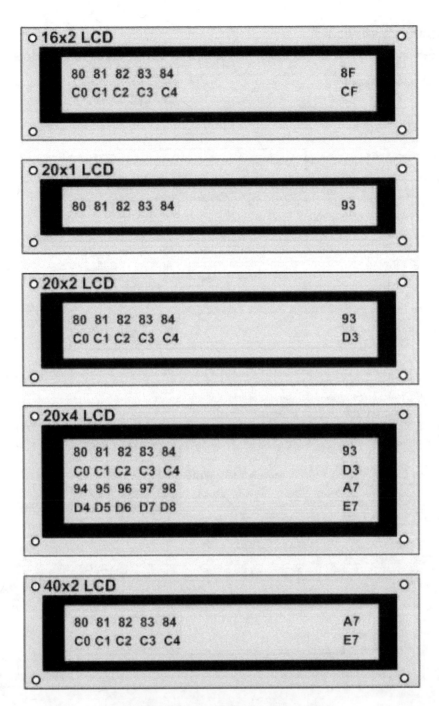

Figure 3-4: Cursor Addresses for Some LCDs

As an example of setting the cursor at the fourth location of line 1 we have the following:

```
LCD_command(0x83);
```

and for the sixth location of the second line we have:

```
LCD_command(0xC5);
```

Notice that the cursor location addresses are in hex and starting at 0 as the first location.

LCD timing and data sheet

Figures 3-5 and 3-6 show timing diagrams for LCD write and read timing, respectively.

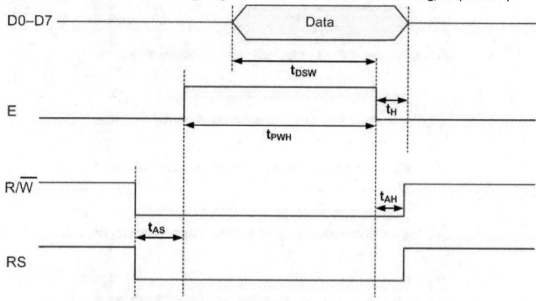

t_{PWH} = Enable pulse width = 230 ns (minimum)
t_{DSW} = Data setup time = 80 ns (minimum)
t_H = Data hold time = 10 ns (minimum)
t_{AS} = Setup time prior to E (going high) for both RS and R/W = 40 ns (minimum)
t_{AH} = Hold time after E has come down for both RS and R/W = 10 ns (minimum)

Figure 3-5: LCD Write Timing

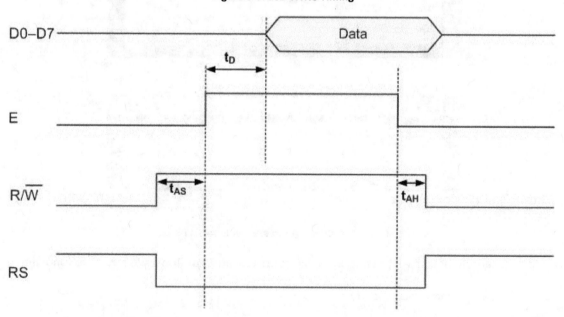

t_D = Data output delay time
t_{AS} = Setup time prior to E (going high) for both RS and R/W = 40 ns (minimum)
t_{AH} = Hold time after E has come down for both RS and R/W = 10 ns (minimum)

Note: Read requires an L-to-H pulse for the E pin.

Figure 3-6: LCD Read Timing

Notice that the write operation happens on the H-to-L transition of the E pin. The microcontroller must have data ready and stable on the data lines before the H-to-L transition of E to satisfy the setup time requirement.

The read operation is activated by the L-to-H pulse of the E pin. After the delay time, the LCD controller will have the data available on the data bus if the R/W line is high. The microcontroller should read the data from the data lines before lowering the E pulse.

Table 3-4 provides a more detailed list of LCD instructions.

Instruction	RS	R/W	DB 7	DB 6	DB 5	DB 4	DB 3	DB 2	DB 1	DB 0	Description	Execution Time (Max)
Clear display	0	0	0	0	0	0	0	0	0	1	Clears entire display and sets DD RAM address 0 in address counter	1.64 ms
Return Home	0	0	0	0	0	0	0	0	1	-	Sets DD RAM address to 0 as address counter. Also returns display being shifted to original positions. DD RAM contents remain unchanged.	1.64 ms
Entry Mode Set	0	0	0	0	0	0	0	1	I/D	S	Sets cursor move direction and specifies shift of display. These operations are performed during data write and read.	40μs
Display On/Off Control	0	0	0	0	0	0	1	D	C	B	Sets On/Off of entire display (D), cursor On/Off (C), and blink of cursor position character (B).	40μs
Cursor or Display shift	0	0	0	0	0	1	S/C	R/L	-	-	Moves cursor and shifts display without changing DD RAM contents.	40μs
Function Set	0	0	0	0	1	DL	N	F	-	-	Sets interface data length (DL), number of display lines (L), and character font (F)	40μs
Set CG RAM Address	0	0	0	1	AGC						Sets CG RAM address. CG RAM data is sent and received after this setting.	40μs
Set DD RAM Address	0	0	1	ADD							Sets DD RAM address. DD RAM data is sent and received after this setting.	40μs

Read Busy Flag & Address	0	1	B F	AC	Reads Busy flag (BF) indicating internal operation is being performed and reads address counter contents.	40µs
Write Data CG or DD RAM	1	0		Write Data	Writes data into DD or CG RAM.	40µs
Read Data CG or DD RAM	1	1		Read Data	Reads data from DD or CG RAM.	40µs

Abbreviations:

    DD RAM: Display data RAM

    CG RAM: Character generator RAM

    AGC: CG RAM address

    ADD: DD RAM address, corresponds to cursor address

    AC: address counter used for both DD and CG RAM addresses

    I/D: 1 = Increment, 0: Decrement

    S =1: Accompanies display shift

    S/C: 1 = Display shift, 0: Cursor move

    R/L: 1: Shift to the right, 0: Shift to the left

    DL: 1 = 8 bits, 0 = 4 bits

    N: 1 = 2-line, 0 = 1-line

    F: 1 = 5 x 10 dots, 0 = 5 x 7 dots

    BF: 1 = Internal operation, 0 = Can accept instruction

Table 3-4: List of LCD Instructions

Review Questions

1. The RS pin is an _____ (input, output) pin for the LCD.
2. The E pin is an _____ (input, output) pin for the LCD.
3. The E pin requires an _____ (H-to-L, L-to-H) transition to latch in information at the data pins of the LCD.
4. For the LCD to recognize information at the data pins as data, RS must be set to _____ (high, low).
5. Give the command codes for line 1, first character, and line 2, first character.

Section 3.2: Interfacing the Keyboard to the CPU

To reduce the microcontroller I/O pin usage, keyboards are organized in a matrix of rows and columns. The CPU accesses both rows and columns through ports; therefore, with two 8-bit ports, an 8 × 8 matrix of 64 keys can be connected to a microprocessor. When a key is pressed, a row and a column make a contact; otherwise, there is no connection between rows and columns. In a PC keyboards, an embedded microcontroller in the keyboard takes care of the hardware and software interfacing of the keyboard. In such systems, it is the function of programs stored in the ROM of the microcontroller to scan the keys continuously, identify which one has been activated, and present it to the main CPU on the motherboard. In this section, we look at the mechanism by which the microprocessor scans and identifies the key. For clarity some examples are provided.

Scanning and identifying the key

Figure 3-7 shows a 4 × 4 matrix connected to two ports. The rows are connected to an output port and the columns are connected to an input port. All the input pins have pull-up resistor connected. If no key has been pressed, reading the input port will yield 1s for all columns. If all the rows are driven low and a key is pressed, the column of that key will read back a 0 since the key pressed shorted that column to the row that is driven low. It is the function of the microprocessor to scan the keyboard continuously to detect and identify the key pressed. How it is done is explained next.

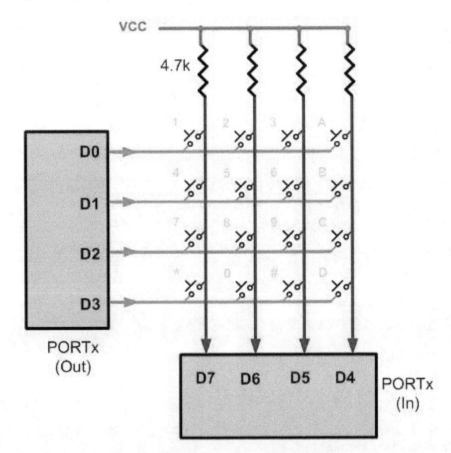

Figure 3-7: Matrix Keyboard Connection to Ports

Key press detection

To detect the key pressed, the microprocessor drives all rows low then it reads the columns. If the data read from the columns is D7–D4 = 1111, no key has been pressed and the process continues until a key press is detected. However, if one of the column bits has a zero, this means that a key was pressed. For example, if D7–D4= 1101, this means that a key in the D5 column has been pressed.

The following program detects whether any of the keys is pressed.

Program 3-4: This program turns on the blue LED when a key is pressed.

```c
/* p3_4.c: Matrix keypad detect
 *
 * This program checks a 4x4 matrix keypad to see whether
 * a key is pressed or not. When a key is pressed, it turns
 * on the LD2 (green LED).
 *
 * PC0-3 are connected to the columns and PC4-7 are
 * connected to the rows of the keypad.
 *
 * This program was tested with Keil uVision v5.24a with DFP v2.11.0
 */

#include "stm32f4xx.h"

void delay(void);
void keypad_init(void);
char keypad_kbhit(void);

int main(void) {
    keypad_init();

    // enable PA5 for green LED
    RCC->AHB1ENR |= 1;                  /* enable GPIOA clock */
    GPIOA->MODER &= ~0xC0000C00;    /* clear pin mode */
    GPIOA->MODER |=  0x00000400;    /* set pin output mode */

    while(1) {
        if (keypad_kbhit() != 0)    /* if a key is pressed */
            GPIOA->BSRR = 0x00000020;   /* turn on green LED */
        else
            GPIOA->BSRR = 0x00200000;   /* turn off green LED */
    }
}

/* this function initializes PC0-3 (column) and PC4-7 (row).
 * The column pins need to have the pull-up resistors enabled.
 */
void keypad_init(void) {
    RCC->AHB1ENR |=  0x14;          /* enable GPIOC clock */
    GPIOC->MODER &= ~0x0000FFFF;    /* clear pin mode to input */
    GPIOC->PUPDR =  0x00000055;     /* enable pull up resistors for column pins */
}

/* This is a non-blocking function.
 * If a key is pressed, it returns 1. Otherwise, it returns a 0.
 */
char keypad_kbhit(void) {
    int col;

    GPIOC->MODER = 0x00005500;      /* make all row pins output */
    GPIOC->BSRR =  0x00F00000;      /* drive all row pins low */
    delay();                        /* wait for signals to settle */
    col = GPIOC->IDR & 0x000F;      /* read all column pins */
    GPIOC->MODER &= ~0x0000FF00;    /* disable all row pins drive */
    if (col == 0x000F)              /* if all columns are high */
        return 0;                   /* no key pressed */
    else
        return 1;                   /* a key is pressed */
```

```
}

/* make a small delay */
void delay(void) {
    int i;
    for (i = 0; i < 20; i++) ;
}
```

Key identification

After a key press is detected, the microprocessor will go through the process of identifying the key. Starting from the top row, the microprocessor drives one row low at a time; then it reads the columns. If the data read is all 1s, no key in that row is pressed and the process is moved to the next row. It drives the next row low, reads the columns, and checks for any zero. This process continues until a row is identified with a zero in one of the columns. The next task is to find out which column the pressed key belongs to. This should be easy since each column is connected to a separate input pin. Look at Example 3-1.

Example 3-1

From Figure 3-7, identify the row and column of the pressed key for each of the following.
(a) D3–D0 = 1110 for the row, D7–D4= 1011 for the column
(b) D3–D0 = 1101 for the row, D7–D4= 0111 for the column

Solution:

From Figure 3-7 the row and column can be used to identify the key.
(a)   The row belongs to D0 and the column belongs to D6; therefore, the key number 2 was pressed.
(b)   The row belongs to D1 and the column belongs to D7; therefore, the key number 4 was pressed.

Figure 3-8 is the flowchart for the detection and identification of the key activation.

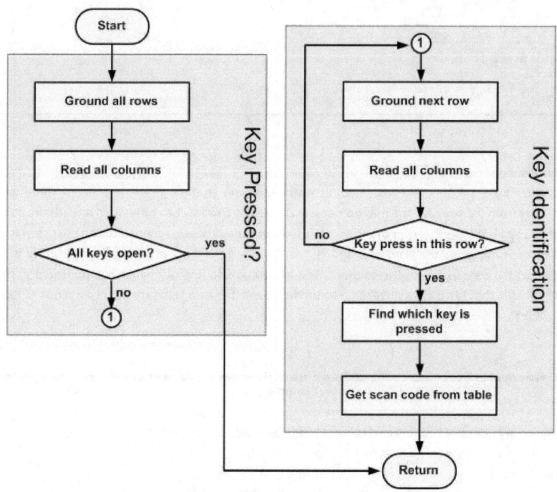

Figure 3-8: The Flowchart for Key Press Detection and Identification

Program 3-5 provides an implementation of the detection and identification algorithm in C language. We will exam it in details here. First for the initialization of the ports, Port C pins 3-0 are used for rows. The Port C pins 7-4 are used for columns. They are all configured as input digital pin to prevent accidental short circuit of two output pins. If output pins are driven high and low and two keys of the same column are pressed at the same time by accident, they will short the output low to output high of the adjacent pins and cause damages to these pins. To prevent this, all pins are configured as input pin and only one pin is configured as output pin at a time. Since only one pin is actively driving the row, shorting two rows will not damage the circuit. The input pins are configured with pull-up enabled so that when the connected keys are not pressed, they stay high and read as 1.

The key scanning function is a non-blocking function, meaning the function returns regardless of whether there is a key pressed or not. The function first drives all rows low and check to see if any key pressed. If no key is pressed, a zero is returned. Otherwise the code will proceed to check one row at a time by driving only one row low at a time and read the columns. If one of the columns is active, it will find out which column it is. With the combination of the active row and active column, the code will find out the key that is pressed and return a unique numeric code. The program below reads a 4x4 keypad and use the key code returned to set the LEDs. LED program is borrowed from P2-7 in Chapter 2.

```
/* p3_5.c: Matrix keypad scanning
 *
 * This program scans a 4x4 matrix keypad and returns a unique
 * number for each key pressed.
 * LD2 (green LED) is used to blink the returned number.
 *
 * PC0-3 are connected to the columns and PC4-7 are
 * connected to the rows of the keypad.
 *
 * This program was tested with Keil uVision v5.24a with DFP v2.11.0
 */

#include "stm32f4xx.h"

void delay(void);
void delayMs(int n);
void keypad_init(void);
char keypad_getkey(void);
void LED_init(void);
void LED_blink(int value);

int main(void) {
    unsigned char key;

    keypad_init();
    LED_init();

    while(1) {
        key = keypad_getkey();   /* read the keypad */
        if (key != 0)
            LED_blink(key);      /* set LEDs according to the key code */
    }
}
/* this function initializes PC0-3 (column) and PC4-7 (row).
 * The column pins need to have the pull-up resistors enabled.
 */
void keypad_init(void) {
    RCC->AHB1ENR |=  0x14;            /* enable GPIOC clock */
    GPIOC->MODER &= ~0x0000FFFF;      /* clear pin mode to input */
    GPIOC->PUPDR =  0x00000055;       /* enable pull up resistors for column pins */
}


/*
 * This is a non-blocking function to read the keypad.
 * If a key is pressed, it returns a unique code for the key.
 * Otherwise, a zero is returned.
 * PC6-9 are used as input and connected to the columns. Pull-up resistors are
 * enabled so when the keys are not pressed, these pins are pulled high.
 * PC4-7 are used as output that drives the keypad rows.
 * First, all rows are driven low and the input pins are read. If no key is
 * pressed, they will read as all one because of the pull up resistors.
 * If they are not all one, some key is pressed.
 * If some key is pressed, the program proceeds to drive only one row low at
 * a time and leave the rest of the rows inactive (float) then read the input pins.
 * Knowing which row is active and which column is active, the program can decide
 * which key is pressed.
```

77

```
 *
 * Only one row is driven so that if multiple keys are pressed and row pins are
 * shorted, the microcontroller will not be damaged. When the row is being
 * deactivated, it is driven high first otherwise the stray capacitance may keep
 * the inactive row low for some time.
 */
char keypad_getkey(void) {
    int row, col;
    const int row_mode[] = {0x00000100, 0x00000400, 0x00001000, 0x00004000}; /* one
row is output */
    const int row_low[] =  {0x00100000, 0x00200000, 0x00400000, 0x00800000}; /* one
row is low */
    const int row_high[] = {0x00000010, 0x00000020, 0x00000040, 0x00000080}; /* one
row is high */

    /* check to see any key pressed */
    GPIOC->MODER = 0x00005500;          /* make all row pins output */
    GPIOC->BSRR =  0x00F00000;          /* drive all row pins low */
    delay();                            /* wait for signals to settle */
    col = GPIOC->IDR & 0x000F;          /* read all column pins */
    GPIOC->MODER &= ~0x0000FF00;        /* disable all row pins drive */
    if (col == 0x000F)                  /* if all columns are high */
        return 0;                            /* no key pressed */

    /* If a key is pressed, it gets here to find out which key.
     * It activates one row at a time and read the input to see
     * which column is active. */
    for (row = 0; row < 4; row++) {
        GPIOC->MODER &= ~0x0000FF00;    /* disable all row pins drive */
        GPIOC->MODER |= row_mode[row];  /* enable one row at a time */
        GPIOC->BSRR = row_low[row];     /* drive the active row low */
        delay();                        /* wait for signal to settle */
        col = GPIOC->IDR & 0x000F;      /* read all columns */
        GPIOC->BSRR = row_high[row];    /* drive the active row high */
        if (col != 0x000F) break;       /* if one of the input is low, some key is
pressed. */
    }
    GPIOC->BSRR = 0x000000F0;           /* drive all rows high before disable them */
    GPIOC->MODER &= ~0x0000FF00;        /* disable all rows */
    if (row == 4)
        return 0;                            /* if we get here, no key is pressed */

    /* gets here when one of the rows has key pressed, check which column it is */
    if (col == 0x000E) return row * 4 + 1;      /* key in column 0 */
    if (col == 0x000D) return row * 4 + 2;      /* key in column 1 */
    if (col == 0x000B) return row * 4 + 3;      /* key in column 2 */
    if (col == 0x0007) return row * 4 + 4;      /* key in column 3 */

    return 0;    /* just to be safe */
}

void LED_init(void) {
    // enable PA5 for green LED
    RCC->AHB1ENR |= 1;                       /* enable GPIOA clock */
    GPIOA->MODER &= ~0xC0000C00;      /* clear pin mode */
    GPIOA->MODER |=  0x00000400;      /* set pin output mode */
}
/* turn on or off the LEDs according to the value */
void LED_blink(int value) {
```

```
        value %= 17;                        /* cap the max count at 16 */

        for (; value > 0; value--) {
            GPIOA->BSRR = 0x00000020;   /* turn on LED */
            delayMs(200);
            GPIOA->BSRR = 0x00200000;   /* turn off LED */
            delayMs(200);
        }
        delayMs(200);
}

/* make a small delay */
void delay(void) {
    int i;
    for (i = 0; i < 20; i++) ;
}

/* 16 MHz SYSCLK */
void delayMs(int n) {
    int i;
    for (; n > 0; n--)
        for (i = 0; i < 3195; i++) ;
}
```

Contact Bounce and Debounce

When a mechanical switch is closed or opened, the contacts do not make a clean transition instantaneously, rather the contacts open and close several times before they settle. This event is called contact bounce (see Figure 3-9). So it is possible when the program first detects a switch in the keypad is pressed but when interrogating which key is pressed, it would find no key pressed. This is the reason we have a return 0 after checking all the rows. Another problem manifested by contact bounce is that one key press may be recognized as multiple key presses by the program. Contact bounce also occurs when the switch is released. Because the switch contacts open and close several times before they settle, the program may detect a key press when the key is released.

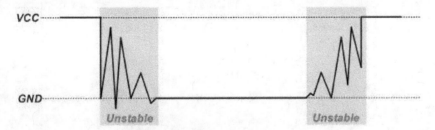

Figure 3-9: Switch contact bounces

For many applications, it is important that each key press is only recognized as one action. When you press a numeral key of a calculator, you expect to get only one digit. A contact bounce results in multiple digits entered with a single key press. A simple software solution is that when a transition of the contact state change is detected such as a key pressed or a key released, the software does a delay for about 10 – 20 ms to wait out the contact bounce. After the delay, the contacts should be settled and stable.

There are IC chips such as National Semiconductor's MM74C923 that incorporate keyboard scanning and decoding all in one chip. Such chips use combinations of counters and logic gates (no microprocessor) to implement the underlying concepts presented in Programs 3-4 and 3-5.

Review Questions

1. True or false. To see if any key is pressed, all rows are driven low.
2. If D3–D0 = 0111 is the data read from the columns, which column does the key pressed belong to?
3. True or false. Key press detection and key identification require two different processes.
4. In Figure 3-7, if the row has D3–D0 = 1110 and the columns are D7–D4 = 1110, which key is pressed?
5. True or false. To identify the key pressed, one row at a time is driven low.

Answers to Review Questions

Section 3-1
1. Input
2. Input
3. H-to-L
4. High
5. 0x80 and 0xC0

Section 3-2
1. True
2. Column 3
3. True
4. A
5. True

Chapter 4: UART Serial Port Programming

Computers transfer data in two ways: parallel and serial. In parallel data transfers, often eight or more lines (wire conductors) are used to transfer data to another device. In serial communication, the data is sent one bit at a time. Years ago, parallel data transfer was preferred for a short distance because it may transfer multiple bits at the same time and provides higher throughput. As technology advances, the data rate of serial communication may exceed parallel communication while parallel communication still retains the disadvantages of the size and cost of cable and connector, the crosstalk between the data lines and the difficulty of synchronizing the arrival time of data lines at a longer distance.

Serial communication and the study of associated chips are the topics of this chapter. Section 4.1 examines the basic concepts of serial communication. The STM Arm serial COM (UART) port programming is covered in Sections 4.2 and 4.3. The other serial data transfer protocols such as SPI and I2C are covered in future chapters.

Section 4.1: Basics of Serial Communication

When a microprocessor communicates with the outside world it usually provides the data in byte-size chunks. For parallel transfer, 8-bit data is transferred at the same time. For serial transfer, 8-bit data is transferred one bit at a time. Figure 4-1 diagrams serial versus parallel data transfers.

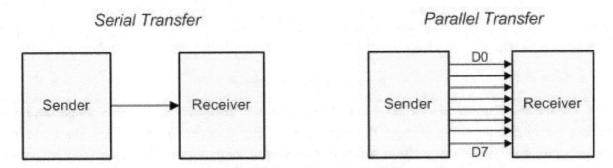

Figure 4-1: Serial vs. Parallel Data Transfer

The fact that in serial communication, a single data line is used instead of the 8-bit data line of parallel communication not only makes it much cheaper but also makes it possible for two computers located in two distant locations to communicate.

For serial data communication to work, the byte of data must be grabbed from the 8-bit data bus of the microprocessor and converted to serial bits using a parallel-in-serial-out shift register; then it can be transmitted over a single data line. This also means that at the receiving end there must be a serial-in-parallel-out shift register to receive the serial data, pack it into a byte, and present it to the system at the receiving end. See Figures 4-2 and 4-3.

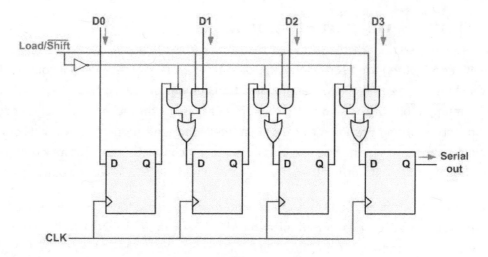

Figure 4-2: Parallel In Serial Out

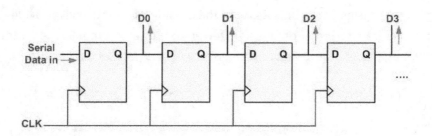

Figure 4-3: Serial In Parallel Out

When the distance is short, the digital signal can be transferred as it is on a simple wire and requires no modulation. This is how PC keyboards transfer data between the keyboard and the motherboard. However, for long-distance data transfers using communication lines such as a telephone, serial data communication requires a modem to modulate (convert from 0s and 1s to audio tones) the data before putting it on the transmission media and demodulate (convert from audio tones to 0s and 1s) at the receiving end.

Serial data communication uses two methods, asynchronous and synchronous. With synchronous communication, the clock is transmitted alongside with the data. With asynchronous communication, no clock is transmitted. The transmitter and receiver agree on a clock speed for data transmission. They may have slight speed difference so the receiver will try to synchronize the clock to the incoming data for every character received. We will see how it works later. The synchronous method usually transfers a block of data (characters) at a time while the asynchronous transfers a single byte at a time.

It is possible to write software to use either of these methods, but the programs can be tedious and inefficient. For this reason, special IC chips are made by many manufacturers for serial data communications. These chips are commonly referred to as UART (universal asynchronous receiver-transmitter) and USART (universal synchronous-asynchronous receiver-transmitter). The COM port in the PC uses an UART. When this function is incorporated into a microcontroller, it is often referred as SCI (Serial Communication Interface).

Half- and full-duplex transmission

In data transmission, a duplex transmission is one in which the data can be transmitted and received. This is in contrast to simplex transmission such as printers, in which the computer only sends data. Duplex transmissions can be half or full duplex. If data is transmitted one way at a time, it is referred to as *half duplex*. If the data can go both ways at the same time, it is *full duplex*. Of course, full duplex requires two wire conductors for the data lines (in addition to ground), one for the transmission and one for the reception, in order to transfer and receive data simultaneously. See Figure 4-4.

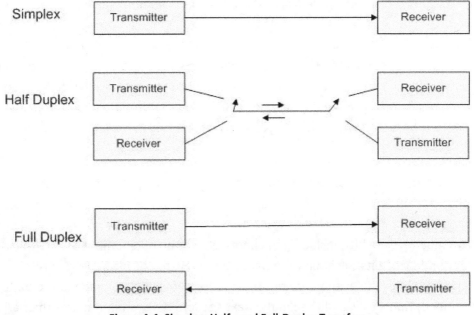

Figure 4-4: Simplex, Half-, and Full-Duplex Transfers

Asynchronous serial communication and data framing

The data coming in at the receiving end of the data line in a serial data transfer is all 0s and 1s; it is difficult to make sense of the data unless the sender and receiver agree on a set of rules, a *protocol*, on how the data is packed, how many bits constitute a character, and when the data begins and ends.

Start and stop bits

Asynchronous serial data communication is widely used for character-oriented transmissions. In the asynchronous method, each character, such as ASCII characters, is packed between the start and stop bits. This is called *framing*. The start bit is always one bit but the stop bit can be one or two bits. The start bit is always a 0 (low) and the stop bit(s) is a 1 (high). For example, look at Figure 4-5 where the ASCII character "A", binary 0100 0001, is framed between the start bit and 2 stop bits. Notice that the LSB is sent out first.

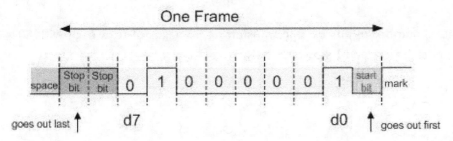

Figure 4-5: Framing ASCII "A" (0x41)

In Figure 4-5, when there is no data transfer, the signal stays 1 (high), which is referred to as a *mark*. The 0 (low) is referred to as *space*. Notice that the transmission begins with a start bit followed by D0, the LSB, and then the rest of the bits until the MSB (D7), finally, the 2 stop bits indicating the end of the character "A" are sent.

In asynchronous serial communications, peripheral chips can be programmed for data that is 5, 6, 7, or 8 bits wide. While in older systems ASCII characters were 7-bit, the modern systems usually send non-ASCII 8-bit data. The old Baud code uses 5- or 6-bit characters but they are rarely seen these days even though some of the hardware still support them. In some older systems, due to the slowness of the receiving mechanical device, 2 stop bits were used to give the device sufficient time to organize itself before transmission of the next byte. However, in modern PCs the use of 1 stop bit is common. Assuming that we are transferring a text file of ASCII characters using 1 stop bit, we have a total of 10 bits for each character since 8 bits are for the ASCII code, and 1 and 2 bits are for start and stop bits, respectively. Therefore, for each 8-bit character, there are extra two bits or 25% overhead. (2/8 x100=25%)

Parity bit

In some systems in order to maintain data integrity, the parity bit of the character byte is included in the data frame. This means that for each character (7- or 8-bit, depending on the system) we have a single parity bit in addition to the start and stop bits. The parity bit may be odd or even. In the case of an odd parity the number of data bits, including the parity bit, has an odd number of 1s. Similarly, in an even parity the total number of bits, including the parity bit, is even. For example, the ASCII character "A", binary 0100 0001, has 0 for the even parity bit. UART chips allow programming of the parity bit for odd, even, and no parity options, as we will see in the next section. If a system requires the parity, the parity bit is transmitted after the MSB, and is followed by the stop bit. Parity bit offers single bit detection but no easy way to recovery. The modern data communication uses a higher level of protocols such as TCP/IP that performs error detection and recovery strategy. Usage of the parity bit is not as useful and if rarely used.

Data transfer rate

The rate of data transfer in serial data communication is specified in *bps* (bits per second). Another often used term for bps is *Baud rate*. However, the baud and bps rates are not necessarily equal. This is due to the fact that baud rate is defined as the number of signal changes per second. In modems, it is possible for each signal to transfer multiple bits of data. As far as the unmodulated signal is concerned, the baud rate and bps are the same, and for this reason, in this book we use the terms bps and baud interchangeably.

Example 4-1

Calculate the total number of bits used in transferring 50 pages of text, each with 80 × 25 characters. Assume 8 bits per character and 1 stop bit.

Solution:

For each character a total of 10 bits is used, 8 bits for the character, 1 stop bit and 1 start bit. Therefore, the total number of bits is 80 × 25 × 10 = 20,000 bits per page. For 50 pages, 1,000,000 bits will be transferred.

Example 4-2

Calculate the time it takes to transfer the entire 50 pages of data in Example 4-1 using a baud rate of:
(a) 9600   (b) 57,600

Solution:

(a) 1,000,000 / 9600 = 104 seconds

(b) 1,000,000 / 57,600 = 17 seconds

Example 4-3

Calculate the time it takes to download a movie of 2 gigabytes using a telephone line. Assume 8 bits, 1 stop bit, no parity, and 57,600 baud rate.

Solution:
$2 \times 2^{30} \times 10 / 57{,}600 = 347{,}222$ seconds = 4 days

---

RS232 and other serial I/O standards

To allow compatibility among data communication equipment made by various manufacturers, an interfacing standard called RS232 was proposed by the Electronics Industries Association (EIA) in 1960, where RS stands for recommended standard. It has several revisions through the years using an alphabet at the end to denote the revision number such as RS232C. It was finally adopted as an EIA standard and renamed EIA232, later on, TIA232 but most of the people still refer to it as RS232.

Today, RS232 is still used for simple serial I/O interfacing. However, since the standard was set long before the advent of the TTL logic family, the input and output voltage levels are not TTL compatible. In the RS232 at the receiver, a 1 is represented by –3V to –25 V, while the 0 bit is +3V to +25 V, making the voltages between –3V to +3V undefined. For this reason, to connect any RS232 to a TTL-level chip (microprocessor or UART) we must use voltage converters such as MAX232 or MAX233 to convert the TTL logic levels to the RS232 voltage level, and vice versa. MAX232 and MAX233 IC chips are commonly referred to as line drivers/receivers. This is shown in Figures 4-6 and 4-7. The MAX232 has two sets of line drivers for transferring and receiving data, as shown in Figure 4-6. The line drivers used for TxD are called T1 and T2, while the line receivers for RxD are designated as R1 and R2. In many applications, only one of each is used. Notice in MAX232 that the T1 line driver has a designation of T1in and T1out on pin numbers 11 and 14, respectively. The T1in pin is the TTL side and is connected to TxD of the USART, while T1out is the RS232 side that is connected to the RxD pin of the RS232 DB connector. The R1 line driver has a designation of R1in and R1out on pin numbers 13 and 12, respectively. The R1in (pin 13) is the RS232 side that is connected to the TxD pin of the RS232 DB connector, and R1out (pin 12) is the TTL side that is connected to the RxD pin of the USART.

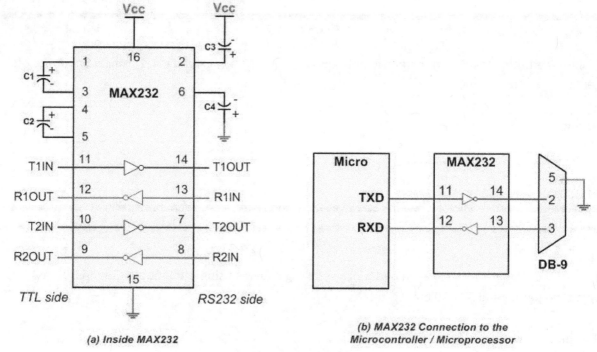

(a) Inside MAX232

(b) MAX232 Connection to the Microcontroller / Microprocessor

Figure 4-6: MAX232

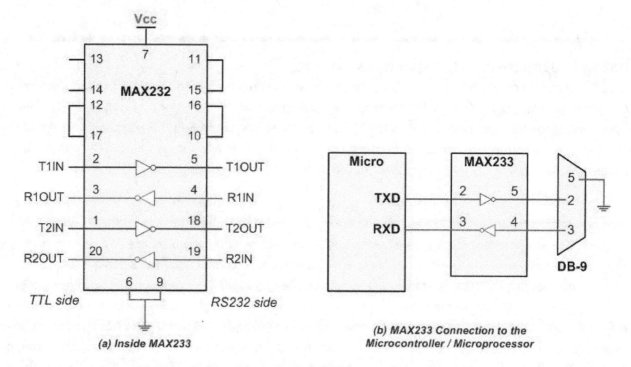

(a) Inside MAX233

(b) MAX233 Connection to the Microcontroller / Microprocessor

Figure 4-7: MAX233

MAX232 requires four capacitors of 1 μF. To save board space, some designers use the MAX233 chip from Maxim. The MAX233 performs the same job as the MAX232 but eliminates the need for capacitors. However, the MAX233 chip is larger and more expensive than the MAX232. See Figure 4-7 for MAX233 with no capacitor used.

RS232 pins

Table 4-1 provides the pins and their labels for the RS232 cable, commonly referred to as the DB-9 connector. The x86 PC 9-pin serial port is shown in Figure 4-8.

Pin	Description
1	Data carrier detect (DCD)
2	Received data (RxD)
3	Transmitted data (TxD)
4	Data terminal ready (DTR)
5	Signal ground (GND)
6	Data set ready (DSR)
7	Request to send (RTS)
8	Clear to send (CTS)
9	Ring indicator (RI)

Table 4-1: RS232 Pins

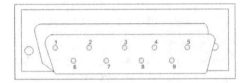

Figure 4-8: 9-Pin Male Connector

Data communication classification

Current terminology classifies data communication equipment as DTE (data terminal equipment) or DCE (data communication equipment). DTE refers to terminals and computers that send and receive data, while DCE refers to communication equipment, such as modems, that is responsible for transferring the data. Notice that all the RS232 pin function definitions of Table 4-1 are from the DTE point of view.

The simplest connection between two PCs (DTE and DTE) requires a minimum of three pins, TxD, RxD, and ground, as shown in Figure 4-9. Notice that the connection between two DTE devices, such as two PCs, requires pins 2 and 3 to be interchanged as shown in Figure 4-9. In looking at Figure 4-9, keep in mind that the RS232 signal definitions are from the point of view of DTE.

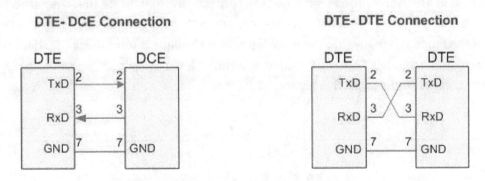

Figure 4-9: DTE-DCE and DTE-DTE Connections

Examining the RS232 handshaking signals

To ensure fast and reliable data transmission between two devices, the data transfer must be coordinated. Some of the pins of the RS-232 are used for handshaking signals. They are described below. Due to the fact that in serial data communication the receiving device may have no room for the data, there must be a way to inform the sender to stop sending data. So some of these handshaking lines may be used for flow control tool

1. **DTR (data terminal ready):** When the terminal (or a PC COM port) is turned on, after going through a self-test, it sends out signal DTR to indicate that it is ready for communication. If there is something wrong with the COM port, this signal will not be activated. This is an active-low signal and can be used to inform the modem that the computer is alive and kicking. This is an output pin from DTE (PC COM port) and an input to the modem.

2. **DSR (data set ready):** When a DCE (modem) is turned on and has gone through the self-test, it asserts DSR to indicate that it is ready to communicate. Therefore, it is an output from the modem (DCE) and an input to the PC (DTE). This is an active-low signal. If for any reason the modem cannot make a connection to the telephone, this signal remains inactive, indicating to the PC (or terminal) that it cannot accept or send data.

3. **RTS (request to send):** When the DTE device (such as a PC) has a byte to transmit, it asserts RTS to signal the modem that it has a byte of data to transmit. RTS is an active-low output from the DTE and an input to the modem.

4. **CTS (clear to send):** In response to RTS, when the modem has room for storing the data it is to receive, it sends out signal CTS to the DTE (PC) to indicate that it can receive the data now. This input signal to the DTE is used by the DTE to start transmission.

5. **CD (carrier detect, or DCD, data carrier detect):** The modem asserts signal DCD to inform the DTE (PC) that a valid carrier has been detected and that contact between it and the other modem is established. Therefore, DCD is an output from the modem and an input to the PC (DTE).

6. **RI (ring indicator):** An output from the modem (DCE) and an input to a PC (DTE) indicates that the telephone is ringing. It goes on and off in synchronization with the ringing sound. Of the six handshake signals, this is the least often used, due to the fact that modems take care of answering the phone. However, if in a given system the PC is in charge of answering the phone, this signal can be used.

From the above description, PC and modem communication can be summarized as follows: While signals DTR and DSR are used by the PC and modem, respectively, to indicate that they are alive and well, it is RTS and CTS that actually control the flow of data. When the PC wants to send data it asserts RTS, and in response, if the modem is ready (has the room) to accept the data, it sends back CTS. If for lack of room, the modem does not activate CTS, the PC will de-assert DTR and try again. RTS and CTS are also referred to as *hardware control flow signals*. See Figure 4-10.

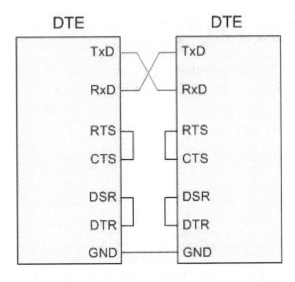

Figure 4-10: Null Modem Connection with Flow Control Signals

This concludes the description of the most important pins of the RS232 handshake signals plus TxD, RxD, and ground. The ground is also referred to as SG (signal ground). In the next section, we will see serial communication programming for the microcontroller.

Review Questions

1. The transfer of data using parallel lines is _____ (more expensive, less expensive).
2. In communications between two PCs in New York and Dallas, we use _____ (serial, parallel) data communication.
3. In serial data communication, which method fits block-oriented data?
4. True or false. Sending data to a printer is duplex.
5. True or false. In duplex we must have two data lines.
6. The start and stop bits are used in the _____ (synchronous, asynchronous) method.
7. Assuming that we are transmitting letter "D", binary 100 0100, with odd-parity bit and 2 stop bits, show the sequence of bits transferred.
8. In Question 7, find the overhead due to framing.
9. Calculate the time it takes to transfer 400 characters as in Question 7 if we use 1200 bps. What percentage of time is wasted due to overhead?
10. True or false. RS232 is not TTL-compatible.

Section 4.2: Programming the UART Ports

In this section, we examine the USART serial port registers of STM Arm and show how to program them to transmit and receive data serially. The STM Arm chips come with many on-chip USART (Universal synchronous/asynchronous receiver transmitter) and they are designated as USARTx, x=1, 2, 3 and so on. STM Arm chips also come with on-chip LPUART (Low-power universal asynchronous receiver transmitter) and are designated as LPUARTx, x=1, 2 and so on. The STM Arm supports SPI and I2C protocols as we will see in future chapters. In the STM Arm trainers such as Nulceo boards, the USART2 port is connected to the ST-Link programming and debugging tool, which is connected to a USB connector. See Figure 4-11. The ST-LINK/V2 is an in-circuit debugger and programmer for the STM32 microcontroller families. The single wire interface module (SWIM) and JTAG/serial wire debugging (SWD) interfaces are used to communicate with any STM32 microcontroller located on an application board. ST-LINK/V2 connection performs three distinct functions among other things:

a) The programming (downloading) of the target device.
b) The debugging using Serial Wire Debug (SWD). The SWD is an alternative to the JTAG standard.
c) Use as a virtual COM port.

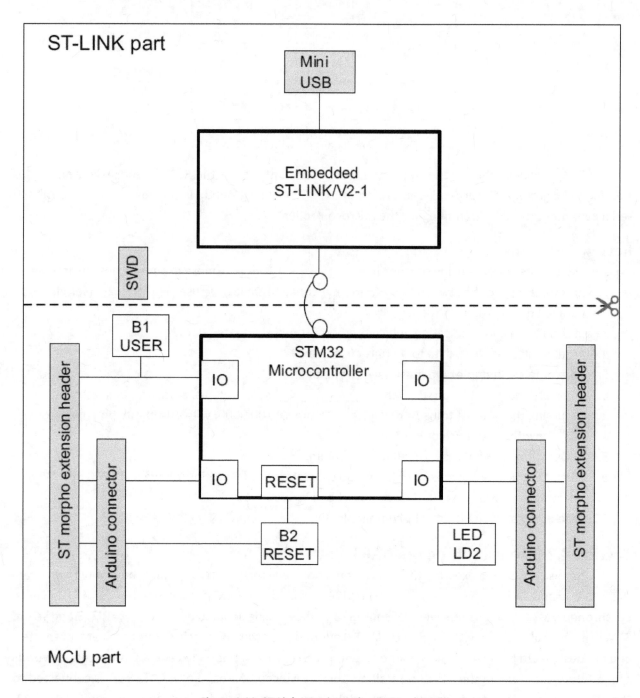

Figure 4-11: ST-Link-V2-1 in Nucleo ST Arm board

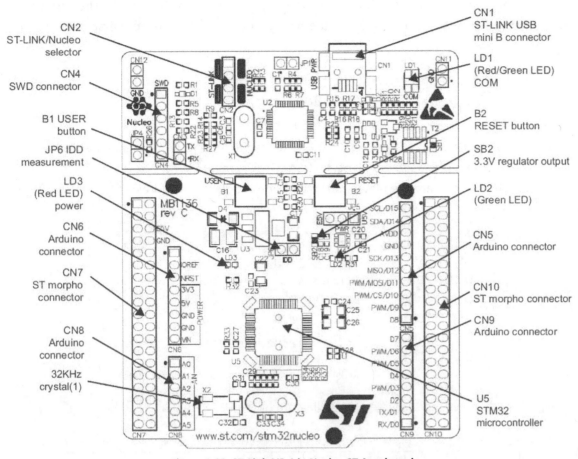

Figure 4-12: ST-Link-V2-1 in Nucleo ST Arm board

When the USB cable connects the PC to the STM Arm trainer board, the device driver at the host PC establishes a virtual connection between the PC and the UART of the target STM Arm device with the ST-LINK in between. On the Nucleo boards, the connection appears as a UART. On the host PC, it appears as a COM/USB port and will work with communication software on the PC such as a terminal emulator. It is called a virtual connection because there is no need for an additional cable to make this connection.

Examining the datasheet of the Nucleo board, we see the UART2 uses PA2 (USART2_TX) and PA3 (USART2_RX) for TxD and RxD, respectively. See Figure 4-13.

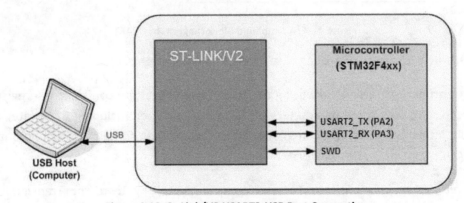

Figure 4-13: St-Link/V2 USART2-USB Port Connection

As we mentioned earlier, the STM Arm has many on-chip Serial COM ports. They are designated as USARTx. The following is the partial list of the base addresses in the memory map for STM32F446RE chip:

- USART1 base address: 0x4001 1000
- USART2 base address: 0x4000 4400
- USART3 base address: 0x4000 4800

For other UART addresses see Table 2-3 in Chapter 2. Check the memory map table for the datasheet of your device. The address offsets for some of the USART registers are shown below. The actual physical addresses of these registers are the offset addresses added to the base addresses.

Register Name	Register Function	Register Address Offset (Hex)
USART_SR	Status Register	0000
USART_DR	Data Register	0004
USART_BRR	Baud Rate Register	0008
USART_CR1	Control Register 1	000C
USART_CR2	Control Register 2	0010
USART_CR3	Control Register 3	0014

Table 4-2: Partial list of USART Registers and their addresses

Figure 4-14 shows the simplified block diagram of the USART units

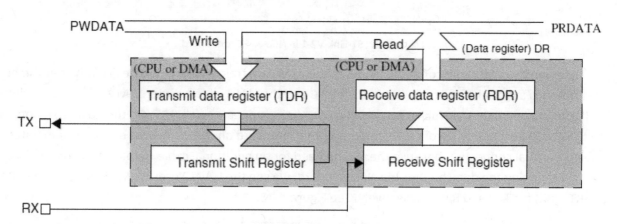

Figure 4-14: A Simplified Block Diagram of USART

In all microcontrollers, there are 3 groups of registers in UART peripherals:

1. **Configuration registers:** Before using the USART peripheral the configuration registers must be initialized. This sets some parameters of the communication including Baud rate, word length, stop bit, interrupts (if needed). In STM Arm microcontroller, some of the configuration registers are: BAUD, Control 1, and Control 2.

2. **Transmit and receive register:** To send data, we simply write to the Transmit Data register (USART_TDR). The USART peripheral sends out the content of the data transmit register through the serial transmit pin (TXD). The received data is stored in the Receive Data register

(USART_RDR). Notice that we have two separate registers for transmit and Receive registers. They have two different addresses. That means you write to the transmit register and you read from the receive register.

3. **_Interrupt and status register:_** the interrupt and status register contains some flags which show the state of sending and receiving data including the availability of the newly received data, the existence of errors in receiving data, the sending unit is ready for new data, Interrupt flag, etc. The interrupt and status register is called as USART_ISR (USART interrupt and status) in the STM Arms.

There are many special function registers associated with each of the USARTs. In this section, first, we will be using the USART2 as an example, since a virtual connection is available on the STM Nucleo trainer boards.

First, we will examine the baud-rate generator registers.

16MHz HSI Clock and SYSCLK

In STM32F446 Arm, there are three different clock sources that can be used to drive the system clock (SYSCLK). They are as follow:

1. HSI (High Speed Internal) RC oscillator clock.

2. HSE (High Speed External) oscillator clock using a crystal value of 4MHz to 26 MHz.

3. PLL clock.

The SYSCLK (system clock) clock is the clock that runs the peripherals such as USART. The SYSCLK itself can come from any of the above sources. In this book, we use the HSI (high speed internal) RC. According to STM32F446 reference manual "The HSI clock signal is generated from an internal 16 MHz RC oscillator and can be used directly as a system clock, or used as PLL input. The HSI RC oscillator has the advantage of providing a clock source at low cost (no external components). It also has a faster startup time than the HSE crystal oscillator however, even with calibration the frequency is less accurate than an external crystal oscillator or ceramic resonator." Again, it must be emphasized that after restart from Reset, the HSI oscillator frequency is set to its default value of 16 MHz and this is the clock frequency we use in this book. See Appendix C for more information on STMF4xx Arm clock. The HSI Oscillator is the default clock source for SYSCLK and is turned on upon Reset. The HSION bit D0 in Figure 4-15 (RCC_CR) shows that.

31	30	29	28	27	26	25	24	23	22	21	20	19	18	17	16
Res	Res	PLLSAI RDY	PLLSAI ON	PLLI2S RDY	PLLI2S ON	PLL RDY	PLL ON	Res	Res	Res	Res	CSS ON	HSE BYP	HSE RDY	HSE ON
		r	rw	r	rw	r	rw					rw	rw	r	rw
15	14	13	12	11	10	9	8	7	6	5	4	3	2	1	0
HSICAL[7:0]								HSITRIM[4:0]					Res	HSI RDY	HSI ON
r	r	r	r	r	r	r	r	rw	rw	rw	rw	rw		r	rw

Bit 1 **HSIRDY**: Internal high-speed clock ready flag

Set by hardware to indicate that the HSI oscillator is stable. After the HSION bit is cleared, HSIRDY goes low after 6 HSI clock cycles.

0: HSI oscillator not ready

1: HSI oscillator ready

Bit 0 **HSION**: Internal high-speed clock enable

Set and cleared by software.

Set by hardware to force the HSI oscillator ON when leaving the Stop or Standby mode or in case of a failure of the HSE oscillator used directly or indirectly as the system clock. This bit cannot be cleared if the HSI is used directly or indirectly as the system clock.

0: HSI oscillator OFF

1: HSI oscillator ON

Figure 4-15: RCC_CR (RCC Control Register) to showing the HSI Clock Source

SYSCLK and Peripheral Clock

As we show in Appendix C, the peripheral bus clocks are derived from the (SYSCLK) System Clock. In order to optimize power consumption, each clock source can be switched on or off independently when it is not used. Figures 4-16 and 4-17 show several prescalers to configure the AHB frequency, the high speed APB (APB2) and the low speed APB (APB1) domains. Each peripheral clock can be enabled by the xxxxEN bit of the RCC_AHBxENR, RCC_APBxENRy registers as we will see soon. Notice from Figures 4-16 and 4-17, the SYSCLK goes through the AHB prescaler. The lowest value for the AHB prescaler can divide by is 1 and the highest is 512 before it goes to APBx prescaler. Bits D7-D4 of RCC clock configuration register (RCC_CFGR) registers dictates that. After going through APBx presacler it is fed to USART2 and other peripherals such as Timer, I2C and so on. Bits D12:D10 of RCC_CFGR gives us the options of dividing HCLK by 1, 2, 4, 8 or 16 before it becomes PCLK1. That means if we use 16MHz SYSCLK default clock, we can have maximum of 16MHz clock source for all the peripherals if we leave these registers unchanged from default. In case of USART we use 16MHz for Baud rate generation, as we will see soon. Notice in Figure 4-16 for RCC_CFGR (Clock Configuration Register) we also have bits D15:D13 for PPRE2 which is for APB high-speed prescaler (APB2) clock divider. In all of the above prescalers the default is to divide the SYSCLK by 1.

31	30	29	28	27	26	25	24	23	22	21	20	19	18	17	16
MCO2[1:0]		MCO2 PRE[2:0]			MCO1 PRE[2:0]				MCO1		RTCPRE[4:0]				
rw		rw	rw	rw	rw	rw	rw		rw		rw	rw	rw	rw	rw
15	14	13	12	11	10	9	8	7	6	5	4	3	2	1	0
PPRE2[2:0]			PPRE1[2:0]						HPRE[3:0]			SWS[1:0]		SW[1:0}	
rw	rw	rw	rw	rw	rw			rw	rw	rw	rw	r	r	rw	rw

Bits 15:13 **PPRE2:** APB high-speed prescaler (APB2)

Set and cleared by software to control APB high-speed clock division factor.

Caution: The software has to set these bits correctly not to exceed 90 MHz on this domain.

The clocks are divided with the new prescaler factor from 1 to 16 AHB cycles after PPRE2 write.

0xx: AHB clock not divided

100: AHB clock divided by 2

101: AHB clock divided by 4

110: AHB clock divided by 8

111: AHB clock divided by 16

Bits 12:10 **PPRE1:** APB Low speed prescaler (APB1)

Set and cleared by software to control APB low-speed clock division factor.

Caution: The software has to set these bits correctly not to exceed 45 MHz on this domain. The clocks are divided with the new prescaler factor from 1 to 16 AHB cycles after PPRE1 write.

0xx: AHB clock not divided

100: AHB clock divided by 2

101: AHB clock divided by 4

110: AHB clock divided by 8

111: AHB clock divided by 16

Bits 9:8 Reserved, must be kept at reset value.

Bits 7:4 **HPRE:** AHB prescaler

Set and cleared by software to control AHB clock division factor.

Caution: The clocks are divided with the new prescaler factor from 1 to 16 AHB cycles after HPRE write.

Caution: The AHB clock frequency must be at least 25 MHz when the Ethernet is used.

0xxx: system clock not divided

1000: system clock divided by 2

1001: system clock divided by 4

1010: system clock divided by 8

1011: system clock divided by 16

1100: system clock divided by 64

1101: system clock divided by 128

1110: system clock divided by 256

1111: system clock divided by 512

Figure 4-16: RCC_CFGR (Clock Configuration Register) Clock Select Resgister bit assignment

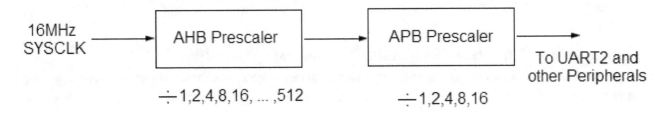

Figure 4-17: Clock Generation for USART2

Note
The clock generation of STM Arm is discussed in more details in the Appendix C.

Enabling Clock to USART2

It must be noted that when the peripheral clock is not active, the peripheral registers read or write accesses are not supported. The GPIO ports discussed in chapters 2 and 3 are connected to AHB2 and its clock can be enabled by using RCC_AHB2_ENR (AHB2 Enable register) bits, as we saw in chapters 2 and 3. Some of the USARTx modules are associated with APB1 bus clock including the USART2 used in this chapter. It must be emphasized that all the peripherals on AHBx and APBx buses have their clocks disabled after reset. Their bus clock has to be enabled before gaining access to the registers in that module. Figure 4-18 shows some of the clock enable bits for various peripherals in the RCC_APB1ENR register. The D17 bit of that register is used to enable the clock to the USART2 used in this chapter. We will see others as we examine the STM Arm peripherals throughout the book.

31	30	29	28	27	26	25	24	23	22	21	20	19	18	17	16
Res.	Res.	DAC EN	PWR EN	CEC EN	CAN2 EN	CAN1 EN	FMPI2C1 EN	I2C3 EN	I2C2 EN	I2C1 EN	UART5 EN	UART4 EN	USART3 EN	USART2 EN	SPDIFRX EN
		rw	rw	rw	rw	rw	rw	rw	rw	rw	rw	rw	rw	rw	rw

15	14	13	12	11	10	9	8	7	6	5	4	3	2	1	0
SPI3 EN	SPI2 EN	Res.	Res.	WWDG EN	Res.	Res.	TIM14 EN	TIM13 EN	TIM12 EN	TIM7 EN	TIM6 EN	TIM5 EN	TIM4 EN	TIM3 EN	TIM2 EN
rw	rw			rw			rw	rw	rw	rw	rw	rw	rw	rw	rw

Bit 20 **UART5EN:** UART5 clock enable
This bit is set and cleared by software.
0: UART5 clock disabled
1: UART5 clock enabled

Bit 19 **UART4EN:** UART4 clock enable
This bit is set and cleared by software.
0: UART4 clock disabled
1: UART4 clock enabled

Bit 18 **USART3EN:** USART3 clock enable
This bit is set and cleared by software.
0: USART3 clock disabled
1: USART3 clock enabled

Bit 17 **USART2EN:** USART2 clock enable
This bit is set and cleared by software.
0: USART2 clock disabled

Figure 4-18: APB1ENR peripheral clock enable register (RCC_APB1ENR) Bit Assignments (Partial Listing)

Transmitter and Receiver Clock in USART baud rate generation

The transmitter uses the transmission clock to pace the data bit output. For each clock pulse, one bit is transmitted. Therefore, the transmitter operates on the clock that runs at the Baud rate. Because USART is asynchronous, the receiver needs to detect the falling edge of the start bit and then samples the consequent bits at the center of the bit time, so it has to run on a faster clock. This is called oversampling.

BAUD Register

In the USART of ST Arm, the baud rate for the receiver and transmitter (Rx and Tx) are both set to the same value as programmed in the USART_BRR register. Although the BAUD register (USART_BRR) is a 32-bit register only the lower 16 bits are used. For BRR register, we have the choices of oversampling of 8 or 16. This is discussed next.

Oversampling by 16 and Baud Register

In case of oversampling by 16 (OVER8 = 0, default), we get BRR = USARTDIV using the following equation:

Tx/Rx baud = Fck / 8 x (2 - OVER8) x USARTDIV

= Fck / 8 x (2 - 0) x USARTDIV

= Fck / 8 x 2 x USARTDIV

USARTDIV = Fck / 16 x Baud

In which Fck is the clock frequency fed to USART and USARTDIV is an unsigned fixed point number that is coded on the USART_BRR register. Notice from Figure 4-19, for the oversampling of 16, the fixed number with both mantissa and fraction are placed in USART_BRR register in a way that the lower 4 bits of the USART_BRR are used for fraction part and the upper 12 bits are set aside for Mantissa. See Example 4-4A.

31	30	29	28	27	26	25	24	23	22	21	20	19	18	17	16
Res	Res	Res	Res	Res	Res	Res	Res	Res	Res	Res	Res	Res	Res	Res	Res

15	14	13	12	11	10	9	8	7	6	5	4	3	2	1	0
DIV_Mantissa[11:0]												DIV_Fraction[3:0]			
rw	rw	rw	rw	rw	rw	rw	rw	rw	rw	rw	rw	rw	rw	rw	rw

Bits 31:16 Reserved, must be kept at reset value

Bits 15:4 **DIV_Mantissa[11:0]**: mantissa of USARTDIV

These 12 bits define the mantissa of the USART Divider (USARTDIV)

Bits 3:0 **DIV_Fraction[3:0]**: fraction of USARTDIV

These 4 bits define the fraction of the USART Divider (USARTDIV). When OVER8=1, the DIV_Fraction3 bit is not considered and must be kept cleared.

Figure 4-19: BAUD (USART_BRR) Register

See Examples 4-4 and 4-5 for the calculations of values to put in USART_BRR Baud register.

Example 4-4

Assume the clock source of 16 MHz is fed to USART Baud rate generator with oversampling rate of 16. Find the values for the USART_BRR register for baud rates of (a) 9,600, (b) 19,200, (c) 57,600, and (d) 115,200.

Solution:

USARTDIV = Fck / 16 x Baud

(a) 16MHz / 16 x 9,600 = 104.166. Now, 104 = 0x68 for upper 12-bits. For fraction part, 0.166 x 16 = 2.656 and we use 3 for the lower 4 bits. Therefore BRR = 0x0683

(b) 16MHz / 16 x 19,200 = 52.08. Now, 52 = 0x034 for upper 12-bits. For fraction part, 0.08 x 16 = 1.28 and we use 1 for lower 4-bits. Therefore BRR = 0x0341

(c) 16MHz / 16 x 57,600 = 17.36. Now, 17 = 0x011 for upper 12-bits. For fraction part, 0.36 x 16 = 5.76 and we use 6 for lower 4 bits. Therefore BRR = 0x0116

(d) 16MHz / 16 x 115,200 = 8.68. Now, 08 = 0x008 for upper 12-bits. For fraction part, 0.68 x 16 = 10.88 and we use 11 = 0xB for lower 4-bits. Therefore BRR = 0x008B.

Some of the standard Baud rates are 9,600, 19,200, 57,600, and 115,200. Tables 4-3 shows the USART_BRR Register values for the different baud rate using oversampling of 16 with 16 MHz Clock frequency.

Baud rate	BRR (in dec)	BRR (in hex)
9,600	104.166	0x0683
19,200	52.06	0x0341
57,600	17.36	0x0116
115,200	8.68	0x008B

Table 4-3: BAUD Rate Register (BRR) Values for Some Baud Rates using OVER=16 and clock of 16MHz.

Oversampling by 8 and Baud Register

In the case of oversampling by 8 (OVER8 = 1), the equation is:

Tx / Rx baud = Fck / 8 x (2 - OVER8) x USARTDIV

= Fck / 8 x (2 - 1) x USARTDIV

= Fck / 8 x USARTDIV

USARTDIV = Fck / 8 x Baud

In case of oversampling by 8 (OVER8=1), the fractional part is coded on 3 bits and programmed by the DIV_fraction[2:0] bits in the USART_BRR register, and bit DIV_fraction[3] must be kept cleared.

Example 4-5

Assume the clock source of 16 MHz is fed to USART Baud rate generator with oversampling rate of 8. Find the values for the USART_BRR register for baud rates of (a) 9,600, (b) 19,200, (c) 57,600, and (d) 115,200.

Solution:

According to STM32F446 reference manual "When OVER8=1, the fractional part is coded on 3 bits and programmed by the DIV_fraction[2:0] bits in the USART_BRR register, and bit DIV_fraction[3] must be kept cleared."

USARTDIV = Fck / 8 x Baud

(a) 16MHz / 8 x 9,600 = 280.33. Now, we use 280 = 0x118 for upper 12-bits. For fraction part, 0.33 x 8 = 2.64 and we use 3 for 3 lower bits. Therefore BRR = 0x1183. Notice the 4th bit must be 0 in oversampling of 8.

(b) 16MHz / 8 x 19,200 = 104.166. Now, we use 104 = 0x068 for upper 12 bits. For fraction part, 0.166 x 8 = 1.328 and we use 1 for 3 lower bits. Therefore BRR = 0x0681

(c) 16MHz / 8 x 57,600 = 34.72. We use 35 = 0x023 for upper 12-bits. For fraction part, 0.72x 8 = 5.77 and we use 6 for lower 3 bits. Therefore BRR = 0x0236

(d) 16MHz / 8 x 115,200 = 17.36. We use 17 = 0x011 for upper 12bits. For fraction part, 0.36 x 8 = 2.88 and we use 3 for lower 3 bits. Therefore BRR = 0x0113

Table 4-4 shows the USART_BRR Register values for the different baud rate using oversampling of 8 with 16 MHz Clock frequency.

Baud rate	BRR (in decimal)	BRR (in hex)
9,600	280.33	0x1183
19,200	104.166	0x0681
57,600	34.72	0x0236
115,200	17.36	0x0113

Table 4-4: BAUD Rate Register (BRR) Values for Some Baud Rates using OVER=8 and clock of 16MHz.

The choice of 16 or 8 oversampling is done via the CR1 Control register. We discuss CR1 control register next.

USART Control 1 (USART_CR1) register

The next important register in USART is the control register. We have several USART control registers. The most important among them are USART Control 1 (USART_CR1) register and USART Control 2 (USART_CR2) register. They are 32-bit registers. The USART_CR1 register is used to set the number of bits per character (data length) in a frame among other things. Notice that the M1 bits of the USART_CR1 register determine the framing of data by specifying the number of bits per character (character size). The default for number of bits in character (word length) is 8. The USART_CR1 register is also used to enable the serial port to send (TE, Transmit Enable) and receive (RE, Receive Enable) data too. USART feature cannot be used unless the UE (USART Enable) bit of CR1 register is set to high. The TE (Transmit Enable), RE (Receive Enable), UE (USART enable) are some of the most important bits in this register. Selection of oversampling (OVER8) for Baud rate is another important bit in this register. Upon Reset, the OVER8=0 which is for oversampling of 16. Many of the other bits in CR1 are used for interrupts, as we will see in Chapter 6. See Figure 4-20.

31	30	29	28	27	26	25	24	23	22	21	20	19	18	17	16
Res	Res	Res	Res	Res	Res	Res	Res	Res	Res	Res	Res	Res	Res	Res	Res

15	14	13	12	11	10	9	8	7	6	5	4	3	2	1	0
OVER8	Res	UE	M	WAKE	PCE	PS	PEIE	TXEIE	TCIE	RXNEIE	IDLEIE	TE	RE	RWU	SBK
rw		rw	rw	rw	rw	rw	rw	rw	rw	rw	rw	rw	rw	rw	rw

Bit 15 **OVER8**: Oversampling mode
   0: oversampling by 16
   1: oversampling by 8
Bit 13 **UE**: USART enable
   When this bit is cleared the USART prescalers and outputs are stopped and the end of the current byte transfer in order to reduce power consumption. This bit is set and cleared by software.
   0: USART prescaler and outputs disabled
   1: USART enabled

Bit 12 **M**: Word length

This bit determines the word length. It is set or cleared by software.

0: 1 Start bit, 8 Data bits, n Stop bit

1: 1 Start bit, 9 Data bits, n Stop bit

Bit 7 **TXEIE**: TXE interrupt enable

This bit is set and cleared by software.

0: Interrupt is inhibited

1: An USART interrupt is generated whenever TXE=1 in the USART_SR register

Bit 6 **TCIE**: Transmission complete interrupt enable

This bit is set and cleared by software.

0: Interrupt is inhibited

1: An USART interrupt is generated whenever TC=1 in the USART_SR register

Bit 5 **RXNEIE**: RXNE interrupt enable

This bit is set and cleared by software.

0: Interrupt is inhibited

1: An USART interrupt is generated whenever ORE=1 or RXNE=1 in the USART_SR register

Bit 4 **IDLEIE**: IDLE interrupt enable

This bit is set and cleared by software.

0: Interrupt is inhibited

1: An USART interrupt is generated whenever IDLE=1 in the USART_SR register

Bit 3 **TE**: Transmitter enable

This bit enables the transmitter. It is set and cleared by software.

0: Transmitter is disabled

1: Transmitter is enabled

Bit 2 **RE**: Receiver enable

This bit enables the receiver. It is set and cleared by software.

0: Receiver is disabled

1: Receiver is enabled and begins searching for a start bit

Figure 4-20: USART CR1 (Control 1 Register) bits definition (Partial Listing)

UART Control 2 register (USART_CR2)

Figure 4-21 describes various bits of the USART Control 2 (USART_CR2) Register. The most important bit in this register is the selection of number of stop bits. The default, upon Reset, is 1 stop bit.

31	30	29	28	27	26	25	24	23	22	21	20	19	18	17	16
Res	Res	Res	Res	Res	Res	Res	Res	Res	Res	Res	Res	Res	Res	Res	Res

15	14	13	12	11	10	9	8	7	6	5	4	3	2	1	0
Res	LINEN	STOP[1:0]		CLKEN	CPOL	CPHA	LBCL	Res.	LBDIE	LBDL	Res	ADD[3:0]			
	rw	rw	rw	rw	rw	rw	rw		rw	rw		rw	rw	rw	rw

Bits 13:12 **STOP**: STOP bits

These bits are used for programming the stop bits.

00: 1 Stop bit

01: 0.5 Stop bit

10: 2 Stop bits

11: 1.5 Stop bit

Note: The 0.5 Stop bit and 1.5 Stop bit are not available for UART4 & UART5.

Bit 11 **CLKEN**: Clock enable

This bit allows the user to enable the SCLK pin.

0: SCLK pin disabled

1: SCLK pin enabled

This bit is not available for UART4 & UART5.

Figure 4-21: USART Control 2 (USART_CTR2) register (Partial Listing)

UART Control 3 register (USART_CR3)

STM Arm reference manual describes various bits of the USART Control 3 (USART_CR3) Register. The USART_CR3 register is mainly concerned with the handshaking signals of RTS and CTS among other things.

UART Data Register

To transmit a byte of data we must place it in USART Data (USART_DR) register. It must be noted that a write to this register initiates a transmission from the USART. Like some other Arm chips, the STM Arm uses the same register for both transmit and receive data and it is called USART_DR (USART Data Register). Notice some of STM Arm chips use different registers for the received and transmit byte. It also must be noted that received data in USART_RD register must be retrieved by reading it before it is lost. Notice this is a 32-bit register and for the 8-bit character size, we use only the lower 8 bits. According to STM32F446 reference manual "The Data register performs a double function (read and write) since it is composed of two registers, one for transmission (TDR) and one for reception (RDR). The TDR register provides the parallel interface between the internal bus and the output shift register"

31	30	29	28	27	26	25	24	23	22	21	20	19	18	17	16
Res.	Res.	Res.	Res.	Res.	Res.	Res.	Res.	Res.	Res.	Res.	Res.	Res.	Res.	Res.	Res.

15	14	13	12	11	10	9	8	7	6	5	4	3	2	1	0
Res.	Res.	Res.	Res.	Res.	Res.	Res.	DR[8:0]								
							rw	rw	rw	rw	rw	rw	rw	rw	rw

Bits 8:0 **DR [8:0]**: Data value

Contains the Received or Transmitted data character, depending on whether it is read from or written to. The Data register performs a double function (read and write) since it is composed of two registers, one for transmission (TDR) and one for reception (RDR) The TDR register provides the parallel interface between the internal bus and the output shift register The RDR register provides the parallel interface between the input shift register and the internal bus. When transmitting with the parity enabled (PCE bit set to 1 in the USART_CR1 register), the value written in the MSB (bit 7 or bit 8 depending on the data length) has no effect because it is replaced by the parity. When receiving with the parity enabled, the value read in the MSB bit is the received parity bit.

Figure 4-22: USART_DR, USART Data Register (D31-D8 are not shown)

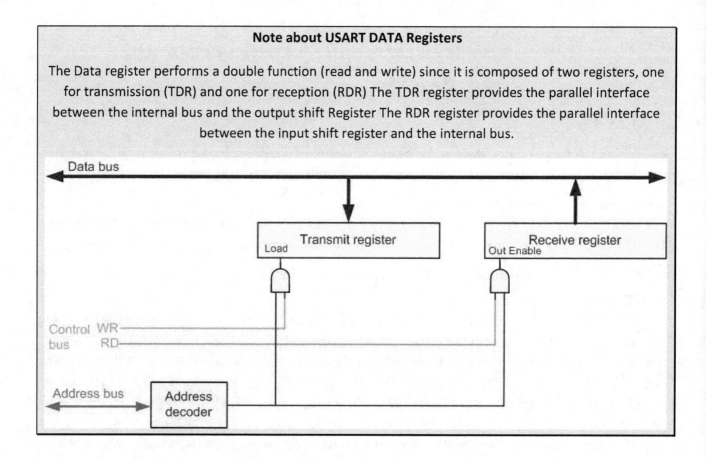

Note about USART DATA Registers

The Data register performs a double function (read and write) since it is composed of two registers, one for transmission (TDR) and one for reception (RDR) The TDR register provides the parallel interface between the internal bus and the output shift Register The RDR register provides the parallel interface between the input shift register and the internal bus.

USART Status Register (USART_SR)

The USART_SR (Status Register) register is very important register. It contains the error flags such as Framing Error (FE), Parity Error (PE), and Overrun Error (ORE). Only when the error flag is set, the program needs to interrogate the USART_SR register for further information about the source of the error. We will not go into details about the errors here. Readers who are interested may refer to the reference manual for more information. The flag bits in USART_SR can also be programmed to generate interrupts. We will discuss the interrupts in Chapter 6. The USART_SR register also contains some other important flags. They are TXE (Transmit Data Register Empty), TC (Transmission Complete), and RXNE (Read Data Register Not Empty). See Figure 4-23.

Figure 4-23 describes various bits of the USART_SR. Three of the USART_SR register bits are used by the USART extensively. The TXE (Transmit Data Register Empty) flag indicates that the transmit data register is empty and is available to take a new byte of data to be transmitted. The RXNE (Read Data Register Not Empty) flag indicates data register has received a new byte of data and needs to be picked up before it is lost. The TC (Transmit Complete) flag indicates that transmission is complete and there is no more data to be transmitted by USART. That means it is ready to accept a new data to be transmitted.

31	30	29	28	27	26	25	24	23	22	21	20	19	18	17	16
Res	Res	Res	Res	Res	Res	Res	Res	Res	Res	Res	Res	Res	Res	Res	Res

15	14	13	12	11	10	9	8	7	6	5	4	3	2	1	0
Res	Res	Res	Res	Res	Res	CTS	LBD	TXE	TC	RXNE	IDLE	ORE	NF	FE	PE
						rc_w0	rc_w0	r	rc_w0	rc_w0	r	r	r	r	r

Bit 7 **TXE**: Transmit data register empty

This bit is set by hardware when the content of the TDR register has been transferred into the shift register. An interrupt is generated if the TXEIE bit =1 in the USART_CR1 register. It is cleared by a write to the USART_DR register.

0: Data is not transferred to the shift register

1: Data is transferred to the shift register)

Bit 6 **TC**: Transmission complete

This bit is set by hardware if the transmission of a frame containing data is complete and if TXE is set. An interrupt is generated if TCIE=1 in the USART_CR1 register. It is cleared by a software sequence (a read from the USART_SR register followed by a write to the USART_DR register). The TC bit can also be cleared by writing a '0' to it. This clearing sequence is recommended only for multibuffer communication.

0: Transmission is not complete

1: Transmission is complete

Bit 5 **RXNE**: Read data register not empty

This bit is set by hardware when the content of the RDR shift register has been transferred to the USART_DR register. An interrupt is generated if RXNEIE=1 in the USART_CR1 register. It is cleared by a read to the USART_DR register. The RXNE flag can also be cleared by writing a zero to it. This clearing sequence is recommended only for multibuffer communication.

0: Data is not received

1: Received data is ready to be read.

Bit 3 **ORE**: Overrun error

This bit is set by hardware when the word currently being received in the shift register is ready to be transferred into the RDR register while RXNE=1. An interrupt is generated if RXNEIE=1 in the USART_CR1 register. It is cleared by a software sequence (an read to the USART_SR register followed by a read to the USART_DR register).

0: No Overrun error

1: Overrun error is detected

Bit 1 **FE**: Framing error

This bit is set by hardware when a de-synchronization, excessive noise or a break character is detected. It is cleared by a software sequence (an read to the USART_SR register followed by a read to the USART_DR register).

0: No Framing error is detected

1: Framing error or break character is detected

Bit 0 **PE**: Parity error

This bit is set by hardware when a parity error occurs in receiver mode. It is cleared by a software sequence (a read from the status register followed by a read or write access to the USART_DR data register). The software must wait for the RXNE flag to be set before clearing the PE bit. An interrupt is generated if PEIE = 1 in the USART_CR1 register.

0: No parity error

1: Parity error

Figure 4-23: Status Register (USART_SR)

The TXE (Transmit Data Register Empty) flag

To transmit a byte of data serially out of the TxD pin, we must write the data into the USART Data Register (USART_DR). The transmit shift register is an internal parallel-in-serial-out shift register whose job is to get the data from the DR, frame it with the start and stop bits, and send it out one bit at a time via the TXD pin. The transmit shift register is not accessible to the programmer. The transmitter is double buffered, that means there is a data register in addition to the shift register that shifts the bits out. While the shift register is shifting the last byte out, the program may write another byte of data to the data register to wait for the shift register to be ready. The transfer of data between the data register and the shift register is automatic and the programmer does not have to be concerned about it. We can only write to the USART_DR register. Whenever the shifter is empty, it gets its new data from the USART_DR register and clears the USART_DR register immediately, so it does not send out the same data twice. When the shifter fetches the data from the USART_DR, it clears the TXE flag to indicate it is empty and the USART_DR register is ready for the next character. We monitor the TXE flag before we write (load) another byte to the USART_DR register.

The TC (Transmit Complete) flag

It must be emphasized that the TC (Transmit Complete) flag indicates both the Transmit Data Register and the shift register are empty and there is no data left for the transmitter to send. This bit is used when the program needs to know that all the data is sent before starting the next task. When TXE flag is set, the Transmit Data Register is empty but the last byte of data may still be in the shift register. If the program is to shut down the transmitter, the last byte of data will be lost and the data could have been half transmitted, which may cause confusion or error on the receiving end. The TC flag is mostly used in error handling and debugging so that the program waits for the data transmission to complete before halting the operation or re-initialize the USART.

The RXNE (Receive Not Empty) flag

The internal serial-in-parallel-out shifter register receives data via the RXD pin. It removes the start and the stop bits and writes the received byte to the USART Data Register (USART_DR). The receiver is also double buffered. After the received data is written to the DR register, the shift register is available to accept another byte of data. This allows the receiver to receive data back-to-back. The program has the time before the next byte is completely shifted in to read the last byte of data. The program should check the RXNE flag frequently to see if data is ready to be read. After the data is read from the USART_DR register, the RXNE flag is cleared automatically. According to ST Arm reference manual "The RXNE bit is set to indicate that the content of the shift register is transferred to the USART_DR. In other words, data has been received and can be read (as well as its associated error flags."

If the program failed to read the data out of the USART_DR register before the next byte is shifted in, a buffer overflow error occurs. A byte of data is lost and the Overrun Error (ORE) flag in USART_SR register is set.

Reset and enabling the USART

As we mentioned earlier, to conserve power many of the on-chip peripherals are disabled coming out of reset. Before enabling the USART, first the bus clock to the USART should be enabled. The enabling of these clocks was described earlier in this section.

The USART module should be configured properly before it is enabled because most of the control registers are enabled-protected, that means they cannot be modified while the module is enabled. One good way to disable the USART before configuring is to use the software reset. By writing a 1 to UE bit (UE, USART Enable) of the CR1 (Control Register 1), all the registers will assume the default value and the module is disabled. When the configuration is done, writing a 1 to USART Enable bit of the CR1 register enables the USART module.

The GPIO pins used for USART TxD and RxD

In addition to the USART registers setup, we must also configure the I/O pins for USART (TxD and RxD) to use their alternate functions. In the last two chapters, we used the I/O pins as general purpose I/O (GPIO). When I/O pins are used for other peripheral functions such as USART, Timer, and ADC, we need to configure them as the alternate peripheral function using the AFRx (Alternative Function Register) registers.

In STM Arm we have maximum of 16 pins for each port. There are two GPIO_AFRx registers of GPIO_AFRL and GPIO_AFRH for each port. Each GPIO_AFRx register is 32 bit long and holds the alternate function selection for 8 pins. Since we have AF15-AF0 (total of 16) selections, we need 4 bits for each entry (16 AFx4=64bits). That means we need two 32-bit registers (32x2=64bits) to take care of all the alternate functions. That explains why we have GPIO_AFRH and GPIO_AFRL registers.

In order for the GPIO_AFRx register selection of the alternate functions to take effect, the GPIO_MODER bits for each pin must be configured first. See Figure 4-24. Upon reset, GPIO_MODER are set as analog functions. That means, we select GPIO_MODER=10 for AF option first and then we choose one of the eight alternate peripheral pin functions using the GPIO_AFRx register. See Figure 4-25. The available functions depend on the pin and are shown in Table 4-5. In the first example program P4-1, PA2 and PA3 pins to be used for USART2_TxD and USART2_RxD signals. The alternate functions of PA2 and PA3 pins are selected by GPIO_AFRx registers. From Table 4-6, you can see that PA2 is for TXD of USART2 and PA3 is used for RXD of USART2. The multiple USARTx options provide some flexibility of choosing TxD and RxD for a given pins.

31	30	29	28	27	26	25	24	23	22	21	20	19	18	17	16
AFRL7[3:0]				AFRL6[3:0]				AFRL5[3:0]				AFRL4[3:0]			
rw	rw	rw	rw	rw	rw	rw	rw	rw	rw	rw	rw	rw	rw	rw	rw
15	14	13	12	11	10	9	8	7	6	5	4	3	2	1	0
AFRL3[3:0]				AFRL2[3:0]				AFRL1[3:0]				AFRL0[3:0]			
rw	rw	rw	rw	rw	rw	rw	rw	rw	rw	rw	rw	rw	rw	rw	rw

Bits 31:0 **AFRLy:** Alternate function selection for port x bit y (y = 0..7)

These bits are written by software to configure alternate function I/Os

AFRLy selection:

0000: AF0	1000: AF8
0001: AF1	1001: AF9
0010: AF2	1010: AF10
0011: AF3	1011: AF11
0100: AF4	1100: AF12
0101: AF5	1101: AF13
0110: AF6	1110: AF14
0111: AF7	1111: AF15

Figure 4-24: GPIO_AFRL (GPIO Alternate Function Register Low)

31	30	29	28	27	26	25	24	23	22	21	20	19	18	17	16
AFRH15[3:0]				AFRH14[3:0]				AFRH13[3:0]				AFRH12[3:0]			
rw	rw	rw	rw	rw	rw	rw	rw	rw	rw	rw	rw	rw	rw	rw	rw
15	14	13	12	11	10	9	8	7	6	5	4	3	2	1	0
AFRH11[3:0]				AFRH10[3:0]				AFRH9[3:0]				AFRH8[3:0]			
rw	rw	rw	rw	rw	rw	rw	rw	rw	rw	rw	rw	rw	rw	rw	rw

Bits 31:0 **AFRHy:** Alternate function selection for port x bit y (y = 8..15)

These bits are written by software to configure alternate function I/Os

AFRHy selection:

0000: AF0	1000: AF8
0001: AF1	1001: AF9
0010: AF2	1010: AF10
0011: AF3	1011: AF11
0100: AF4	1100: AF12
0101: AF5	1101: AF13
0110: AF6	1110: AF14
0111: AF7	1111: AF15

Figure 4-25: GPIO_AFRH (GPIO Alternate Function Register High)

PIN	TXD	RXD	AF

106

PA0	USART4		AF8
PA1		USART4	AF8
PA2	USART2		AF7
PA3		USART2	AF7
PA9	USART1		AF7
PA10		USART1	AF7
PB6	USART1		AF7
PB7		USART1	AF7
PB10	USART3		AF7
PB11		USART3	AF7

Table 4-5: partial list of STM Arm Pins Used for USART (See Appendix B and Table 4-6)

31	30	29	28	27	26	25	24	23	22	21	20	19	18	17	16
MODER15[1:0]		MODER14[1:0]		MODER13[1:0]		MODER12[1:0]		MODER11[1:0]		MODER10[1:0]		MODER9[1:0]		MODER8[1:0]	
rw	rw	rw	rw	rw	rw	rw	rw	rw	rw	rw	rw	rw	rw	rw	rw

15	14	13	12	11	10	9	8	7	6	5	4	3	2	1	0
MODER7[1:0]		MODER6[1:0]		MODER5[1:0]		MODER4[1:0]		MODER3[1:0]		MODER2[1:0]		MODER1[1:0]		MODER0[1:0]	
rw	rw	rw	rw	rw	rw	rw	rw	rw	rw	rw	rw	rw	rw	rw	rw

Bits 2y:2y+1 **MODERy[1:0]:** Port x configuration bits (y = 0..15)

These bits are written by software to configure the I/O direction mode.

00: Input (reset state)

01: General purpose output mode

10: Alternate function mode

11: Analog mod

Figure 4-26: GPIOx_MODER (GPIO Mode) for Direction Register (x=A, B, C,..)

Port		AF7	AF8	AF9	AF10	AF11	AF12	AF13	AF14	AF15
		SPI2/3/ USART1/ 2/3/UART 5/SPDIFR X	SAI/ USART6/ UART4/5/ SPDIFRX	CAN1/2 TIM12/13/ 14/ QUADSPI	SAI2/ QUADSPI/ OTG2_HS/ OTG1_FS	OTG1_FS	FMC/ SDIO/ OTG2_FS	DCMI	-	SYS
Port A	PA0	USART2_ CTS	UART4_ TX	-	-	-	-	-	-	EVENT OUT
	PA1	USART2_ RTS	UART4_ RX	QUADSPI_ BK1_IO3	SAI2_ MCLK_B	-	-	-	-	EVENT OUT
	PA2	USART2_ TX	SAI2_ SCK_B	-	-	-	-	-	-	EVENT OUT
	PA3	USART2_ RX	-	-	OTG_HS_ ULPI_D0	-	-	-	-	EVENT OUT
	PA4	USART2_ CK	-	-	-	-	OTG_HS_ SOF	DCMI_ HSYNC	-	EVENT OUT
	PA5	-	-	-	OTG_HS_ ULPI_CK	-	-	-	-	EVENT OUT
	PA6	-	-	TIM13_CH1	-	-	-	DCMI_ PIXCLK	-	EVENT OUT
	PA7	-	-	TIM14_CH1	-	-	FMC_ SDNWE	-	-	EVENT OUT
	PA8	USART1_ CK	-	-	OTG_FS_ SOF	-	-	-	-	EVENT OUT
	PA9	USART1_ TX	-	-	-	-	-	DCMI_D0	-	EVENT OUT
	PA10	USART1_ RX	-	-	OTG_FS_ ID	-	-	DCMI_D1	-	EVENT OUT
	PA11	USART1_ CTS	-	CAN1_RX	OTG_FS_ DM	-	-	-	-	EVENT OUT
	PA12	USART1_ RTS	SAI2_ FS_B	CAN1_TX	OTG_FS_ DP	-	-	-	-	EVENT OUT
	PA13	-	-	-	-	-	-	-	-	EVENT OUT
	PA14	-	-	-	-	-	-	-	-	EVENT OUT
	PA15	-	UART4_RT S	-	-	-	-	-	-	EVENT OUT

**Table 4-6: Alternate Functions (AF) Pin Multiplexing for Port A in STM32F446 Arm. See Appendix B for other Ports.
(See AF table for your device)**

Example 4-6

In a given ST Miro Arm trainer USART2 port is used for serial ports. Find the values for registers GPIO_MODER and GPIO_AFRL if pins PA2 and PA3 are used for TxD and RxD.

Solution:

We use the option C (10=0x2) in the GPIO_MODER register to allow each of PA2 and PA3 pins to be used for USART2_TxD and USART2_RxD signals, respectively:

```
GPIOA->MODER  &= ~0x0030;
GPIOA->MODER  |= 0x0020;  /* enable alternate function for PA2 */
GPIOA->MODER  &= ~0x00C0;
GPIOA->MODER  |= 0x0080;  /* enable alternate function for PA3 */
```

Also, peripheral function needs to be enabled in GPIOA_AFRL register:

```
GPIOA->AFR[0] &= ~0xF000;
GPIOA->AFR[0] |= 0x7000;        /* alt7 for USART2 */
GPIOA->AFR[0] &= ~0x0F00;
GPIOA->AFR[0] |= 0x0700;        /* alt7 for USART2 */
```

Steps to configure USART2 for transmitting data

Here are the steps to configure the USART2 and transmit a byte of data for STM Nucleo board:

1) Enable the Clock to GPIOA.
2) Enable the Clock to USART2.
3) Select the peripheral function AF7 for PA2 (USART2_TxD) pin using the GPIO_MODER and GPIO_AFRL registers.
4) Set the baud rate for USART2 using USART2_BRR register.
5) Configure the CR1 (Control 1) register for oversampling rate, character size (8-bit or 9-bit) and enabling transmit (TE).
6) Configure the CR2 (Control 2) register for number of stop bit(s) and so on.
7) Configure the CR3 (Control 3) register for no hardware flow control and so on.
8) Enable USART2 after configuration complete.
9) Wait until the TXE (Transmit Empty) bit of the USART_SR register is set.
10) Write a byte to DR Register to be transmitted.
11) To transfer the next character, go to step 9.

Program 4-1 sends the characters "YES" to the terminal emulator program (Tera Term) on a PC. You need to install Tera Term (or other terminal programs such as HyperTerminal or Putty) on your PC to receive the output. For Tera Term download and tutorial see:

http://MicroDigitalEd.com/tutorials/Tera_Terminal.pdf

```c
/* p4_1.c Send a string "YES" to USART2
 *
 * USART2 is connected to the ST-Link virtual COM port.
 * Use Tera Term to see the message "YES" on a PC.
 *
 * By default, the clock is running at 16 MHz.
 * The UART2 is configured for 9600 Baud.
 * PA2 - USART2 TX (AF7)
 *
 * This program was tested with Keil uVision v5.24a with DFP v2.11.0
 */
#include "stm32F4xx.h"

void USART2_init(void);
void USART2_write(int c);
void delayMs(int);

/*-------------------------------------------------------------------------
  MAIN function
  *-----------------------------------------------------------------------*/
int main (void) {
    USART2_init();              /* initialize USART2 */

    while(1) {                  /* Loop forever */
        USART2_write('Y');
        USART2_write('e');
        USART2_write('s');
        delayMs(10);            /* leave a gap between messages */
    }
}

/*-------------------------------------------------------------------------
  Initialize UART pins, Baudrate
  *-----------------------------------------------------------------------*/
void USART2_init (void) {
    RCC->AHB1ENR |= 1;          /* Enable GPIOA clock */
    RCC->APB1ENR |= 0x20000;    /* Enable USART2 clock */

    /* Configure PA2 for USART2_TX */
    GPIOA->AFR[0] &= ~0x0F00;
    GPIOA->AFR[0] |=  0x0700;   /* alt7 for USART2 */
    GPIOA->MODER  &= ~0x0030;
    GPIOA->MODER  |=  0x0020;   /* enable alternate function for PA2 */

    USART2->BRR = 0x0683;       /* 9600 baud @ 16 MHz */
    USART2->CR1 = 0x0008;       /* enable Tx, 8-bit data */
    USART2->CR2 = 0x0000;       /* 1 stop bit */
    USART2->CR3 = 0x0000;       /* no flow control */
    USART2->CR1 |= 0x2000;      /* enable USART2 */
}


/* Write a character to USART2 */
void USART2_write (int ch) {
    while (!(USART2->SR & 0x0080)) {}   // wait until Tx buffer empty
    USART2->DR = (ch & 0xFF);
}
```

110

```
void delayMs(int n) {
    int i;
    for (; n > 0; n--)
        for (i = 0; i < 2000; i++) ;
}
```

The importance of the TXE (Transmit Data Register Empty) flag

To understand the importance of the role of TXE, look at the following sequence of steps that the STM Arm goes through in transmitting a character via DR register:

1. The character to be transmitted is written into the DR (data Register) register.
2. The TXE flag is set to 0 automatically to indicate that the DR register has a character and will not accept another character until this one is vacated.
3. The transmit shift register reads the character from the DR register and begins to transfer the character.
4. The TXE flag is set to 1 as soon as the character is moved to the shift register to indicate that the DR register is ready to accept another character.
5. The program may load another character into the DR register while the last character is still shifting out.
6. When the last character is shifted out, the new character in the DR register is moved to the shift register and immediately started being transmitted.

By monitoring the TXE flag, the program can keep the DR register full all the time and the transmission of characters can be done back-to-back to achieve the full throughput.

Steps to configure USART for receiving data

Here are the steps to configure the USART2 and receive a byte of data to STM Nucleo board:

1) Enable the Clock to GPIOA.
2) Enable the Clock to USART2.
3) Select the peripheral function AF7 for PA3 (USART2_RxD) pin using the GPIO_MODER and GPIO_AFRL registers.
4) Set the baud rate for USART2 using USART2_BRR register.
5) Configure the CR1 (Control 1) register for oversampling rate, character size (8-bit or 9-bit) and enabling receive (RE).
6) Configure the CR2 (Control 2) register for number of stop bit(s) and so on.
7) Configure the CR3 (Control 3) register for no hardware flow control and so on.
8) Enable USART2 after configuration complete.
9) Wait until the RXNE (Receive Not Empty) bit of the USART_SR register is set.
10) Read a byte from USART2_DR register that was received.
11) To receive the next character, go to step 9.

Program 4-2 receives the bytes of data via USART2 and displays it on the LEDs.

```
/* p4_2.c UART on USART2 Receive at 115200 Baud
 *
 * Receive key strokes from terminal emulator (TeraTerm) of the
 * host PC to the USART2 of the Nucleo-F446RE board.
 * USART2 is connected to the ST-Link virtual COM port.
 * Launch Tera Term on a PC and hit any key.
 * The LED program from P3_5 of Chapter 3 is used to blink the green LED
 * according to the key received.
 * You need to wait till the blinking stops before hitting another key.
 * Received key is not echoed back to the terminal, so you will not see
 * the character displayed.
 *
 * By default, the clock is running at 16 MHz.
 * The UART2 is configured for 115200 Baud.
 * PA3 - USART2 RX (AF7)
 *
 * This program was tested with Keil uVision v5.24a with DFP v2.11.0
 */
#include "stm32F4xx.h"

void USART2_init(void);
char USART2_read(void);
void LED_blink(int value);
void delayMs(int);

/*-----------------------------------------------------------------------
  MAIN function
 *---------------------------------------------------------------------*/
int main (void) {
    char c;

    RCC->AHB1ENR |=  1;              /* enable GPIOA clock */
    GPIOA->MODER &= ~0x00000C00;     /* clear pin mode */
    GPIOA->MODER |=  0x00000400;     /* set pin to output mode */

    USART2_init();                   /* initialize USART2 */

    while(1) {                       /* Loop forever */
        c = USART2_read();           /* wait for a character received */
        LED_blink(c);                /* blink the LED */
    }
}

/*-----------------------------------------------------------------------
  Initialize UART pins, Baudrate
 *---------------------------------------------------------------------*/
void USART2_init (void) {
    RCC->AHB1ENR |= 1;          /* Enable GPIOA clock */
    RCC->APB1ENR |= 0x20000;    /* Enable USART2 clock */

    /* Configure PA3 for USART2 RX */
    GPIOA->AFR[0] &= ~0xF000;
    GPIOA->AFR[0] |=  0x7000;   /* alt7 for USART2 */
    GPIOA->MODER  &= ~0x00C0;
    GPIOA->MODER  |=  0x0080;   /* enable alternate function for PA3 */
```

```
    USART2->BRR = 0x008B;       /* 115200 baud @ 16 MHz */
    USART2->CR1 = 0x0004;       /* enable Rx, 8-bit data */
    USART2->CR2 = 0x0000;       /* 1 stop bit */
    USART2->CR3 = 0x0000;       /* no flow control */
    USART2->CR1 |= 0x2000;      /* enable USART2 */
}


/* Read a character from USART2 */
char USART2_read(void) {
    while (!(USART2->SR & 0x0020)) {}    // wait until char arrives
    return USART2->DR;
}

/* turn on or off the LEDs according to the value */
void LED_blink(int value) {
    value %= 16;                         /* cap the max count at 15 */

    for (; value > 0; value--) {
        GPIOA->BSRR = 0x00000020;    /* turn on LED */
        delayMs(200);
        GPIOA->BSRR = 0x00200000;    /* turn off LED */
        delayMs(200);
    }
    delayMs(800);
}

void delayMs(int n) {
    int i;
    for (; n > 0; n--)
        for (i = 0; i < 2000; i++) ;
}
```

Importance of the RXNE (Receive Not Empty) flag bit

In receiving bits via its RXD pin, the STM Arm goes through the following steps:

1. The receiver's shift register receives the start bit indicating that the next bit is the first bit of the character it is about to receive.
2. The character is received one bit at a time. When the stop bit is received, a character is formed and placed in DR register and the RXNE flag is set indicating that an entire character has been received.
3. If another character is coming in, the shift register will start receiving the next character.
4. By checking the RXNE flag, we know that a character has been received and is sitting in the DR register. The program reads the DR register contents and saves it in a register or a variable before the next character received is complete.
5. The RXNE flag is cleared automatically when the DR data register is read.

Using other USART port

The previous two programs showed how to use the USART2 on STM Nucleo board, which is connected to the host computer through the USB cable. To use other USART ports, you can use a USB-to-Serial module (or cable) and connect to any USARTx port. The side of the USB-to-Serial module connected to the USARTx pins on the Nucleo board should be 3.3V logic level signals for TxD and RxD. The other USB side is connected to the PC USB port. Here are some of the USB-to-Serial connections on the market:

https://www.sparkfun.com/products/9893, https://www.sparkfun.com/products/9717,

http://www.adafruit.com/products/284 or http://www.adafruit.com/products/70.

Make sure you are using a 3.3V logic level converter or configure the converter to use 3.3V. Many TTL-level serial to USB converters produce output higher than 3.6V. They may appear functional in the short term but will damage the Arm input pins.

Program 4-3 is modified from Program 4-1 to use UART4. (UART module is like the USART module but does not support synchronous communication.) Comparing them you will find that the initialization of the associated port is changed. Program 4-3 also demonstrates how to initialize an array of characters and send the message string to a UART.

Program 4-3: Sending "Hello" to Tera Term via UART4

```c
/* p4_3.c Send a string "YES" to UART4
 *
 * UART4 Tx signal is connected to pin PA0. To see the output of UART4
 * on a PC, you need to use a USB-serial module. Connect the Rx pin of
 * the module to the PA0 pin of the STM32F446 Nucleo board. Make sure
 * the USB-serial module you use has a 3.3V interface.
 *
 * By default, the clock is running at 16 MHz.
 * The UART is configured for 9600 Baud.
 * PA0 - UART4 TX (AF8)
 *
 * This program was tested with Keil uVision v5.24a with DFP v2.11.0
 */
#include "stm32F4xx.h"

void UART4_init(void);
void UART4_write(int c);
void delayMs(int);

/*-------------------------------------------------------------------
  MAIN function
 *-----------------------------------------------------------------*/
int main (void) {
    char message[] = "Hello\r\n";
    int i;

    UART4_init();

    while (1) {
        for (i = 0; i < 7; i++) {
            UART4_write(message[i]); /* send a char */
        }
        delayMs(10);                 /* leave a gap between messages */
    }
}
```

```
/*---------------------------------------------------------------------------
   Initialize UART pins, Baudrate
 *---------------------------------------------------------------------------*/
void UART4_init (void) {
    RCC->AHB1ENR |= 1;              /* Enable GPIOA clock */
    RCC->APB1ENR |= 0x80000;       /* Enable UART4 clock */

    /* Configure PA0 for UART4 TX */
    GPIOA->AFR[0] &= ~0x000F;
    GPIOA->AFR[0] |=  0x0008;       /* alt8 for UART4 */
    GPIOA->MODER  &= ~0x0003;
    GPIOA->MODER  |=  0x0002;       /* enable alternate function for PA0 */

    UART4->BRR = 0x0683;           /* 9600 baud @ 16 MHz */
    UART4->CR1 = 0x0008;           /* enable Tx, 8-bit data */
    UART4->CR2 = 0x0000;           /* 1 stop bit */
    UART4->CR3 = 0x0000;           /* no flow control */
    UART4->CR1 |= 0x2000;          /* enable UART4 */
}


/* Write a character to UART4 */
void UART4_write (int ch) {
    while (!(UART4->SR & 0x0080)) {}   // wait until Tx buffer empty
    UART4->DR = (ch & 0xFF);
}

void delayMs(int n) {
    int i;
    for (; n > 0; n--)
        for (i = 0; i < 2000; i++) ;
}
```

Program 4-4 combines the UART transmit with UART receive. When a key on the PC is pressed with a terminal emulator program, the keyed character is sent to STM Nucleo board. The character received is echoed back out through UART to the terminal emulator on the PC.

Program 4-4: Echoing the received data from UART4

```
/* p4_4.c UART4 echo at 9600 Baud
 *
 * This program receives a character from UART4 receiver
 * then sends it back through UART4 transmitter.
 * UART4 is connected to PA0-Tx and PA1-Rx.
 * A 3.3V signal level to USB cable is used to connect PA0/PA1
 * to the host PC COM port.
 * PA0 - UART4 TX (AF8)
 * PA1 - UART4 RX (AF8)
 * Use Tera Term on the host PC to send keystrokes and observe the display
 * of the characters echoed.
 *
 * By default, the clock is running at 16 MHz.
 *
 * This program was tested with Keil uVision v5.24a with DFP v2.11.0
 */
#include "stm32F4xx.h"
```

```c
void UART4_init(void);
void UART4_write(int c);
void delayMs(int);
char UART4_read(void);

int main (void) {
    char c;
    UART4_init();

    while (1) {
        c = UART4_read();
        UART4_write(c);
    }
}

/* initialize UART4 to transmit at 9600 Baud */
void UART4_init (void) {
    RCC->AHB1ENR |= 1;          /* Enable GPIOA clock */
    RCC->APB1ENR |= 0x80000;    /* Enable UART4 clock */

    /* Configure PA0, PA1 for UART4 TX, RX */
    GPIOA->AFR[0] &= ~0x00FF;
    GPIOA->AFR[0] |= 0x0088;    /* alt8 for UART4 */
    GPIOA->MODER  &= ~0x000F;
    GPIOA->MODER  |= 0x000A;    /* enable alternate function for PA0, PA1 */

    UART4->BRR = 0x0683;        /* 9600 baud @ 16 MHz */
    UART4->CR1 = 0x000C;        /* enable Tx, Rx, 8-bit data */
    UART4->CR2 = 0x0000;        /* 1 stop bit */
    UART4->CR3 = 0x0000;        /* no flow control */
    UART4->CR1 |= 0x2000;       /* enable UART4 */
}

/* Write a character to UART4 */
void UART4_write (int ch) {
    while (!(UART4->SR & 0x0080)) {}   // wait until Tx buffer empty
    UART4->DR = (ch & 0xFF);
}

/* Read a character from UART4 */
char UART4_read(void) {
    while (!(UART4->SR & 0x0020)) {}   // wait until char arrives
    return UART4->DR;
}
```

Baud rate error calculation

In calculating the baud rate, we can use the integer number for the BRR (Baud) register and drop the fraction. By dropping the decimal fraction portion of the calculated values, we run the risk of introducing error into the baud rate. Even when we use the fraction in Baud rate generation, it allows only four bits for the fraction. See STM Arm reference manual for further information on this topic.

$$BAUD = 65,536 \times (1 - 8 \times 9,6001\ MHz) = 60,502.835 \frac{1\ MHz}{8} \left(1 - \frac{60503}{65536}\right)$$ **Interrupt-based data transfer**

By now you might have noticed that it is a waste of the microcontroller's time to poll the TXE and RXNE flags. In order to avoid wasting the microcontroller's time, we use interrupts instead of polling. In Chapter 6, we will show how to use interrupts to program the serial communication port.

Break character and auto-baud

In the reference manuals, we see the mention of some terminology such as break. The break character is when the USART sends out a low signal much longer than one frame, that is ten zeros when the data size is 8-bit. The break character is used to force a framing error at the receiver for the testing purpose and auto-baud.

Auto-baud was fairly popular in the days when telephone modem dial-up connection was used between the user terminal and the mainframe computer. Because of the quality of the telephone line and modem equipment, users had different maximal baud rate they might use. Instead of forcing all users to use the lowest common baud rate, the main-frame computers support several different baud rates. When the modem connection is established, the user hit the enter key. If the computer recognized the enter key (when they have the same baud rate), it responds with a message and the user proceeds to log in the system. If the message is unintelligible (when they have the different baud rate), the user hit the break key and sends a break character to the computer. Upon receiving the break, a framing error is detected and the computer will change the baud rate and resend the message again. The process repeats until they find the same baud rate.

STM Arm USART ports support hardware auto-baud for LIN (Local Interconnect Network). Readers should refer to the datasheet for the detailed information.

Review Questions

1. On STM Nucleo board, which USART is used for Virtual Serial Com port?
2. On STM Nucleo board, pins ___ and ___ are used for TxD and RxD of USART2.
3. Which register is used to set the data size and number of stop bits?
4. How do we know if the transmit buffer is empty before we load in another byte?
5. How do we know if a new byte has been received?

Section 4.3: Using C Library Console I/O

C library provides some standard console I/O functions that are convenient for use such as getchar(), putchar(), gets(), puts(), printf(), and scanf(). These functions rely on the hardware to provide input and output. In the Keil MDK-Arm, the hardware interface is handled by two functions: fgetc() and fputc(). The embedded programmers are required to implement these two functions for the I/O. The implementation of these functions are usually in the part of the software named Board Support Package (BSP). In the example program P4-5 below, we use USART2 as the console and direct fgetc() and fputc() to USART2_read() and USART2_write() so all the console I/O will use USART2, which is connected to the host PC by the virtual console through the ST-Link on the Nucleo board. Using a terminal emulator like Tera Term will allow the user interface to the console I/O of the embedded program. The return value of

USART2_write() and USART2_read() are modified from P4-1 and P4-2 to match the function prototypes of the C library.

Program 4-5: C library Console I/O using USART2 in Keil

```c
/* p4_5.c C library Console I/O using USART2 at 9600 Baud
 *
 * This program demonstrates the use of C library console I/O.
 * The functions fputc() and fgetc() are implemented using
 * USART2_write() and USART2_read() for character I/O.
 * In the fgetc(), the received character is echoed and if a '\r'
 * is received, a pair of '\r', '\n' is echoed.
 * In fputc() and fgetc(), the file descripter is not checked. All
 * file I/O's are directed to the console.
 *
 * By default, the clock is running at 16 MHz.
 * The USART is configured for 9600 Baud.
 * PA2 - USART2 TX (AF7)
 * PA3 - USART2 RX (AF7)
 * Use Tera Term on the host PC to send keystrokes and observe the display
 * of the characters echoed.
 *
 * This program was tested with Keil uVision v5.24a with DFP v2.11.0
 */
#include "stm32F4xx.h"
#include <stdio.h>

void USART2_init(void);
void delayMs(int);
int USART2_write(int c);
int USART2_read(void);

int main(void) {
    int n;
    char str[80];

    USART2_init();

    printf("Test stdio library console I/O functions\r\n");
    fprintf(stdout, "    test for stdout\r\n");
    fprintf(stderr, "    test for stderr\r\n");

    while (1) {
        printf("please enter a number: ");
        scanf("%d", &n);
        printf("the number entered is: %d\r\n", n);
        printf("please type a character string: ");
        gets(str);
        printf("the character string entered is: ");
        puts(str);
        printf("\r\n");
    }
}

/* initialize USART2 to transmit at 9600 Baud */
void USART2_init (void) {
    RCC->AHB1ENR |= 1;          /* Enable GPIOA clock */
```

```c
    RCC->APB1ENR |= 0x20000;       /* Enable USART2 clock */

    /* Configure PA2, PA3 for USART2 TX, RX */
    GPIOA->AFR[0]  &= ~0xFF00;
    GPIOA->AFR[0]  |=  0x7700;     /* alt7 for USART2 */
    GPIOA->MODER   &= ~0x00F0;
    GPIOA->MODER   |=  0x00A0;     /* enable alt. function for PA2, PA3 */

    USART2->BRR = 0x0683;          /* 9600 baud @ 16 MHz */
    USART2->CR1 = 0x000C;          /* enable Tx, Rx, 8-bit data */
    USART2->CR2 = 0x0000;          /* 1 stop bit */
    USART2->CR3 = 0x0000;          /* no flow control */
    USART2->CR1 |= 0x2000;         /* enable USART2 */
}

/* Write a character to USART2 */
int USART2_write (int ch) {
    while (!(USART2->SR & 0x0080)) {}   // wait until Tx buffer empty
    USART2->DR = (ch & 0xFF);
    return ch;
}

/* Read a character from USART2 */
int USART2_read(void) {
    while (!(USART2->SR & 0x0020)) {}   // wait until char arrives
    return USART2->DR;
}

/* The code below is the interface to the C standard I/O library.
 * All the I/O are directed to the console, which is UART3.
 */
struct __FILE { int handle; };
FILE __stdin  = {0};
FILE __stdout = {1};
FILE __stderr = {2};

/* Called by C library console/file input
 * This function echoes the character received.
 * If the character is '\r', it is substituted by '\n'.
 */
int fgetc(FILE *f) {
    int c;

    c = USART2_read();        /* read the character from console */

    if (c == '\r') {          /* if '\r', after it is echoed, a '\n' is appended*/
        USART2_write(c);      /* echo */
        c = '\n';
    }

    USART2_write(c);          /* echo */

    return c;
}

/* Called by C library console/file output */
int fputc(int c, FILE *f) {
    return USART2_write(c);   /* write the character to console */
```

```
        }
```

The program P4-5 is a simple implementation to use the C library console I/O. The Keil uVision IDE run-time environment has console I/O under Compiler->I/O->STDIN, STDOUT, and STDERR. This topic is beyond the scope of this book.

Answer to Review Questions

Section 4-1

1. more expensive
2. serial
3. synchronous
4. False; it is simplex.
5. True
6. Asynchronous
7. With 100 0100 binary we have 1 as the odd-parity bit. The bits as transmitted in the sequence are:

   (a) 0 (start bit)   (b) 0   (c) 0   (d) 1
   (e) 0   (f) 0   (g) 0   (h) 1
   (i) 1 (parity)   (j) 1 (first stop bit)   (k) 1 (second stop bit)
8. 4 bits (a, i, j, k)
9. $400 \times 11 = 4400$ bits total bits transmitted. $4400/1200 = 3.667$ seconds, $4/7 = 58\%$.
10. True

Section 4-2

1. USART2
2. PA2 and PA3
3. USARTx_CR1 and USARTx_CR2
4. The TXE flag from the USART2_SR register goes high.
5. The RXNE flag from the USART2_SR register goes high.

Chapter 5: STM Arm Timer Programming

In Section 5-1, the counter and timer concepts are reviewed. Section 5-2 covers the System Tick Timer which is available in all Arm Cortex microcontrollers. In Section 5-3, 32-bit timers of STM Arm are covered. We also cover STM 16-bit feature and show how to create a delay. Section 5-4 shows the output compare mode. In Section 5-5, input capturing is discussed and the pulse width and frequency measuring are covered. Section 5-6 shows event counter feature.

Section 5.1: Introduction to counters and timers

In the digital design course, you connected many flip-flops (FFs) together to create up counter/down counter. For example, connecting 3 FFs together we can count up to 7 (000-111 in binary). This is called *3-bit counter*. The same way, to create a 4-bit counter (counting up to 15, or 0000-1111 in binary) we need 4 FFs. For 16-bit counter, we need 16 FFs and it counts up to $2^{16} - 1$. Figure 5- shows the T flip-flop connection and pulse outputs for all three flip-flops.

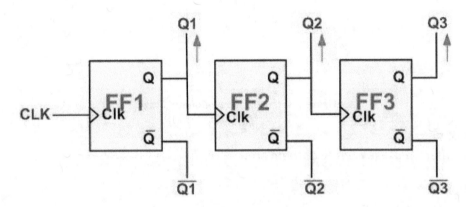

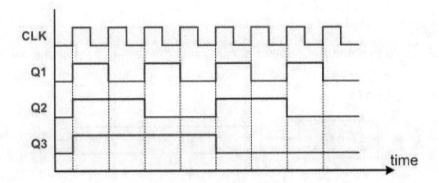

Figure 5-1: A 3-bit Counter

Regarding Figure 5-1, notice the following points:

1) The Q outputs give the down counter.
2) The $\bar{Q}$ (Q not) outputs give us up counter.
3) The frequency on Q3 is 1/8 of the Clock fed to FF1.
4) We can use the circuit in Figure 5-1 to divide clock frequency.
5) We can use the circuit in Figure 5-1 to count the number of pulses fed to CLK pin of FF1.

An up counter begins counting from 0 and its value increases on each clock until it reaches its maximum value. Then, it overflows and rolls over to zero in the next clock. The following figure shows the stages which an 8-bit counter goes through.

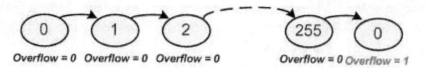

Figure 5-2: an 8-bit Up-Counter Stages

A down counter begins counting from its maximum value and decreases on each clock until it reaches to 0. Then, it underflows and rolls over to its maximum value in the next clock. The following figure shows the stages which an 8-bit down counter goes through.

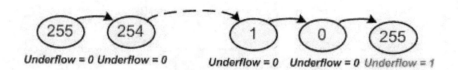

Figure 5-3: an 8-bit Down-Counter Stages

Counter Usages

Counters have different usages. Some of them are:

1. Counting events
2. Making delays (Using Counter as a Timer)
3. Measuring the time between 2 events

1. Counting events

You might need to count the number of cars going through a street or the number of spaghetti packages which produced in a factory. To do so, you can connect the output of a sensor to a counter, as shown in the following figure.

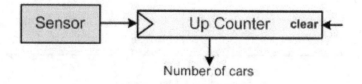

Figure 5-4: Counting Events Using a Counter

2. Making delays (Using Counter as a timer)

While controlling devices, it is a common practice to start or terminate a task when a desired amount of time elapsed. For example, a washing machine or an oven do each task for a determined amount of time. To do timing, we can connect a clock generator to a counter, and wait until a desired amount of time elapses. For example, in the following picture, the clock generator makes a 1 Hz signal and the counter increasing every second. The counter reaches to 60 after 60 seconds.

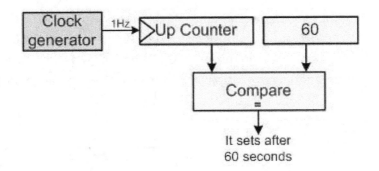

Figure 5-5: Using Counter as a Timer

3. Measuring the time between 2 events

You might need to measure the time between 2 events. For example, the amount of time it takes a marathon runner to go from the start to the finish point. In such cases we can use a circuit similar to the following:

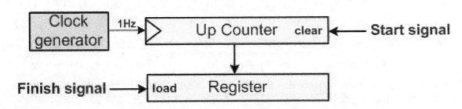

Figure 5-6: Capturing

The counter is cleared at the start. Then, it increases on each clock pulse. The value of the counter is loaded into another register when the runner passes the finish line.

Counters and Timers in microcontrollers

Nowadays, all the microcontrollers come with on-chip Timer/Counter. If the clock to the Timer comes from an internal source such as PLL, XTAL, and RC, then it is called a *Timer*. If the clock source comes from an external source, such as pulses fed to the CPU pin, then it is called a *Counter*. By Counter, it is meant event-counter since it counts the event happening outside the CPU. In many microcontrollers, the Timers can be used as Timer or Counter.

Review Questions

1. With 5 FFs maximum count value we can get is _____.
2. With 5 FFs we can divide the frequency by maximum of _____.
3. When pulses are fed to a timer from the outside it is called _____.
4. When clocks pulses are fed to a timer from inside it is called _____.
5. If we need to divide a frequency by 500, we need _____ flip-flops.

Section 5.2: System Tick Timer

Every Arm Cortex-M comes with a System tick timer. System tick timer allows the system to initiate an action on a periodic basis. This action is performed internally at a fixed rate without external signal. For example, in a given application we can use SysTick to read a sensor every 200 msec. SysTick is used widely by operating systems so that the system software may interrupt the application software periodically (often at 10 ms interval) to monitor and control the system operations. The SysTick is a 24-bit down counter driven by the processor clock (AHB clock, the clock that feeds the CPU). It counts from an initial value down to 0. When it reaches 0, in the next clock, it underflows and it raises a flag called COUNT and reloads the initial value and starts over again. We can set the initial value to a value between 0x000000 to 0xFFFFFF. See the following figure.

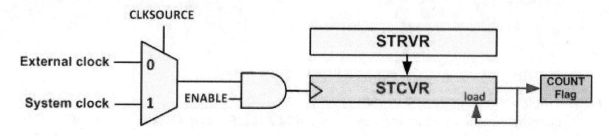

Figure 5-7: System Tick Timer Internal Structure

The down counter is named as STCVR (SysTick Current Value Register) in Arm Cortex-M devices. The counter receives clock from the system clock or the external clock. The clock source is chosen using the CLKSOURCE bit of STCSR (SysTick Control & Status Register) register. In the STM32F4, the external clock is connected to a prescaler that divides the AHB clock by 8. The clock is ANDed with the ENABLE bit of STCSR register so it counts down when the ENABLE bit is set. The STCSR register is shown in Figure 5-.

SysTick Registers

Next, we will describe the SysTick registers. There are three registers in the SysTick module: SysTick Control and Status register, SysTick Reload Value register, and SysTick Current Value register.

The STCTRL (SysTick Control and Status) register is located at 0xE000E010. We use it to start the SysTick counter among other things.

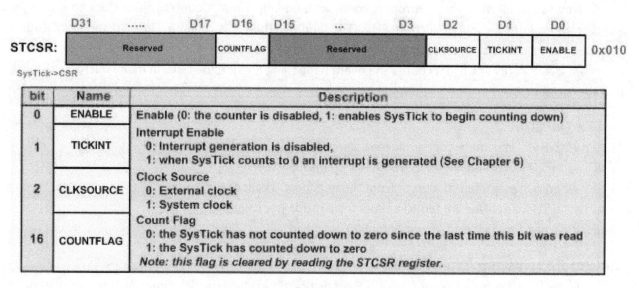

Figure 5-8: STCTRL (System Tick Control)

ENABLE (D0): enables or disables the counter. When the *ENABLE* bit is set the counter initializes the STCVR (*SysTick Current Value Register*) with the value of the *STRVR (SysTick Reload Value Register)*

register and it counts down until it reaches to zero. Then, in the next clock, it underflows which sets the *COUNTFLAG* flag to high and the counter reloads the STCVR with the value of the *STRVR* register and then the process is repeated. See the following figure.

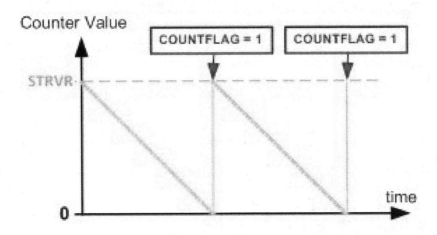

Figure 5-9: System Tick Counting

TICKINT (Tick Interrupt): If TICKINT=1, an interrupt occurs when the COUNTFLAG flag is set. See Chapter 6.

CLKSOURCE (Clock Source): The Arm core provides the choices of the clock coming from system clock or External clock. If CLKSOURCE=0 then the clock comes from External source. If CLKSOURCE=1, then the processor clock provides the clock source to SysTick down counter. When the CLKSOURCE bit is cleared, the SysTick will run at the 1/8 frequency of the processor clock.

COUNTFLAG: Counter counts down from the initial value and when it reaches 0, the counter is reloaded with the value in STRVR and the COUNTFLAG is set high. See Figure 5-9. The flag remains high until it is cleared by software. The flag can be cleared by reading the STCSR register or writing to the STCVR register.

Example 5-1

Find the value for STCSR register, to start counting down with the internal clock.

Solution:

STCSR:	000000000000000	0	0000000000000	1	0	1
	Reserved	COUNTFLAG	Reserved	CLKSOURCE	TICKINT	Enable

SysTick Reload Value Register (STRVR)

The STRVR (SysTick Reload Value) register is used to program the starting value of SysTick down counter. The STRVR should contain the value N − 1 for the COUNT to fire every N clock cycles because the counter counts down to 0 and stay at 0 for one clock cycle before reloading. For example, if we need 1000 clock interval, then we make STRVR = 999. Although this is a 32-bit register, only the lower 24 bits are used. That means the highest value that can be loaded into this register is 0x00FF FFFF or 16,777,216 decimal. See Figures 5-7 and 5-10.

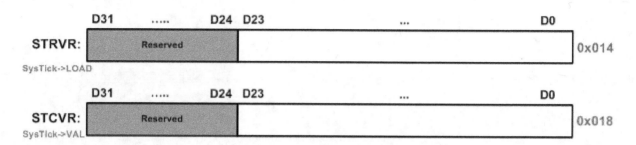

Figure 5-10: STRVR vs. STCVR

Program 5-1 loads the initial value to the maximum and dumps the current value of the SysTick as it counts down onto an LED. The value of STCVR (SysTick->VAL) is shifted to the right from bit 23 (the MSB of SysTick->VAL) to bit 5 (the LED is connected to pin PA5) so that it is aligned with the user LED. SysTick is configured to use default system clock at 16 MHz. The STRVR (SysTick->LOAD) register has 24 bits and is set to the maximal value 0xFFFFFF. So the LED is toggling at the frequency of

$$\frac{16,000,000 \ Hz}{2^{23}} = \frac{16,000,000 \ Hz}{8,388,608} = 1.907 \ Hz$$

And the frequency of the user LED is 0.954 Hz (half of the frequency of toggles).

Program 5-1: Monitoring the value of STCVR of SysTick on LEDs

```
/* p5_1.c Toggle Green LED (LD2) on STM32F446RE Nucleo64 using SysTick

 * This program configures SysTick to be a 24-bit free-running
 * down-counter. Bit 23 of SysTick current value is written to
 * the LED (PA5) continuously.
 * SysTick is based on system clock running at 16 MHz.
 * So bit 23 of SysTick current value toggles about 1 Hz
 * (16,000,000 Hz / 2^23 = 1.907 Hz).
 *
 * This program was tested with Keil uVision v5.24a with DFP v2.11.0
 */
#include "stm32f4xx.h"

void delayMs(int n);

int main(void) {
    RCC->AHB1ENR |=  1;           /* enable GPIOA clock */
    GPIOA->MODER &= ~0x00000C00;  /* clear pin mode */
```

```
    GPIOA->MODER |=  0x00000400;    /* set pin to output mode */

    /* Configure SysTick */
    SysTick->LOAD = 0xFFFFFF;        /* reload with max value */
    SysTick->CTRL = 5;      /* enable it, no interrupt, use system clock */

    while (1) {
        /* take bit 23 of SysTick current value and shift it to bit 5
            then write it to PortA */
        GPIOA->ODR = (SysTick->VAL >> (23 - 5)) & 0x00000020;
    }
}
```

See the following examples.

Example 5-2

In an Arm microcontroller system clock = 8MHz. Calculate the delay which is made by the following function.

```
void delay(){
    SysTick->LOAD = 9;
    SysTick->VAL = 0;    /* clear current value register */
    SysTick->CTRL = 5;   /* Enable the timer */

    while((SysTick->CTRL &0x10000) == 0) /*wait until the COUNTFLAG is set */
        {}
    SysTick->CTRL = 0; /*Stop the timer (Enable = 0) */
}
```

Solution:

The timer is initialized with 9. So, it goes through the following 10 stages:

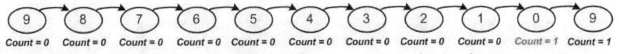

Since the system clock is chosen as the clock source, each clock lasts $\frac{1}{sysclk} = \frac{1}{8MHz} = 0.125\mu s$.

So, the program makes a delay of $9 \times 0.125\mu s = 1.125\mu s$.

Note: the function call and the instructions execution take few clock cycles as well. If you want to calculate the exact amount of delay, you should include this overhead, as well. The value of SysTick->VAL chosen in this example is small for ease of illustration. In real applications, you would want to choose a larger delay so that the overhead is negligible compared to the delay.

Note: Because the COUNTFLAG is set when the counter reaches zero, it takes 9 cycles for the COUNTFLAG to set. If periodic (repetitive) operation is used, the period will be equal to 10 cycles because the counter stays at 0 for one clock cycle before reloading.

Example 5-3

In an Arm microcontroller, the SYSCLK clock is chosen as the clock source for the System tick timer. Calculate the delay which is made by the timer if the STRVR register is loaded with N.

Solution:

The timer is initialized with N. So, it goes through N cycles.
Since the system clock is chosen as the clock source, each clock lasts 1 / SYSCLK
So, the program makes a delay of N × (1/ SYSCLK) = N / SYSCLK.

Example 5-4

Using the SysTick timer, write a function that makes a delay of 1ms. Assume SYSCLK = 16MHz.

Solution:

From the equation derived in Example 5-2
delay = N / SYSCLK
N = delay × SYSCLK = 0.001 sec × 16 MHz = 16,000
N = 16,000

```
void delay1ms(void){
    SysTick->LOAD = 16000;
    SysTick->VAL = 0;    /* clear current value register */
    SysTick->CTRL = 0x5;  /* Enable the timer */

    while((SysTick->CTRL & 0x10000) == 0) /* wait until the COUNTFLAG is set */
      {}
    SysTick->CTRL = 0; /* Stop the timer (Enable = 0) */

}
```

The Program 5-2 uses the SysTick to toggle PA5 pin 5 times every second. We need the STRVR (Reload) value of 3,200,000 − 1 since 16MHz / 5 = 3,200,000. We assume the System clock is 16 MHz. Notice, every 3,200,000 clocks the down counter reaches 0, and COUNTFLAG is raised. Then the STRVR register is loaded with 3,200,000 − 1 automatically. The COUNTFLAG is clear when the STCTRL (SysTick->CTRL) register is read.

Program 5-2: Toggle user LED at 5 Hz using the SysTick Counter

```c
/* p2_2.c Toggle Green LED (LD2) on STM32F446RE Nucleo64 using SysTick
 *
 * This program uses SysTick to generate 500 ms delay to
 * toggle the LED. System clock is running at 16 MHz.
 * SysTick is configure to count down from 3199999 to zero
 * to give a 500 ms delay.
* This program was tested with Keil uVision v5.24a with DFP v2.11.0
 */
#include "stm32f4xx.h"
int main(void) {
    RCC->AHB1ENR |= 1;              /* enable GPIOA clock */
    GPIOA->MODER &= ~0x00000C00;    /* clear pin mode */
    GPIOA->MODER |= 0x00000400;     /* set pin to output mode */
    /* Configure SysTick */
    SysTick->LOAD = 3200000 - 1; /* reload with number of clocks per second */
    SysTick->VAL = 0;
    SysTick->CTRL = 5;        /* enable it, no interrupt, use system clock */

    while (1) {
        if (SysTick->CTRL & 0x10000) {  /* if COUNT flag is set */
            GPIOA->ODR ^= 0x00000020;   /* toggle green LED */
        }
    }
}
```

In Program 5-3, SysTick is used to generate multiple of 1 millisecond delay. STRVR value of 16,000 is used since 0.001 sec × 16MHz = 16,000.

Program 5-3: Making delays using SysTick

```c
/* p5_3.c Toggle Green LED (LD2) on STM32F446RE Nucleo64 using SysTick
 *
 * This program uses SysTick to generate multiples of millisecond delay.
 * System clock is running at 16 MHz. SysTick is configure
 * to count down from 16000 to zero to give a 1 ms delay.
 * A for loop counts how many millisecond the delay should be.
 * When 1000 is used for loop count, the delay is 1000 ms or 1 second.
 *
 * This program was tested with Keil uVision v5.24a with DFP v2.11.0
 */
#include "stm32f4xx.h"

void delayMs(int n);

int main(void) {
    RCC->AHB1ENR |= 1;              /* enable GPIOA clock */
    GPIOA->MODER &= ~0x00000C00;    /* clear pin mode */
    GPIOA->MODER |= 0x00000400;     /* set pin to output mode */

    while (1) {
        delayMs(1000);              /* delay 1000 ms */
        GPIOA->ODR ^= 0x00000020;   /* toggle red LED */
    }
}
```

```
void delayMs(int n) {
    int i;

    /* Configure SysTick */
    SysTick->LOAD = 16000;  /* reload with number of clocks per millisecond */
    SysTick->VAL = 0;        /* clear current value register */
    SysTick->CTRL = 0x5;     /* Enable the timer */

    for(i = 0; i < n; i++) {
        while((SysTick->CTRL & 0x10000) == 0) /* wait until the COUNTFLAG is set */
            { }
    }
    SysTick->CTRL = 0;        /* Stop the timer (Enable = 0) */
}
```

The System Tick Timer has a very simple structure and is the same across all the Arm Cortex-M chips regardless of who makes them. In addition, STM32F4xx has its own timers which are covered in the next sections.

Review Questions

1. The highest number we can place in STRVR register is _____.
2. Assume CPU frequency of 16MHz. Find the value for STRVR register if we want 5 ms elapsed time.
3. The SysTick is _____-bit wide.
4. Which bit of STCSR is used to enable the SysTick.
5. The SysTick is (down or up) counter.

Section 5.3: Timer and Delay Generation in STM32F4xx

In addition to SysTick timers, STM32Fxx Arm comes with a large number of timers. The timers are called TIMx where x=0, 1, 2, 3, 4, and so on. They fall into three categories: a) Advanced Control Timer, b) General Purpose Timer, and c) Basic Timer. See table 5-1. Advanced Control Timer is mostly used for PWM and DC motor control and is covered in Chapter 11. The TIMx are used for a wide range of generic timer/counter applications. While most timers in STM Arm are 16-bit, there are one or two 32-bit timers too. The 32-bit timers are in the general purpose timers group and usually designated as TIM2 and TIM5. The 32-bit Timers discussed first in this section. Other aspects of timers will be discussed in later part of this section.

TIMx has a counter similar to SysTick timer with additional features including:

- To slow down the speed of timer counting, it has a prescaler.
- It can be used to generate an output of programmable frequency and pulse-width modulation.
- It can capture the frequency and pulse width of an input signal.
- It can be used as event counter.
- On a counter overflow, compare match, or capture, it can generate interrupts or events

We will discuss the details of these features in the coming sections. See table below.

130

Timer type	Timer	Counter resolution	Counter type	Prescaler factor	Capture/ compare channels
Advanced-control	TIM1, TIM8	16-bit	Up, Down, Up/down	Any integer between 1 and 65536	4
General purpose	TIM2, TIM5	32-bit	Up, Down, Up/down	Any integer between 1 and 65536	4
	TIM3, TIM4	16-bit	Up, Down, Up/down	Any integer between 1 and 65536	4
	TIM9	16-bit	Up	Any integer between 1 and 65536	2
	TIM10, TIM11	16-bit	Up	Any integer between 1 and 65536	1
	TIM12	16-bit	Up	Any integer between 1 and 65536	2
	TIM13, TIM14	16-bit	Up	Any integer between 1 and 65536	1
Basic	TIM6, TIM7	16-bit	Up	Any integer between 1 and 65536	0

Table 5-1: STMF466RE Arm timers

Timer Clock

As we discuss in Appendix C, the SYSCLK goes through AHB and APB prescaler before it is fed to peripheral modules such as timers. The AHB prescaler can divide the SYSCLK by up to maximum of 512. After SYSCLK goes through AHB prescaler it can be divided again by another prescaler associated with the APB prescaler. The values that APB prescaler can divide by are 1, 2, 4, 8, and 16. This is the case for all peripherals. However, in the case of STM Arm timers, we have another stage. If the APB prescaler is 1 (no division), the timer clock frequencies are the same frequency as APB. If the APB prescaler is 2, 4, 8, 16 (divided by 2, 4, 8, 16), timer clock frequencies are set to twice the frequency of the APB.

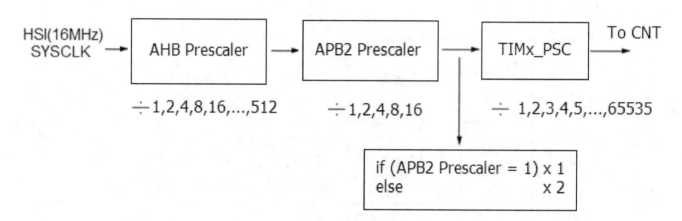

Figure 5-11: STM32F4xx Timer Prescale Options

In STM32F4xx, all the timers are connected to APB buses. The RCC_APB1ENR and APB2ENR registers are used to enable or disable the clock to individual TIMx timers. Bits 8-0 of RCC_APB1ENR register are used to enable the clock to some of TIMx timers. These bits are cleared after reset. Without the clock enabled, the CPU will not be able to communicate with the timer. So the program needs to enable these clocks first. Figures 5-12 and 5-13 show portion of the RCC_APB1ENR and RCC_APB2ENR registers. The register is 32-bit wide but the figure only shows the bits that are related to the TIMx timers.

31	30	29	28	27	26	25	24	23	22	21	20	19	18	17	16
Res.	Res.	DAC EN	PWR EN	CEC EN	CAN2 EN	CAN1 EN	FMPI2C1 EN	I2C3 EN	I2C2 EN	I2C1 EN	UART5 EN	UART4 EN	USART3 EN	USART2 EN	SPDIFRX EN
		rw	rw	rw	rw	rw	rw	rw	rw	rw	rw	rw	rw	rw	rw

15	14	13	12	11	10	9	8	7	6	5	4	3	2	1	0
SPI3 EN	SPI2 EN	Res.	Res.	WWDG EN	Res.	Res.	TIM14 EN	TIM13 EN	TIM12 EN	TIM7 EN	TIM6 EN	TIM5 EN	TIM4 EN	TIM3 EN	TIM2 EN
rw	rw			rw			rw	rw	rw	rw	rw	rw	rw	rw	rw

Bit 8 **TIM14EN:** TIM14 clock enable
This bit is set and cleared by software.
0: TIM14 clock disabled
1: TIM14 clock enabled
Bit 7 **TIM13EN:** TIM13 clock enable
This bit is set and cleared by software.
0: TIM13 clock disabled

1: TIM13 clock enabled
Bit 6 **TIM12EN:** TIM12 clock enable
This bit is set and cleared by software.
0: TIM12 clock disabled
1: TIM12 clock enabled
Bit 5 **TIM7EN:** TIM7 clock enable
This bit is set and cleared by software.

0: TIM7 clock disabled

1: TIM7 clock enabled

Bit 4 **TIM6EN**: TIM6 clock enable

This bit is set and cleared by software.

0: TIM6 clock disabled

1: TIM6 clock enabled

Bit 3 **TIM5EN**: TIM5 clock enable

This bit is set and cleared by software.

0: TIM5 clock disabled

1: TIM5 clock enabled

Bit 2 **TIM4EN**: TIM4 clock enable

This bit is set and cleared by software.

0: TIM4 clock disabled

1: TIM4 clock enabled

Bit 1 **TIM3EN**: TIM3 clock enable

This bit is set and cleared by software.

0: TIM3 clock disabled

1: TIM3 clock enabled

Bit 0 **TIM2EN**: TIM2 clock enable

This bit is set and cleared by software.

0: TIM2 clock disabled

1: TIM2 clock enabled

Figure 5-12: RCC_APB1ENR Register is used to enable timer clock

31	30	29	28	27	26	25	24	23	22	21	20	19	18	17	16
Res.	Res.	Res.	Res.	Res.	Res.	Res.	Res.	SAI2 EN	SAI1 EN	Res.	Res.	Res.	TIM11 EN	TIM10 EN	TIM9 EN
								rw	rw				rw	rw	rw

15	14	13	12	11	10	9	8	7	6	5	4	3	2	1	0
Res.	SYSCFG EN	SPI4 EN	SPI1 EN	SDIO EN	ADC3 EN	ADC2 EN	ADC1 EN	Res.	Res.	USART6 EN	USART1 EN	Res.	Res.	TIM8 EN	TIM1 EN
	rw	rw	rw	rw	rw	rw	rw			rw	rw			rw	rw

Bit 18 **TIM11EN**: TIM11 clock enable

This bit is set and cleared by software.

0: TIM11 clock disabled

1: TIM11 clock enabled

Bit 17 **TIM10EN**: TIM10 clock enable

This bit is set and cleared by software.

0: TIM10 clock disabled

1: TIM10 clock enabled

Bit 16 **TIM9EN**: TIM9 clock enable

This bit is set and cleared by software.

0: TIM9 clock disabled

1: TIM9 clock enabled

Bit 1 **TIM8EN**: TIM8 clock enable

This bit is set and cleared by software.

0: TIM8 clock disabled

1: TIM8 clock enabled

Bit 0 **TIM1EN**: TIM1 clock enable

This bit is set and cleared by software.

0: TIM1 clock disabled

1: TIM1 clock enabled

Figure 5-13: RCC_APB2ENR Register is used to enable timer clock

For example, we can use the following code to enable the clock to TIM2:

```
RCC->APB1ENR |= 1;        /* enable TIM2 clock */
```

Timer counter clock

At the heart of each timer, there is a counter. The clock that drives the counter (CK_CNT) may come from an event, external source, or an internal clock (CK_INT) via the prescaler. We will discuss the event in the last sections. Before that, we will focus on the clock from CK_INT.

The STM32F4xx clock system is very flexible and complex. Appendix C describes it in more details. To simplify the discussion and programming examples here, we use 16MHz as SYSCLK. This is done automatically upon powered-up reset.

TIM2 32-bit Timer

While most of the timers in the STM32 Arm are 16-bit, there is also at least one 32-bit timer. The 32-bit is called TIM2 and is present with the same name in all family members of the STM32 Arm chips. Some of the STM32F4 chips such as STM32F446RE have two 32-bit timers. They are called TIM2 and TIM5. We can also create 32-bit timers by pairing together two 16-bit timers.

Table 5-2 shows some of the TIMx registers. The size of registers varies.

Offset	Register Name
0x00	TIMx_CR1 (Control 1)
0x04	TIMx_CR2 (Control 2)
0x10	TIMx_SR (Status)
0x18	TIMx_CCMR1
0x1C	TIMx_CCMR2
0x20	TIMx_CCER
0x24	TIMx_CNT (Count)
0x28	TIMx_PSC(Presacler)
0x2C	TIM_ARR (Auto Reload)
0x34	TIMx_CCR1
0x38	TIMx_CCR2
0x3C	TIMx_CCR3
0x40	TIMx_CCR4
0x20	TIMx_CCER

Table 5-2: Some of the STM32F4xx Timer Registers

The STM32F4xx TIMx counter can be up-counter or down-counter. The CK_INT goes through multiple prescalers before it is fed to the timer. The last prescaler can divide CK_INT by values 1 to 65,536.

CONTROL 1 Register (CR1)

Using the CR1 (Control 1) register, we can control the counter direction, one-shot, or disable/enable. After TIMx configuration is done, the TIMx should be enabled by writing a 1 to the CEN (Counter Enable) bit to start its function. We can make the Counter to count up (DIR=0, default) or down (DIR=1) by using the DIR bit of CR1. See figure below and Table 5-3.

15	14	13	12	11	10	9	8	7	6	5	4	3	2	1	0
Res.	Res.	Res.	Res.	Res.	Res.	CKD[1:0]		ARPE	CMS[1:0]		DIR	OPM	URS	UDIS	CEN
						rw	rw	rw	rw	rw	rw	rw	rw	rw	rw

Figure 5-14: CR1 (Control 1) Register

bit	Name	Description
0	CEN	**Counter enable** 0: Counter disabled 1: Counter enabled
3	OPM	**One-pulse mode** 0: Counter is not stopped at update event 1: Counter stops counting at the next update event (clearing the bit CEN)
4	DIR	**Direction** 0: Counter used as up counter 1: Counter used as down counter

Table 5-3: Some of the CR1 register bits

CEN (Counter Enable, D0): enables or disables the counter. When the CEN bit is set, the timer starts to count. It counts up or down depending on the DIR bit.

DIR (Direction, D4): This bit configures the Timer/Counter as an up or down counter. If the DIR bit is 0, the timer counts up. If the DIR bit is 1, the counter counts down.

Example 5-5

Find the value for CR1 register, to enable the TIM2 for up counter.

Solution:

15	14	13	12	11	10	9	8	7	6	5	4	3	2	1	0
Res.	Res.	Res.	Res.	Res.	Res.	CKD[1:0]		ARPE	CMS[1:0]		DIR	OPM	URS	UDIS	CEN
						rw	rw	rw	rw	rw	rw	rw	rw	rw	rw

TIM2_CR1 = 0b010001 = 0x0011

TIMxSR (Status Register)

UIF (D0): This is like overflow flag in other microcontrollers. When the timer counts down from a starting value and reaches 0, the UIF is set high. In the case of up counter, the UIF goes HIGH when it reaches the top value and wraps around to zero. The UIF flag remains high until it is cleared by software.

15	14	13	12	11	10	9	8	7	6	5	4	3	2	1	0
Res.	Res.	Res.	CC4OF	CC3OF	CC2OF	CC1OF	Res.	BIF	TIF	COMIF	CC4IF	CC3IF	CC2IF	CC1IF	UIF
			rc_w0	rc_w0	rc_w0	rc_w0		rc_w0	rc_w0	rc_w0	rc_w0	rc_w0	rc_w0	rc_w0	rc_w0

Figure 5-15: TIMxSR Register

bit	Name		Description

0	UIF	Update interrupt Flag
		This bit is set by hardware on an update event. It is cleared by software.
		No update occurred. 0:
		Update interrupt pending. 1:

Table 5-4: TIMx_SR (Staus) Register UIF Bit

TIMx_CNT (COUNT) Register

The TIMx_CNT Count register shows the current counter value. The TIMx_CNT register can be 16-bit or 32-bit depending on which TIMx we are using. As we mention earlier, timers are basically a counter. In the case of a 16-bit timer, TIMx_CNT is a 16-bit counter and can take values between 0 to 0xFFFF. For the 32-bit timers such as TIM2, the TIM2_CNT is 32 bit wide. The TIM2_CNT can take values between 0 and 0xFFFF FFFF. See Figure 5-16.

31	30	29	28	27	26	25	24	23	22	21	20	19	18	17	16
CNT[31:16] (depending on timers)															
rw	rw	rw	rw	rw	rw	rw	rw	rw	rw	rw	rw	rw	rw	rw	rw

15	14	13	12	11	10	9	8	7	6	5	4	3	2	1	0
CNT[15:0]															
rw	rw	rw	rw	rw	rw	rw	rw	rw	rw	rw	rw	rw	rw	rw	rw

Figure 5-16: TIMx counter (TIMx_CNT)

Timer Auto-reload Register (TIMxARR)

The counter is an up counter by default. It counts up from 0 to the auto-reload value (content of the TIMx_ARR, Auto Reload Register) then restarts from 0 and generates a counter overflow event. In 32-bit, TIMxARR count could be the maximum count which is 0xFFFFFFFF. For 16-bit TIMx maximum count is 0xFFFF. See Figure 5-17. Notice that when the counter reaches the TIM_ARR value, the UIF flag in TIM_SR (status) register is set HIGH, the counter value is wrapped around to zero, then continues to count up again. Figure 5-18 shows the up counting in 32-bit mode.

31	30	29	28	27	26	25	24	23	22	21	20	19	18	17	16
ARR[31:16] (depending on timers)															
rw	rw	rw	rw	rw	rw	rw	rw	rw	rw	rw	rw	rw	rw	rw	rw
15	14	13	12	11	10	9	8	7	6	5	4	3	2	1	0
ARR[15:0]															
rw	rw	rw	rw	rw	rw	rw	rw	rw	rw	rw	rw	rw	rw	rw	rw

Figure 5-17: TIMx auto-reload register (TIMx_ARR)

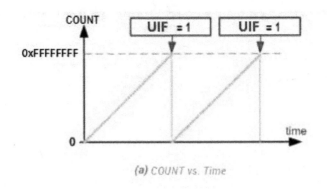

(a) COUNT vs. Time

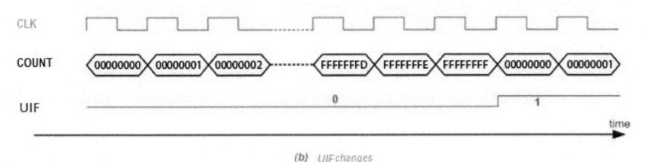

(b) UIF changes

Figure 5-18: TIM2_CNT counter counting for 32-bit

When the DIR bit of CR1 (Control 1) register is set (DIR=1), the counter counts from the auto-reload value (content of the TIMx_ARR register) down to 0, then restarts from the auto-reload value and generates a counter underflow and the UIF flag is set.

Timer Prescaler Register (TIMx_PSC)

TIMx_PSC: The prescaler slows down the counting speed of the timer by dividing the input clock of the timer. As mentioned earlier and shown in Figure 5-20, the CK_INT clock is divided by the prescaler to become CK_INC, which drives the TIMx counter. The prescaler TIMx_PSC can be programmed to divide the clock further. TIM_PSC can divide by 1 to 0xFFFF (65,535).

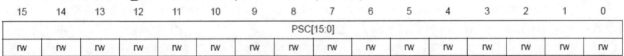

Figure 5-19: TIMx prescaler (TIMx_PSC)

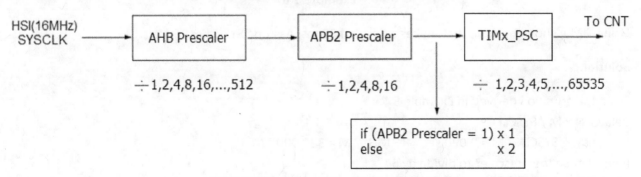

Figure 5-20: TIMx Options for Prescaler

137

Example 5-6

In a STM32F4xx microcontroller with SYSCLK = 16MHz, calculate the delay which is made by the following code. Assume counter clock comes from the 16 MHz SYSCLK clock.

```
RCC->APB1ENR |= 1;        /* enable TIM2 clock */
TIM2->PSC = 1600 - 1;     /* divided by 1600 */
TIM2->ARR = 6;            /* divided by 6 */
TIM2->CNT = 0;
TIM2->CR1 = 1;            /* enable timer2 */
```

Solution:

Since the system clock is chosen as the clock source, each clock lasts $\frac{1}{SYSCLK} = \frac{1}{16\ MHz} = 62.5$ns.

The prescaler (PSC) is set to divide by 1,600, so the timer makes a delay of $1,600 \times 62.5$ns $\times 6 = 600,000$ns.

Example 5-7

In an STM32F4xx microcontroller, the SYSCLK is chosen as the clock source for the Timer/Counter. Derive the formula of delay which is made by the timer if the TIMx_CNT register is loaded with N and the prescaler (PSC) is divided by M.

Solution:

The timer is initialized with N. So, it goes through (N + 1) stages.
Since the SYSCLK clock is chosen as the clock source, each incoming clock lasts (1 / SYSCLK). The PSC prescaler divides the incoming clock by M, therefore, the counter clock period is (M / SYSCLK).
So, the program makes a delay of CNT × M / SYSCLK.

Example 5-8

Using TIM2, show the code that makes a delay of 20 ms. Assume SYSCLK = 16 MHz.

Solution:

From the equation derived in Example 5-7
delay = N × M / SYSCLK
N = delay × SYSCLK / M = 0.020 sec × 16 MHz / M = 320,000 / M
If we choose the prescaler to divide by 64,
N = 320,000 / 64 = 5,000

```
RCC->APB1ENR |= 1;              /* enable TIM2 clock */
TIM2->PSC = 64 - 1;             /* divided by 64 */
TIM2->ARR = 5000 - 1;           /* divided by 5000 */
TIM2->CNT = 0;
TIM2->CR1 = 1;                  /* enable timer2 */
```

The Program 5-4 uses the TIM2 to toggle the LED at 1 Hz. The 16MHz SYSCLK is divided by 1600 by the PSC prescaler. The TIM2_ARR value is set at (10,000 − 1) so that 16 MHz / 1600 / 10,000 = 1 Hz.

The 32-bit TIM2 is configured as up counter. Every time the counter overflows, the UIF flag in TIM2_SR register is set. The program polls the UIF flag. When the flag is set, the program clears it and toggles LED.

Program 5-4: Toggle the LED at 1 Hz using TIM2

```c
/* p5_4.c Toggle Green LED (LD2) on STM32F446RE Nucleo64 using TIM2
 *
 * This program configures TIM2 with prescaler divides by 1600
 * and counter wraps around at 10000. So the 16 MHz system clock
 * is divided by 1600 then divided by 10000 to become 1 Hz.
 * Every time the counter wraps around, it sets UIF flag
 * (bit 0 of TIM2_SR register). The program waits for the
 * UIF to set then toggles the LED (PA5).
 *
 * This program was tested with Keil uVision v5.24a with DFP v2.11.0
 */
#include "stm32f4xx.h"

int main(void) {
    // configure PA5 as output to drive the LED
    RCC->AHB1ENR |=  1;              /* enable GPIOA clock */
    GPIOA->MODER &= ~0x00000C00;     /* clear pin mode */
    GPIOA->MODER |=  0x00000400;     /* set pin to output mode */

    // configure TIM2 to wrap around at 1 Hz
    RCC->APB1ENR |= 1;               /* enable TIM2 clock */
    TIM2->PSC = 1600 - 1;            /* divided by 1600 */
    TIM2->ARR = 10000 - 1;           /* divided by 10000 */
    TIM2->CNT = 0;                   /* clear timer counter */
    TIM2->CR1 = 1;                   /* enable TIM2 */

    while (1) {
        while(!(TIM2->SR & 1)) {}    /* wait until UIF set */
        TIM2->SR &= ~1;              /* clear UIF */
        GPIOA->ODR ^= 0x00000020;    /* toggle green LED */
    }
}
```

Generating large time delays using 32-bit Timer

One way to prolong the delay is to repeat a short delay multiple times. This method is used when the timer counter is 8-bit or 16-bit without much of the prescaler. In the case of STM32F4xx, a 32-bit timer with all the prescalers set to maximum will take more than 100 years to wrap around even when the system clock is running at the top speed of 180 MHz. There seems no point of employing other methods when the timers are capable of handling such a large range of timing needs.

Example 5-9

(a) Calculate the largest delay time in 16-bit mode with and without prescaler at clock = 16 MHz.

(b) Calculate the largest delay time in 32-bit mode with and without prescaler at clock = 16 MHz.

(c) Find the TIMx_CNT value with clock = 16 MHz to generate a delay of 2 minutes. Use the smallest divisor in the prescaler.

Solution:

(a) 1 / 16 MHz = 62.5 ns.

The largest TIMx_ARR count in 16-bit mode is 65,536.

Without prescaler, 65,536 × 62.5 ns = 4.096 ms

With prescaler, the largest divisor is 65536; 65536 × 65536 × 62.5 ns = 268.4 s

(b) The largest TIMxARR count in 32-bit mode is 2^{32}.

Without prescaler, 2^{32} × 62.5 ns = 268.4 s

With prescaler, the largest divisor is 65535; 2^{32} × 65,535 × 62.5 ns = 17,589,594 sec (That is 203 days!)

(c) With prescaler PSC set to 1 we have:

2 minutes = 120 sec

120 sec / 62.5 ns = 1,920,000,000.

The mode that can hold the number this large is 32-bit mode.

The next program uses TIM3 the same way as the previous program. Because the value we need to set the AAR register is less than 16 bits, these two programs are identical.

Program 5-5: Toggle LED using TIM3 in 16-bit mode

```
/* p5_5.c Toggle Green LED (LD2) on STM32F446RE Nucleo64 using TIM3
 *
 * This program configures TIM3 with prescaler divides by 1600
 * and counter wraps around at 10000. So the 16 MHz system clock
 * is divided by 1600 then divided by 10000 to become 1 Hz.
 * Every time the counter wraps around, it sets UIF flag
 * (bit 0 of TIM3_SR register). The program waits for the
 * UIF to set then toggles the LED (PA5).
 *
```

```
 * This program was tested with Keil uVision v5.24a with DFP v2.11.0
 */
#include "stm32f4xx.h"

int main(void) {
    // configure PA5 as output to drive the LED
    RCC->AHB1ENR |=  1;                 /* enable GPIOA clock */
    GPIOA->MODER &= ~0x00000C00;        /* clear pin mode */
    GPIOA->MODER |=  0x00000400;        /* set pin to output mode */

    // configure TIM3 to wrap around at 1 Hz
    RCC->APB1ENR |= 2;                  /* enable TIM3 clock */
    TIM3->PSC = 1600 - 1;               /* divided by 1600 */
    TIM3->ARR = 10000 - 1;              /* divided by 10000 */
    TIM3->CNT = 0;                      /* clear timer counter */
    TIM3->CR1 = 1;                      /* enable TIM3 */

    while (1) {
        while(!(TIM3->SR & 1)) {}       /* wait until UIF set */
        TIM3->SR &= ~1;                 /* clear UIF */
        GPIOA->ODR ^= 0x00000020;       /* toggle green LED */
    }
}
```

Review Questions

1. True or false. STM32F4xx Arm timers supports both up and down counter.
2. True or false. Timers in STM32F4xx support maximum of 16-bit.
3. True or false. Timer PSC prescalers can divide the clock by maximum of 256.
4. In up mode, the 32-bit counter rolls over when the counter reaches _____.
5. Which register holds the UIF overflow flag?

Section 5.4: Compare Registers and Waveform Output

So far, we have been generating output waveform by monitoring the overflow flag and toggling an output pin in software every time the UIF is set. It is very inefficient to poll the status of the overflow flag or any other status for that matter. In the next chapter, we will see how to use an interrupt to notify the program when the status of the hardware changes. But for the timers, we can generate output waveform without software intervention once it is configured. The waveform output is accomplished by the compare function.

The Compare function uses register called CCRx(Compare/Capture) register. The size of the register is identical to the CNT and ARP. For a 16-bit timer, they are 16-bit wide, and for a 32-bit timer, they are 32-bit wide. The CCRx register content is compared with the value of the counter (CNT register) continuously. When the values of the CNT register and CCRx register are equal, the corresponding pin performs an action. Upon a match between the CNT counter and the value in CCRx registers, the output pin associated with this CCRx register can be configured to set, clear, or toggle depending on the configuration. See Figure 5-21. Just like the previous cases, the ARP register holds the original value.

141

The compare function can be used to generate pulse width modulation output (PWM), which we will discuss in details in chapter 11. In this section, we will limit the discussion to output compare operation.

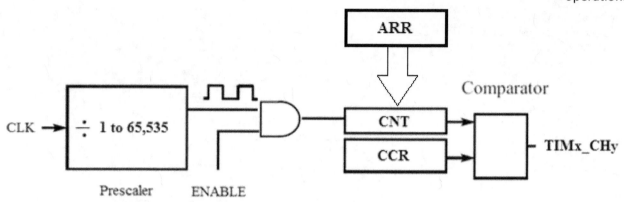

Figure 5-21: CNT, ARR and Compare registers (CCR) with Waveform Output

Notice we have four CCRx registers (CCR1, CCR2, CCR3 and CCR4) for each timer regardless of using a 32-bit timer (TIM2) or a 16-bit timer (TIM3). The output pins are called TIMx_CHy, in which the x is for TIMx and can be 1, 2, 3, 4, 5, 6, and so on depending on how many on-chip timers a given STM Arm chip has. The CHy can be CH1, CH2, CH3, and CH4 only, as we will see soon. Four channels of a given timer can work independently of each other. They are shown below.

31	30	29	28	27	26	25	24	23	22	21	20	19	18	17	16
CCR1[31:16] (depending on timers)															
rw	rw	rw	rw	rw	rw	rw	rw	rw	rw	rw	rw	rw	rw	rw	rw
15	14	13	12	11	10	9	8	7	6	5	4	3	2	1	0
CCR1[15:0]															
rw	rw	rw	rw	rw	rw	rw	rw	rw	rw	rw	rw	rw	rw	rw	rw

31	30	29	28	27	26	25	24	23	22	21	20	19	18	17	16
CCR2[31:16] (depending on timers)															
rw	rw	rw	rw	rw	rw	rw	rw	rw	rw	rw	rw	rw	rw	rw	rw
15	14	13	12	11	10	9	8	7	6	5	4	3	2	1	0
CCR2[15:0]															
rw	rw	rw	rw	rw	rw	rw	rw	rw	rw	rw	rw	rw	rw	rw	rw

31	30	29	28	27	26	25	24	23	22	21	20	19	18	17	16
CCR3[31:16] (depending on timers)															
rw	rw	rw	rw	rw	rw	rw	rw	rw	rw	rw	rw	rw	rw	rw	rw
15	14	13	12	11	10	9	8	7	6	5	4	3	2	1	0
CCR3[15:0]															
rw	rw	rw	rw	rw	rw	rw	rw	rw	rw	rw	rw	rw	rw	rw	rw

31	30	29	28	27	26	25	24	23	22	21	20	19	18	17	16
CCR4[31:16] (depending on timers)															
rw	rw	rw	rw	rw	rw	rw	rw	rw	rw	rw	rw	rw	rw	rw	rw

15	14	13	12	11	10	9	8	7	6	5	4	3	2	1	0
CCR4[15:0]															
rw	rw	rw	rw	rw	rw	rw	rw	rw	rw	rw	rw	rw	rw	rw	rw

Figure 5-22: TIMx capture/compare registers (TIMx_CCRy)

Waveform Output

The OCxM bits in TIMx_CCMRy register are used to decide the output operation. Here are the options for output pin:

000: Frozen
001: Set output to active HIGH level when TIMx_CNT=TIMx_CCRy.
010: Set output to inactive LOW level when TIMx_CNT=TIMx_CCRy.
011: Toggle when TIMx_CNT=TIMx_CCRy.
100: Forced LOW.
101: Forced HIGH.
110: PWM mode 1. (See Chapter 11)
111: PWM mode 2. (See Chapter 11)

Notice we have two TIMx_CCMR1 and TIM_CCMR2 for each timer. The TIMx_CCMR1 takes care of CH1 and CH2 and TIMx_CCMR2 is set aside for the CH3 and CH4 of each timer.

15	14	13	12	11	10	9	8	7	6	5	4	3	2	1	0
OC2CE	OC2M[2:0]			OC2PE	OC2FE	CC2S[1:0]		OC1CE	OC1M[2:0]			OC1PE	OC1FE	CC1S[1:0]	
	IC2F[3:0]			IC2PSC[1:0]					IC1F[3:0]			IC1PSC[1:0]			
rw	rw	rw	rw	rw	rw	rw	rw	rw	rw	rw	rw	rw	rw	rw	rw

OCxCE: Output compare x clear enable
OCxM: Output compare x mode
   when TIMx_CNT=TIMx_CCRy.
   010: Set output to inactive LOW level when TIMx_CNT=TIMx_CCRy.
   011: Toggle when TIMx_CNT=TIMx_CCRy.
   100: Forced LOW.
   101: Forced HIGH.
   110: PWM mode 1. (See Chapter 11)
   111: PWM mode 2. (See Chapter 11)
OCxPE: Output compare x preload enable
CCxS: Capture/Compare x selection
This bit-field defines the direction of the channel (input/output) as well as the used input.
00: CCx channel is configured as output

Fig 5-23: TIMx_CCMR1 for output option

15	14	13	12	11	10	9	8	7	6	5	4	3	2	1	0
OC4CE	OC4M[2:0]			OC4PE	OC4FE	CC4S[1:0]		OC3CE	OC3M[2:0]			OC3PE	OC3FE	CC3S[1:0]	
IC4F[3:0]				IC4PSC[1:0]				IC3F[3:0]				IC3PSC[1:0]			
rw	rw	rw	rw	rw	rw	rw	rw	rw	rw	rw	rw	rw	rw	rw	rw

OCxCE: Output compare x clear enable

OCxM: Output compare x mode

       The OCxM bits in TIMx_CCMRy register are used to decide the output operation. Here are the options for output pin:

       000: Frozen

       001: Set output to active HIGH level when TIMx_CNT=TIMx_CCRy.

       010: Set output to inactive LOW level when TIMx_CNT=TIMx_CCRy.

       011: Toggle when TIMx_CNT=TIMx_CCRy.

       100: Forced LOW.

       101: Forced HIGH.

       110: PWM mode 1. (See Chapter 11)

       111: PWM mode 2. (See Chapter 11)

OCxPE: Output compare x preload enable

CCxS: Capture/Compare x selection

This bit-field defines the direction of the channel (input/output) as well as the used input.

00: CCx channel is configured as output

Fig 5-24 TIMx_CCMR2 for output option

Channel Enable

       The TIMx_CCER (TIMx capture/compare enable register) is a 16-bit register. It allows us to enable any of the 4 channels either as input capture or output compare. Notice every 4 bits takes care of one of the channels. Also notice this is different from the TIMx enable. See figure below.

15	14	13	12	11	10	9	8	7	6	5	4	3	2	1	0
CC4NP	Res	CC4P	CC4E	CC3NP	Res	CC3P	CC3E	CC2NP	Res	CC2P	CC2E	CC1NP	Res	CC1P	CC1E
rw		rw	rw	rw		rw	rw	rw		rw	rw	rw		rw	rw

       Bit 15 CC4NP: Capture/Compare 4 output Polarity. Refer to CC1NP description

       Bit 14 Reserved, must be kept at reset value.

       Bit 13 CC4P: Capture/Compare 4 output Polarity. Refer to CC1P description

       Bit 12 CC4E: Capture/Compare 4 output enable. Refer to CC1E description

       Bit 11 CC3NP: Capture/Compare 3 output Polarity. Refer to CC1NP description

       Bit 10 Reserved, must be kept at reset value.

       Bit 9 CC3P: Capture/Compare 3 output Polarity. Refer to CC1P description

       Bit 8 CC3E: Capture/Compare 3 output enable. Refer to CC1E description

       Bit 7 CC2NP: Capture/Compare 2 output Polarity. Refer to CC1NP description

       Bit 6 Reserved, must be kept at reset value.

       Bit 5 CC2P: Capture/Compare 2 output Polarity. Refer to CC1P description

       Bit 4 CC2E: Capture/Compare 2 output enable. Refer to CC1E description

       Bit 3 CC1NP: Capture/Compare 1 output Polarity.

CC1 channel configured as output:

CC1NP must be kept cleared in this case.

CC1 channel configured as input:

This bit is used in conjunction with CC1P to define TI1FP1/TI2FP1 polarity. Refer to CC1P description.

Bit 2 Reserved, must be kept at reset value.

Bit 1 CC1P: Capture/Compare 1 output Polarity.

CC1 channel configured as output:

0: OC1 active high

1: OC1 active low

CC1 channel configured as input:

CC1NP/CC1P bits select TI1FP1 and TI2FP1 polarity for trigger or capture operations.

00: noninverted/rising edge

Circuit is sensitive to TIxFP1 rising edge (capture, trigger in reset, external clock or trigger mode), TIxFP1 is not inverted (trigger in gated mode, encoder mode).

01: inverted/falling edge

Circuit is sensitive to TIxFP1 falling edge (capture, trigger in reset, external clock or trigger mode), TIxFP1 is inverted (trigger in gated mode, encoder mode).

10: reserved, do not use this configuration.

11: noninverted/both edges

Circuit is sensitive to both TIxFP1 rising and falling edges (capture, trigger in reset, external clock or trigger mode), TIxFP1 is not inverted (trigger in gated mode). This configuration must not be used for encoder mode.

Bit 0 CC1E: Capture/Compare 1 output enable.

CC1 channel configured as output:

0: Off - OC1 is not active

1: On - OC1 signal is output on the corresponding output pin

CC1 channel configured as input:

This bit determines if a capture of the counter value can actually be done into the input capture/compare register 1 (TIMx_CCR1) or not.

0: Capture disabled

1: Capture enabled

Fig 5-25: TIMx_CCER (TIMx capture/compare enable register)

Pin Selection for waveform Output

STMF4xx has many timer/counters and each one can have up to four Compare channels. Now, Table 5-5 shows the output pins associated with the Timer/Counter Compare channels for Ports A and B in an STMF466RE chip. As we saw in Chapter 4, to use a PORT pin for a multiplex function, the alternative function option in MODER register needs to be enabled. All the Timer/Counters use of the alternative function for CH1-CH4 are shown in Appendix B.

31	30	29	28	27	26	25	24	23	22	21	20	19	18	17	16
MODER15[1:0]		MODER14[1:0]		MODER13[1:0]		MODER12[1:0]		MODER11[1:0]		MODER10[1:0]		MODER9[1:0]		MODER8[1:0]	
rw	rw	rw	rw	rw	rw	rw	rw	rw	rw	rw	rw	rw	rw	rw	rw

15	14	13	12	11	10	9	8	7	6	5	4	3	2	1	0
MODER7[1:0]		MODER6[1:0]		MODER5[1:0]		MODER4[1:0]		MODER3[1:0]		MODER2[1:0]		MODER1[1:0]		MODER0[1:0]	
rw	rw	rw	rw	rw	rw	rw	rw	rw	rw	rw	rw	rw	rw	rw	rw

Bits 2y:2y+1 **MODERy[1:0]:** Port x configuration bits (y = 0..15)

These bits are written by software to configure the I/O direction mode.

00: Input (reset state)

01: General purpose output mode

10: Alternate function mode

11: Analog mode

Figure 5-26: MODER Register is used to select alternative pin functions

31	30	29	28	27	26	25	24	23	22	21	20	19	18	17	16
AFRL7[3:0]				AFRL6[3:0]				AFRL5[3:0]				AFRL4[3:0]			
rw	rw	rw	rw	rw	rw	rw	rw	rw	rw	rw	rw	rw	rw	rw	rw

15	14	13	12	11	10	9	8	7	6	5	4	3	2	1	0
AFRL3[3:0]				AFRL2[3:0]				AFRL1[3:0]				AFRL0[3:0]			
rw	rw	rw	rw	rw	rw	rw	rw	rw	rw	rw	rw	rw	rw	rw	rw

Bits 31:0 **AFRLy:** Alternate function selection for port x bit y (y = 0..7)

These bits are written by software to configure alternate function I/Os

AFRLy selection:

0000: AF0   1000: AF8

0001: AF1   1001: AF9

0010: AF2   1010: AF10

0011: AF3   1011: AF11

0100: AF4   1100: AF12

0101: AF5   1101: AF13

0110: AF6   1110: AF14

0111: AF7   1111: AF15

Figure 5-27: GPIOx_AFRL Register

Port		AF0 SYS	AF1 TIM1/2	AF2 TIM3/4/5	AF3 TIM8/9/10/11/CEC
Port A	PA0	-	TIM2_CH1/TIM2_ETR	TIM5_CH1	TIM8_ETR
	PA1	-	TIM2_CH2	TIM5_CH2	-
	PA2	-	TIM2_CH3	TIM5_CH3	TIM9_CH1
	PA3	-	TIM2_CH4	TIM5_CH4	TIM9_CH2
	PA4	-	-	-	-
	PA5	-	TIM2_CH1/TIM2_ETR	-	TIM8_CH1N
	PA6	-	TIM1_BKIN	TIM3_CH1	TIM8_BKIN
	PA7	-	TIM1_CH1N	TIM3_CH2	TIM8_CH1N
	PA8	MCO1	TIM1_CH1	-	-
	PA9	-	TIM1_CH2	-	-
	PA10	-	TIM1_CH3	-	-
	PA11	-	TIM1_CH4	-	-
	PA12	-	TIM1_ETR	-	-
	PA13	JTMS-SWDIO	-	-	-
	PA14	JTCK-SWCLK	-	-	-
	PA15	JTDI	TIM2_CH1/TIM2_ETR	-	-

Port		AF0 SYS	AF1 TIM1/2	AF2 TIM3/4/5	AF3 TIM8/9/10/11/CEC
Port B	PB0	-	TIM1_CH2N	TIM3_CH3	TIM8_CH2N
	PB1	-	TIM1_CH3N	TIM3_CH4	TIM8_CH3N
	PB2	-	TIM2_CH4	-	-
	PB3	JTDO/TRACESWO	TIM2_CH2	-	-
	PB4	NJTRST	-	TIM3_CH1	-
	PB5	-	-	TIM3_CH2	-
	PB6	-	-	TIM4_CH1	HDMI_CEC
	PB7	-	-	TIM4_CH2	-
	PB8	-	TIM2_CH1/TIM2_ETR	TIM4_CH3	TIM10_CH1
	PB9	-	TIM2_CH2	TIM4_CH4	TIM11_CH1
	PB10	-	TIM2_CH3	-	-
	PB11	-	TIM2_CH4	-	-
	PB12	-	TIM1_BKIN	-	-
	PB13	-	TIM1_CH1N	-	-
	PB14	-	TIM1_CH2N	-	TIM8_CH2N
	PB15	RTC_REFIN	TIM1_CH3N	-	TIM8_CH3N

Note: PA5 for Timer2_CH1 uses AF1

Note: PA6 for Timer3_CH1 uses AF2

Note: PB8 for Timer2_ETR uses AF1

Table 5-5: STMF466RE Alternative Function Table for Ports A and B (See Appendix B for other Ports)

147

Program 5-6 below demonstrates the generation of waveform output using the compare of TIM2 Channel 1. The counter clock uses the 16 MHz system clock. The prescaler and the AAR register are set to count with wrapping around between 0 and AAR value once per second as the previous program. CH1 is configured to compare mode so when the counter CNT value matches the value of CCR1 the corresponding output pin will perform the function prescribed by CCMR register. In CCMR the CH1 is set to toggle the output pin on a match. If the CCR1 register is programmed with any value between 0 and the value of AAR, during the counting, the counter value will have a match once every cycle.

In Program 5-6, you will see that once the TIM2_CCR1 is configured, the waveform output generation does not require the software anymore.

Program 5-6: Generating Waveform Output Using Compare Mode

```
/* p5_6.c Toggle Green LED using TIM2 Compare mode
 *
 * This program configures TIM2 with prescaler divides by 1600
 * and counter wraps around at 10000. So the 16 MHz system clock
 * is divided by 1600 then divided by 10000 to become 1 Hz.
 * The channel 1 is configured for compare mode to toggle the output
 * pin every time the timer counter matches the CCR1 register.
 * The output pin of TIM2 CH1 is PA5 and the alternate function
 * of PA5 should be set to AF1.
 *
 * This program was tested with Keil uVision v5.24a with DFP v2.11.0
 */
#include "stm32f4xx.h"

int main(void) {
    // configure PA5 as output to drive the LED
    RCC->AHB1ENR |= 1;              /* enable GPIOA clock */
    GPIOA->MODER &= ~0x00000C00;    /* clear pin mode */
    GPIOA->MODER |= 0x00000800;     /* set pin to alternate function */
    GPIOA->AFR[0] &= 0x00F00000;    /* clear pin AF bits */
    GPIOA->AFR[0] |= 0x00100000;    /* set pin to AF1 for TIM2 CH1 */


    // configure TIM2 to wrap around at 1 Hz
       // and toggle CH1 output when the counter value is 0
    RCC->APB1ENR |= 1;              /* enable TIM2 clock */
    TIM2->PSC = 1600 - 1;           /* divided by 1600 */
    TIM2->ARR = 10000 - 1;          /* divided by 10000 */
    TIM2->CCMR1 = 0x30;             /* set output to toggle on match */
    TIM2->CCR1 = 0;                 /* set match value */
    TIM2->CCER |= 1;                /* enable CH1 compare mode */
    TIM2->CNT = 0;                  /* clear counter */
    TIM2->CR1 = 1;                  /* enable TIM2 */

    while (1) {
    }
}
```

Review Questions

1. True or false. The Timer also has the waveform Output feature.
2. In STMF4xx Timer, which pin is used for the TIM2_CCR1 waveform Output?
3. Which register is used to configure the waveform Output option?
4. True or false. TIM2_CCR1 Compare/Capture register is 32-bit.

Section 5.5: Using Timer/Counter for Input Capture

The STMF4xx timer can be used for output compare and input capture. We examined the output compare features in the last section. This section examines the input capture feature. For most of the microcontrollers, in input capture mode, the timer/counter is used to capture the signal transitions of an I/O pin and take a timestamp of each transition. In this section, we will describe how to capture the signal transitions of an I/O pin. We use many of the same registers used in the output compare covered in the last section.

To use the input capture option of the STMF4xx, the CCxS (Capture/Compare Selection) bits of the TIMx_CCMRx register are used. Each of the four channels has its own input pin (TIx) and input channel(IC). The inputs are designated as TI1, TI2, TI3, and TI4. TIx stands for timer input. The channels are designated as ICx(input channel). Examining the CCxS bits of TIMx_CCMR1 we see the following options for input capture:

01: CC1 channel is configured as input, IC1 is mapped on TI1.

10: CC2 channel is configured as input, IC2 is mapped on TI2.

The following shows the options for TIMxCCMR2 register:

01: CC3 channel is configured as input, IC3 is mapped on TI3.

10: CC4 channel is configured as input, IC4 is mapped on TI4.

Notice in the last section we used the default option (00) of CCxS bits in TIMx_CCMRx to select output compare. Now, to use the timer for input capture we need to select the signal transitions of an input pin. The desired transition is selected by two bits of CCxNP and CCP in TIMxCCER register. The choices are in the table below. It may be rising edge or falling edge or both.

CCxNP	CCxP	
0	0:	rising edge
0	1:	falling edge
1	0:	reserved, do not use this configuration.
1	1:	both edges

Table 5-6: Choices of input pin transition in TIMx_CCER register when timers are used for Input capture

The above choices are valid only wen the channels are used as input capture.

15	14	13	12	11	10	9	8	7	6	5	4	3	2	1	0
CC4NP	Res	CC4P	CC4E	CC3NP	Res	CC3P	CC3E	CC2NP	Res	CC2P	CC2E	CC1NP	Res	CC1P	CC1E
rw		rw	rw	rw		rw	rw	rw		rw	rw	rw		rw	rw

Bit 15 **CC4NP**: Capture/Compare 4 output Polarity. Refer to CC1NP description

Bit 14 Reserved, must be kept at reset value.

Bit 13 **CC4P**: Capture/Compare 4 output Polarity. Refer to CC1P description

Bit 12 **CC4E**: Capture/Compare 4 output enable. Refer to CC1E description

Bit 11 **CC3NP**: Capture/Compare 3 output Polarity. Refer to CC1NP description

Bit 10 Reserved, must be kept at reset value.

Bit 9 **CC3P**: Capture/Compare 3 output Polarity. Refer to CC1P description

Bit 8 **CC3E**: Capture/Compare 3 output enable. Refer to CC1E description

Bit 7 **CC2NP**: Capture/Compare 2 output Polarity. Refer to CC1NP description

Bit 6 Reserved, must be kept at reset value.

Bit 5 **CC2P**: Capture/Compare 2 output Polarity. Refer to CC1P description

Bit 4 **CC2E**: Capture/Compare 2 output enable. Refer to CC1E description

Bit 3 **CC1NP**: Capture/Compare 1 output Polarity.

CC1 channel configured as output:

CC1NP must be kept cleared in this case.

CC1 channel configured as input:

This bit is used in conjunction with CC1P to define TI1FP1/TI2FP1 polarity. See CC1P description.

Bit 2 Reserved, must be kept at reset value.

Bit 1 **CC1P**: Capture/Compare 1 output Polarity.

CC1 channel configured as output:

0: OC1 active high

1: OC1 active low

CC1 channel configured as input:

CC1NP/CC1P bits select TI1FP1 and TI2FP1 polarity for trigger or capture operations.

00: noninverted/rising edge

Circuit is sensitive to TIxFP1 rising edge (capture, trigger in reset, external clock or trigger mode), TIxFP1 is not inverted (trigger in gated mode, encoder mode).

01: inverted/falling edge

Circuit is sensitive to TIxFP1 falling edge (capture, trigger in reset, external clock or trigger mode), TIxFP1 is inverted (trigger in gated mode, encoder mode).

10: reserved, do not use this configuration.

11: noninverted/both edges

Circuit is sensitive to both TIxFP1 rising and falling edges (capture, trigger in reset, external clock or trigger mode), TIxFP1 is not inverted (trigger in gated mode). This configuration must not be used for encoder mode.

Bit 0 **CC1E**: Capture/Compare 1 output enable.

CC1 channel configured as output:

0: Off - OC1 is not active

1: On - OC1 signal is output on the corresponding output pin

CC1 channel configured as input:

This bit determines if a capture of the counter value can actually be done into the input capture/compare register 1 (TIMx_CCR1) or not.

0: Capture disabled

1: Capture enabled

Figure 5-28: TIM_CCER Register (Notice the input capture)

15	14	13	12	11	10	9	8	7	6	5	4	3	2	1	0
OC2CE	OC2M[2:0]			OC2PE	OC2FE	CC2S[1:0]		OC1CE	OC1M[2:0]			OC1PE	OC1FE	CC1S[1:0]	
	IC2F[3:0]			IC2PSC[1:0]					IC1F[3:0]			IC1PSC[1:0]			
rw	rw	rw	rw	rw	rw	rw	rw	rw	rw	rw	rw	rw	rw	rw	rw

15	14	13	12	11	10	9	8	7	6	5	4	3	2	1	0
OC4CE	OC4M[2:0]			OC4PE	OC4FE	CC4S[1:0]		OC3CE	OC3M[2:0]			OC3PE	OC3FE	CC3S[1:0]	
	IC4F[3:0]			IC4PSC[1:0]					IC3F[3:0]			IC3PSC[1:0]			
rw	rw	rw	rw	rw	rw	rw	rw	rw	rw	rw	rw	rw	rw	rw	rw

Figure 5-29: TIMx_CCMR1 and TIMx_CCMR2 (register details are shown in the last section)

Timer Input Capture

To capture events by the timer/counter, these steps need to be followed:

- Enable and configure the input pin to timer alternate function
- Enable clock to timer
- Set the prescaler to desired value
- Set the capture mode in CCMRx register
- Set the capture edge(s) in CCER register
- Enable timer in CR1 register

In Program 5-7, TIM3 is configured to do input capture. Pin PA6 is configured to be the input pin of TIM3 CH1. The prescaler of TIM3 is set to divide by 16,000 to slow down the clock so that the captured result is easier to see in the debugger. With the prescaler, the clock to the counter will be running at 1 kHz. In TIM3_CCMR1, the timer is configured for capture mode with no capture pre-scaling. CCMRx register also allows setting noise filtering of the input signal but with a short jumper wire, noise should not be an issue. The TIM3_CCER is used to enable the capture mode (CC1E bit) and set the polarity and edge of capture (CC1P, CC1NP bits) to non-inverting rising edge. Each time the input signal goes from low to high, a capture occurs.

TIM2 is configured to toggle the output of PA5 as the same in Program 5-6 for a test signal. A jumper wire should be installed between the output PA5 pin and input PA6 pin. Since TIM2 toggles the output at 1 Hz, every two seconds, there will be a rising edge.

In the program, the infinite loop waits for the capture flag to set in the TIM3 status register. When the capture occurs, the program reads the captured counter value (TIM3_CCR1) and stores it in a global variable. You may put a breakpoint in the infinite loop in the debugger. Right click the global variable "timestamp" and add it to a watch window. Every time the breakpoint is hit, the watch window is updated. Hit the Run button or F5 key on the keyboard to continue program execution as soon as the breakpoint is hit. You will see the value of "timestamp" is incrementing by 2000. The TIM3 counter is driven by a 1 kHz clock. It counts up by 2000 for every two seconds by a rising edge of the input signal.

ST-Link debugger does not do live watch of the variables. The program execution must be stopped for the watch window to update its display. When the CPU execution is stopped, the TIM2 output compare and the TIM3 input capture do not stop. If you waited too long to resume the program execution, you might miss reading one or more captured counter values. In that case, you will see the value of "timestamp" incremented by a multiple of 2000. The status register of TIM3 will have the overflow bit (CC1OF) set to alert you that a captured value was lost.

The program could be tested by an external periodic signal. To do so, you need to remove the jumper between PA5 and PA6 and drive the capture input PA6 by a function generator. The STMF4xx operates on a 3.3V logic level. The input test signal should be within 3.3V and 0V. Driving the pin beyond that voltage range may damage the pin or the device.

Program 5-7: Using Timer input capture for the event of the rising edges

```c
/* p5_7.c TIM3 Input Capture

 * This program configures TIM2 CH1 to toggle PA5 as was done in p5_6.
 * The TIM3 CH1 is set to do Input Capture from PA6. The program waits
 * for capture flag (CC1IF) to set then stores the captured value in a
 * global variable to be watched by the debugger. The flag is cleared
 * by reading CCR1.
 * A jumper should be used to connect PA5 to PA6.
 *
 * This program was tested with Keil uVision v5.24a with DFP v2.11.0
 */
#include "stm32f4xx.h"

int timestamp = 0;
int hold = 1;

int main(void) {
    // configure PA5 as output of TIM2 CH1
    RCC->AHB1ENR |= 1;                  /* enable GPIOA clock */
    GPIOA->MODER &= ~0x00000C00;        /* clear pin mode */
    GPIOA->MODER |= 0x00000800;         /* set pin to alternate function */
    GPIOA->AFR[0] &= ~0x00F00000;       /* clear pin AF bits */
    GPIOA->AFR[0] |= 0x00100000;        /* set pin to AF1 for TIM2 CH1 */

    // configure TIM2 to wrap around at 1 Hz
        // and toggle CH1 output when the counter value is 0
    RCC->APB1ENR |= 1;                  /* enable TIM2 clock */
    TIM2->PSC = 1600 - 1;               /* divided by 1600 */
    TIM2->ARR = 10000 - 1;              /* divided by 10000 */
    TIM2->CCMR1 = 0x30;                 /* set output to toggle on match */
    TIM2->CCR1 = 0;                     /* set match value */
    TIM2->CCER |= 1;                    /* enable ch 1 compare mode */
    TIM2->CNT = 0;                      /* clear counter */
    TIM2->CR1 = 1;                      /* enable TIM2 */

    // configure PA6 as input of TIM3 CH1
    RCC->AHB1ENR |= 1;                  /* enable GPIOA clock */
    GPIOA->MODER &= ~0x00003000;        /* clear pin mode */
    GPIOA->MODER |= 0x00002000;         /* set pin to alternate function */
    GPIOA->AFR[0] &= ~0x0F000000;       /* clear pin AF bits */
    GPIOA->AFR[0] |= 0x02000000;        /* set pin to AF2 for TIM3 CH1 */

    // configure TIM3 to do input capture with prescaler ...
```

```
RCC->APB1ENR |= 2;                    /* enable TIM3 clock */
TIM3->PSC = 16000 - 1;                /* divided by 16000 */
TIM3->CCMR1 = 0x41;                   /* set CH1 to capture at every edge */
TIM3->CCER = 1;                       /* enable CH 1 capture rising edge */
TIM3->CR1 = 1;                        /* enable TIM3 */

while (1) {
    while (!(TIM3->SR & 2)) {}        /* wait until input edge is captured */
    timestamp = TIM3->CCR1;           /* read captured counter value */
}
}
```

Applications of Input Capture

By calculating the time difference between two consecutive rising edges or two consecutive falling edges, we can get the period of the input signal as demonstrated in the program 5-8. With the period, the frequency can be calculated. If we capture the pulses from the rotary encoder of the wheel axle, the speed of the vehicle can be derived.

If we capture and calculate the time difference between a rising edge and the following falling edge, the pulse width can be calculated. With period and pulse width, the duty cycle can be calculated.

If two periodic signals of the same frequency are captured by two channels of the same timer, the phase between these two signals can be calculated.

In Program 5-8, TIM2 is used to generate a signal that toggles every 300 milliseconds. TIM3 is configured to do input capture of both edges with the clock running at 1 kHz. When a capture event occurs, the last captured value is subtracted from the captured value to give the period of the 300 milliseconds. And since the TIM3 counter clock is running at 1 kHz with 1 millisecond period, the difference between two consecutive captured values should be 300. The frequency of the capture (twice the frequency of the input signal since both edges are captured) is 1000 / period, where 1000 is the frequency of the TIM3 clock. Both period and frequency are stored in global variables so that they can be observed by the debugger.

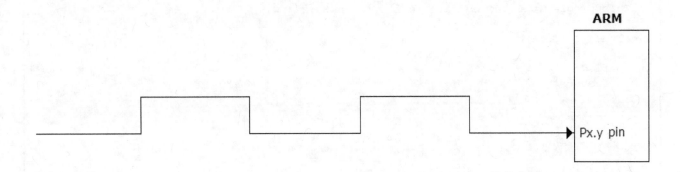

Figure 5-30: Inputing Signal

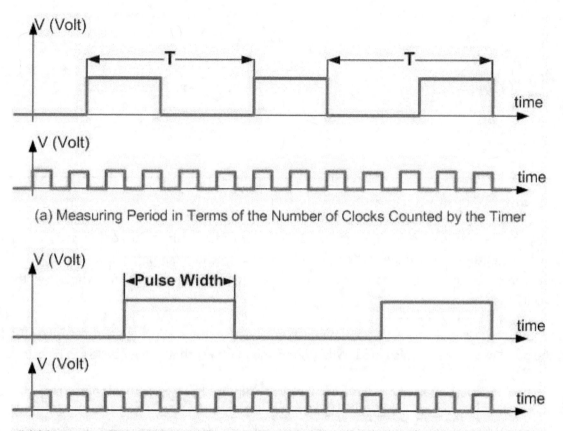

(a) Measuring Period in Terms of the Number of Clocks Counted by the Timer

(b) Measuring Pulse Width in Terms of the Number of Clocks Counted by the Timer

Figure 5-31: Messuring Period and Puls Width

Program 5-8: Using Timer to measure period and frequency

```c
/* p5_8.c TIM3 Measuring Period and Frequency

 * This program configures TIM2 CH1 to toggle PA5 as was done in p5_6.
 * The TIM3 CH1 is set to do Input Capture from PA6. The program waits
 * for capture flag (CC1IF) to set then calculates the period and
 * frequency of the input signal.
 * A jumper should be used to connect PA5 to PA6.
 *
 * This program was tested with Keil uVision v5.24a with DFP v2.11.0
 */
#include "stm32f4xx.h"

int period;
float frequency;

int main(void) {
    int last = 0;
    int current;

    // configure PA5 as output of TIM2 CH1
    RCC->AHB1ENR |=  1;             /* enable GPIOA clock */
    GPIOA->MODER &= ~0x00000C00;    /* clear pin mode */
```

```
GPIOA->MODER   |=  0x00000800;    /* set pin to alternate function */
GPIOA->AFR[0]  &= ~0x00F00000;    /* clear pin AF bits */
GPIOA->AFR[0]  |= 0x00100000;     /* set pin to AF1 for TIM2 CH1 */

// configure TIM2 to wrap around at 1 Hz
   // and toggle CH1 output when the counter value is 0
RCC->APB1ENR |= 1;                /* enable TIM2 clock */
TIM2->PSC = 1600 - 1;             /* divided by 1600 */
TIM2->ARR = 3000 - 1;             /* divided by 3000 */
TIM2->CCMR1 = 0x30;               /* set output to toggle on match */
TIM2->CCR1 = 0;                   /* set match value */
TIM2->CCER |= 1;                  /* enable ch 1 compare mode */
TIM2->CNT = 0;                    /* clear counter */
TIM2->CR1 = 1;                    /* enable TIM2 */

// configure PA6 as input of TIM3 CH1
RCC->AHB1ENR |=  1;               /* enable GPIOA clock */
GPIOA->MODER &= ~0x00003000;      /* clear pin mode */
GPIOA->MODER |=  0x00002000;      /* set pin to alternate function */
GPIOA->AFR[0] &= ~0x0F000000;     /* clear pin AF bits */
GPIOA->AFR[0] |= 0x02000000;      /* set pin to AF2 for TIM3 CH1 */

// configure TIM3 to do input capture with prescaler ...
RCC->APB1ENR |= 2;                /* enable TIM3 clock */
TIM3->PSC = 16000 - 1;            /* divided by 16000 */
TIM3->CCMR1 = 0x41;               /* set CH1 to capture at every edge */
TIM3->CCER = 0x0B;                /* enable CH 1 capture both edges */
TIM3->CR1 = 1;                    /* enable TIM3 */

while (1) {
    while (!(TIM3->SR & 2)) {}    /* wait until input edge is captured */
    current = TIM3->CCR1;         /* read captured counter value */
    period = current - last;      /* calculate the period */
    last = current;
    frequency = 1000.0f / period;
    last = current;
}
}
```

Review Questions

1. True or false. To measure the frequency of a signal, the time interval between a falling edge and a rising edge are needed.

2. True or false. If the time interval between two consecutive falling edges is measured, the frequency of the periodic signal can be calculated.

3. True or False. The STMF4xx supports both rising and falling edge detection.

Section 5.6: Pulse Counter programming

Another application of the timer is counting the number of external input pulses. In other words, the external input signal becomes the clock for the counter.

Internally, the timer counter is always clocked at the rising edge of the signal but the external input signal can be inverted before feeding it to the counter so that the counter may clock at the falling edge of the signal. A prescaler for the external signal is available to divide the external signal by 1, 2, 4, or 8. The timer counter prescaler has no effect on the external signal. All the configuration bits for external pulse counting are in the Slave Mode Control Register (TIMx_SMCR). Not all the timers support external input clock. You need to consult the reference manual to find out which ones do.

The counter wraps around when the value matches the AAR on the up count and set to the value of AAR when down count to 0. It sets the UIF when the count wraps around. It sets CCxIF when the value matches the CCRx register.

The external pulse counter mode can be used in conjunction with a rotary encoder to count the revolutions per minute (RPM) of the engine or the wheels. With the circumference of the wheel, the RPM can be used to calculate the speed of the vehicle.

Program 5-9 below uses PB8 as the external input clock for STM2. The least significant bit of the counter is used to turn on or off the LED. When the counter is counting, the LSB of the counter is toggling at every clock. You may use an external pulse generator to drive the clock input or you may use a jumper between PC13 and PB8 and use the user push-button switch to pulse the counter.

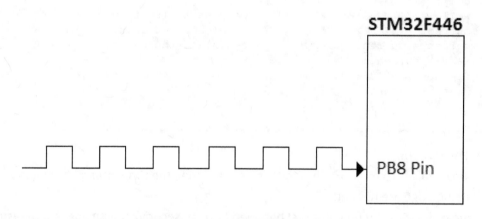

Figure 5-32: Counting Pulses

Program 5-9: using Timer as an event counter

```c
/* p5_9.c TIM2 External Event Counting

 * This program configures TIM2 to use external input PB8 as the
 * counter clock source. Each rising edge of the input signal
 * increments the TIM2 counter by 1.
 * Use an external signal to drive PB8 for testing or use a jumper
 * between PC13 and PB8. PC13 is connected to the user switch.
 *
 * This program was tested with Keil uVision v5.24a with DFP v2.11.0
 */
#include "stm32f4xx.h"
int main(void) {
    // configure PA5 output for the LED
    RCC->AHB1ENR |= 1;                   /* enable GPIOA clock */
    GPIOA->MODER &= ~0x00000C00;    /* clear pin mode */
    GPIOA->MODER |= 0x00000400;     /* set pin to output mode */


    // configure PB8 as input of TIM2 ETR
    RCC->AHB1ENR |= 2;                   /* enable GPIOB clock */
    GPIOB->MODER &= ~0x00030000;    /* clear pin mode */
    GPIOB->MODER |= 0x00020000;     /* set pin to alternate function */
    GPIOB->AFR[1] &= ~0x0000000F;   /* clear pin AF bits */
    GPIOB->AFR[1] |= 0x00000001;    /* set pin to AF1 for TIM2 ETR */


    // configure TIM2 to use external input as counter clock source
    RCC->APB1ENR |= 1;                   /* enable TIM2 clock */
    TIM2->SMCR = 0x4377;                 /* use ETR input as clock, no prescaler */
    TIM2->CNT = 0;                       /* clear counter */
    TIM2->CR1 = 1;                       /* enable TIM2 */

    while (1) {
        // use bit 0 to turn LED on/off
        if (TIM2->CNT & 1)
            GPIOA->ODR |= 0x20;      /* turn on LED */
        else
            GPIOA->ODR &= ~0x20;     /* turn off LED */
    }
}
```

Before we finish this section, we need to state an important point. You might think to monitor the flags to toggle the LED (or other tasks) is a waste of the CPU time. You are right. There is a solution to this: the use of interrupts. Using interrupts enables us to do other things with the microcontroller while waiting for the flag to change. When a timer interrupt flag such as UIF is raised, it will trigger an interrupt. This important and powerful feature of the microcontroller is discussed in Chapter 6.

Review Questions

1. True or false. The timer can also be used as an event counter.
2. True or false. The STMF4xx timer counts both rising and falling edges.
3. True or false. To use the timer as even-counter, we must configure it input capture mode.
4. True or false. Any pin can be used for input capture to count pulses.

Answer to Review Questions

Section 5-1
11. 31
12. 32
13. event counter
14. Timer
15. 9

Section 5-2
1. 0xFFFFFF
2. 1/16MHz=62.5 nsec. Now, 5 msec/62.5nsec=80,000. Therefore, RELOAD=80,000 − 1 =79,999
3. 24
4. The bit 0 of STCTRL (the Enable)
5. Down counter

Section 5-3
1. True
2. False, 32-bit
3. False, 65,536
4. the value of AAR register
5. TIMx_SR

Section 5-4
1. True
2. PA5
3. CCMR1
4. True

Section 5-5
1. False
2. True
3. True

Section 5-6
1. True, for some of the timers
2. True
3. True
4. True

Chapter 6: Interrupt and Exception Programming

This chapter examines the interrupts in Arm. We also discuss sources of hardware interrupts in the STM32 Arm chip. In Section 6.1 we discuss the concept of interrupts in the Arm CPU, and then we look at the interrupt assignments of the Arm Cortex-M. Section 6.2 examines the NVIC interrupt controller and discusses the Thread and Handler mode in Arm Cortex-M. The interrupts for I/O ports are discussed in Section 6.3. Section 6.4 examines the interrupt for UART. Timer's interrupts are explored in Section 6.5. The SysTick interrupt is covered in Section 6.6. The interrupt priority is discussed in Section 6.7.

Section 6.1: Interrupts and Exceptions in Arm Cortex-M

In this section, we examine the difference between polling and interrupt first then describe the various interrupts of the Arm Cortex.

Interrupts vs. polling

A single microprocessor can serve several devices. There are two ways to do that: interrupts and polling. In the *interrupt* method, whenever a device needs service, the device notifies the CPU by sending an interrupt signal. Upon receiving an interrupt signal, the CPU interrupts whatever it is doing and serves the device. In *polling*, the CPU continuously monitors the status of a given device; when the status condition is met, it performs the service. After that, it moves on to monitor the next device until each one is serviced. See Figure 6-1.

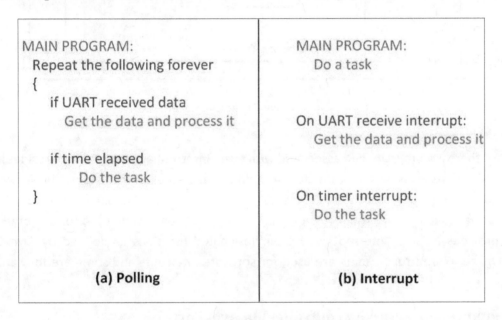

Figure 6-1: Polling vs. Interrupts

Although polling can monitor the status of several devices and serve each of them as certain conditions are met, it is not an efficient use of the CPU time. The polling method wastes much of the CPU's time by polling devices when they do not need service. So, in order to avoid tying down the CPU, interrupts are used. For example with polling, in Timer we might wait until a determined amount of time elapses, and while we were waiting we do not do anything else. That is a waste of the CPU's time that could have been used to perform some useful tasks. In the case of the Timer, if we use the interrupt method, the CPU can go about doing other tasks, and when the time is up the Timer will interrupt the CPU to let it know. See Figure 6-1.

Interrupt service routine (ISR)

For every interrupt, there must be a program associated with it. When an interrupt occurs, this program is executed to perform certain service for the interrupt. This program is commonly referred to as an *interrupt service routine* (ISR) or an *interrupt handler*. When an interrupt occurs, the CPU runs the interrupt service routine. Now, the question is how the ISR gets executed?

As shown in Figure 6-2, in the Arm CPU there are pins that are associated with hardware interrupts. They are input signals into the CPU. When the signals are triggered, CPU pushes the PC register onto the stack and loads the PC register with the address of the interrupt service routine. This causes the ISR to get executed.

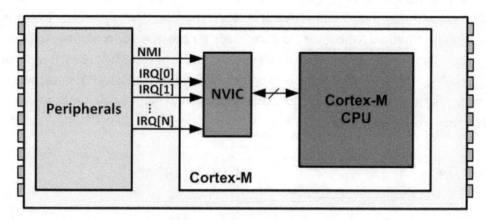

Figure 6-2: NVIC in Arm Cortex-M

Interrupt Vector Table

Since there is a program (ISR) associated with every interrupt and this program resides in memory (RAM or ROM), there must be a look-up table to hold the addresses of these ISRs. This look-up table is called *interrupt vector table*. In the Arm Cortex-M4 by default, the lowest 1024 bytes (256 × 4 = 1024) of memory space are set aside for the interrupt vector table and must not be used for any other function. Table 6-1 provides a list of interrupts and their designated functions as defined by Arm Cortex-M4 products. Of the 47 interrupts, some are used for software interrupts and some are for hardware IRQ interrupts.

NVIC (nested vector interrupt controller) In Arm Cortex-M

The Cortex-M has an on-chip interrupt controller called NVIC (Nested Vector Interrupt Controller). See Figure 6-2. This allows some degree of standardization among the Arm Cortex-M (M0, M0+, M1, M3, M4, and M7) family members. The classical Arm chips and Cortex-A and Cortex-R series do not have this NVIC interrupt controller, therefore Arm manufacturers' implementation of the interrupt handling varies. This chapter focuses on the interrupts for Arm Cortex-M series. It must be noted that there are substantial differences between the Arm Cortex-M series and classical Arm versions as far as interrupt handling are concerned. The study of classical Arm and Arm Cortex A and R series interrupts are left to the reader since they are used for high-performance systems using complex OS and real-time system.

Interrupt and Exception assignments in Arm Cortex-M

The NVIC of the Arm Cortex-M4 has room for a total of 255 interrupts and exceptions. The interrupt numbers are also referred to INT type (or INT#) in which the type can be from 1 to 255 or 0x01 to 0xFF. That is INT1 to INT255. The NVIC in Arm Cortex-M4 assigns the first 15 interrupts for internal use. The memory locations 0-3 are used to store the value to be loaded into the stack pointer when the device is coming out of reset. See Table 6-1. Although Arm Cortex-M4 core allocates 255 interrupt numbers, not all of them are used by the STMF4 devices. We will see the used interrupts in Table 6-7.

INT #	Interrupt	Memory Location
	Stack Pointer initial value	0x00000000
1	Reset	0x00000004
2	NMI	0x00000008
3	Hard Fault	0x0000000C
4	Reserved	0x00000010
5	Reserved	0x00000014
6	Reserved	0x00000018
7	Reserved	0x0000001C
8	Reserved	0x00000020
9	Reserved	0x00000024
10	Reserved	0x00000028
11	SVCall	0x0000002C
12	Reserved	0x00000030
13	Reserved	0x00000034
14	PendSV	0x00000038
15	SysTick	0x0000003C
16	IRQ0 for peripherals	0x00000040
17	IRQ1 for peripherals	0x00000044
...	...	...
255	IRQ239 for peripherals	0x000003FC

Table 6-1: Interrupt Vector Table for Arm Cortex-M4

The predefined Interrupts (INT0 to INT15)

The followings are the first 15 interrupts in Arm Cortex-M:

Reset

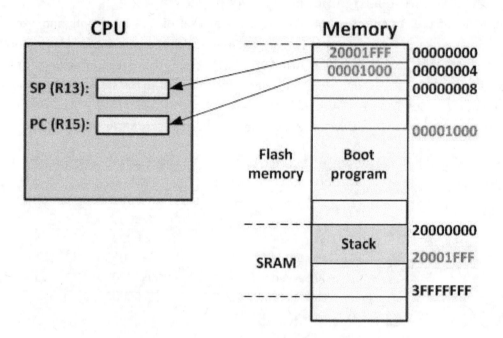

Figure 6-3: Going from Reset to Boot Program

The Arm devices have a reset pin. It is usually tied to a circuit that keeps the pin low for a while when the power is coming on. This is the power-up reset or power-on reset (POR). On the Arm trainer board, there is often a push-button switch to lower the signal. The reset signal is normally high after the power is on and when reset is activated during power-on or when the reset button is pressed, it goes low and the CPU goes to a known state with all the registers loaded with the predefined values. When the device is coming out of reset, the Arm Cortex-M loads the program counter from memory location 0x00000004. In Arm Cortex-M system we must place the starting address of the program at the 0x00000004 to get the program running. Notice in Table 6-1, the addresses 0x00000000 to 0x00000003 are set aside for the initial stack pointer value. This ensures that the Arm has access to stack immediately coming out of the reset.

Non-maskable interrupt

As shown in Figure 6-2, there are pins in the Arm chip that are associated with hardware interrupts. They are IRQs (interrupt request) and NMI (non-maskable interrupt). IRQ is an input signal into the CPU, which can be masked (ignored) and unmasked through the use of software. However, NMI, which is also an input signal to the CPU, cannot be masked by software, and for this reason, it is called a *non-maskable interrupt*. Arm Cortex-M NVIC has assigned "INT02" into the Arm CPU to be used only for NMI. Whenever the NMI pin is activated, the CPU will go to memory location 0x00000008 to get the address of the interrupt service routine (ISR) associated with NMI. Memory locations 0x00000008-0x0000000B contain the 4 bytes of address associated with the ISR belonging to NMI.

Exceptions (Faults)

There is a group of interrupts belongs to the category referred to as *fault* or exception *interrupts*. Internally, they are invoked by the microprocessor whenever there are conditions (exceptions) that the CPU is unable to handle.

Hard Fault

One such situation is an attempt to execute an instruction that is not implemented in this CPU. Since the result is undefined, and the CPU has no way of handling it, it automatically invokes the invalid instruction exception. The undefined instruction fault is an attempt to execute an instruction that is not implemented in the CPU. As we discussed in Chapter 6 of Volume 1, the unaligned data memory access for word or half-word can cause an exception too.

Arm Cortex-M4 processor does not distinguish the source of these faults. They share the same vector of HardFault.

SVCall

An ISR can be called upon as a result of the execution of SVC (supervisor call) instruction. This is referred to as a *software interrupt* since it was invoked from software, not from a fault exception, or any peripheral IRQ interrupt. Whenever the SVC instruction is executed, the CPU will go to memory location 0x0000002C to get the address of the ISR associated with SVC. The SVC is widely used by the operating system to call the OS kernel functions and services that can be provided only by the privileged access mode of the OS. In many systems, the API and function calls needed by various User applications are handled by the SVCall to make sure the OS is protected. In the classical Arm literature, SVC was called SWI (software interrupt), but the Arm Cortex-M has renamed it as SVC.

PendSV (pendable service call)

The PendSV (pendable service call) can be used to do the same thing as the SVC to get the OS services. However, the SVC is an instruction and is executed right away just like all Arm instructions. The PendSV is an interrupt that waits until NVIC has time to service it after other urgent higher priority interrupts are being taken care. Examine the concept of nested interrupt and pending interrupts at end of this section to see how NVIC handles multiple pending interrupts.

SysTick

In the multitasking OS, we need a real-time interrupt clock to notify the CPU that it needs to service the other tasks. The clock ticks happen at a regular interval and are used mainly by the OS system. The SysTick in Arm Cortex is designed for this purpose.

IRQ Peripheral interrupts

An ISR can be launched as a result of an event at the peripheral devices such as timer timeout or analog-to-digital converter (ADC) conversion complete. The largest number of the interrupts in the Arm Cortex-M belongs to this category. Notice from Table 6-1 that Arm Cortex-M NVIC has set aside the first 15 interrupts (INT1 to INT15) for internal use and is not available to the chip designer. The Reset, NMI, HardFault, and so on are part of this group of exceptions. The rest of the interrupts are used for peripherals. INT16 to INT47 (IRQ0 to IRQ31) are used by the chip manufacturer to be assigned to various peripherals such as timers, ADC, Serial COM, external hardware interrupts, and so on. There is no standard in assigning the INT16 to INT47 to the peripherals. Different manufacturers assign different interrupts to different peripherals. Not all the interrupts are assigned. You need to examine the datasheet for your Arm Cortex-M chip. Each peripheral module has a group of special function registers that must be used to configure the functions of the peripheral module. For a given peripheral interrupt to take effect, the interrupt for that peripheral must be enabled. The special function registers for that device provide the way to enable the interrupts.

Fast context saving in task switching

Most of the interrupts are asynchronous, that means they may happen anytime in the middle of program execution. When the interrupt is acknowledged and the interrupt service routine is launched, the interrupt service routine will need some CPU resource, mainly the CPU registers, to execute the code. In order not to corrupt the register content of the program that was running before the interrupt occurs, these CPU registers need to be preserved. This saving of the CPU contents before switching to interrupt handler is called context switching (or context saving). The use of the stack as a place to save the CPU's contents is tedious and time-consuming. It takes time to save all the registers. In executing an interrupt service routine, each task generally needs some key registers such as PC (R15), LR (R14), and CPSR (flag register) in addition to some working registers. For that reason, the Arm Cortex-M automatically saves the registers of CPSR, PC, LR, R12, R3, R2, R1, and R0 on the stack when an interrupt is acknowledged. See Figure 6-4 for the stack after the registers are saved. If the interrupt service routine needs to use more registers than those preserved, the program has to save the contents before using the other registers. The choice of the registers automatically saved adheres to the Arm Architecture Procedure Call Standard (AAPCS) so that an interrupt handler may be written as a plain C function without the need of any special provision.

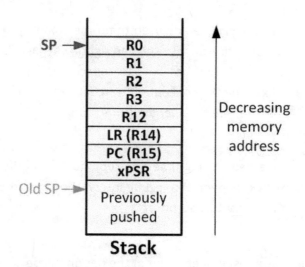

Figure 6-4: Arm Cortex-M Stack Frame upon Interrupt

Processing interrupts in Arm Cortex-M

When the Arm Cortex-M processes any interrupt (from either Fault Exceptions or peripheral IRQs), it goes through the following steps:

1. The Current processor status register (CPSR) is pushed onto the stack and SP is decremented by 4 since CPSR is a 4-byte register.
2. The current PC (R15) is pushed onto the stack and SP is decremented by 4.
3. The current LR (R14) is pushed onto the stack and SP is decremented by 4.
4. The current R12 is pushed onto the stack and SP is decremented by 4.
5. The current R3 is pushed onto the stack and SP is decremented by 4.
6. The current R2 is pushed onto the stack and SP is decremented by 4.
7. The current R1 is pushed onto the stack and SP is decremented by 4.
8. The current R0 is pushed onto the stack and SP is decremented by 4.
9. The CPU goes into the Handler Mode (details will be described later). LR is loaded with a number with bits 31-5 all 1s.
10. The INT number (type) is multiplied by 4 to get the offset of the location within the vector table to fetch the program counter of the interrupt service routine (interrupt handler).
11. From the memory locations pointed to by this new PC, the CPU starts to fetch and execute instructions belonging to the ISR program.
12. When one of the return instructions is executed in the interrupt service routine, the CPU recognizes that it is in the Handler Mode from the value of the LR (LR is loaded with a number with bits 31-5 all 1s when entering ISR). It then restores the registers saved when entering ISR including the program counter from the stack and makes the CPU run the code where it left off when the interrupt occurred. See Figure 6-5.

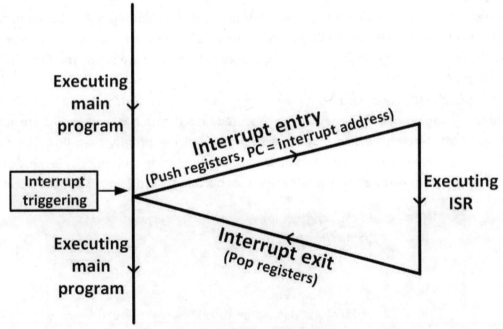

Figure 6-5: Main Program gets interrupted

Difference between interrupt and a subroutine call

If the execution of an interrupt saves the program counter of the following instruction and jumps indirectly to the subroutine associated with the interrupt, what is the difference between that and a BL instruction, which also saves the program counter and jumps to the desired subroutine (procedure)? The differences can be summarized as follows:

1. A "BL" instruction can take an argument and jump to any location within the 4-gigabyte address range of the Arm CPU, but "INT" goes to a fixed memory location in the interrupt vector table to get the address of the interrupt service routine.
2. A "BL" instruction is used by the programmer in the sequence of instructions in the program but an externally activated hardware interrupt can come in at any time, requesting the attention of the CPU.
3. A "BL" instruction cannot be masked (disabled), but "INT#" belonging to externally activated hardware interrupts can be masked.
4. A "BL" instruction automatically saves the PC of the next instruction in register LR, while "INT#" saves SP, R12, R3–R0, CPSR (flag register) in addition to PC of the next instruction.
5. An interrupt puts the CPU in the Handler Mode while the "BL" instruction does not change the CPU execution mode.
6. When returning from the end of the subroutine that has been called by the "BL" instruction, the PC is restored to the address of the next instruction after the "BL" instruction. When returning from the interrupt handler, the CPU will restore the registers saved when the CPU entered into ISR (the CPSR, R15, R14, R12, R3–R0 registers) from the top of stack.

Interrupt priority

The next topic in this section is the concept of priority for exceptions and IRQs. What happens if two interrupts want the attention of the CPU at the same time? Which has priority? In the Arm Cortex-M the Reset, NMI and Hard Fault exceptions have fixed priority levels and are set by the Arm itself and not subject to change. Among the Reset, NMI, and Hard Fault, the Reset has the highest priority. As we can see from Table 6-2, the NMI and Hard Fault have lower priority than Reset, meaning if all three of them are activated at the same time, the Reset will be executed first. If both NMI and an IRQ are activated at the same time, NMI is acknowledged first since NMI has a higher priority than IRQ. The rest of the exceptions and IRQs have lower priority and are configurable, meaning their priority levels can be set by the programmer. Programmable priority levels are values between 0 and 3 with 3 has the lowest priority.

INT #	Interrupt	Priority Level
0	*Stack Pointer initial value*	
1	Reset	-3 Highest
2	NMI	-2
3	Hard Fault	-1
4	Memory Management Fault	Reserved
5	Bus Fault	Reserved
6	Usage Fault	Reserved
7	Reserved	Reserved
8	Reserved	Reserved
9	Reserved	Reserved

10	Reserved	Reserved
11	SVCall	Programmable
12	Reserved	Reserved
13	Reserved	Reserved
14	PendSV	Programmable
15	SysTick	Programmable
16	IRQ 0 for peripherals	Programmable
17	IRQ 1 for peripherals	Programmable
...	...	Programmable
255	IRQ 239 for peripherals	Programmable

Table 6-2: Interrupt Priority for Arm Cortex-M4

Table 6-2 shows interrupt assignments for Arm Cortex-M4. Not all Cortex-M4 chips have all the first 15 interrupts. For the hardware IRQs coming through NVIC, the NVIC resolves priority depending on the way the NVIC is programmed. Also, not all the IRQs are used in all the chips. The STM32F466 uses IRQ0 to IRQ96 (INT16-INT112).

Interrupt latency

The time from the moment the event triggers an interrupt signal to the moment the CPU starts to execute the ISR code is called the interrupt latency. The duration of interrupt latency can also be affected by the type of the instruction which the CPU was executing when the interrupt occurs. It takes longer in cases where the instruction being executed lasts for many instruction cycles compared to the instructions that last for only one instruction cycle time. In the Arm Cortex-M, we also have extra clocks added to the latency due to the fact that it saves the content of registers CPSR, PC, LR, R12, and R0-R3 on the stack.

Another source of the interrupt latency is the interrupt priority. As mentioned earlier, when several interrupts occur at the same time, the interrupt with the highest priority is acknowledged first. All other interrupts have to wait. But when a low priority interrupt is being served, a higher priority interrupt can preempt it, which we will discuss next.

Interrupt inside an interrupt handler (nested interrupt)

What happens if the Arm is executing an ISR belonging to an interrupt and another interrupt is activated? In many older CPUs when an interrupt service routine is launched, all other interrupts are masked. All interrupts happened at this time have to wait. If the interrupt service routine runs too long, there is a risk some interrupts may be lost. The interrupt service routine may unmask the interrupts. But in doing so, it will allow all the interrupts to preempt itself. With Arm Cortex-M, the higher priority interrupt will stop the lower priority interrupt handler and launch the higher priority interrupt handler. In the Arm Cortex-M systems, it is up to the software engineer to configure the priority level for each exception and IRQ (except NMI and HardFault) and set the policy of how to support nested interrupt.

The Arm Cortex-M allows only the higher priority interrupts to preempt the lower priority interrupt service routine. The programmer is responsible for assigning the proper priority to each IRQ to determine whether an interrupt may preempt the other's interrupt handler. The NVIC in Arm Cortex-M has the ability to capture the pending interrupts and keeps track of each one until all are serviced.

Review Questions
1. True or false. When any interrupt is activated, the CPU jumps to a predefined address.
2. There are _____ bytes of memory in the interrupt vector table for each interrupt.
3. How many bytes of memory are used by the interrupt vector table for 48 interrupts, and what are the beginning and ending addresses of the table for the first 48 interrupts?
4. The program associated with an interrupt is also referred to as _____.
5. What is the function of the interrupt vector table?
6. What memory locations in the interrupt vector table hold the address for INT16 ISR?
7. The Arm Cortex-M has assigned INT2 to NMI. Can that be changed?

Section 6.2: Arm Cortex-M Processor Modes
In this section, we examine various operation modes in Arm Cortex-M.

Arm Cortex Thread (application) and Handler (exception) modes
The Arm Cortex-M can run in one of the two modes at any given time. They are (1) Thread (Application) mode and (2) Handler (Exception) mode. The differences can be stated as follows:

1. When the Arm Cortex-M is powered on and coming out of reset, it automatically goes to the Thread mode. The Thread mode is the mode that vast majority of the applications programs are executed in. The CPU spends most of its time in Thread mode and gets interrupted only to execute ISR for exceptions or peripheral IRQs.

2. The Arm Cortex-M switches to Handler mode only when an exception (of course other than the Reset) or an IRQ interrupt from a peripheral is activated to get the attention of the CPU to execute an ISR (interrupt handler). Upon returning from ISR, the CPU automatically changes from Handler mode back to Thread mode. It must be noted that of all the exceptions and IRQs in the Table 6-1, only the Reset forces the CPU into Thread mode and the rest of the interrupt handlers are executed in Handler mode.

A big advantage of having Handler mode is that when returning from Handler mode, the CPU will pop the stack and restore the registers saved during entry to Handler mode. With this, the interrupt handlers are written just like any other functions as we will see in the examples soon.

There are two Stacks in Arm Cortex
The classical Arm has a single stack pointer (R13) to be used to point to RAM area for the purpose of the stack. With a multi-threaded operating system, every thread should have their own stack so does the operating system itself. It is much more efficient to have separate stack pointers for the system and the thread. The Arm Cortex-M has two stack pointer registers. They are called PSP (processor stack pointer) and MSP (main stack pointer). Threads running in Thread mode should use the process stack and the kernel and exception handlers should use the main stack.

The bit 1, ASP (active stack pointer), of the special function register, called CONTROL register gives the option of choosing MSP or PSP for stack pointer. Upon Reset the ASP=0, meaning that R13 is the Main Stack pointer (MSP) and its value comes from the first 4 bytes of the interrupt vector table starting at 0x00000000 address location. By making the ASP=1, the R13 is the same as PSP (processor stack pointer). Next, we examine the privilege levels in Arm Cortex-M.

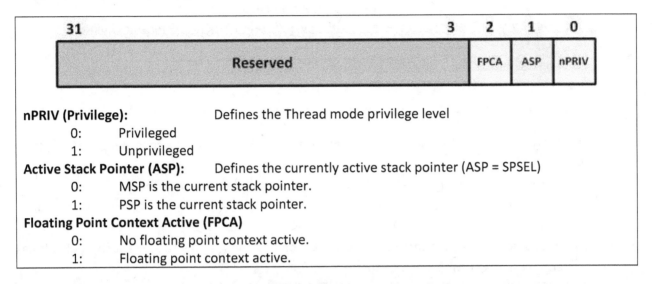

nPRIV (Privilege):   Defines the Thread mode privilege level
    0:     Privileged
    1:     Unprivileged
Active Stack Pointer (ASP):   Defines the currently active stack pointer (ASP = SPSEL)
    0:     MSP is the current stack pointer.
    1:     PSP is the current stack pointer.
Floating Point Context Active (FPCA)
    0:     No floating point context active.
    1:     Floating point context active.

Figure 6-6: CONTROL Register in Arm Cortex-M4

Processor Mode	Software	Privilege level
Thread	Applications	Privileged and Unprivileged
Handler	ISR for Exceptions and IRQs	Always Privileged
In Thread mode, use bit 0 of the CONTROL register to select Privileged or Unprivileged		

Table 6-3: Privileged level Execution and Processor Modes in Arm Cortex-M

Privileged and Unprivileged levels in Arm Cortex-M

There are two privilege levels in Arm Cortex-M. They are called privileged and unprivileged. The Privileged level in Arm Cortex-M can be used to limit the CPU access to special registers and protected memory area to prevent the system from getting corrupted due to error in coding or malicious user. Here are summary of the Privileged level software:

1. The privileged level software has access to all registers including the special function registers for interrupts.
2. The privileged level software has access to every region of memory.
3. The privileged level software has access to system timer, NVIC, and system resources.
4. The Privileged level software can execute all the Arm Cortex-M instructions including the MRS, MSR, and CPS.
5. The Handlers for fault exceptions and IRQs can be executed only in Privileged level.

6. Only the Privileged software can access the CONTROL register to see whether execution is in Privileged or Unprivileged mode. In Unprivileged mode one can switch from unprivileged level to Privileged level by using SVC instruction.

Processor Mode	Software	Stack Usage
Thread	Applications	MSP or PSP
Handler	ISR for Exceptions and IRQs	MSP
Note: In Thread mode, use bit 1 of the Control register to select MSP or PSP for stack pointer.		

Table 6-4: Processor Modes and Stack Usage in Arm Cortex-M

Here is the summary of the unprivileged level software:

1. The unprivileged level software has no access to some registers such the special function registers for interrupts.
2. The unprivileged level software has limited access to some regions of memory.
3. The unprivileged level software is blocked from accessing system timer, NVIC, and system control block and resources.
4. The Unprivileged level software cannot execute some of the Arm instructions such as CPS. It has limited access to the MRS and MSR instructions.
5. While Handler mode is always executed in the Privileged level, the Thread mode software can be executed in privileged or unprivileged level. The bit 0 of the special a function register called CONTROL register gives the option of running the software in Privileged or Unprivileged mode.
6. In the unprivileged mode, one can use SVC instruction to make a supervisor call to switch from the unprivileged level to Privileged level.

Mode	Privilege	Stack Pointer	Typical Example usage
Handler	Privileged	Main	Exception Handling
Handler	Unprivileged	Any	Reserved since Handler is always Privileged
Thread	Privileged	Main	Operating system kernel
Thread	Privileged	Process	
Thread	Unprivileged	Main	
Thread	Unprivileged	Process	Application threads

Table 6-5: Processor Mode, Privilege, and Stack in Arm Cortex

Special Function Registers in Arm Cortex

Besides the traditional general purpose registers of R0–R15, the Arm Cortex-M core has several new special function registers. These registers are used in programs written for the Cortex-M based embedded systems. See Figure 6-7.

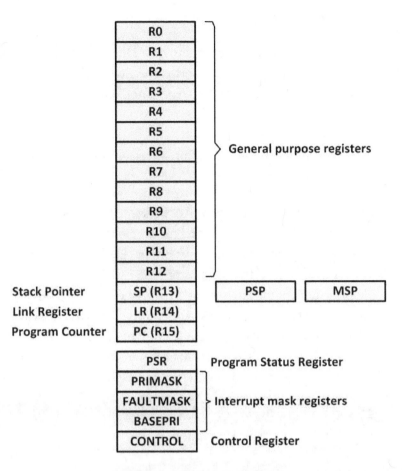

Figure 6-7: Arm Cortex-M Registers

While the general purpose registers of R0–R15 can be accessed using the MOV, LDR, and STR instructions, these new special function registers can be accessed only with the two new instructions MSR and MRS. To manipulate (clear or set) the bits of special function registers, first we must use the MSR to move them to a general purpose register and after changing their values they are moved back by using MRS instruction. Table 6-6 shows special function registers.

Register name	Privilege Usage
MSP (main stack pointer)	Privileged
PSP (processor stack pointer)	Privileged or Unprivileged
PSR (Processor status register)	Privileged
APSR (application processor status register)	Privileged or Unprivileged
ISPR (interrupt processor status register)	Privileged
EPSR (execution processor status register)	Privileged
PRIMASK (Priority Mask register)	Privileged
FAULTMASK (fault mask register)	Privileged
BASEPRI (base priority register)	Privileged
CONTROL (control register)	Privileged
Note: We must use MSR and MRS instructions to access the above registers	

Table 6-6: Special function registers of Arm Cortex-M

Review Questions

1. True or false. After the Reset pin is activated, the Arm CPU wakes up in Thread mode.
2. How many processor modes are in the Arm Cortex-M? Give their names.
3. How many bytes of data are fetched into CPU from interrupt vector table when Arm Cortex-M is Reset, and what are they?
4. Another name for ISR is _____.
5. True or false. When an interrupt comes in from an exception or IRQ, the Arm CPU switches to Handler mode automatically.

Section 6.3: STM32 Arm I/O Port Interrupt Programming

In Chapter 2, we showed how to use GPIO ports for simple I/O. We also showed a simple program polling an input switch status and using it to turn on or off an LED. In this section, we will demonstrate how to program the interrupt capability of the I/O pins of the STM32F4xx chip.

Let's examine the interrupt vector table of the STM32F4xx microcontroller first. Table 6-7 shows the peripheral interrupt assignments. The I/O pin interrupts come through the External Interrupts (EXTIx), which are assigned to IRQ6 (EXTI0), IRQ7 (EXTI1), IRQ8 (EXTI2), IRQ9 (EXTI3), IRQ10(EXTI4), IRQ23 (EXTI5-9), and IRQ40 (EXTI10-15). Notice the first five EXTIx lines are mapped one to one to the interrupts but the last two interrupts each handles a group of five EXTIx lines (IRQ23-EXTI9-5, IRQ40-EXTI15-10).

INT#	IRQ#	Vector location	Device
1-15		0800 0000 to 0800 003C	CPU Exception
16	0	0800 0040	Window Watchdog interrupt
17	1	0800 0044	PVD through EXTI line detection interrupt
18	2	0800 0048	Tamper and TimeStamp interrupts through the EXTI line
19	3	0800 004C	RTC Wakeup interrupt through the EXTI line
20	4	0800 0050	Flash global interrupt
21	5	0800 0054	RCC global interrupt
22	6	0800 0058	EXTI Line0 interrupt (EXTI0)
23	7	0800 005C	EXTI Line1 interrupt (EXTI1)
24	8	0800 0060	EXTI Line2 interrupt (EXTI2)
25	9	0800 0064	EXTI Line3 interrupt (EXTI3)
26	10	0800 0068	EXTI Line4 interrupt (EXTI4)
27	11	0800 006C	DMA1 Stream0 global interrupt
28	12	0800 0070	DMA1 Stream1 global interrupt
29	13	0800 0074	DMA1 Stream2 global interrupt
30	14	0800 0078	DMA1 Stream3 global interrupt
31	15	0800 007C	DMA1 Stream4 global interrupt
32	16	0800 0080	DMA1 Stream5 global interrupt
33	17	0800 0084	DMA1 Stream6 global interrupt
34	18	0800 0088	ADC1, ADC2 and ADC3 global interrupts

35	19	0800 008C	CAN1 TX interrupts
36	20	0800 0090	CAN1 RX0 interrupts
37	21	0800 0094	CAN1 RX1 interrupt
38	22	0800 0098	CAN1 SCE interrupt
39	23	0800 009C	EXTI9_5 (EXTI Line[9:5])
40	24	0800 00A0	TIM1_BRK_TIM9
41	25	0800 00A4	TIM1_UP_TIM10
42	26	0800 00A8	TIM1_TRG_COM_TIM11
43	27	0800 00AC	TIM1_CC
44	28	0800 00B0	TIM2 (TIM2 global interrupt)
45	29	0800 00B4	TIM3 (TIM3 global interrupt)
46	30	0800 00B8	TIM4 (TIM4 global interrupt)
47	31	0800 00BC	I2C1_EV (I2C1 event interrupt)
48	32	0800 00C0	I2C1_ER (I2C1 error interrupt)
49	33	0800 00C4	I2C2_EV (I2C2 event interrupt)
50	34	0800 00C2	I2C2_ER (I2C2 error interrupt)
51	35	0800 00CC	SPI1 (SPI1 global interrupt)
52	36	0800 00D0	SPI2 (SPI2 global interrupt)
53	37	0800 00D4	USART1 (USART1 global interrupt)
54	38	0800 00D8	USART2 (USART2 global interrupt)
55	39	0800 00DC	USART3 (USART3 global interrupt)
56	40	0800 00E0	EXTI15_10 (EXTI Line[15:10])

Table 6-7: IRQ assignment in STM32F4xx (Partial Listing – For complete list see STM32F4 ref. manual)

STM32F4xx Memory Map

Arm vendors are free to implement the Arm memory and I/O map as they please as long as they follow some guideline from the Arm Corp. We often see the I/O map address locations for peripherals varies greatly among the vendors. However, for the memory map locations, they mostly follow the guideline set by Arm Corp. In the case of the memory map for the Flash memory, most vendors use the location 0000 as the default starting location after Power-on reset, as we saw in the earlier part of this section. For the STM32F4xx Arm chip the Flash memory addresses are different than what we saw in Section 6.1. Examine the memory locations below:

0x2000 0000 - 0x2001 BFFF SRAM

0x0800 0000 - 0x081F FFFF Flash memory

Notice the Flash memory starting address is 0x0800 0000 instead of 0x0000 0000.

When you start a project in the Keil MDK-Arm IDE, the memory addresses will be handled by the project wizard when the project is created and the linker will assign the memory addresses accordingly. As a C programmer, you do not have to do anything to build the project properly but you do need to be aware of the final memory locations when you debug the programs.

The memory addresses for STM32F4xx are much more complex. The devices have several different boot modes and the memory allocations are different in different boot mode. Although the default location of flash memory starts at 0x0800 0000, it also has the alias address starting at 0. Last but not least, the interrupt vector table starting address is relocatable. These topics are all beyond the scope of this book so we will not elaborate further here.

As discussed earlier, the peripheral interrupts are generated from the peripheral modules. These interrupt signals enter the CPU by the Nested Vector Interrupt Controller (NVIC). In case multiple interrupts occur at the same time, NVIC determines which interrupt to be passed on to the CPU according to the priority assigned to each interrupt. Finally, there is a global mask that may block all the interrupts. Upon reset, all the interrupts are disabled at the peripheral modules. To activate any interrupt, we need to enable the interrupt generation for a specific peripheral module then enable the interrupt at the NVIC module. We will go through each of these components of interrupt handling in this section.

External Interrupt Controller

All the I/O pins of STM32F4xx may generate an external interrupt. To use external interrupt lines, the port pin must be configured in input mode. As we saw in Chap2, we use GPIOx_MODER to make a pin an input pin.

Each of the EXTI0 (External Interrupt 0) to EXTI15 (External Interrupt 15) interrupt is assigned to a group of I/O pins. In STM32F4xx Arm chips, all the Px0 (PA0, PB0, PC0,... and so on) pins are grouped together and fed to EXTI0 (External Interrupt 0). In other words, there is not a separate interrupt assigned to each I/O pin of each port. Table 6-7 shows IRQ6 is assigned EXTI0 (External Interrupt 0) and IRQ7 is assigned to EXTI1 (External Interrupt 1) and so on. That means if pin 0 of any port (Px0) is used for an external interrupt it is directed to the EXTI0. Table 6-8 shows the External interrupt line mapping of I/O pins to EXTIx signals. There are up to 16 pins for each port, therefore there are 16 external interrupt lines (EXTIx). In STM32F446 Arm chip we have 23 external interrupts. While 16 of them (EXTI0-EXIT15) are dedicated to I/O pins of the ports, the other 7 are used for functions such as than RTC0 wake-up and others.

Although multiple pins are mapped into a single EXTIx signal but only one can be responded to at a time. The port pin that will be responded to is selected by a multiplexer using bits from SYSCFG_EXTICRx registers. There are four EXTICRx registers (EXTICR1 – EXTICR4). Each register handles four EXTI lines and each EXTI line has four bits to select from up to eight possible ports. For example, bits 3-0 of SYSCFG_EXTICR1 select port for EXTI0 line, bits 7-4 of SYSCFG_EXTICR1 select port for EXTI1 line, and so on.

EXTIx[3:0]	Port
0000	PAx pin
0001	PBx pin
0010	PCx pin
0011	PDx pin
0100	PEx pin
0101	PFx pin
0110	PGx pin
0111	PHx pin

Table 6-8: External Interrupts Assignments to various Ports

To configure PC13 to generate interrupts, we need to set bits 7-4 of SYSCFG_EXTICR4 to 0010. We do that with the next two statements, the first one clears all the four bits and the second statement sets the bits to 0010. Notice the register name in the C statement for SYSCFG_EXTICR4 is SYSCFG->EXTICR[3].

```
SYSCFG->EXTICR[3] &= ~0x00F0;
SYSCFG->EXTICR[3] |= 0x0020;
```

To configure Px.y pin to generate interrupts, the pin needs to be configured as an input. This is done by using GPIOx_MODER register of PORTx. The statement below makes PC13 (which is connected to the user push button switch on the Nucleo board) an input pin.

```
GPIOC->MODER &= ~0x0C000000;        /* clear pin mode to input mode */
```

EXTI0[3:0] bits in the SYSCFG_EXTICR1 register

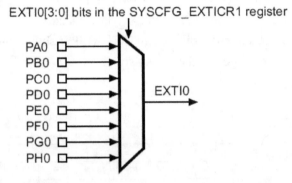

EXTI1[3:0] bits in the SYSCFG_EXTICR1 register

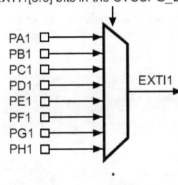

EXTI15[3:0] bits in the SYSCFG_EXTICR4 register

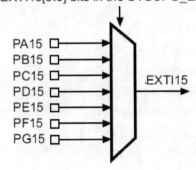

Figure 6-8: External interrupt/event GPIO mapping

I/O Pin	EXTIx	I/O Pin	EXTIx	I/O Pin	EXTIx	I/O Pin	EXTIx
PA0	EXTI0	PA1	EXTI1	PA2	EXTI2	PA3	EXTI3
PB0	EXTI0	PB1	EXTI1	PB2	EXTI2	PB3	EXTI3
PC0	EXTI0	PC1	EXTI1	PC2	EXTI2	PC3	EXTI3
PD0	EXTI0	PD1	EXTI1	PD2	EXTI2	PD3	EXTI3
PE0	EXTI0	PE1	EXTI1	PE2	EXTI2	PE3	EXTI3
PF0	EXTI0	PF1	EXTI1	PF2	EXTI2	PF3	EXTI3
PG0	EXTI0	PG1	EXTI1	PG2	EXTI2	PG3	EXTI3
PH0	EXTI0	PH1	EXTI1				

Table 6-9: Associations of I/O pins to EXTINT signals (External interrupt/event GPIO mapping)

To complete the configuration of an interrupt, we need the following procedure:

1) Enable the mask bit of the interrupt line in EXTI_IMR register.

2) Select the trigger by the selection bits of the EXTI_RTSR (rising trigger selection register) and/or EXTI_FTSR (falling trigger selection register) registers.

3) Enable the interrupt in NVIC registers.

31	30	29	28	27	26	25	24	23	22	21	20	19	18	17	16
Res	Res	Res	Res	Res	Res	Res	Res	Res	MR22	MR21	MR20	MR19	MR18	MR17	MR16
									rw	rw	rw	rw	rw	rw	rw

15	14	13	12	11	10	9	8	7	6	5	4	3	2	1	0
MR15	MR14	MR13	MR12	MR11	MR10	MR9	MR8	MR7	MR6	MR5	MR4	MR3	MR2	MR1	MR0
rw	rw	rw	rw	rw	rw	rw	rw	rw	rw	rw	rw	rw	rw	rw	rw

Bits 31:23 Reserved, must be kept at reset value.

Bits 22:0 **MRx:** Interrupt mask on line x

　　　0: Interrupt request from line x is masked

　　　1: Interrupt request from line x is not masked

Figure 6-9A: Interrupt Mask Register (EXTI_IMR)

31	30	29	28	27	26	25	24	23	22	21	20	19	18	17	16
Res	Res	Res	Res	Res	Res	Res	Res	Res	PR22	PR21	PR20	PR19	PR18	PR17	PR16
									rc_w1	rc_w1	rc_w1	rc_w1	rc_w1	rc_w1	rc_w1

15	14	13	12	11	10	9	8	7	6	5	4	3	2	1	0
PR15	PR14	PR13	PR12	PR11	PR10	PR9	PR8	PR7	PR6	PR5	PR4	PR3	PR2	PR1	PR0
rc_w1	rc_w1	rc_w1	rc_w1	rc_w1	rc_w1	rc_w1	rc_w1	rc_w1	rc_w1	rc_w1	rc_w1	rc_w1	rc_w1	rc_w1	rc_w1

Bits 31:23 Reserved, must be kept at reset value.

Bits 22:0 **PRx:** Pending bit on line x

　　　　0: No trigger request occurred

　　　　1: selected trigger request occurred

　　　　This bit is set when the selected edge event arrives on the external interrupt line.

　　　　This bit is cleared by programming it to '1'.

Figure 6-9B: Pending Interrupt Register (EXTI_PR)

31	30	29	28	27	26	25	24	23	22	21	20	19	18	17	16
Res.	Res.	Res.	Res.	Res.	Res.	Res.	Res.	Res.	Res.	Res.	Res.	Res.	Res.	Res.	Res.

15	14	13	12	11	10	9	8	7	6	5	4	3	2	1	0
EXTI3[3:0]				EXTI2[3:0]				EXTI1[3:0]				EXTI0[3:0]			
rw	rw	rw	rw	rw	rw	rw	rw	rw	rw	rw	rw	rw	rw	rw	rw

Bits 31:16 Reserved, must be kept at reset value.

Bits 15:0 **EXTIx[3:0]**: EXTI x configuration (x = 0 to 3)

These bits are written by software to select the source input for the EXTIx external interrupt.

Note:

0000: PA[x] pin   0100: PE[x] pin

0001: PB[x] pin   0101: PF[x] pin

0010: PC[x] pin   0110: PG[x] pin

0011: PD[x] pin   0111: PH[x] pin

Figure 6-9C: SYSCFG external interrupt configuration register 1 (SYSCFG_EXTICR1)

Rising or Falling Edge Trigger Interrupt

The input signal for external interrupt coming from I/O pins has edge detectors for generating event/interrupt requests. We can set to triggered on rising or falling edge or both. See registers below.

31	30	29	28	27	26	25	24	23	22	21	20	19	18	17	16
Res.	Res.	Res.	Res.	Res.	Res.	Res.	Res.	Res.	TR22	TR21	TR20	Res.	TR18	TR17	TR16
									rw	rw	rw		rw	rw	rw

15	14	13	12	11	10	9	8	7	6	5	4	3	2	1	0
TR15	TR14	TR13	TR12	TR11	TR10	TR9	TR8	TR7	TR6	TR5	TR4	TR3	TR2	TR1	TR0
rw	rw	rw	rw	rw	rw	rw	rw	rw	rw	rw	rw	rw	rw	rw	rw

Bits 31:23 Reserved, must be kept at reset value.

Bits 22:20 **TRx**: Rising trigger event configuration bit of line x

0: Rising trigger disabled (for Event and Interrupt) for input line

1: Rising trigger enabled (for Event and Interrupt) for input line

Bit 19 Reserved, must be kept at reset value.

Bits 18:0 **TRx**: Rising trigger event configuration bit of line x

0: Rising trigger disabled (for Event and Interrupt) for input line

1: Rising trigger enabled (for Event and Interrupt) for input line

Figure 6-10A: Rising trigger selection register (EXTI_RTSR)

31	30	29	28	27	26	25	24	23	22	21	20	19	18	17	16
Res.	Res.	Res.	Res.	Res.	Res.	Res.	Res.	Res.	TR22	TR21	TR20	Res.	TR18	TR17	TR16
									rw	rw	rw		rw	rw	rw

15	14	13	12	11	10	9	8	7	6	5	4	3	2	1	0
TR15	TR14	TR13	TR12	TR11	TR10	TR9	TR8	TR7	TR6	TR5	TR4	TR3	TR2	TR1	TR0
rw	rw	rw	rw	rw	rw	rw	rw	rw	rw	rw	rw	rw	rw	rw	rw

Bits 31:23 Reserved, must be kept at reset value.

Bits 22:20 **TRx:** Falling trigger event configuration bit of line x

    0: Falling trigger disabled (for Event and Interrupt) for input line

    1: Falling trigger enabled (for Event and Interrupt) for input line.

Bit 19 Reserved, must be kept at reset value.

Bits 18:0 **TRx:** Falling trigger event configuration bit of line x

    0: Falling trigger disabled (for Event and Interrupt) for input line

    1: Falling trigger enabled (for Event and Interrupt) for input line.

Figure 6-10B: Falling trigger selection register (EXTI_FTSR)

To generate interrupts, the corresponding bit in Interrupt Mask (EXTI_IMR) register needs to be set. Writing a 1 to the register will enable the corresponding EXTIx interrupt. The interrupt can be disabled by writing 0 to the same bit in (EXTI_IMR) register. We must also set the rising or falling edge detection using EXTI_RTSR and EXTI_FTSR registers.

Notice again that the EXTI_IMR register is 32-bit wide but only bits D22-D0 are used to enable the 23 external interrupts. The following program statements configure EXTI13 as a rising-edge interrupt for pin PC13.

```
EXTI->IMR  |= 0x2000;        /* unmask EXTI13 */
EXTI->FTSR |= 0x2000;        /* select falling edge trigger */
```

Nested Vector Interrupt Controller

In Arm Cortex, all the peripheral interrupts enter NVIC where they may be enabled or disable and also have their priority sorted out. There is an interrupt enable bit for each IRQ. These enable bits are controlled by the registers in NVIC. There is one register used for setting the enable bits (Interrupt Set Enable Register or ISER[x]) and there is a register used for clearing the enable bits (Interrupt Clear Enable Register or ICER[x]). Each register covers 32 IRQ interrupts. See Figure 6-11. Each interrupt can be enabled by writing a 1 to the corresponding bit in the ISER register. Writing 0 to the ISER register has no effect on its value.

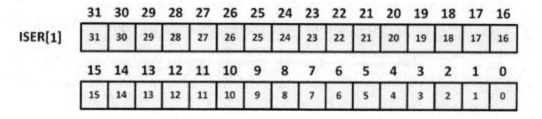

Figure 6-11: Set Enable Register (ISER[1]) for IRQ 32–63

In a Cortex-M4 device, there are eight ISER registers. The same goes for the Interrupt Clear Enable Register (ICER) that will be discussed later.

As we can see in the interrupt vector table in Table 6-3, EXTI13 is grouped with EXTI15_10 for IRQ40. Therefore, to enable the interrupts associated with PC13, we need the following statement:

NVIC->ISER[1] = 0x00000100;   /* enable IRQ40 (bit 8 of ISER[1]) */

Alternatively, the interrupts can be enabled using the following function, as well:

void NVIC_EnableIRQ(IRQn_Type IRQn);

This function is defined in the file core_cm4.h which is included in the stm32f446xx.h header file. To enable an interrupt using this function, the IRQ number of the interrupt should be passed as the argument to the function. For example, the following statement enables EXTI15_10 interrupt:

NVIC_EnableIRQ(40);

Since the IRQ numbers for all the interrupts are defined in the stm32f446xx.h, we can use their names instead of their numbers for a more meaningful code. For example, to enable EXTI15_10 interrupt the following statement can be used as well:

NVIC_EnableIRQ(EXTI15_10_IRQn);

To disable the same interrupt there is another register ICER1. See the Figure 6-12.

	31	30	29	28	27	26	25	24	23	22	21	20	19	18	17	16
ICER[1]	31	30	29	28	27	26	25	24	23	22	21	20	19	18	17	16

15	14	13	12	11	10	9	8	7	6	5	4	3	2	1	0
15	14	13	12	11	10	9	8	7	6	5	4	3	2	1	0

Figure 6-12: Clear Enable Register (ICER[1]) for IRQ 32–63

Each interrupt can be disabled by writing a 1 to the corresponding bit in the ICER register. Writing 0 to the ICER register has no effect on their value. For example, the following instruction disables EXTI15_10 interrupt, keeping the other interrupts unchanged:

NVIC->ICER[1] = 0x00000100;   /* enable IRQ40 (bit 8 of ISER[1]) */

For example, the following statement disables the EXTI15_10 interrupt:

NVIC_DisableIRQ(EXTI15_10_IRQn);

In fact, each bit of the ISER register together with its corresponding bit in the ICER register is connected to a J-K Flip-Flop, as shown below:

179

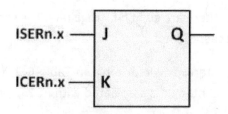

Figure 6-13: Enabling and Disabling an Interrupt

Global Interrupt Enable

Global interrupt enable/disable allows us with a single instruction to mask all interrupts during the execution of some critical task such as manipulating a common pointer shared by multiple threads. In Arm Cortex-M devices, the global interrupt mask is located in the PRIMASK register in the CPU. Two special instructions are used to modify the mask bit in the PRIMASK register, CPSID I (Change Processor State Interrupt Disable) and CPSIE I (Change Processor State Interrupt Enable). To eliminate the need to write assembly instructions in the program, the Keil MDK toolchain added two pseudo-functions in C language which will be replaced by CPSIE I or CPSID I instruction by the compiler:

```
__enable_irq();   /* Enable interrupt Globally */
```

and

```
__disable_irq();   /* Disable interrupt Globally */
```

It may not always be necessary but is a good idea to disable all interrupts during the initialization and enable interrupts only after all the initializations are complete especially when some other resources need to be initialized before interrupt handler can run properly.

The following lines of code enable the interrupt for PA15 pin at all three levels:

```
EXTI->IMR  |= 0x2000;              /* unmask EXTI13 */

NVIC_EnableIRQ(EXTI15_10_IRQn);   /* enable interrupt in NVIC */

__enable_irq();                   /* global enable IRQs */
```

IRQ Priority

As describe earlier, Arm Cortex-M supports nested interrupt handling, higher priority interrupt may preempt the lower interrupt handler, it is important that each interrupt is assigned a proper priority before they are enabled. The IRQ interrupt priorities are controlled by the NVIC IPR registers. For each IRQ number, there is one byte corresponding to that IRQ to assign its priority. The priority levels are ranging from 0 to 7 in an STM32F4 Arm device and they are defined by three bits left justified in that byte. There are 60 IPR registers to hold the priority of 240 IRQs. One needs to identify the byte and the register to set the IRQ priority. We will describe it in more details in Section 6.7. If left untouched, these registers contain zero, so all the interrupts have the same priority.

Interrupt Handler and Interrupt Vector

In program 6-1, the main function sets up the interrupt from pin PC13, which is connected to the user switch on the STM32F446 Nucleo board. Notice that in various STM32F4xx Discovery and Nucleo boards the user switch is connected to a different pin. Check the user manual for your board and modify the program. The Px.y pin is configured as input with pull-up resistor so that the pin stays high when the switch is not pressed. The switch when depressed will connect Px.y pin to the ground. There is a 100nF capacitor in series with a 100 Ohm resistor across the switch to reduce the contact bounce. The signal from the input pin is routed through External Interrupt Controller to generate an EXTI interrupt. After the initialization, the interrupt is enabled and the main function goes into an infinite loop waiting for an interrupt to occur. When an interrupt happens, the interrupt handler is called. The interrupt handler blinks the onboard LED twice using a dummy loop delay. It is a very poor practice to do delay or wait for something to happen in an interrupt handler because while the handler is stalling, all other programs except higher priority interrupts are blocked. We use it here just to simplify the example. It is important that the interrupt source is cleared before leaving the interrupt handler, otherwise, the program execution will return back to the interrupt handler immediately and no other program except the handler is executed.

The interrupt vector for EXTI in the interrupt vector table needs to hold the starting address of the interrupt handler. The task of installing the vector turns out to be very simple with Keil MDK-Arm. As we discussed earlier, an interrupt handler is written as a function in C. The name of the function in C represents the starting address of the function execution. What needs to be done is to put this address into the interrupt vector table. With Keil MDK-Arm, when a new project is created, a startup assembly file startup_STM32f446xx.s is added to the project. In this file, all the interrupt vectors are initialized with a dummy interrupt handler. The dummy interrupt handlers are declared with the attribute of "WEAK", meaning they can be overwritten by another interrupt handler. If an interrupt handler is written with the same name as the dummy handler, the linker will change the interrupt vector to point to the new interrupt handler instead of the dummy handler. So the programmer only has to look up the interrupt handler name in the file startup_STM32f446xx.s and reuse the name for a function that is intended for an interrupt handler. In this case, the interrupt handler's name is EXTI15_10_IRQHandler.

Program 6-1: interrupt from the switch on the Nucleo Board

```
/* p6_1.c using SW0 interrupt
 *
 * User Switch B1 is used to generate interrupt through PC13.
 * The user button is connected to PC13. It has a pull-up resitor
 * so PC13 stays high when the button is not pressed.
 * When the button is pressed, PC13 becomes low.
 * The falling-edge of PC13 (when switch is pressed) triggers an
 * interrupt from External Interrupt Controller (EXTI).
 * In the interrupt handler, the user LD2 is blinked twice.
 * It serves as a crude way to debounce the switch.
 * The green LED (LD2) is connected to PA5.
 *
 * This program was tested with Keil uVision v5.24a with DFP v2.11.0.
```

```c
*/

#include "stm32f4xx.h"

void delayMs(int n);

int main(void) {
    __disable_irq();                    /* global disable IRQs */

    RCC->AHB1ENR |= 4;                      /* enable GPIOC clock */
    RCC->AHB1ENR |= 1;                  /* enable GPIOA clock */
    RCC->APB2ENR |= 0x4000;             /* enable SYSCFG clock */

    /* configure PA5 for LED */
    GPIOA->MODER &= ~0x00000C00;        /* clear pin mode */
    GPIOA->MODER |=  0x00000400;        /* set pin to output mode */

    /* configure PC13 for push button interrupt */
    GPIOC->MODER &= ~0x0C000000;        /* clear pin mode to input mode */

    SYSCFG->EXTICR[3] &= ~0x00F0;       /* clear port selection for EXTI13 */
    SYSCFG->EXTICR[3] |= 0x0020;        /* select port C for EXTI13 */

    EXTI->IMR |= 0x2000;                /* unmask EXTI13 */
    EXTI->FTSR |= 0x2000;               /* select falling edge trigger */

//    NVIC->ISER[1] = 0x00000100;         /* enable IRQ40 (bit 8 of ISER[1]) */
    NVIC_EnableIRQ(EXTI15_10_IRQn);

    __enable_irq();                     /* global enable IRQs */

    while(1) {
    }
}

void EXTI15_10_IRQHandler(void) {
        GPIOA->BSRR = 0x00000020;    /* turn on green LED */
        delayMs(250);
        GPIOA->BSRR = 0x00200000;    /* turn off green LED */
        delayMs(250);
        GPIOA->BSRR = 0x00000020;    /* turn on green LED */
        delayMs(250);
        GPIOA->BSRR = 0x00200000;    /* turn off green LED */
        delayMs(250);

        EXTI->PR = 0x2000;           /* clear interrupt pending flag */
}

/* 16 MHz SYSCLK */
void delayMs(int n) {
    int i;
    for (; n > 0; n--)
        for (i = 0; i < 3195; i++) ;
}
```

When a configured I/O pin signal meets the trigger condition, it sends an EXTIx signal to set the corresponding bit in the Pending register (EXTI_PR). If the associated bit in EXTI_IMR is set, an interrupt is generated. If there are more than one pin with interrupt enabled in the group, the interrupt handler should interrogate the EXTI_PR register to find which EXTIx signal is interrupting. The sequence the interrupt handler polls the EXTI_PR bits determines the priority the I/O pin is served. The Program 6-2 uses two pins (PC13 and PB10) to generate interrupts. PC13 is connected to the user push button switch on the Nucleo board. PB10 has the pull-up resistor enabled. Connect PB10 to ground will generate an interrupt. In the interrupt handler, the PC13 interrupt blinks the LED twice and the PB10 interrupt blinks the LED three times.

| Program 6-2: Rewrite of the interrupt handler in Program 6-1 to distinguish the interrupt pin |

```c
/* p6_2.c Interrupts from two input pins
 *
 * User Switch PB10 is used to generate interrupt through PC13.
 * PB10 is configured to generate interrupt. It is has the
 * pull-up resistor enabled. Use a jumper wire to ground the
 * pin to generate interrupts.
 * In the interrupt handler, the interrupt pending bits are
 * checked. If the interrupt is from PC13, the LED blinks twice.
 * If the interrupt is from PB10, the LED blinks three times.
 * The green LED (LD2) is connected to PA5.
 *
 * This program was tested with Keil uVision v5.24a with DFP v2.11.0.
 */

#include "stm32f4xx.h"

void delayMs(int n);

int main(void) {
    __disable_irq();                    /* global disable IRQs */

    RCC->AHB1ENR |= 4;                  /* enable GPIOC clock */
    RCC->AHB1ENR |= 2;                  /* enable GPIOB clock */
    RCC->AHB1ENR |= 1;                  /* enable GPIOA clock */
    RCC->APB2ENR |= 0x4000;             /* enable SYSCFG clock */

    /* configure PA5 for LED */
    GPIOA->MODER &= ~0x00000C00;        /* clear pin mode */
    GPIOA->MODER |=  0x00000400;        /* set pin to output mode */

    /* configure PC13 for push button interrupt */
    GPIOC->MODER &= ~0x0C000000;        /* clear pin mode to input mode */

    SYSCFG->EXTICR[3] &= ~0x00F0;       /* clear port selection for EXTI13 */
    SYSCFG->EXTICR[3] |= 0x0020;        /* select port C for EXTI13 */

    EXTI->IMR  |= 0x2000;               /* unmask EXTI13 */
    EXTI->FTSR |= 0x2000;               /* select falling edge trigger */

    /* configure PB10 for interrupt */
    GPIOB->MODER &= ~0x00030000;        /* clear pin mode to input mode */
    GPIOB->PUPDR &= ~0x00300000;
    GPIOB->PUPDR |=  0x00100000;        /* enable pull up resistor */

    SYSCFG->EXTICR[2] &= ~0x0F00;       /* clear port selection for EXTI10 */
    SYSCFG->EXTICR[2] |= 0x0100;        /* select port B for EXTI10 */
```

```c
    EXTI->IMR |= 0x0400;                  /* unmask EXTI10 */
    EXTI->FTSR |= 0x0400;                 /* select falling edge trigger */

    NVIC_EnableIRQ(EXTI15_10_IRQn);       /* enable interrupt in NVIC */
    __enable_irq();                       /* global enable IRQs */

    while(1) {
    }
}

void EXTI15_10_IRQHandler(void) {
    if (EXTI->PR == 0x2000) {             /* interrupt from PC13 */
        GPIOA->BSRR = 0x00000020;         /* turn on green LED */
        delayMs(250);
        GPIOA->BSRR = 0x00200000;         /* turn off green LED */
        delayMs(250);
        GPIOA->BSRR = 0x00000020;         /* turn on green LED */
        delayMs(250);
        GPIOA->BSRR = 0x00200000;         /* turn off green LED */
        delayMs(250);

        EXTI->PR = 0x2000;                /* clear interrupt pending flag */
    }
    else if (EXTI->PR == 0x0400) {        /* interrupt from PB10 */
        GPIOA->BSRR = 0x00000020;         /* turn on green LED */
        delayMs(250);
        GPIOA->BSRR = 0x00200000;         /* turn off green LED */
        delayMs(250);
        GPIOA->BSRR = 0x00000020;         /* turn on green LED */
        delayMs(250);
        GPIOA->BSRR = 0x00200000;         /* turn off green LED */
        delayMs(250);
        GPIOA->BSRR = 0x00000020;         /* turn on green LED */
        delayMs(250);
        GPIOA->BSRR = 0x00200000;         /* turn off green LED */
        delayMs(250);

        EXTI->PR = 0x0400;                /* clear interrupt pending flag */
    }
}

/* 16 MHz SYSCLK */
void delayMs(int n) {
    int i;
    for (; n > 0; n--)
        for (i = 0; i < 3195; i++) ;
}
```

Review Questions

1. IRQ6 is assigned to the interrupt of which device?
2. True or false. There is an interrupt assigned to each pin of every I/O pin.
3. True or false. The I/O ports in STM32F4xx support both level and edge trigger interrupts.
4. We use _____ in C to enable the interrupts globally.
5. Show 3 levels of interrupt enabling we must go through before we start using it.

Section 6.4: USART Serial Port Interrupt Programming

In Chapter 4, we showed the programming of USART2 in STM32F446 Arm using polling. This chapter shows how to do the same thing using interrupts. Using interrupt frees up the CPU from having to poll the status of USART. From Table 6-7 interrupt vector table we see the IRQ38 is assigned to USART2. The USART2 global interrupt is located at the address 0x0000 00D8 in the interrupt vector location. We use it next.

USART2 Interrupt Programming to receive data

Program 4-2 in Chapter 4 showed how USART2 receives data by polling Receive Complete (RXNE) flag. The disadvantage with that program is that it ties down the CPU while polling the flag. We can modify it to make it an interrupt driven program. Examining the USARTx_CR1 (Control 1) register, we see RXNEIE (RX No Empty Interrupt Enable) bit allows us to enable the receive interrupt. If the RXNEI interrupt is enabled and a byte is received, the receiver RXNEI flag goes high and that in turn generates an interrupt to NVIC and causes the interrupt handler associated with the USART2 to be executed. In the USART2 interrupt handler, we must read the received character. Reading the received character from the DR (DATA Register) clears the RXNE flag.

31	30	29	28	27	26	25	24	23	22	21	20	19	18	17	16
Res	Res	Res	Res	Res	Res	Res	Res	Res	Res	Res	Res	Res	Res	Res	Res

15	14	13	12	11	10	9	8	7	6	5	4	3	2	1	0
OVER8	Res	UE	M	WAKE	PCE	PS	PEIE	TXEIE	TCIE	RXNEIE	IDLEIE	TE	RE	RWU	SBK
rw		rw	rw	rw	rw	rw	rw	rw	rw	rw	rw	rw	rw	rw	rw

Bit 5 **RXNEIE**: RXNE interrupt enable

This bit is set and cleared by software.

0: Interrupt is inhibited

1: An USART interrupt is generated whenever ORE=1 or RXNE=1 in the USART_SR register

Figure 6-14: USARTx_CR1 to Enable Register to Enable RX interrupt

The initialization of USART2 in Program 6-4 is identical to Program 4-2 except at the end, RXNEIE interrupt is enabled. The polling of the RXNE flag is removed from the infinite loop. The USART2 interrupt handler is added. In the interrupt handler, the data is read and used to blink the LEDs. Reading the data automatically clears the interrupt flag. In this simple example, only RXNE interrupt is enabled so there is no need to check other flags. In real applications, it may be desirable to check the error flag and handle the error conditions.

With Program 6-3, pressing a key at the terminal emulator causes the PC to send the ASCII code of the key to the STM32F4xx board. When the character is received by USART2, the interrupt handler blinks the LED.

Program 6-3: Using the USART2 interrupt

```
/* p6_3.c UART on USART2 Receive at 115200 Baud
```

```c
 *
 * Receive key strokes from terminal emulator (Tera Term) of the
 * host PC to the UART on USART2 of the Nucleo-F446RE board and
 * use the key value to blink the LED.
 * Same program as p4_2 but is interrupt driven.
 *
 * By default, the clock is running at 16 MHz.
 * The UART is configured for 115200 Baud.
 * PA3 - USART2 RX (AF7)
 *
 * This program was tested with Keil uVision v5.24a with DFP v2.11.0
 */
#include "stm32F4xx.h"

void USART2_init(void);
void LED_blink(int value);
void delayMs(int);

/*-------------------------------------------------------------------
  MAIN function
 *-----------------------------------------------------------------*/
int main (void) {
    __disable_irq();                    /* global disable IRQs */

    RCC->AHB1ENR |=  1;                 /* enable GPIOA clock */
    GPIOA->MODER &= ~0x00000C00;        /* clear pin mode */
    GPIOA->MODER |=  0x00000400;        /* set pin to output mode */

    USART2_init();                      /* initialize USART2 */

    USART2->CR1 |= 0x0020;              /* enable Rx interrupt */
    NVIC_EnableIRQ(USART2_IRQn);        /* enable interrupt in NVIC */
    __enable_irq();                     /* global enable IRQs */

    while(1) {                          /* Loop forever */
    }
}

/*-------------------------------------------------------------------
  Initialize UART pins, Baudrate
 *-----------------------------------------------------------------*/
void USART2_init (void) {
    RCC->AHB1ENR |= 1;          /* Enable GPIOA clock */
    RCC->APB1ENR |= 0x20000;    /* Enable USART2 clock */

    /* Configure PA2 for USART2 TX */
    GPIOA->AFR[0] &= ~0xF000;
    GPIOA->AFR[0] |=  0x7000;   /* alt7 for USART2 */
    GPIOA->MODER  &= ~0x00C0;
    GPIOA->MODER  |=  0x0080;   /* enable alternate function for PA3 */

    USART2->BRR = 0x008B;       /* 115200 baud @ 16 MHz */
    USART2->CR1 = 0x0004;       /* enable Rx, 8-bit data */
    USART2->CR2 = 0x0000;       /* 1 stop bit */
    USART2->CR3 = 0x0000;       /* no flow control */
    USART2->CR1 |= 0x2000;      /* enable USART2 */
}
```

```c
void USART2_IRQHandler(void) {
    char c;

    if (USART2->SR & 0x0020) {
        c = USART2->DR;                 /* Read a character from USART2 */
        LED_blink(c);                   /* blink the LED */
    }
}

/* turn on or off the LEDs according to the value */
void LED_blink(int value) {
    value %= 16;                        /* cap the max count at 15 */

    for (; value > 0; value--) {
        GPIOA->BSRR = 0x00000020;       /* turn on LED */
        delayMs(200);
        GPIOA->BSRR = 0x00200000;       /* turn off LED */
        delayMs(200);
    }
    delayMs(800);
}

void delayMs(int n) {
    int i;
    for (; n > 0; n--)
        for (i = 0; i < 2000; i++) ;
}
```

USART2 Interrupt Programming to transmit data

Also, notice that in Program 6-3 there is only a single interrupt for both receiver and transmitter. If we want to implement both transmitter and receiver interrupts, we also have to enable TXEIE (TXE interrupt enable) bit in USARTx_CR1 register. This way a USART interrupt is generated whenever TXE=1 in the USART_SR register. We can also use TCIE (Transmission complete interrupt enable) in the USARTx_CR1 register then a USART interrupt is generated whenever TC=1 in the USART_SR register. In the interrupt handler, we must poll to see the source of the interrupt.

Using interrupts to transmit data is more complex than receiving data. The program needs to create a first-in-first-out buffer to store the characters to be transmitted. After the character is transmitted, the TXE or TC flag becomes set and the interrupt is triggered. In the interrupt handler, the data in the buffer is moved to the transmit DR (DATA) register. If the buffer is empty, transmit interrupt needs to be disabled. When new data is added to the buffer, the transmit interrupt is enabled again.

Review Questions

1. In STM32F4xx, Which IRQ is assigned to USART2?
2. True or false. There is only one interrupt for both Receiver and Transmitter.
3. What address locations in vector table is assigned to USART2 in STM32F4xx Arm chip?
4. We use register _____ to enable the interrupt associated with USART2.
5. True or false. Upon Reset, USART2 is enabled and ready to go.

Section 6.5: SysTick Programming and Interrupt

Another useful interrupt in Arm is the SysTick. The SysTick timer was discussed in Chapter 5. Next, you learn how to use the SysTick interrupt. See figure below.

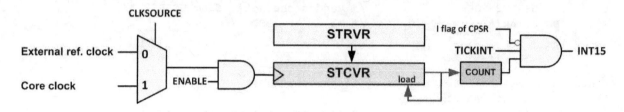

Figure 6-15: SysTick Internal Structure

If TICKINT=1, when the COUNT flag is set, it generates an interrupt. TICKINT is D1 of the CSR register, as shown in Figure 6-16.

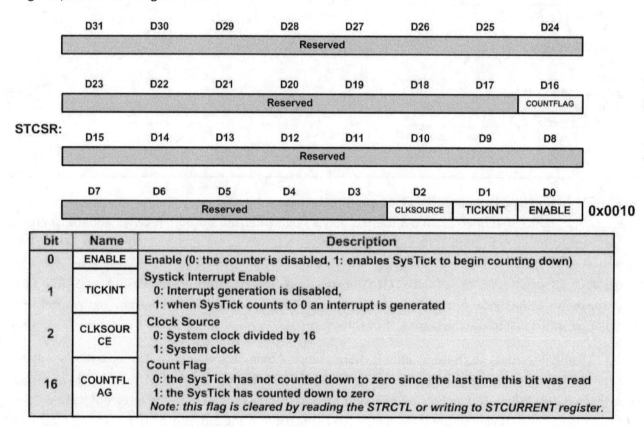

bit	Name	Description
0	ENABLE	Enable (0: the counter is disabled, 1: enables SysTick to begin counting down)
1	TICKINT	Systick Interrupt Enable 0: Interrupt generation is disabled, 1: when SysTick counts to 0 an interrupt is generated
2	CLKSOURCE	Clock Source 0: System clock divided by 16 1: System clock
16	COUNTFLAG	Count Flag 0: the SysTick has not counted down to zero since the last time this bit was read 1: the SysTick has counted down to zero Note: this flag is cleared by reading the STRCTL or writing to STCURRENT register.

Figure 6-16: SysTick Control and Status Register (SYST_CSR)

The SysTick interrupt can be used to initiate an action on a periodic basis. This action is performed at a fixed rate without external signal. For example, in a given application we can use SysTick to read a sensor every 200 msec. SysTick is used widely for an operating system so that the system software may interrupt the application software periodically (often at 10 ms interval) to monitor and control the system operations.

Using SysTick with Interrupt

The Program 6-4 uses the SysTick to toggle an LED every second. We need the RELOAD value of 16,000,000-1. The CLK_SRC bit of CTRL register is set so the system clock is used as the clock source of SysTick. In the STM32F4xx Arm, the alternative clock for SysTick is connected to a prescaler that divides the system clock by 16. The system clock is running at 16 MHz. The COUNT flag is raised every 16,000,000 clocks and an interrupt occurs. Then the RELOAD register is loaded with 16,000,000-1 automatically.

The interrupt is enabled in SysTick Control and Status register. Examining interrupt vector table for Arm Cortex, we see that the SysTick is assigned to INT15. Because SysTick is an interrupt below INT16, the enable/disable and the priority are not managed by the NVIC. Its priority is controlled by a System Handler Priority register (SHPR) of System Control Block (SCB). Instead for finding out which register to use, we may use NVIC_SetPriority(SysTick_IRQn, prio) function defined in core_cm4.h to change the priority. Although the function name has NVIC in it, it modifies SHP registers for interrupts below 16. There is no need to clear interrupt flag in the interrupt handler for SysTick.

```
                    Program 6-4: SysTick interrupt

/* p6_4.c Toggle the LED using the SysTick interrupt
 *
 * This program sets up the SysTick to interrupt at 1 Hz.
 * The system clock is running at 16 MHz.
 * 1 sec/1 us = 16,000,000-1 for RELOAD register.
 * In the interrupt handler, the LED is toggled.
 *
 * This program was tested with Keil uVision v5.24a with DFP v2.11.0
 */
#include "stm32F4xx.h"

int main(void) {
    __disable_irq();                    /* global disable IRQs */

    RCC->AHB1ENR |=  1;                 /* enable GPIOA clock */
    GPIOA->MODER &= ~0x00000C00;        /* clear pin mode */
    GPIOA->MODER |=  0x00000400;        /* set pin to output mode */

    /* Configure SysTick */
    SysTick->LOAD = 16000000-1;         /* reload with number of clocks per second */
    SysTick->VAL = 0;
    SysTick->CTRL = 7;                  /* enable SysTick interrupt, use system clock */
    __enable_irq();

    while (1) {
    }
}

void SysTick_Handler(void) {
    GPIOA->ODR ^= 0x00000020;    /* turn on LED */
}
```

Review Questions

1. Which interrupt is assigned to SysTick in Arm Cortex M chip?
2. Which register of Systick is used to enable the interrupt associated with SysTick.

3. True or false. We use ISER in NVIC register to enable SysTick interrupt.

Section 6.6: Timer Interrupt Programming

In Chapter 5, we showed how to program the timers. In those programming examples, we used polling to see if a timer counter update occurred. In this section, we give an interrupt-based version of that program.

Timer Counter Update Interrupt

Examine the programs in Section 5.3 of Chapter 5. In those programs, inside the infinite loop, the program continuously polls the interrupt flag until the flag is set. At the same time, the program does not do anything useful. In this section, we are going to use the timer interrupt to notify the program that the timer counter update happen. At the meantime, the program is free to do other useful tasks. To do that, we use the TIMx DMA/Interrupt enable register (TIMx_DIER). In the interrupt enable register, the UIE (Update interrupt enable) is set to 1 to trigger an interrupt when timer counter update occurs. From Table 6-7 we see the IRQ28 is assigned to TIM2 interrupt. The IRQ28 (TIM2 global interrupt) is located at the vector table address of 0x0000 00B0.

15	14	13	12	11	10	9	8	7	6	5	4	3	2	1	0
Res	TDE	COMDE	CC4DE	CC3DE	CC2DE	CC1DE	UDE	BIE	TIE	COMIE	CC4IE	CC3IE	CC2IE	CC1IE	UIE
	rw	rw	rw	rw	rw	rw	rw	rw	rw	rw	rw	rw	rw	rw	rw

Bit 0 **UIE**: Update interrupt enable

0: Update interrupt disabled

1: Update interrupt enabled

Figure 6-17: TIMx DMA/Interrupt enable register (TIMx_DIER) to Enbale Timer interrupt

Program 6-5 is modified from the polling program 5-4. Timer interrupt is enabled and an LED is blinked in the interrupt handler.

```
                    Program 6-5: Toggling the LED using the Timer 2  reload interrupt

/* p6_5.c Timer TIM2 interrupt
 *
 * Timer TIM2 is configured as an up-counter. By default, the system clock is
 * running at 16 MHz. The prescaler is set to divide by 16,000 that gives a
 * 1 kHz clock to the counter. The counter auto-reload is set to 999. When
 * the counter counts to 999, it updates the counter to zero and sets the
 * update interrupt flag (UIF). The UIE bit of TIM2->DIER is set so that
 * the UIF triggers a timer interrupt. The interrupt frequency is 1 Hz.
 * In the timer interrupt handler, the green LED (PA5) is toggled and
 * the UIF is cleared.
 *
 * This program was tested with Keil uVision v5.24a with DFP v2.11.0
 */
#include "stm32f4xx.h"

void delayMs(int n);

int main(void) {
```

```
        __disable_irq();             /* global disable IRQs */
        RCC->AHB1ENR |=  1;          /* enable GPIOA clock */


        GPIOA->MODER &= ~0x00000C00;
        GPIOA->MODER |=  0x00000400;


        /* setup TIM2 */
        RCC->APB1ENR |= 1;           /* enable TIM2 clock */
        TIM2->PSC = 16000 - 1;       /* divided by 16000 */
        TIM2->ARR = 1000 - 1;        /* divided by 1000 */
        TIM2->CR1 = 1;               /* enable counter */

        TIM2->DIER |= 1;             /* enable UIE */
        NVIC_EnableIRQ(TIM2_IRQn);   /* enable interrupt in NVIC */

        __enable_irq();              /* global enable IRQs */

        while(1) {
        }
}

void TIM2_IRQHandler(void) {
        TIM2->SR = 0;                /* clear UIF */
        GPIOA->ODR ^= 0x20;              /* toggle LED */
}
```

Timer Output Compare Interrupt

Recall in Chapter 5, when operating in Output Compare operation, when the counter value matches the content of CCRx register, the output of the associated pin can be configured to change in several different ways. Here we are going to trigger an interrupt in addition to the output change. In the interrupt handler, a value in added to the CCRx register so that the output compare match will occur after the number of the clocks determined by the value added.

For example, when the CCR1 register contains 750, an output compare match of channel 1 occurs when the counter counts to 750. If 345 is added to CCR1, the CCR1 will have 1095. The next time an output compare match occurs is when the counter reaches 1095, exactly 345 clock cycles after the last output compare match. In the program 6-6 below, the output compare is set to toggle the output and the output is connected to the LED. In the interrupt handler, 1000 is added to the CCR1. The time clock is configured to run at 1 kHz (with 16 MHz system clock and the prescaler divided by 16,000). The output compare occurs once every second.

We added a constant 1000 to the CCR1 to generate a square wave output. In other applications, you may add a series of different intervals to create a different waveform output.

Program 6-6: Toggling the yellow LED using two Timer interrupts

```
/* p6_6.c Timer TIM2 interrupt
 *
 * Timer TIM2 is configured as an up-counter. By default, the system clock is
 * running at 16 MHz. The prescaler is set to divide by 16,000 that gives a
 * 1 kHz clock to the counter.
```

```
 * The timer is set up for output compare interrupt for channel 1. When the
 * counter matches the CCR1 register, the output toggles and an interrupt
 * is triggered. In the interrupt handler, the PERIOR value is added CCR1
 * so that the next CCR1 match occurs after the PERIOR count.
 * When the PERIOD is set to 1000, the output toggles at 1 Hz.
 * The output of TIM2 Channel 1 is PA5 which is connected to the LED.
 *
 * This program was tested with Keil uVision v5.24a with DFP v2.11.0
 */
#include "stm32f4xx.h"

#define PERIOD 1000
void delayMs(int n);

int main(void) {
    __disable_irq();                     /* global disable IRQs */
    RCC->AHB1ENR |= 1;                     /* enable GPIOA clock */

    GPIOA->MODER &= ~0x00000C00;
    GPIOA->MODER |= 0x00000800;          /* use alternate function */
    GPIOA->AFR[0] = 0x00100000;          /* PA5 TIM2-CH1 */

    /* setup TIM2 */
    RCC->APB1ENR |= 1;                   /* enable TIM2 clock */
    TIM2->PSC = 16000 - 1;               /* divided by 16000 */
    TIM2->ARR = 0xFFFF;                  /* max count */
    TIM2->CCR1 = PERIOD;
    TIM2->CNT = 0;
    TIM2->CCMR1 = 0x30;                  /* Output compare toggle */
    TIM2->CCER = 1;                      /* CC1 enable */
    TIM2->CR1 = 1;                       /* enable counter */

    TIM2->DIER |= 2;                     /* enable CC1IE */
    NVIC_EnableIRQ(TIM2_IRQn);           /* enable interrupt in NVIC */

    __enable_irq();                      /* global enable IRQs */

    while(1) {
    }
}

void TIM2_IRQHandler(void) {
    TIM2->SR = 0;                                  /* clear UIF */
    TIM2->CCR1 = (TIM2->CCR1 + PERIOD) & 0xFFFF;     /* update CCR1 */
}
```

Review Questions

1. For STM32F4xx chip, which IRQ is assigned to TIM2?
2. True or false. There is only one interrupt for both TIM2 and TIM3.
3. We use register _____ in TIM2 to enable the interrupt associated with TIM2.
4. True or false. Upon Reset, TIM2 interrupt is enabled and ready to go.

Section 6.7: Interrupt Priority Programming in STM32 Arm

The implementation of interrupts varies from vendor to vendor. While Arm has control over the standardization of the first 15 interrupts (INT1 to INT15), the Arm licensees are free to implement the peripheral interrupts of INT16 – INT255 (the IRQs). The first three interrupts are Reset, NMI, and Hard Fault. For these three interrupts, Reset has the highest priority (with -3 priority number), then NMI (with -2), and Hard Fault (with -1), in that order. In Arm, the lower value has higher priority. The priorities of interrupts 11, 14, and 15 are controlled by the System handler Priority Register 2 and 3 in the System Control Block. We have talked about the priority setting of SysTick, which is INT15, in Section 6.5. You can explore them by reading the Arm Cortex data sheet. In this section, we deal with the priority of peripheral interrupts of INT16 (IRQ0) to INT56 (IRQ40). We must pay attention to the IRQ# since this is used to index into the registers in the NVIC to change the priority of the interrupt.

When more than one interrupt is pending, the interrupt with the highest priority is acknowledged first. While an interrupt handler is running, another interrupt with higher priority will interrupt the current interrupt handler and start its own interrupt handler (nested interrupts).

The IPR registers and the Interrupt Priority

The priority of an IRQ is assigned in one of the interrupt priority registers (IPRx) in NVIC. If we do not assign a priority to an IRQ, by default, it has priority 0 that is the highest priority for the IRQ. Each IRQ uses one byte in one of the interrupt priority registers. Therefore, each interrupt priority register holds priorities for four IRQ. For example, IPR0 (IPR zero) register holds the priorities of IRQ3, IRQ2, IRQ1 and IRQ0. In the same way, the priorities of IRQ7, IRQ6, IRQ5 and IRQ4 are assigned in IPR1 register. For 240 IRQs, 60 interrupt priority registers are used. The STM32F4 Arm devices use only the four most significant bits of the byte in the interrupt priority register. With four bits, there can be 16 different priorities, 0 to 15. The lower the number the higher the priority is.

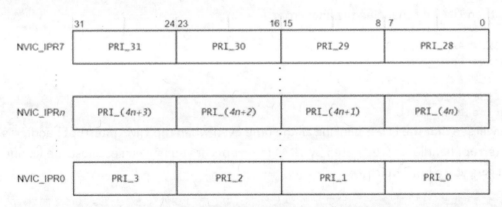

Figure 6-18: IPRn Registers

Notice, there is a pattern in the IPRn and IRQ# assignments. It follows the following formula:

IPRn   IRQ(4n+3), IRQ(4n+2), IRQ(4n+1), and IRQ(4n)

To find the IPR number simply divide the IRQ number by 4 and the remainder will determine which byte it is in the register. Because only the highest four bits are used for priority, the priority number needs to be multiplied by 16 (or left shift 4 bits) before loading into the proper byte. For example, for priority 2, the value 32 should be loaded. To ease the calculation of finding the correct bits of the correct register to set the proper value for the priority, the NVIC_IPRx registers are defined as an array of 8-bit registers IP[x] in the core_cm4.h. This way, the priority of IRQx is controlled by IP[x].

For example, if we want to set the TIM2 interrupt priority to 3, first we need to find out the IRQ number of a TIM2 interrupt, which is IRQ28. Then the C statement is simply:

```
NVIC->IP[28] = 3 << 4;
```

There is also a function NVIC_SetPriority(IRQ#) defined in core_cm4.h to set the priority of an IRQ in NVIC. To set the priority of TIM2 to 3:

```
NVIC_SetPriority(TIM2_IRQn, 3);
```

TIM2_IRQn is defined in stm32f446xx.h.

Program 6-7 illustrates two interrupts with different priorities. In this example, delay function is called in the interrupt handler to demonstrate the preemption by a higher priority interrupt. (In the real world, it is a bad practice to call delay function in an interrupt handler.) TIM3 is programmed to interrupt at about 1-second interval. In the interrupt handler, pin PB3 is turned on for 500 ms. TIM4 is programmed to interrupt at about 100 ms interval and in its interrupt handler, pin PB4 and the LED are turned on for 25 ms. The frequencies of two interrupts are intentionally made slightly off the multiple of 10 so that the phase relationship of two interrupts will be changing and their interactions can be observed with an oscilloscope. Since TIM3 has higher priority, you will observe that the LED is not blinking when the TIM3 interrupt handler is running (once every second for half a second). Now, change the priority of the TIM4 to be higher than TIM3 by changing the lines from

```
#define PRIO_TIM3 3
#define PRIO_TIM4 4
to
#define PRIO_TIM3 4
#define PRIO_TIM4 3
```

You will see that the LED is blinking all the time even when the TIM3 interrupt handler is running. The TIM3 interrupt handler is preempted by TIM4 interrupts. If you have an oscilloscope, connect to PB3 and PB4 will give you a better picture.

Program 6-7: Interrupt priority demonstration

```
/* p6_7.c Demonstrate Nested Interrupts
 *
 * TIM3 is setup to interrupt at about 1 Hz. In the interrupt handler,
 * PB3 is turned on and a delay function of 500 ms is called.
 * PB3 is turned off at the end of the delay.
 *
 * TIM4 is setup to interrupt at about 10 Hz. In the interrupt handler,
```

```
 * PB4 and the LED0 is turned on and a delay function of 25 ms is called.
 * PB4 and the LED0 is turned off at the end of the delay.
 *
 * When TIM3 has the higher priority (the way this code is), the TIM4
 * interrupts are blocked by TIM3 interrupt handler and the LED stops
 * blinking intermittently. You can see their interactions better
 * with an oscilloscope on PB3 and PB4.
 *
 * When TIM4 has the higher priority (you need to switch the priority of
 * the two timers at the #define statements), the TIM3 interrupt handler is
 * preempted by TIM4 interrupts and the LED is blinking all the time.
 *
 * This program was tested with Keil uVision v5.24a with DFP v2.11.0
 */

#include "stm32f4xx.h"

void delayMs(int n);

/* priority of TIM3 and TTIM4 should be between 0 and 15 */
#define PRIO_TIM3 3
#define PRIO_TIM4 4

int main (void) {
    __disable_irq();                /* global disable IRQs */
    RCC->AHB1ENR |= 1;              /* enable GPIOA clock */
    RCC->AHB1ENR |= 2;              /* enable GPIOB clock */

    GPIOA->MODER &= ~0x00000C00;    /* pin PA5 (LED) output */
    GPIOA->MODER |= 0x00000400;
    GPIOB->MODER &= ~0x000003C0;    /* pins PB3, PB4 output */
    GPIOB->MODER |= 0x00000140;

    /* setup TIM3 */
    RCC->APB1ENR |= 2;              /* enable TIM3 clock */
    TIM3->PSC = 1000 - 1;           /* divided by 1000 */
    TIM3->ARR = 15500 - 1;          /* divided by 15500 */
    TIM3->CR1 = 1;                  /* enable counter */

    TIM3->DIER |= 1;                /* enable UIE */
    NVIC_SetPriority(TIM3_IRQn, PRIO_TIM3);
    NVIC_EnableIRQ(TIM3_IRQn);      /* enable interrupt in NVIC */

    /* setup TIM4 */
    RCC->APB1ENR |= 4;              /* enable TIM4 clock */
    TIM4->PSC = 1000 - 1;           /* divided by 1000 */
    TIM4->ARR = 1562 - 1;           /* divided by 1562 */
    TIM4->CR1 = 1;                  /* enable counter */

    TIM4->DIER |= 1;                /* enable UIE */
    NVIC_SetPriority(TIM4_IRQn, PRIO_TIM4);
    NVIC_EnableIRQ(TIM4_IRQn);      /* enable interrupt in NVIC */

    __enable_irq();                 /* enable interrupt globally */

    while(1) {
    }
```

```
    }

void TIM3_IRQHandler(void) {
    GPIOB->BSRR = 0x00000008;        /* turn on PB3 */
    delayMs(500);
    GPIOB->BSRR = 0x00080000;        /* turn off PB3 */
    TIM3->SR = 0;                    /* clear UIF */
}

void TIM4_IRQHandler(void) {
    GPIOA->BSRR = 0x00000020;        /* turn on LED */
    GPIOB->BSRR = 0x00000010;        /* turn on PB4 */
    delayMs(25);
    GPIOA->BSRR = 0x00200000;        /* turn off LED */
    GPIOB->BSRR = 0x00100000;        /* turn off PB4 */
    TIM4->SR = 0;                    /* clear UIF */
}

/* 16 MHz SYSCLK */
void delayMs(int n) {
    int i;
    for (; n > 0; n--)
        for (i = 0; i < 3195; i++) ;
}
```

Review Questions

1. In Arm, which interrupt has the highest priority?
2. True or false. Upon Reset, all the IRQs have the same priority.
3. We use register _____ to modify the interrupt priority of IRQ28.
4. To assign priority to IRQ28, we need to write to the IP[__] register.

Answer to Review Questions

Section 6.1

1. True
2. 4
3. 192 byte beginning at 0x00000000 and ending at 0x000000BF
4. Interrupt service routine (ISR) or interrupt handler
5. To hold the starting address of each ISR
6. 0x00000040, 41, 42, and 43
7. No; it is embedded internally in the CPU.

Section 6.2

1. True
2. 2; Thread mode and Handler mode
3. 8 bytes. 4 bytes for the address of the stack (loaded into the Stack Pointer) and 4 bytes for the address of beginning of the program (loaded in Program Counter).

4. Interrupt handler
5. True

Section 6.3

1. EXTI0
2. False; all I/O pins are mapped to 16 EXTIx and all 16 EXTIx are mapped to 7 IRQs.
3. True
4. __enable_irq();
5. (a) on the peripheral device module level. (b) on the system level with ISER register in NVIC. (c) on the global level with the __enable_irq(); statement.

Section 6.4

1. IRQ38
2. True
3. 0x0800 00D8
4. USART2_CR1
5. False

Section 6.5

1. INT15
2. SYST_CSR
3. False. NVIC_ISER register is used for IRQs (external interrupts) and SysTick is not part of them.

Section 6.6

1. IRQ28
2. False
3. TIM2_DIER
4. False

Section 6.7

1. Reset
2. True, by default all IRQs have priority of 0.
3. NVIC_IPR7
4. IP[28]

Chapter 7: ADC, DAC, and Sensor Interfacing

Most of the things in the world is analog but the computer is digital. For the computer to interact with the surrounding world, an analog-to-digital converter (ADC) and a digital-to-analog converter (DAC) are needed. This chapter explores ADC, DAC, and sensors and how to interface the STM Arm to these devices. In Section 7.1, we describe analog-to-digital converter. We will program the ADC module of the STM32 Arm chip in Section 7.2. In Section 7.3, we show the interfacing of sensors and discuss the issue of signal conditioning. The characteristics and programming of DAC chips are discussed in Section 7.4.

Section 7.1: ADC Characteristics

This section will explore the ADC in general. First, we describe some general aspects of the ADC itself, then focus on the functionality of some important signals in an ADC.

ADC devices

Analog-to-digital converters are essential for data acquisition. Digital computers use binary (discrete) values, but in the physical world, everything is analog (continuous). Temperature, pressure, humidity, and velocity are a few examples of physical quantities that we deal with every day. A physical quantity is converted to electrical (voltage, current) signals using a device called a *transducer*. Transducers used to generate electrical outputs are also referred to as *sensors*. Sensors for temperature, velocity, pressure, light, and many other physical quantities produce an output that is voltage (or current). Therefore, we need an analog-to-digital converter to translate the analog signals to digital numbers so that the microcontroller can read and process the numbers. See Figures 7-1 and 7-2.

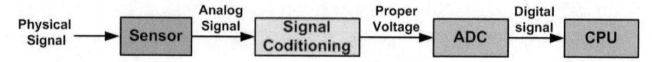

Figure 7-1: Microcontroller Connection to Sensor via ADC

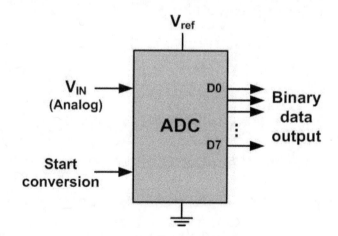

Figure 7-2: An 8-bit ADC Block Diagram

Some of the major characteristics of the ADC

Resolution

The ADC has an *n*-bit resolution, where *n* can be 8, 10, 12, 16, or even 24 bits. Higher-resolution ADCs provide a smaller step size, where *step size* is the smallest change that can be discerned by an ADC. Some widely used resolutions and their step sizes for ADCs are shown in Table 7-1. Although the resolution of an ADC is decided at the time of its design and cannot be changed, we can control the step size with the help of what is called V_{ref}. This is discussed below.

n-bit	Number of steps	Step size
8	256	5V /256 = 19.53 mV
10	1,024	5V /1,024 = 4.88 mV
12	4,096	5V /4,096 = 1.22 mV
16	65,536	5V /65,536 = 0.0763 mV
Note: V_{ref} = 5V		

Table 7-1: Resolution versus Step Size for ADC (Vref = 5V)

Vref

Vref is an input voltage used for the reference of the converter. The voltage connected to this pin, along with the resolution of the ADC chip, determine the step size. For an 8-bit ADC, the step size is Vref / 256 because it is an 8-bit ADC, and 2 to the power of 8 gives us 256 steps. See Table 7-1. For example, if the analog input range needs to be 0 to 4 volts, Vref is connected to 4 volts. That gives 4 V / 256 = 15.62 mV for the step size of an 8-bit ADC. In another case, if we need a step size of 10 mV for an 8-bit ADC, then V_{ref} = 2.56 V, because 2.56 V / 256 = 10 mV. For the 10-bit ADC, if the V_{ref} = 5V, then the step size is 4.88 mV as shown in Table 7-1. Tables 7-2 and 7-3 show the relationship between the V_{ref} and step size for the 8- and 10-bit ADCs, respectively. In some applications, we need the differential reference voltage where $V_{ref} = V_{ref(+)} - V_{ref(-)}$. If differential reference is not necessary, the $V_{ref(-)}$ pin is connected to ground and the $V_{ref(+)}$ pin is used as the V_{ref}. Voltage reference devices are commonly available to be used.

V_{ref} (V)	V_{in} in Range (V)	Step Size (mV)
5.00	0 to 5	5 / 256 = 19.53
4.00	0 to 4	4 / 256 = 15.62
3.00	0 to 3	3 / 256 = 11.71
2.56	0 to 2.56	2.56 / 256 = 10
2.00	0 to 2	2 / 256 = 7.81
1.28	0 to 1.28	1.28 / 256 = 5
1.00	0 to 1	1 / 256 = 3.90
Note: In an 8-bit ADC, step size is V_{ref}/256		

Table 7-2: Vref Relation to Vin Range for an 8-bit ADC

Vref (V)	V_{in}Range (V)	Step Size (mV)
5.00	0 to 5	5 / 1024 = 4.88
4.96	0 to 4.096	4.096 / 1024 = 4
3.00	0 to 3	3 / 1024 = 2.93
2.56	0 to 2.56	2.56 / 1024 = 2.5
2.00	0 to 2	2 / 1024 = 2
1.28	0 to 1.28	1.28 / 1024 = 1.25
1.024	0 to 1.024	1.024 / 1024 = 1
Note: In a 10-bit ADC, step size is V_{ref}/1024		

Table 7-3: Vref Relation to Vin Range for an 10-bit ADC

Conversion time

In addition to resolution, conversion time is another major factor in selecting an ADC. *Conversion time* is defined as the time it takes the ADC to convert the analog input to a digital number. The conversion time is dictated by the clock source connected to the ADC in addition to the method used for data conversion and technology used in the fabrication of the ADC. Generally, the higher the resolution, the longer it takes to do a conversion.

Digital data output

In an 8-bit ADC, we have an 8-bit digital data output of D0–D7, while in the 10-bit ADC the data output is D0–D9. To calculate the output value, we use the following formula:

$$D_{out} = V_{in} / StepSize$$

Where D_{out} is the digital data output (a numeric value) and V_{in} is the analog input voltage. Figure 7-3 shows a simple 2-bit ADC. In the circuit, the voltage between Vref(+) and Vref(-) is divided into 4 since resistors have the same values. As a result, the step size is $(V_{ref(+)} - V_{ref(-)}) / 4$.

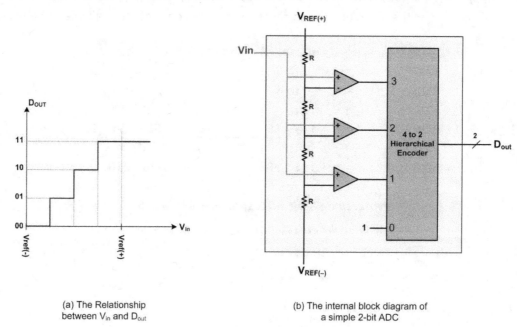

(a) The Relationship
between V_{in} and D_{out}

(b) The internal block diagram of
a simple 2-bit ADC

Figure 7-3: A Simultaneous 2-bit ADC

200

If V_{in} is below one step size all the comparators send out zeros. When V_{in} is between one step size and step size × 2, the lowest comparator sends out 1 and the encoder gives 01.

If V_{in} is between step size × 2 and step size × 3, the second comparator and the first comparator sends out 1. Since the encoder is a hierarchical priority encoder, it sends out the highest value in cases that more than 1 input is high. As a result, 2 (10 in binary) will be sent out.

When V_{in} is bigger than step size × 3, the third comparator becomes high and 3 will be sent out.

See Example 7-1. This data is brought out of the ADC chip either one bit at a time (serially) or in one chunk, using a parallel line of outputs. This is discussed next.

Example 7-1

For a given 8-bit ADC (e.g. ADC0848), we have V_{ref} = 2.56 V. Calculate the D0–D7 output if the analog input is: (a)1.7 V, and (b) 2.1 V.

Solution:

Since the step size is 2.56/256 = 10 mV, we have the following.
(a)D_{out} = 1.7V/10 mV = 170 in decimal, which gives us 10101011 in binary for D7–D0.
(b)D_{out} = 2.1V/10 mV = 210 in decimal, which gives us 11010010 in binary for D7–D0.

Parallel versus serial ADC

The ADC chips are either parallel or serial. In parallel ADC, we have 8 or more pins dedicated to bringing out the binary data, but in serial ADC we have only one pin for data out. The D0–D7 data pins of the 8-bit ADC provide an 8-bit parallel data path between the ADC chip and the CPU. In the case of the 16-bit parallel ADC chip, we need 16 pins for the data path. In order to save pins, many 12- and 16-bit ADCs use pins D0–D7 to send out the upper and lower bytes of the binary data. In recent years, for many applications where space is a critical issue, using such a large number of pins for data is not feasible. For this reason, serial devices such as the serial ADC are common. While the serial ADCs use fewer pins and their smaller packages take much less space on the circuit board, more CPU time is needed to get the converted data from the ADC because the CPU must get data one bit at a time, instead of in one single read operation as with the parallel ADC. The Serial Peripheral Interface (SPI) module is designed to clock in the data so that the CPU does not have to spend time directly on acquiring the data. We will cover SP in Chapter 8. ADC0848 is an example of a parallel ADC with 8 pins for the data output, while the MAX1112 is an example of a serial ADC with a single pin for D_{out}. Figures 7-4 and 7-5 show the block diagram for ADC0848 and MAX1112, respectively.

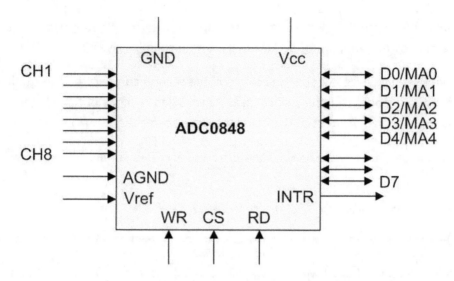

Figure 7-4: ADC0848 Parallel ADC Block Diagram

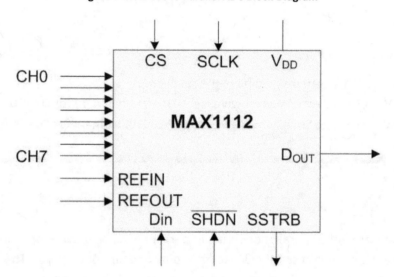

Figure 7-5: MAX1112 Serial ADC Block Diagram

Analog input channels

Many data acquisition applications need more than one analog input. For this reason, we see ADC chips with 2, 4, 8, or even 16 channels on a single chip. Instead of having many ADCs, multiplexing of analog inputs is often used as shown in the ADC848 and MAX1112. In these chips, we have 8 channels of analog inputs, allowing us to monitor multiple quantities such as temperature, pressure, flow, and so on. The SAMD2x devices have up to 20 single-ended input analog channels for the on-chip ADC.

Start conversion and end-of-conversion signals

For the conversion to be controlled by the CPU, there are needs for start conversion (SC) and end-of-conversion (EOC) signals. When SC is activated, the ADC starts converting the analog input value of V_{in} to a digital number. The amount of time it takes to convert varies depending on the conversion method, clock speed, and resolution. When the data conversion is complete, the end-of-conversion signal notifies the CPU that the converted data is ready to be picked up.

Successive Approximation ADC

Successive Approximation is a broadly used method of converting an analog input to digital output. It has three main components: (a) successive approximation register (SAR), (b) comparator, and (c) control unit. See the figure below.

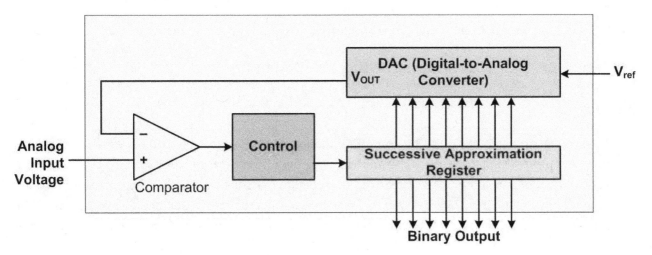

Figure 7-6: Successive Approximation ADC

The successive approximation register is loaded with only the most significant bit set at the start. An internal digital-to-analog converter converts the value of SAR to an analog voltage which is used to compare to the input voltage. If the input voltage is higher, the bit is kept. If the voltage is lower, the bit is cleared. The next bit is tried and the DAC and compare are exercised. This process is repeated for all bits of the SAR. Assuming a step size of 10 mV, the 8-bit successive approximation ADC will go through the following steps to convert an input of 1 Volt:

(1) It starts with binary number 10000000. Since 128 × 10 mV = 1.28 V is greater than the 1 V input, bit 7 is cleared (dropped).
(2) 01000000 gives us 64 × 10 mV = 640 mV and bit 6 is kept since it is smaller than the 1 V input.
(3) 01100000 gives us 96 × 10 mV = 960 mV and bit 5 is kept since it is smaller than the 1 V input,
(4) 01110000 gives us 112 × 10 mV = 1120 mV and bit 4 is dropped since it is greater than the 1 V input.
(5) 01101000 gives us 108 × 10 mV = 1080 mV and bit 3 is dropped since it is greater than the 1 V input.
(6) 01100100 gives us 100 × 10 mV = 1000 mV = 1 V and bit 2 is kept since it is equal to input. Even though the answer is found it does not stop.
(7) 011000110 gives us 102 × 10 mV = 1020 mV and bit 1 is dropped since it is greater than the 1 V input.
(8) 01100101 gives us 101 × 10 mV = 1010 mV and bit 0 is dropped since it is greater than the 1 V input.

Notice that the Successive Approximation method goes through all the steps even if the answer is found in one of the earlier steps. The advantage of the Successive Approximation method is that the conversion time is fixed since it has to go through all the steps. Also, it only takes one more clock cycle to get one more bit of resolution.

Review Questions

1. Give two factors that affect the step size calculation.
2. The ADC0848 is a(n) _____-bit converter.
3. True or false. While the ADC0848 has 8 pins for Dout, the MAX1112 has only one Dout pin.
4. Find the step size for an 8-bit ADC, if Vref = 1.28 V.
5. For question 4, calculate the output if the analog input is: (a) 0.7 V, and (b) 1 V.

Section 7.2: ADC Programming with STM32 Arm

In this section, we discuss the ADC features of the STM32F4xx Arm and show how it is programmed.

The STM32F4xx Arm chip has three on-chip ADC modules. It can support up to 16 external analog input channels and three internal sources using multiplexing. The ADC has 12-bit resolution. To program them, we need to understand some of the major registers. Figure 7-7 shows a simplified block diagram of the main (master) ADC in STM32F4xx chip. In the reference manual the ADCs are designated as ADC1 (master), ADC2 (slave) and ADC3 (slave). In this chapter we focus on the ADC1, the main one since it has everything we need.

The base address of the ADC is located at 0x4001 2000. Below are some of the major registers and their offset addresses of STM32F4xx ADC.

Offset Address	Register
0x00	ADC_SR (Status Register)
0x04	ADC_CR1(Control Register1)
0x08	ADC_CR2(Control Register2)
0x0C	ADC_SMPR1
0x10	ADC_SMPR2
0x4C	ADC_DR (Data Register)

Table 7-4: Some of the STM32F4xx Registers

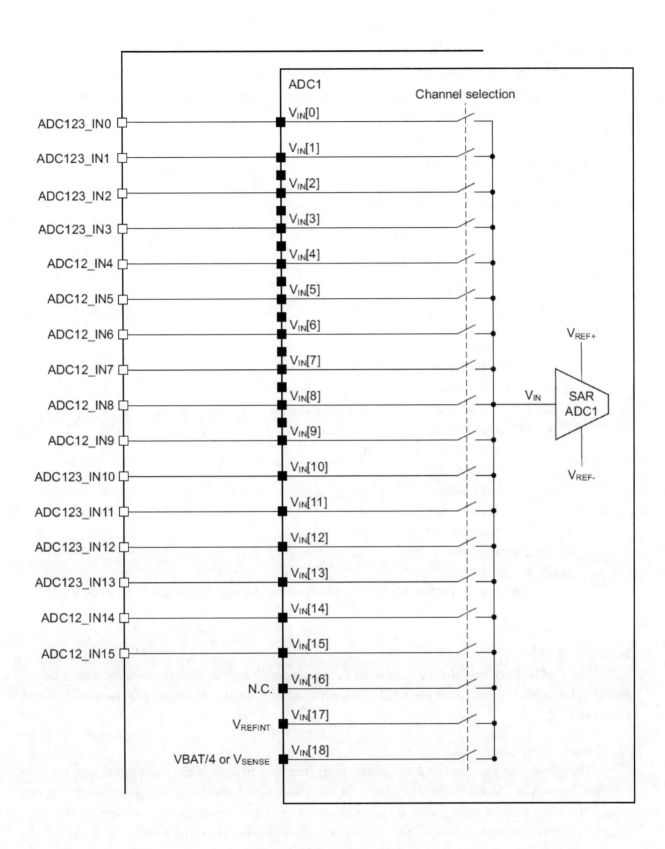

Figure 7-7: Simplified Block Diagram of STM32F4xx chip

Configure Clock Sources

Like other peripheral modules, the ADC needs a clock to drive the conversion. The ADC clock is enabled by bits of RCC_APB2ENR (RCC APB2 peripheral clock enable register) register in the Reset and Control (RCC) section of the CPU. The conversion clock is derived from the SYSCLK. The following statement enables the clock to ADC1.

```
RCC_APB2ENR |= 0x00000100;        /* enable clock for ADC1 */
```

31	30	29	28	27	26	25	24	23	22	21	20	19	18	17	16
Res	Res	Res	Res	Res	Res	Res	Res	SAI2 EN	SAI1 EN	Res	Res	Res	TIM11 EN	TIM10 EN	TIM9 EN
								rw	rw				rw	rw	rw

15	14	13	12	11	10	9	8	7	6	5	4	3	2	1	0
Res	SYSCFG EN	SPI4 EN	SPI1 EN	SDIO EN	ADC3 EN	ADC2 EN	ADC1 EN	Res	Res	USART6 EN	USART1 EN	Res	Res	TIM8 EN	TIM1 EN
	rw	rw	rw	rw	rw	rw	rw			rw	rw			rw	rw

Bit 10 **ADC3EN**: ADC3 clock enable

This bit is set and cleared by software.

0: ADC3 clock disabled

1: ADC3 clock disabled

Bit 9 **ADC2EN**: ADC2 clock enable

This bit is set and cleared by software.

0: ADC2 clock disabled

1: ADC2 clock disabled

Bit 8 **ADC1EN**: ADC1 clock enable

This bit is set and cleared by software.

0: ADC1 clock disabled

1: ADC1 clock disabled

Fig 7-8: RCC_APB2ENR (RCC APB2 peripheral clock enable register) to enable clock to ADC

Conversion Clock

The SYSCLK clock source may be divided by the divider chosen by AHB and APB prescalers before it is fed to the ADC. The output of the APB1 divider is used to clock the ADC core and the sample timer. See Appendix C.

ADC Conversion Time

The conversion time for the ADC has two parts, the time to sample the input signal, and the time to do the conversion. Most of the ADC does not work well when the input signal is changing during conversion. A sample and hold circuit is added between the input signal and the converter. The input signal is sampled and held in a capacitor. The input is disconnected from the holding capacitor for the duration of the conversion so that the fluctuation of the input signal does not affect the input of the converter. During the sampling phase, the input signal is charging the holding capacitor. The longer the sampling time, the closer the holding voltage is to the input signal. But the longer the sampling time also decreases the conversion rate. If the input is from a single channel and the sampling rate is high, the consecutive samples have very close voltages, short sampling time will suffice. On the other hand, if two or more different input signals are sampled alternatively, the sampling time needs to be lengthened to reduce the crosstalk between input channels.

The number of clock cycles for sampling time can be programmed using ADC_SMPRx (Sample Time Register) register. We have two ADC_SMPRx registers to covers all the 18 ADC channels. The ADC_SMPR2 is used for channels 0 to 9 and ADC_SMPR1 is used for channels 10 to 18. The sampling time length can go from 3 clocks (default upon reset) to 480 clocks. See Figures 7-9A and 7-9B.

31	30	29	28	27	26	25	24	23	22	21	20	19	18	17	16
Res	Res	Res	Res	Res	SMP18[2:0]			SMP17[2:0]			SMP16[2:0]			SMP15[2:1]	
					rw	rw	rw	rw	rw	rw	rw	rw	rw	rw	rw

15	14	13	12	11	10	9	8	7	6	5	4	3	2	1	0
SMP15_0	SMP14[2:0]			SMP13[2:0]			SMP12[2:0]			SMP11[2:0]			SMP10[2:0]		
rw	rw	rw	rw	rw	rw	rw	rw	rw	rw	rw	rw	rw	rw	rw	rw

000: 3 cycles	100: 84 cycles
001: 15 cycles	101: 112 cycles
010: 28 cycles	110: 144 cycles
011: 56 cycles	111: 480 cycles

Fig 7-9A: ADC sample time register (ADC_SMPR1) to set sampling time

31	30	29	28	27	26	25	24	23	22	21	20	19	18	17	16
Res	Res	SMP9[2:0]			SMP8[2:0]			SMP7[2:0]			SMP6[2:0]			SMP5[2:1]	
		rw	rw	rw	rw	rw	rw	rw	rw	rw	rw	rw	rw	rw	rw

15	14	13	12	11	10	9	8	7	6	5	4	3	2	1	0
SMP5_0	SMP4[2:0]			SMP3[2:0]			SMP2[2:0]			SMP1[2:0]			SMP0[2:0]		
rw	rw	rw	rw	rw	rw	rw	rw	rw	rw	rw	rw	rw	rw	rw	rw

000: 3 cycles	100: 84 cycles
001: 15 cycles	101: 112 cycles
010: 28 cycles	110: 144 cycles
011: 56 cycles	111: 480 cycles

Fig 7-9B: ADC sample time register (ADC_SMPR2) to set sampling time

In the conversion phase, the analog input is converted to binary numbers. In this phase, the number of clocks required depends on ADC resolution namely the number of bits of the binary output 6, 8, 10, or 12. For a successive approximation converter in the STM32F4xx chips, the time is proportional to the number of bits. For example, if we use the default of 3 clock cycle for sample time with the 8-bit ADC resolution, the total number of clocks needed for ADC conversion is 11 clocks.

Selecting Bit Resolution

We use RES bits (D25-D24) of ADC_CR1 register to select 6, 8, 10, or 12-bit ADC resolution. The default is 12-bit. See Figure 7-10 and Table 7-5.

207

31	30	29	28	27	26	25	24	23	22	21	20	19	18	17	16
Res	Res	Res	Res	Res	OVRIE	RES		AWDEN	JAWDEN	Res	Res	Res	Res	Res	Res
					rw	rw	rw	rw	rw						

15	14	13	12	11	10	9	8	7	6	5	4	3	2	1	0
DISCNUM[2:0]			JDISCEN	DISCEN	JAUTO	AWDSGL	SCAN	JEOCIE	AWDIE	EOCIE	AWDCH[4:0]				
rw	rw	rw	rw	rw	rw	rw	rw	rw	rw	rw	rw	rw	rw	rw	rw

Bit 26 **OVRIE:** Overrun interrupt enable

This bit is set and cleared by software to enable/disable the Overrun interrupt.

0: Overrun interrupt disabled

1: Overrun interrupt enabled. An interrupt is generated when the OVR bit is set.

Bits 25:24 **RES[1:0]:** Resolution

These bits are written by software to select the resolution of the conversion.

00: 12-bit (minimum 15 ADCCLK cycles)

01: 10-bit (minimum 13 ADCCLK cycles)

10: 8-bit (minimum 11 ADCCLK cycles)

11: 6-bit (minimum 9 ADCCLK cycles)

Bit 23 **AWDEN:** Analog watchdog enable on regular channels

This bit is set and cleared by software.

0: Analog watchdog disabled on regular channels

1: Analog watchdog enabled on regular channels

Bit 5 **EOCIE:** Interrupt enable for EOC

This bit is set and cleared by software to enable/disable the end of conversion interrupt.

0: EOC interrupt disabled

1: EOC interrupt enabled. An interrupt is generated when the EOC bit is set.

Bits 4:0 **AWDCH[4:0]:** Analog watchdog channel select bits

These bits are set and cleared by software. They select the input channel to be guarded by the analog watchdog.

Note: 00000: ADC analog input Channel0

00001: ADC analog input Channel1

...

01111: ADC analog input Channel15

10000: ADC analog input Channel16

10001: ADC analog input Channel17

10010: ADC analog input Channel18

Other values reserved

Figure 7-10: Control 1 (ADC_CR1) Register (Not all bits are shown)

RES (bits 25-24)	Description
0x0	12-bit result
0x1	10-bit result
0x2	8-bit result
0x3	6-bit result

Table 7-5: ADC bit Resolution Selection in ADC_CR1 register

Choosing input channel

The STM32F4xx Arm chip supports up to 16 ADC Input (AIN0-AIN15) single-ended channel pins connected to external analog signals. It also supports few more internal ADC options such as on-chip temperature sensor. In order to disable the digital functions, the pins selected as analog input must have their pin multiplexing (discussed in Chapter 2) set as analog input (option 11 in GPIOx_MODER). Just like other cases, we use GPIOx_MODER registers to select pin multiplexing. After making sure that the input pin is set for the analog option, we use the ADC_CR1 register to select the desired channel to convert to digital. The AWDCH (Analog watchdog channel select) bits (D4-D0) of ADC_CR1 register shows all the ADC options supported by the STM32F4xx. Notice that in addition to STM32F4xx pins usable for analog input, it also supports the temperature and VBAT use by ADC. We will discuss the temperature option at the end of this section. Table 7-8 lists the mapping between the analog input channels to the I/O pins.

Bit	Description		
	ADC Channel Input Selection		
	AWDCH[4:0]	Port PIN	Analog Input Channel
	0x00	PA0	ADC AIN0
	0x01	PA1	ADC AIN1
	0x02	PA2	ADC AIN2
	0x03	PA3	ADC AIN3
	0x04	PA4	ADC AIN4
	0x05	PA5	ADC AIN5
	0x06	PA6	ADC AIN6
	0x07	PA7	ADC AIN7
4-0	0x08	PB0	ADC AIN8
	0x09	PB1	ADC AIN9
	0x0A	PC0	ADC AIN10
	0x0B	PC1	ADC AIN11
	0x0C	PC2	ADC AIN12
	0x0D	PC3	ADC AIN13
	0x0E	PC4	ADC AIN14
	0x0F	PC5	ADC AIN15
	0x10	Temperature (internal)	ADC AIN16
	0x11	VREFINT (internal)	ADC AIN17
	0x12	VBAT (internal)	ADC AIN18

Table 7-6: Control R1 (ADC_CR1) Register bits for ADC Channel Selection

I/O Pin	ADC	I/O Pin	ADC
PA0	AIN[0]	PC0	AIN[10]
PA1	AIN[1]	PC1	AIN[11]
PA2	AIN[2]	PC2	AIN[12]
PA3	AIN[3]	PC3	AIN[13]

PA4	AIN[4]	**PC4**	AIN[14]
PA5	AIN[5]	**PC5**	AIN[15]
PA6	AIN[6]		
PA7	AIN[7]		
PB0	AIN[8]		
PB1	AIN[9]		

Table 7-7: Analog input pin assignment in STM32F4xx

31	30	29	28	27	26	25	24	23	22	21	20	19	18	17	16
MODER15[1:0]		MODER14[1:0]		MODER13[1:0]		MODER12[1:0]		MODER11[1:0]		MODER10[1:0]		MODER9[1:0]		MODER8[1:0]	
rw	rw	rw	rw	rw	rw	rw	rw	rw	rw	rw	rw	rw	rw	rw	rw

15	14	13	12	11	10	9	8	7	6	5	4	3	2	1	0
MODER7[1:0]		MODER6[1:0]		MODER5[1:0]		MODER4[1:0]		MODER3[1:0]		MODER2[1:0]		MODER1[1:0]		MODER0[1:0]	
rw	rw	rw	rw	rw	rw	rw	rw	rw	rw	rw	rw	rw	rw	rw	rw

Bits 2y:2y+1 **MODERy[1:0]:** Port x configuration bits (y = 0..15)

These bits are written by software to configure the I/O direction mode.

00: Input (reset state)

01: General purpose output mode

10: Alternate function mode

11: Analog mode

Figure 7-11: GPIO_MODER Register

ADC Conversion Result Register

Upon the completion of a conversion, the result is placed in the DATA registers. Although the DATA register is a 32-bit wide but only the lower 12 bits are used and upper 18 bits are unused. For the ADC, we have the options of 6- ,8-, 10-, and 12-bit for a single-ended unsigned result. When ADC is configured for 12-bit, the result is right-justified and the unused bits are filled with 0s. That means for 12-bit option the bits D11-D0 hold the binary output result of ADC conversion and D31-D12 bits are zeroes. In the case of 10-bit, D31-D10 bits are zeroes, and D9-D0 has the result. For 8-bit the D7-D0 is our converted data while D31-D8 are all 0s. See Figure 7-14.

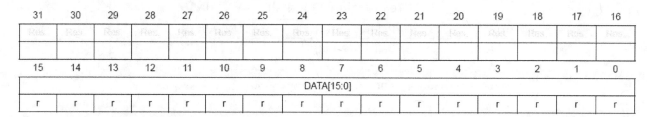

Bits 31:16 Reserved, must be kept at reset value.

Bits 15:0 **DATA[15:0]:** Regular data

These bits are read-only. They contain the conversion result from the regular channels.

The data are left- or right-aligned.

Figure 7-12: ADC_DR (ADC Data Register) register holds conversion result

Right or Left Justified Result

Another important bit of the Control 2 (ADC_CR2) register is the ALIGN bit. The ALIGN bit in CR2 register allows the binary output result of ADC conversion to be moved to the left. The left justified option makes the signed value calculation easier. The default is right justified. See figure below.

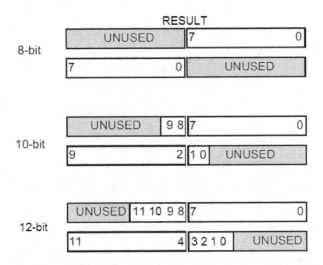

Figure 7-13: ADC_DR (DATA) Register has the result and can be Right and Left Justified

Enable the ADC

The ADC is "off" upon reset. Bit D0 of ADC_CR2 register is used to turn on the ADC module. See Figure 7-14.

31	30	29	28	27	26	25	24	23	22	21	20	19	18	17	16
Res	SWSTART	EXTEN		EXTSEL[3:0]				Res	JSWSTART	JEXTEN		JEXTSEL[3:0]			
	rw	rw	rw	rw	rw	rw	rw		rw	rw	rw	rw	rw	rw	rw

15	14	13	12	11	10	9	8	7	6	5	4	3	2	1	0
Res	Res	Res	Res	ALIGN	EOCS	DDS	DMA	Res	Res	Res	Res	Res	Res	CONT	ADON
				rw	rw	rw	rw							rw	rw

Bit 11 **ALIGN:** Data alignment

This bit is set and cleared by software. Refer to *Figure 75* and *Figure 76*.

0: Right alignment

1: Left alignment

Bit 10 **EOCS:** End of conversion selection

This bit is set and cleared by software.

0: The EOC bit is set at the end of each sequence of regular conversions. Overrun detection is enabled only if DMA=1.

1: The EOC bit is set at the end of each regular conversion. Overrun detection is enabled.

Bit 1 **CONT:** Continuous conversion

This bit is set and cleared by software. If it is set, conversion takes place continuously until it is cleared.

0: Single conversion mode

1: Continuous conversion mode

Bit 0 **ADON:** A/D Converter ON / OFF

This bit is set and cleared by software.

Note: 0: Disable ADC conversion and go to power down mode

1: Enable ADC

Figure 7-14: ADC_CR2 (ADC Control 2) register

Start Conversion trigger options

There are two ways to start an A-to-D conversion in STM32F4xx. They are manually and automatically. The manual trigger is done by writing a 1 to the SWSTART (Start conversion of regular channels) in ADC_CR1 register. The ADC can also be triggered automatically by an event. Using a timer event to trigger the conversion will give a more precise sampling interval.

A free-running mode could be used by setting the CONT (Continuous conversion) bit in ADC_CR1 register. This bit is set and cleared by software. If it is set, a conversion takes place continuously of an input channel. There is no need for a trigger to start the conversion. It will start automatically at the end of the previous conversion.

Conversion Complete (End of Conversion, EOC)

The end-of-conversion (EOC) is indicated by the EOC flag bit in ADC_SR (ADC Status Register) register. This bit is set by ADC itself at the end of each conversion of a channel. It is cleared by software or by reading the ADC_DR (ADC Data) register. See Figure 7-15 and Table 7-8.

31	30	29	28	27	26	25	24	23	22	21	20	19	18	17	16
Res.	Res.	Res.	Res.	Res.	Res.	Res.	Res.	Res.	Res.	Res.	Res.	Res.	Res.	Res.	Res.

15	14	13	12	11	10	9	8	7	6	5	4	3	2	1	0
Res.	Res.	Res.	Res.	Res.	Res.	Res.	Res.	Res.	Res.	OVR	STRT	JSTRT	JEOC	EOC	AWD
										rc_w0	rc_w0	rc_w0	rc_w0	rc_w0	rc_w0

Figure 7-15: ADC_SR(ADC Status g) Register for End-of-Conversion (See table below)

Bit	Field	Descriptions
5	OVR	Overrun This bit is set by hardware when data are lost. This happens if we do not read the result of the last conversion from the Data Register (ADC_DR). It is cleared by software. 0: No overrun occurred 1: Overrun has occurred
1	EOC	End of Conversion 0: Conversion not complete 1: Conversion complete Writing a zero to this bit will clear it or by reading the ADC_DR register.

Table 7-8: ADC_SR (Status) Register Bits

Upon the completion of a conversion, the EOC flag bit goes high indicating that the conversion Data result register is loaded with a new value. By polling this flag, we know if the conversion is complete and we can read the value in the DATA register. This flag bit is cleared (goes LOW) when the result in ADC_DR (ADC Data register) register is read. In this section, we use polling to see if the conversion result is ready. We can also use an interrupt to inform us that the conversion is complete. We can use EOCIE (EOC Interrupt enable) bit in ADC_CR1 register to enable the interrupt option. By default, the interrupt option is not enabled since an interrupt handler is required before the interrupt can be enabled.

To avoid data loss if more than one conversion is enabled, the conversion result must be read as it becomes available (EOC is set in ADC_SR register). Failing to do so will result in an overrun error condition, indicated by the OVR (Overrun) flag bit in the ADC_SR status register.

V_{ref} in STM32F4xx

In the STM32F4xx Arm chip, the reference voltage pins for ADC are called VREF+ and VREF-. The external reference VREF+ can be connected to external reference voltage such as VDD and the VREF- is connected to ground. Notice that ADC input(Vin) range must not exceed VREF $-\ \leqslant$ VIN $\leqslant$ VREF+. There is also internal reference voltage, which can be programmed. See the STM32F4xx reference manual.

If we connect the VREF(+) to an external voltage other than the V_{DD} of the chip, it cannot go beyond the V_{DD} voltage. The positive reference voltage (VREF+) for the ADC must be in the range of 1.8 V $\leqslant$ VREF+ $\leqslant$ VDDA while the negative reference voltage for the ADC is VREF− = VSSA. With VREF+=3.3V, we have the step size of 3.3V / 4,096 = 0.8 mV since the maximum ADC resolution for STM32F4xx is 12-bit. See Example 7-2.

Example 7-2

Give the digital converted output if the ADC input channel voltage is 1.2V for the STM32F4xx with VREF+ = 3.3V.

Solution:

Since the step size is 3.3V / 4,096 = 0.8 mV, we have 1.2V / 0.80 mV = 1,489 = 0x5D1 as ADC output.

Configuring ADC and reading ADC channel

The following steps are used to configure the ADC to perform A-to-D conversion on analog channel x (pin Px.y). These steps are implemented in Program 7-1.

1. Enable ADC clock to ADC in RCC_APB2ENR register.
2. Configure ADC right adjusted result (ALIGN), free running conversion (CONT, continuous conversion) using ADC_CR2 register.
3. Using ADC_CR1 register, select the resolution and the analog input channel.
4. Use GPIOx_MODER register to configure input pin for analog input channel.

5. Using ADC_CR2 register Enable the ADC (ADON) and START (SWSTART) to start the conversion.
6. Monitor the EOC flag in the ADC_SR register for end-of-conversion.
7. When the EOC flag goes HIGH, read the ADC data result from the ADC_DR register and save it.
8. Repeat steps 6 through 7 for the next conversion.

Program 7-1 illustrates the steps for ADC conversion shown above. Figure 7-16 shows the hardware connection for Program 7-1.

Program 7-1: Using ADC to convert an input channel

```
/* p7_1.c: A to D conversion of channel 1

 * This program converts the analog input from channel 1.
 * Channel 1 is connected to input from PA1.
 * Clock prescaler is left at 0 (divided by 2) and Sampling
 * time is also left at default of 3 cycles.
 * Software trigger is used. The bit 8 of the conversion
 * result is used to turn on/off the LED0. For the full
 * scale of the reference voltage, the LED0 should be on
 * for 8 times.
 *
 * This program was tested with Keil uVision v5.24a with DFP v2.11.0.
 */

#include "stm32f4xx.h"

int main (void) {
    int result;

    /* set up pin PA5 for LED */
    RCC->AHB1ENR |= 1;                  /* enable GPIOA clock */
    GPIOA->MODER &= ~0x00000C00;        /* clear pin mode */
    GPIOA->MODER |= 0x00000400;         /* set pin to output mode */

    /* set up pin PA1 for analog input */
    RCC->AHB1ENR |= 1;                  /* enable GPIOA clock */
    GPIOA->MODER |= 0xC;                /* PA1 analog */

    /* setup ADC1 */
    RCC->APB2ENR |= 0x00000100;         /* enable ADC1 clock */
    ADC1->CR2 = 0;                      /* SW trigger */
    ADC1->SQR3 = 1;                     /* conversion sequence starts at ch 1 */
    ADC1->SQR1 = 0;                     /* conversion sequence length 1 */
    ADC1->CR2 |= 1;                     /* enable ADC1 */

    while (1) {
        ADC1->CR2 |= 0x40000000;        /* start a conversion */
        while(!(ADC1->SR & 2)) {}       /* wait for conv complete */
        result = ADC1->DR;              /* read conversion result */
        if (result & 0x100)
            GPIOA->BSRR = 0x00000020;   /* turn on LED */
        else
            GPIOA->BSRR = 0x00200000;   /* turn off LED */
    }
```

```
}
```

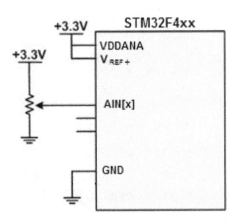

Figure 7-16: ADC Connection for Program 7-1

Internal Temperature sensor

The STM32F4xx chip comes with an internal temperature sensor on-chip. It is connected to channel 0x16. The on-chip temperature sensor is controlled by the ADC_CCR register. In order to use the temperature sensor, we need to turn on the TSVREFE (Temperature Sensor and VREF internal) bit in the ADC common control register (ADC_CCR) register. See Figure 7-17 and Table 7-9.

31	30	29	28	27	26	25	24	23	22	21	20	19	18	17	16
Res.	Res.	Res.	Res.	Res.	Res.	Res.	Res.	TSVREFE	VBATE	Res.	Res.	Res.	Res.	ADCPRE	
								rw	rw					rw	rw

15	14	13	12	11	10	9	8	7	6	5	4	3	2	1	0
DMA[1:0]		DDS	Res	DELAY[3:0]				Res	Res	Res	MULTI[4:0]				
rw	rw	rw		rw	rw	rw	rw				rw	rw	rw	rw	rw

Figure 7-17: ADC common control register (ADC_CCR) register (See table below)

Bit	Field	Descriptions
22	TSVREFE:	**Temperature Sensor and VREINT Enable** This bit is set and cleared by software to enable/disable the temperature sensor and the VREFINT channel. 0: Temperature sensor and VREFINT channel disabled. 1: Temperature sensor and VREFINT channel enabled.
23	VBATE: VBAT enable	**VBAT enable** 0: VBAT channel disabled. 1: VBAT channel enabled.

17:16	**ADCPRE:** ADC prescaler Set and cleared by software to select the frequency of the clock to the ADC. The clock is common for all the ADCs. 00: PCLK2 divided by 2 01: PCLK2 divided by 4 10: PCLK2 divided by 6 11: PCLK2 divided by 8

Table 7-9: ADC common control register (ADC_CCR) register

To use the sensor:

1. Select ADC1_ 18 input channel.

2. Select a sampling time greater than the minimum sampling time specified in the datasheet.

3. Set the TSVREFE bit in the ADC_CCR register to wake up the temperature sensor from power down mode

4. Start the ADC conversion by setting the SWSTART bit (or by external trigger)

5. Read the resulting VSENSE data in the ADC data register

6. Calculate the temperature using the following formula:

Temperature (in °C) = {(VSENSE – V25) / Avg_Slope} + 25

Where:

– V25 = VSENSE value for 25° C

– Avg_Slope = average slope of the temperature vs. VSENSE curve (given in mV/°C or µV/°C)

The next program shows how to convert the internal temperature sensor output. The conversion result is stored in a global variable result for observation by the debugger.

Program 7-2: Converting the on-chip temperature sensor with timer trigger

```
/* p7_2.c: On-chip temperature sensor
 * This program converts the on-chip temperature sensor output
 * and display the temperture in Celcius on the console.
 * Timer TIM2 is configured to generate 1 Hz output, which is
 * used to trigger the A/D conversion. The internal temperature
 * sensor is connected to channel 18 of ADC1 Master. The sensor
 * is turned on at bit 23 of ADC_CCR register.
 *
 * The conversion result is displayed as Celcius using the
 * formula and parameters in the datasheet on the console.
 * The console UART driver is from Program 4-5.
 *
 * This program was tested with Keil uVision v5.24a with DFP v2.11.0.
 */

#include "stm32f4xx.h"
#include <stdio.h>

void USART2_init(void);
int USART2_write(int c);

int main(void) {
    int data;
```

```c
    double volt, temp;

    RCC->AHB1ENR |= 1;                  /* enable GPIOA clock */


    /* setup TIM2 */
    RCC->APB1ENR |= 1;                  /* enable TIM2 clock */
    TIM2->PSC = 1600 - 1;               /* divided by 1600 */
    TIM2->ARR = 10000 - 1;              /* divided by 10000, sample at 1 Hz */
    TIM2->CNT = 0;
    TIM2->CCMR1 = 0x00006800;           /* pwm1 mode,  preload enable */
    TIM2->CCER = 0x0010;                /* ch2 enable */
    TIM2->CCR2 = 50 - 1;
    TIM2->CR1 = 1;                      /* enable timer2 */


    /* setup ADC1 */
    RCC->APB2ENR |= 0x00000100;         /* enable ADC1 clock */
    /* turn on the temp sensor */
    ADC->CCR |= 0x800000;
    ADC->CCR &= ~0x400000;              /* VBATE must be disabled for temp sensor */
    /* configure A to D converter */
    ADC1->SMPR1 = 0x4000000;            /* sampling time minimum 10 us */
    ADC1->SQR3 = 18;                    /* ch18 - internal temp sensor, single channel */
    ADC1->CR2 = 0x13000000;             /* trigger: EXTEN rising edge, EXTSEL 3 = tim2.2
*/
    ADC1->CR2 |= 1;                     /* enable ADC1 */


    /* initialize USART2 for output */
    USART2_init();
    printf("ADC internal temperature sensor \r\n");


    while(1) {
        while(!(ADC1->SR & 2)) {}
        data = ADC1->DR;
        /* Temperature (in °C) = {(VSENSE - V25) / Avg_Slope} + 25 */
        /* V25 = 0.76V, slope = 2.5 mV/C */
        volt = (double)data / 4095 * 3.3;   /* convert ADC output to voltage */
        temp = (volt - 0.76) / 0.0025 + 25; /* convert voltage to temperature C */
        printf("%d, %.2f\370C\r\n", data, temp);    /* octal 370 is degree sign in
extended ASCII */
    }
}

/* initialize USART2 to transmit at 9600 Baud */
void USART2_init (void) {
    RCC->AHB1ENR |= 1;              /* Enable GPIOA clock */
    RCC->APB1ENR |= 0x20000;        /* Enable USART2 clock */


    /* Configure PA2 for USART2_TX */
    GPIOA->AFR[0] &= ~0x0F00;
    GPIOA->AFR[0] |=  0x0700        /* alt7 for USART2 */
    GPIOA->MODER  &= ~0x0030;
    GPIOA->MODER  |=  0x0020;       /* enable alternate function for PA2 */


    USART2->BRR = 0x0683;           /* 9600 baud @ 16 MHz */
    USART2->CR1 = 0x000C;           /* enable Tx, Rx, 8-bit data */
    USART2->CR2 = 0x0000;           /* 1 stop bit */
    USART2->CR3 = 0x0000;           /* no flow control */
```

```
        USART2->CR1 |= 0x2000;        /* enable USART2 */
}

/* Write a character to USART2 */
int USART2_write (int ch) {
    while (!(USART2->SR & 0x0080)) {}    /* wait until Tx buffer empty */
    USART2->DR = ch;
    return ch;
}

/* The code below is the interface to the C standard I/O library.
 * All the I/O are directed to the console, which is UART2.
 */
struct __FILE { int handle; };
FILE __stdout = {1};

/* Called by C library console/file output */
int fputc(int c, FILE *f) {
    return USART2_write(c);   /* write the character to console */
}
```

Multiple Conversions Accumulation and Averaging

The ADC in STM32F4xx is capable of performing sequences of multiple conversions of a given channel and provides the average of the results. Signal averaging is a way of increasing the signal to noise ratio for random noise. When multiple samples are added together, the random noise tends to cancel each other. The cost of doing signal averaging is the reduced maximum sampling rate because multiple conversions are needed for one result. For the details of programming the multiple conversion option, we will leave it to the reader.

Analog Comparator

In some applications such as a thermostat, the actual value of the analog input signal is not important rather whether the input voltage is higher or lower than a preset value is essential for the operation. In these cases, a comparator is more efficient than doing a conversion than compare the result against the preset value.

Many microcontrollers come with analog comparator for monitoring an analog input voltage. Using the analog comparator, we can monitor an analog input against two threshold values to determine whether the analog input value is above the high threshold, between the two threshold values, or below the low threshold. When the analog input falls in the selected region, the comparator may trigger an interrupt to get the attention of the CPU. Using analog comparator, the software does not have to continuously monitor the analog input.

For example, we may program the comparator for the on-chip temperature sensor. When the temperature exceeds a preset threshold, the cooling fan is turned on. When the temperature drops below the threshold, the cooling fan is turned off. The software only has to set the thresholds once and handle the interrupts. It does not have to use the ADC to monitor the temperature continuously. If the microcontroller has no other tasks to run, it may go into the low power mode to conserve energy.

For the details of programming the analog comparator unit, we will leave it to the reader.

Differential versus Single-Ended

In some applications, our interest is in the differences between two analog signal voltages (the differential voltages). Rather than converting two channels and calculate the differences between them, the STM32F4xx has the option of converting the differential voltages of two analog channels. Upon Reset, the default is the single-ended input and we will leave it at that. In single-ended mode, the input voltage must be positive and can use the full 12-bit conversion output. The negative input should be connected to ground.

Review Questions

1. The ADC in STM32F4xx is _____bit.
2. In STM32F4xx, the highest number we can get for the ADC output is_____ in hex.
3. Assume VREF+= 3.3V. Find the ADC output in decimal and hex if V_{in} of analog input is 1.9V. Assume 12-bit resolution.
4. In STM32F4xx, which register provides the ADC output converted data?
5. In STM32F4xx, we have resolution choices of _____.

Section 7.3: Sensor Interfacing and Signal Conditioning

This section will show how to interface external sensors to the microcontroller. We examine some popular temperature sensors and then discuss the issue of signal conditioning. Although we concentrate on temperature sensors, the principles discussed in this section are the same for other types of sensors such as light or pressure sensors.

Temperature sensors

Sensors convert physical parameters such as temperature, light intensity, flow, and speed to electrical signals. Depending on the sensor, the output produced is in the form of voltage, current, resistance, or capacitance. For example, the temperature may be converted to electrical signals using a sensor called thermistor. A thermistor responds to temperature change by changing its resistance, but its response is not linear, as seen in Table 7-10 and Figure 7-18.

Temperature ('C)	Tf (K ohms)
0	29.490
25	10.000
50	3.893
75	1.700
100	0.817

Table 7-10: Thermistor Resistance vs. Temperature

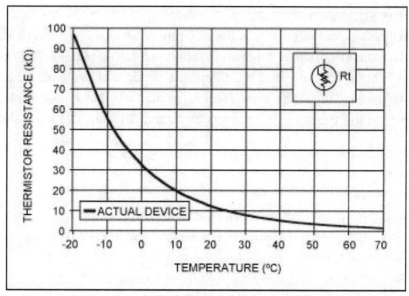

Figure 7-18: Thermistor (Copied from http://www.maximintegrated.com)

The resistance of a thermistor is typically modeled by Steinhart-Hart equation and requires a logarithmic amplifier to produce a linear output. The complexity associated with the circuit for such nonlinear devices has led some manufacturers to market linear temperature sensors. Simple and widely used linear temperature sensors include the LM34 and LM35 from Texas Instruments. They are discussed next.

LM34 and LM35 temperature sensors

The LM34 sensor is a precision integrated-circuit temperature sensor whose output voltage is linearly proportional to the temperature in Fahrenheit. See Figure 7-19. The LM34 requires no external calibration because it is internally calibrated. It outputs 10 mV for each degree of Fahrenheit temperature.

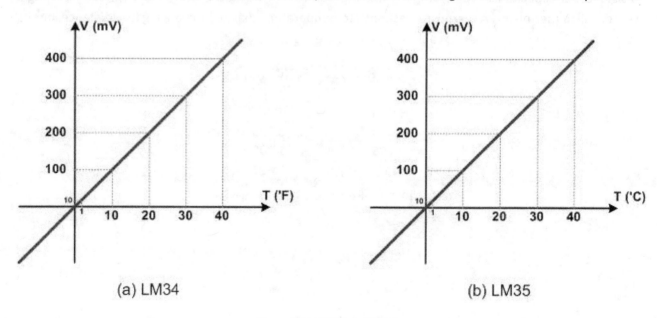

Figure 7-19: LM34 and LM35

The LM35 sensor is similar to LM34 except that the output voltage is linearly proportional to the temperature in Celsius (centigrade). It outputs 10 mV for each degree of Celsius temperature.

Signal conditioning

The common transducers produce an output in the form of voltage, current, charge, capacitance, or resistance. In order to perform A-to-D conversion on these signals, they need to be converted to voltage unless the transducer output is already voltage. In addition to the conversion to voltage, the signal may also need gain and offset adjustments to achieve optimal dynamic range. A low-pass analog filter is often incorporated in the signal conditioning circuit to eliminate the high frequency to avoid aliasing. Figure 7-20 shows a block diagram of the input of a data acquisition system.

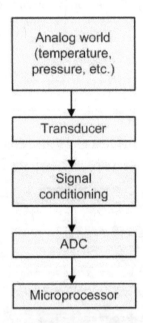

Figure 7-20: Getting analog data to the CPU

Interfacing the LM34 to the STM32F4xx Arm Microcontroller

The A/D of STM32F4xx Arm Microcontroller has 12-bit resolution with a maximum of 4,096 steps, and the LM34 produces 10 mV for every degree of temperature change. The maximum operating temperature of the LM34 is 300 degrees F, so the highest output will be 3,000 mV (3.00 V), which is below 3.3V of V_{ref+}. The LM34/35 can be connected to the microcontroller as shown in Figure 7-21.

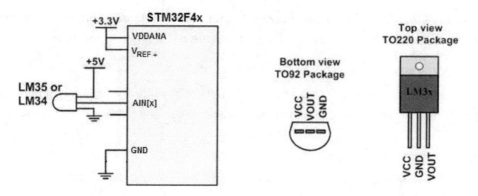

Figure 7-21: LM34/35 Connection to Arm and Its Pin Configuration

To convert the ADC result to temperature in degree, use the following equation:

$$temperature = \frac{result \times 330}{4096}$$

Reading and displaying temperature

Programs 7-3 shows the code for reading and displaying temperature in F with the LM34. Notice that in Figure 7-21, the LM34 (or LM35) must be connected to PC0 (channel 10) 12-bit conversion is used.

Program 7-3: Reading Temperature Sensor of LM34

```
/* p7_3.c: LM34 Fahrenheit temperature sensor
 *
 * LM34 is a Fahrenheit temperature sensor with the output of
 * 10 mV/degreeF. The program assumes an LM34 connected to
 * pin PC0 (channel 10). The conversion result is displayed one
 * the console as degree Fahrenheit.
 * The console UART driver is from Program 4-5.
 * This program was tested with Keil uVision v5.24a with DFP v2.11.0.
 */

#include "stm32f4xx.h"
#include <stdio.h>

void USART2_init(void);
int USART2_write(int c);
void delayMs(int n);

int main (void) {
    int result;
    double temp;

    /* set up pin PC0 for analog input */
    RCC->AHB1ENR |=  4;                 /* enable GPIOC clock */
    GPIOC->MODER |=  3;                 /* PC0 analog */

    /* setup ADC1 */
    RCC->APB2ENR |= 0x00000100;         /* enable ADC1 clock */
    ADC1->CR2 = 0;                      /* SW trigger */
    ADC1->SQR3 = 10;                    /* single conversion ch 10 */
```

```c
        ADC1->SQR1 = 0;                        /* conversion sequence length 1 */
        ADC1->CR2 |= 1;                        /* enable ADC1 */

        /* initialize USART2 for output */
        USART2_init();
        printf("LM34 Temperature Sensor\r\n");

        while (1) {
            ADC1->CR2 |= 0x40000000;           /* start a conversion */
            while(!(ADC1->SR & 2)) {}          /* wait for conv complete */
            result = ADC1->DR;                 /* read conversion result */
            temp = (double)result / 4095 * 330;
            printf("%d, %.2f\r\n", result, temp);
            delayMs(1000);
        }
}
/* initialize USART2 to transmit at 9600 Baud */
void USART2_init (void) {
        RCC->AHB1ENR |= 1;              /* Enable GPIOA clock */
        RCC->APB1ENR |= 0x20000;       /* Enable USART2 clock */

        /* Configure PA2 for USART2_TX */
        GPIOA->AFR[0] &= ~0x0F00;
        GPIOA->AFR[0] |=  0x0700;      /* alt7 for USART2 */
        GPIOA->MODER  &= ~0x0030;
        GPIOA->MODER  |=  0x0020;      /* enable alternate function for PA2 */
        USART2->BRR = 0x0683;          /* 9600 baud @ 16 MHz */
        USART2->CR1 = 0x000C;          /* enable Tx, Rx, 8-bit data */
        USART2->CR2 = 0x0000;          /* 1 stop bit */
        USART2->CR3 = 0x0000;          /* no flow control */
        USART2->CR1 |= 0x2000;         /* enable USART2 */
}
/* Write a character to USART2 */
int USART2_write (int ch) {
        while (!(USART2->SR & 0x0080)) {}   // wait until Tx buffer empty
        USART2->DR = ch;
        return ch;
}
/* The code below is the interface to the C standard I/O library.
 * All the I/O are directed to the console, which is UART2.
 */
struct __FILE { int handle; };
FILE __stdout = {1};

/* Called by C library console/file output */
int fputc(int c, FILE *f) {
        return USART2_write(c);  /* write the character to console */
}

/* 16 MHz SYSCLK */
void delayMs(int n) {
        int i;
        for (; n > 0; n--)
            for (i = 0; i < 3195; i++) ;
}
```

Review Questions

1. True or false. The transducer must be connected to signal conditioning circuitry before its signal is sent to the ADC.
2. The LM35 provides ____ mV for each degree of _____ (Fahrenheit, Celsius) temperature.
3. The LM34 provides ____ mV for each degree of _____ (Fahrenheit, Celsius) temperature.
4. What is the temperature if the ADC output is 0000 0011 1110?

Section 7.4: Interfacing to a DAC

This section will discuss the fundamentals of a digital-to-analog converter (DAC). Then we demonstrate how to generate a sawtooth wave and a sine wave using the DAC.

Digital-to-analog (DAC) converter

The digital-to-analog converter (DAC) is a device used to convert digital signals to analog signals. In this section we discuss the basics of a DAC.

Recall from digital electronics, the two methods of making a DAC: binary weighted and R/2R ladder. The vast majority of integrated circuit DACs, including the DAC0808 in this section, use the R/2R method since it can achieve a much higher degree of precision. The first criterion for selecting a DAC is its resolution, which is a function of the number of bits of the digital input. The common ones are 8, 10, and 12 bits. The number of digital input bits decides the resolution of the DAC since the number of analog output levels is equal to 2^n, where n is the number of digital input bits. Therefore, the 8-bit DAC such as the DAC0808 provides 256 discrete voltage (or current) levels of output. See Figure 7-22.

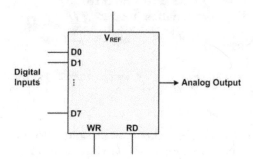

Figure 7-22: DAC Block Diagram

Similarly, the 12-bit DAC provides 4096 discrete voltage levels. Although there are 16-bit and 18-bit DACs, they are much more expensive.

DAC0808

In the DAC0808, the digital inputs are converted to current (I_{OUT}). By connecting a resistor to the I_{OUT} pin, we convert the conversion result current to voltage. The total current provided by the I_{OUT} is a function of the binary numbers at the D0–D7 inputs of the DAC0808 and the reference current (I_{ref}), and is as follows:

$$I_{OUT} = I_{ref} \times \left(\frac{D7}{2} + \frac{D6}{4} + \frac{D5}{8} + \frac{D4}{16} + \frac{D3}{32} + \frac{D2}{64} + \frac{D1}{128} + \frac{D0}{256}\right) = I_{ref} \times \frac{Data}{256}$$

where D0 is the LSB, D7 is the MSB for the inputs, and I_{ref} is the reference input current that must be applied to pin 14. The I_{ref} current is generally set to 2.0 mA. Figure 7-23 shows the generation of current reference (setting I_{ref} = 2 mA) by using the standard 5-V power supply and 5K ohm resistors.

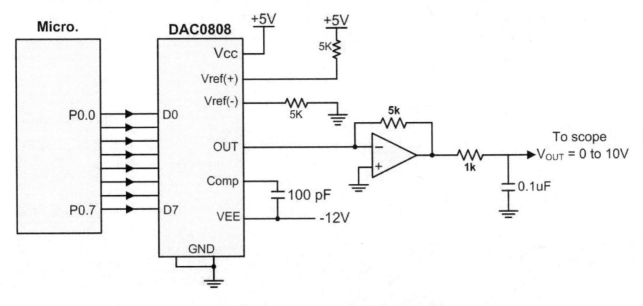

Figure 7-23: Microcontroller Connection to DAC0808

Some also use the Zener diode reference voltage device (LM336), which overcomes fluctuations associated with the power supply voltage. Now assuming that I_{ref} = 2 mA, if all the input bits to the DAC are high, the maximum output current is 1.99 mA (verify this for yourself).

Converting I_{out} to voltage in DAC0808

We connect the output pin I_{OUT} to a resistor, convert this current to voltage, and monitor the output on the scope. However, in real life this can cause inaccuracy since the input resistance of the load will also affect the output voltage. For this reason, the I_{ref} current output is buffered by connecting it to an op-amp with R_f = 5K ohms for the feedback resistor. Assuming that R = 5K ohms, by changing the binary input, the output voltage changes as shown in Example 7-4.

Example 7-4

Assuming that R = 5K and I_{ref} = 2 mA, calculate V_{out} for the following binary inputs:
(a) 10011001 binary (0x99)   (b) 11001000 (0xC8)

Solution:
(a) I_{out} = 2 mA (153/255) = 1.195 mA and V_{out} = 1.195 mA × 5K = 5.975 V
(b) I_{out} = 2 mA (200/256) = 1.562 mA and V_{out} = 1.562 mA × 5K = 7.8125 V

225

STM32 Arm On-chip DAC

Many of the STM32F4xx Arm chips have on-chip digital-to-analog converters (DACs). The STM32F446RE comes with two on-chip DACs. They can be configured for independent or simultaneous conversions. They are designated as DAC1 and DAC2. Each one has its own analog output pin. In STM32F446RE, the analog out pins are PA4 and PA5 for chan1 and chan2, respectively. On-chip DAC has 12-bit resolution but it can also be configured as an 8-bit DAC too. That means digital data loaded into DAC register can be 8- or 12-bit. The digital data can be right-justified or left-justified. The on-chip DACs use the same Vref+ voltage source as the ADC. See figure below.

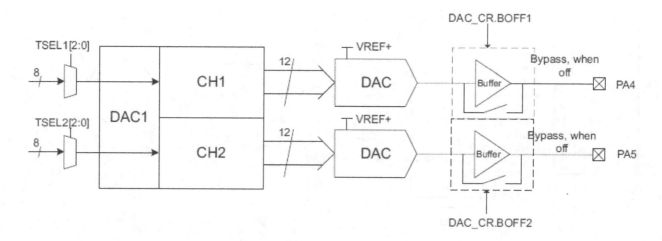

Figure 7-24: STM32F4xx DAC Block Diagram

The output voltage from the DAC can be calculated using the following formula:

$$V_{DAC} = \frac{DATA}{4096} \cdot VREF$$

The on-chip DACs use the same Vref+ voltage source as the ADC. Just like ADC, the reference voltage can internal or can come from outside source. Figure below shows the ADC_CR (ADC Control Register) register.

31	30	29	28	27	26	25	24	23	22	21	20	19	18	17	16
Res	Res	DMAU DRIE2	DMA EN2		MAMP2[3:0]			WAVE2[1:0]			TSEL2[2:0]		TEN2	BOFF2	EN2
		rw	rw	rw	rw	rw	rw	rw	rw	rw	rw	rw	rw	rw	rw

15	14	13	12	11	10	9	8	7	6	5	4	3	2	1	0
Res	Res	DMAU DRIE1	DMA EN1		MAMP1[3:0]			WAVE1[1:0]			TSEL1[2:0]		TEN1	BOFF1	EN1
		rw	rw	rw	rw	rw	rw	rw	rw	rw	rw	rw	rw	rw	rw

Bit 18 **TEN2**: DAC channel2 trigger enable

This bit is set and cleared by software to enable/disable DAC channel2 trigger

0: DAC channel2 trigger disabled and data written into the DAC_DHRx register are transferred one APB1 clock cycle later to the DAC_DOR2 register

1: DAC channel2 trigger enabled and data from the DAC_DHRx register are transferred three APB1 clock cycles later to the DAC_DOR2 register

Bit 17 **BOFF2**: DAC channel2 output buffer disable

This bit is set and cleared by software to enable/disable DAC channel2 output buffer.

0: DAC channel2 output buffer enabled

1: DAC channel2 output buffer disabled

Bit 16 **EN2**: DAC channel2 enable

This bit is set and cleared by software to enable/disable DAC channel2.

0: DAC channel2 disabled

1: DAC channel2 enabled

Figure 7-25: DAC_CR (DAC Conntrol Register)

The most important bit in DAC_CR is the enable bit. From DAC_CR register notice each channel has its own Enable bit of EN1 and EN2. The conversion can be triggered a) internally by software, b) an external signal, or c) by one of the timers such as TIM2. The default is internally by software. The TENx bits in DAC_CR register is used to enable/disable DAC channelx trigger. In DAC_CR register, only if we make TENx=1, the TSELx (trigger selection) bits in DAC_CR are used for DAC trigger selection. If TENx=0, then we use bits of DAC software trigger register (DAC_SWTRIGR) to trigger the conversion from digital data to analog output.

To make programming easier, the STM32 Arm uses a large number of data registers. We separate registers for each of 12-bit right and left justified. The same for 8-bit option. The registers are called DAC Data Holding Registers (DAC_DHR). Writing new data into DAC holing register starts a conversion. Beside holding register, we also have DAC Data Output registers (DAC_DOR). We can only write to DAC_DHR register. According to STM32 reference manual "Data stored in the DAC_DHRx register are automatically transferred to the DAC_DORx register after one clock cycle." Again, according to reference manual "The Digital inputs are converted to output voltages on a linear conversion between 0 and VREF+. The analog output voltages on each DAC channel pin are determined by the following equation:

$$DACoutput = V_{REF} \times \frac{DOR}{4096}$$

DAC channel1 8-bit right aligned data holding register (DAC_DHR8R1)

31	30	29	28	27	26	25	24	23	22	21	20	19	18	17	16
Res.	Res.	Res.	Res.	Res.	Res.	Res.	Res.	Res.	Res.	Res.	Res.	Res.	Res.	Res.	Res.

15	14	13	12	11	10	9	8	7	6	5	4	3	2	1	0
Res.	Res.	Res.	Res.	Res.	Res.	Res.	Res.	DACC1DHR[7:0]							
								rw	rw	rw	rw	rw	rw	rw	rw

DAC channel2 8-bit right-aligned data holding register (DAC_DHR8R2)

31	30	29	28	27	26	25	24	23	22	21	20	19	18	17	16
Res	Res	Res	Res	Res	Res	Res	Res	Res	Res	Res	Res	Res	Res	Res	Res

15	14	13	12	11	10	9	8	7	6	5	4	3	2	1	0
Res	Res	Res	Res	Res	Res	Res	Res	DACC2DHR[7:0]							
								rw	rw	rw	rw	rw	rw	rw	rw

DAC channel1 12-bit right-aligned data holding register (DAC_DHR12R1)

31	30	29	28	27	26	25	24	23	22	21	20	19	18	17	16
Res	Res	Res	Res	Res	Res	Res	Res	Res	Res	Res	Res	Res	Res	Res	Res

15	14	13	12	11	10	9	8	7	6	5	4	3	2	1	0
Res	Res	Res	Res	DACC1DHR[11:0]											
				rw	rw	rw	rw	rw	rw	rw	rw	rw	rw	rw	rw

DAC channel2 12-bit right aligned data holding register (DAC_DHR12R2)

31	30	29	28	27	26	25	24	23	22	21	20	19	18	17	16
Res	Res	Res	Res	Res	Res	Res	Res	Res	Res	Res	Res	Res	Res	Res	Res

15	14	13	12	11	10	9	8	7	6	5	4	3	2	1	0
Res	Res	Res	Res	DACC2DHR[11:0]											
				rw	rw	rw	rw	rw	rw	rw	rw	rw	rw	rw	rw

Figure 7-26: DAC channel-x data holding- register (DAC_DHRx)

It must be emphasized that "The DAC_DORx cannot be written directly and any data transfer to the DAC channelx must be performed by loading the DAC_DHRx register."

DAC output buffer enable

According to the reference manual" The DAC integrates two output buffers that can be used to reduce the output impedance, and to drive external loads directly without having to add an external operational amplifier. Each DAC channel output buffer can be enabled and disabled using the corresponding BOFFx bit in the DAC_CR register."

31	30	29	28	27	26	25	24	23	22	21	20	19	18	17	16
Res	Res	Res	Res	Res	Res	Res	Res	Res	Res	Res	Res	Res	Res	Res	Res

15	14	13	12	11	10	9	8	7	6	5	4	3	2	1	0
Res	Res	Res	Res	DACC1DOR[11:0]											
				r	r	r	r	r	r	r	r	r	r	r	r

Figure 7-27: DAC channel1 data output register (DAC_DOR1)

31	30	29	28	27	26	25	24	23	22	21	20	19	18	17	16
Res	Res	Res	Res	Res	Res	Res	Res	Res	Res	Res	Res	Res	Res	Res	Res

15	14	13	12	11	10	9	8	7	6	5	4	3	2	1	0
Res	Res	Res	Res	DACC2DOR[11:0]											
				r	r	r	r	r	r	r	r	r	r	r	r

Figure 7-28: DAC channel2 data output register (DAC_DOR2)

31	30	29	28	27	26	25	24	23	22	21	20	19	18	17	16
Res	Res	Res	Res	Res	Res	Res	Res	Res	Res	Res	Res	Res	Res	Res	Res

15	14	13	12	11	10	9	8	7	6	5	4	3	2	1	0
Res	Res	Res	Res	Res	Res	Res	Res	Res	Res	Res	Res	Res	Res	SWTRIG2	SWTRIG1
														w	w

Bit 1 **SWTRIG2**: DAC channel2 software trigger

This bit is set and cleared by software to enable/disable the software trigger.

0: Software trigger disabled

1: Software trigger enabled

Note: This bit is cleared by hardware (one APB1 clock cycle later) once the DAC_DHR2 register value has been loaded into the DAC_DOR2 register.

Bit 0 **SWTRIG1**: DAC channel1 software trigger

This bit is set and cleared by software to enable/disable the software trigger.

0: Software trigger disabled

1: Software trigger enabled

Note: This bit is cleared by hardware (one APB1 clock cycle later) once the DAC_DHR1 register value has been loaded into the DAC_DOR1 register.

Figure 7-29: DAC software trigger register (DAC_SWTRIGR)

Enabling Clock to DAC

To save power no clock is fed to DAC upon Reset. To use the on-chip, DAC we must enable the clock to DAC using RCC APB1 peripheral clock enable register (RCC_APB1ENR). See Figure 7-30.

31	30	29	28	27	26	25	24	23	22	21	20	19	18	17	16
Res	Res	DAC EN	PWR EN	CEC EN	CAN2 EN	CAN1 EN	FMPI2C1 EN	I2C3 EN	I2C2 EN	I2C1 EN	UART5 EN	UART4 EN	USART3 EN	USART2 EN	SPDIFRX EN
		rw	rw	rw	rw	rw	rw	rw	rw	rw	rw	rw	rw	rw	rw

15	14	13	12	11	10	9	8	7	6	5	4	3	2	1	0
SPI3 EN	SPI2 EN	Res	Res	WWDG EN		Res	TIM14 EN	TIM13 EN	TIM12 EN	TIM7 EN	TIM6 EN	TIM5 EN	TIM4 EN	TIM3 EN	TIM2 EN
rw	rw			rw			rw	rw	rw	rw	rw	rw	rw	rw	rw

Bit 29 **DACEN:** DAC interface clock enable

This bit is set and cleared by software.

0: DAC interface clock disabled

1: DAC interface clock enable

Figure 7-30: RCC APB1 Peripheral Clock Enable Register (RCC_APB1ENR) to enable clock to DAC

Generating a sawtooth ramp

Program 7-4 uses the on-chip DAC to generate a sawtooth waveform. The loop counter i is incremented every iteration and written into the DAC_DHR register to create the ramp. To see the resulting waveform, connect the output to an oscilloscope. Figure 7-31 shows the output. Checking the STM32F446RE datasheet, we see the analog output pins are PA4 and PA5 for DAC1_output and DAC2_output, respectively. Check the analog output pin for your STM32F4 Arm device using the datasheet. It might not be the same as STM32F446RE chip.

```
Program 7-4: Generating Sawtooth Waveform
```

```c
/* p7_4.c: Use DAC to generate sawtooth waveform
 * The DAC is initialized with no buffer or trigger, so every
 * write to the DAC data register will change the analog output.
 * The data is incremented in the loop and written to the DAC.
 * The output of DAC is on pin PA4.
 *
 * This program was tested with Keil uVision v5.24a with DFP v2.11.0.
 */
#include "stm32f4xx.h"

int main(void) {
    int data;
    RCC->AHB1ENR |=  1;                 /* enable GPIOA clock */
    GPIOA->MODER |=  0x00000300;     /* PA4 analog */
    /* setup DAC */
    RCC->APB1ENR |= 1 << 29;          /* enable DAC clock */
    DAC->CR |= 1;                         /* enable DAC */

    while(1) {
        DAC->DHR12R1 = data++ & 0x0FFF;
    }
}
```

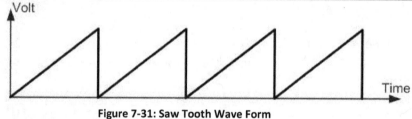

Figure 7-31: Saw Tooth Wave Form

Generating a sine wave

To generate a sine wave, we first need a table whose values represent the magnitude of the sine of angles between 0 and 360 degrees. The values for the sine function vary from -1.0 to +1.0 for 0 to 360 degree angles. Therefore, the table values are integer numbers representing the voltage magnitude for the sine of the angle. This method ensures that only integer numbers are output to the DAC by the processor. Table 7-11 shows the angles, the sine values, the voltage magnitudes, and the integer values representing the voltage magnitude for each angle with 30-degree increments.

Angle Θ (degrees)	Sin Θ	V$_{OUT}$ (Voltage Magnitude) 1. 65V + (1. 65V × sin Θ)	Values Sent to DAC (decimal) (Voltage Mag. × 310)

0	0	1.65	2048
30	0.5	2.475	3071
60	0.866	3.0789	3821
90	1.0	3.3	4095
120	0.866	3.0789	3821
150	0.5	2.475	3071
180	0	1.65	2048
210	-0.5	0.825	1024
240	-0.866	0.2211	274
270	-1.0	0	0
300	-0.866	0.2211	274
330	-0.5	0.825	1024
360	0	1.65	2048

Table 7-11: Angle vs. Voltage Magnitude for Sine Wave

To generate Table 7-11, we assumed the full-scale voltage of 3.3V for the DAC output. The full-scale output of the DAC is achieved when all the data input bits of the DAC are high. Therefore, to achieve the full-scale 3.3V output, we use the following equation:

$$V_{out} = 1.65V + (1.65V \times sin\theta)$$

To find the value sent to the DAC for various angles, we simply multiply the V_{OUT} voltage by 1,241 because the digital input range is 0-4095 (12-bit) and full-scale V_{OUT} is 3.3 volts. Therefore, 4095/3.3 =1241 steps per volt. To further clarify this, look at Example 7-5.

Example 7-5

Verify the values of Table 7-11 for the following angles: (a) 30 (b) 60.

Solution:

(a) V_{OUT} = 1.65 V + (1.65 V × sin Θ) = 1.65 V + 1.65 × sin 30 = 1.65 V +1.65 × 0.5 = 2.475 V
   DAC input values = 2.475 V × 1241 = 3071 (decimal)

(b) V_{OUT} = 1.65 V + (1.65 V × sin Θ) = 1.65 V +1.65 × sin 60 = 1.65 V + 1.65 × 0.866 = 3.079 V
   DAC input values = 3.079 V × 1241 = 3821 (decimal)

The following program sends the values of Table 7-11 to the DAC.

```
Program 7-5: Generating Sine Wave

/* p7_5.c: Use DAC to generate sine waveform
 *
 * This program uses a pre-calculated lookup table to generate a
 * sine wave output through a DAC.
 * The DAC is initialized with no buffer or trigger, so every
 * write to the DAC data register will change the analog output.
 * The index of the lookup table is incremented in the loop and
 * the data is written to the DAC.
```

```
 * The output of DAC is on pin PA4.
 *
 * This program was tested with Keil uVision v5.24a with DFP v2.11.0.
 */
#include "stm32f4xx.h"

void delayUs(int n);

int main(void) {
    int i;
    const static int sineWave[] =
        {2048,3071,3821,4095,3821,3071,2048,1024,274,0,274,1024};

    RCC->AHB1ENR |= 1;                      /* enable GPIOA clock */
    GPIOA->MODER |= 0x00000300;     /* PA4 analog */

    /* setup DAC */
    RCC->APB1ENR |= 1 << 29;          /* enable DAC clock */
    DAC->CR |= 1;                           /* enable DAC */

    while(1) {
        for (i = 0; i < sizeof(sineWave)/sizeof(int); i++)
        {
            DAC->DHR12R1 = sineWave[i]; /* write value of sinewave to DAC */
            delayUs(10);
        }
    }
}

/* 16 MHz SYSCLK */
void delayUs(int n) {
    int i;
    for (; n > 0; n--)
        for (i = 0; i < 3; i++) ;
}
```

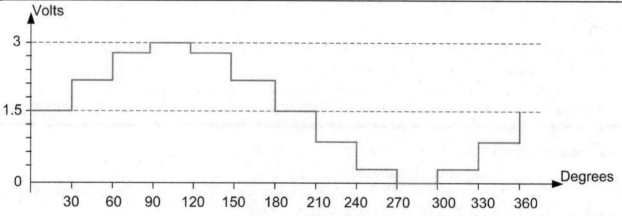

Figure 7-32: Angle vs. Voltage Magnitude for Sine Wave (for 3V)

Program 7-6 uses the C math library functions to generate the lookup table at initialization time.

```c
/* p7_6.c: Use DAC to generate sine waveform
 *
 * This program calculates a lookup table at the initialization to be used
 * to generate a sine wave output through a DAC.
 * The DAC is initialized with no buffer or trigger, so every
 * write to the DAC data register will change the analog output.
 * The index of the lookup table is incremented in the loop and
 * the data is written to the DAC.
 * The output of DAC is on pin PA4.
 *
 * This program was tested with Keil uVision v5.24a with DFP v2.11.0.
 */
#include "stm32f4xx.h"

void delayUs(int n);
#include <math.h>

#define WAVEFORM_LENGTH 256
int sinewave[WAVEFORM_LENGTH];

int main (void) {
    int i;
    double Radians;
    const double M_PI = 3.1415926535897;

    /* construct data table for a sine wave */
    Radians = 2 * M_PI / WAVEFORM_LENGTH;

    for (i = 0; i < WAVEFORM_LENGTH; i++) {
        sinewave[i] = 2000 * (sin(Radians * i) + 1);
    }

    RCC->AHB1ENR |= 1;                 /* enable GPIOA clock */
    GPIOA->MODER |= 0x00000300;     /* PA4 analog */

    /* setup DAC */
    RCC->APB1ENR |= 1 << 29;        /* enable DAC clock */
    DAC->CR |= 1;                   /* enable DAC */

    while (1) {
        for (i = 0; i < WAVEFORM_LENGTH; i++) {
            DAC->DHR12R1 = sinewave[i]; /* write value of sinewave to DAC */
            delayUs(10);
        }
    }
}

/* 16 MHz SYSCLK */
void delayUs(int n) {
    int i;
    for (; n > 0; n--)
        for (i = 0; i < 3; i++) ;
}
```

See Chapter 8 for the Arm connection and programming of LTC1661 DAC using SPI bus.

Review Questions

1. In a DAC, input is _____ (digital, analog) and output is _____ (digital, analog).
2. DAC0808 is a(n) _____-bit D-to-A converter.
3. The output of DAC808 is in _____ (current, voltage).
4. The on-chip DAC of STM32F4xx has _____-bit resolution.
5. True or false. The on-chip DAC for STM32F446RE chip has two channels of DAC1 and DAC2.

Answers to Review Questions

Section 7.1

1. Number of steps (resolution) and V_{ref} voltage
2. 8
3. True
4. 1.28 V / 256 = 5 mV
5.
   (a) 0.7 V / 5 mV = 140 in decimal and D7–D0 = 10001100 in binary
   (b) 1 V/ 5 mV = 200 in decimal and D7–D0 = 11001000 in binary.

Section 7.2

1. 12
2. 0xFFF
3. Step size is 3.3V / 4096 = 0.8057 mV and 1.9V / 0.8057mv = 2,358 in decimal or 0x936.
4. ADC_DR
5. 6-, 8-, 10-, and 12-bit.

Section 7.3

1. False, if the output of the sensor is a voltage in the range of the ADC input and there is no concern of aliasing such as the temperature sensor example here, the signal conditioning circuitry may be omitted.
2. 10, Celsius
3. 10, Fahrenheit
4. 00111110 (binary) = 62 → Temperature = 62 × 330 / 4096 = 5

Section 7.4

1. Digital, analog
2. 8
3. Current
4. 12
5. True

Chapter 8: SPI Protocol and DAC Interfacing

The SPI (serial peripheral interface) is a bus interface incorporated in many devices such as ADC, DAC, and EEPROM. In Section 8.1 we will examine the signals of the SPI bus and show how the read and write operations in the SPI work. Section 8.2 examines the STM32 Arm SPI registers. In Section 8.3 we show LTC1661 DAC interfacing to Arm using SPI bus.

Section 8.1: SPI Bus Protocol

The SPI bus was originally started by Motorola (later became Freescale then acquired by NXP), but in recent years has become widely used by many semiconductor chip companies. SPI devices use only 2 pins for data transfer, called SDI (Din) and SDO (Dout), instead of the 8 or more pins used in traditional buses. This reduction of data pins reduces the package size and power consumption drastically, making them ideal for many applications in which space or pin count is a major concern. The SPI bus has the SCLK (serial clock) pin to synchronize the data transfer between two chips. The last pin of the SPI bus is CE (chip enable), which is used to initiate and terminate the data transfer. These four pins, SDI, SDO, SCLK, and CE, make the SPI a 4-wire interface. See **Figure 8-**.

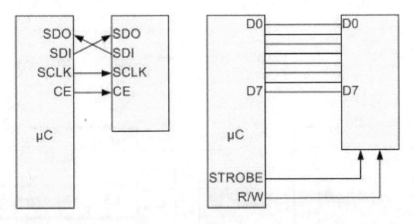

Figure 8-1: SPI Bus vs. Traditional Parallel Bus Connection to Microcontroller

In many chips, the SDI, SDO, SCLK, and CE signals are alternatively named as MOSI, MISO, SCK, and SS as shown in Figure 8- (compared with Figure 8-). There is also a widely used standard called a 3-wire interface bus. In a 3-wire interface bus, we have SCLK and CE, and only a single pin for data transfer. The SPI 4-wire bus can become a 3-wire interface when the SDI and SDO data pins are tied together. However, there are some major differences between the SPI and 3-wire devices in the data transfer protocol. For that reason, a device must support the 3-wire protocol internally in order to be used as a 3-wire device. Many devices support both SPI and 3-wire protocols.

How SPI works

SPI consists of two shift registers, one in the master and the other in the slave. Also, there is a clock generator in the master side that generates the clock for the shift registers.

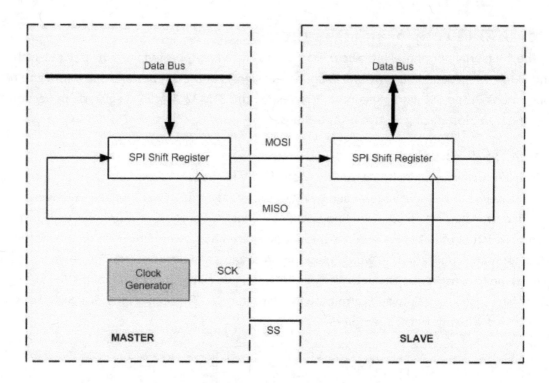

Figure 8-2: SPI Architecture

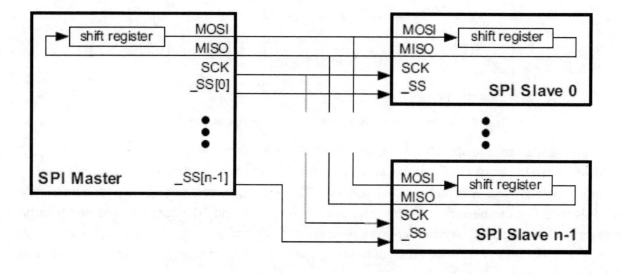

Figure 8-3: Master SPI Connection to multiple slaves SPI in Parallel

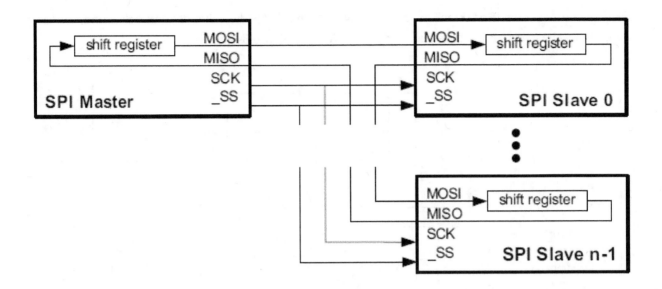

Figure 8-4: Master SPI Connection to multiple slaves SPI in serial

Figures 8-2, 8-3 and 8-4 shows SPI Master and Slave connections. As you can see in Figure 8-2, serial-out pin of the master shift register is connected to the serial-in pin of the slave shift register by MOSI (Master Out Slave In) and the serial-in pin of the master shift register is connected to the serial-out pin of the slave shift register by MISO (Master In Slave Out). The master clock generator provides a clock to shift register in both master and slave shift registers. The clock input of the shift registers can be falling- or rising-edge triggered. This will be discussed shortly.

In SPI, the shift registers are 8 bits long. It means that after 8 clock pulses, the contents of the two shift registers are interchanged. When the master wants to send a byte of data, it places the byte in its shift register and generates 8 clock pulses. After 8 clock pulses, the byte is transmitted to the slave shift register. When the master wants to receive a byte of data, the slave side should place the byte in its shift register and after 8 clock pulses, the data will be received by the master shift register. It must be noted that SPI is full duplex meaning that it may send and receive data at the same time.

Clock polarity and phase in SPI device

As we mentioned before in UART communication, transmitter and receiver must agree on a clock frequency (baud rate). In SPI communication, both master and slave use the same clock but the master and slave must agree on the clock polarity and phase with respect to the data. Clock polarity implies the clock signal level when the clock is idling. Each clock pulse has two edges, the leading edge, and the trailing edge. Clock phase determines whether leading edge or trailing edge is used to sample the data.

With clock polarity as 0, the idle value of the clock is zero while with clock polarity as 1 the idle value of the clock is one. When clock phase is 0, data is sampled on the leading (first) clock edge; while clock phase is 1, data is sampled on the trailing (second) clock edge. Notice that if the idle value of the clock is zero the leading (first) clock edge is a rising edge but if the idle value of the clock is one, the leading (first) clock edge is a falling edge. See Table 8-1 and Figure 8-4 and 8-5.

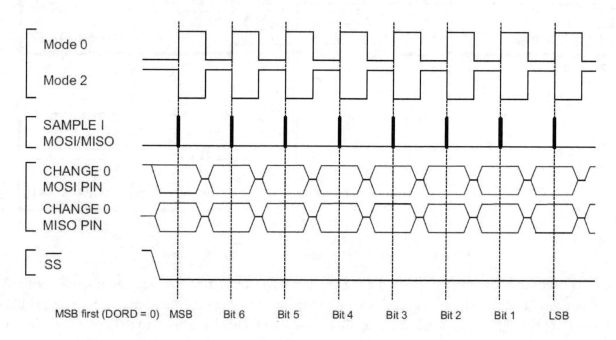

Figure 8-5: SPI Clock Polarity and phase Mode 0 (CPOL = 0, CPHA = 0) and Mode 2 (CPOL = 1, CPHA = 0)

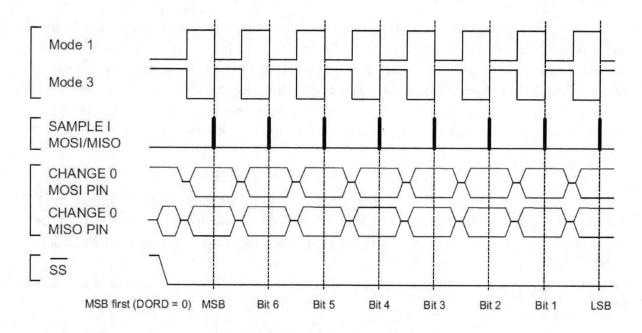

Figure 8-6: SPI Clock Polarity and phase Mode 1 (CPOL = 0, CPHA = 1) and Mode 3 (CPOL = 1, CPHA = 1)

Clock Polarity	Clock Phase	Data read and change time	SPI Mode
0	0	read on rising edge, changed on a falling edge	0
0	1	read on falling edge, changed on a rising edge	1
1	0	read on falling edge, changed on a rising edge	2
1	1	read on rising edge, changed on a falling edge	3

Table 8-1: SPI Clock Polarity and phase

Review Questions

1. True or false. SPI is an asynchronous protocol.
2. True or false. In the SPI protocol, the clock is always generated by the master device.
3. True or false. SPI shares a clock while USART does not.
4. True or false. To connect multiple devices to a single master we use chip select.

Section 8.2: SPI programming in STM32 Arm

The STM32F4xx chip comes with multiple on-chip SPI modules. STM32F4xx Arm SPI module also supports the I2S (Inter IC Sound) protocol. The I2S is used for serial connection of digital audio devices. In this section, we examine the SPI module and show how to program it. The exploration of the I2S feature is left to the readers. The SPI modules are located at the following base addresses:

SPI Module	Base Address
SPI1	0x4001 3000 - 0x4001 33FF
SPI2	0x4000 3800 - 0x4000 3BFF
SPI3	0x4000 3C00 - 0x4000 3FFF

Table 8-2: STM32F4xx Arm SPI Module Base Addresses

SPI Register

To program the SPI, we need to examine the registers associated with it. Table 8-3 shows some of the registers. Notice that SPI is called synchronous since a clock used to synchronize the data transfer between the CPU chip and SPI devices such as DAC, as we will see soon. Recall from Chapter 4 that there was no such a clock for UART. UART used TxD and RxD and common ground between the STM32F4xx chip and the PC for terminal emulator such as the TeraTerm.

Register Name	Register Function	Register Address Offset
SPI_CR1	Control 1	0x00
SPI_CR2	Control 2	0x04
SPI_SR	Status	0x08
SPI_DR	Data	0x0C

Table 8-3: STM32F4xx SPI Registers

Configuring the SPI Module

Enabling the clock to SPI

The SPI clock must be enabled before the registers in the SPI module become accessible. The SPI is connected to the APBx peripheral clock. The STM32F4xx Arm chip comes with four on-chip SPI modules. They are SPI1, SPI2, SPI3, and SPI4. Depending on which of SPIx we want to use, we use either RCC_APB1ENR or RCC_APB2ENR registers to enable the clock to the desired SPI module. The SPI2 and SPI3 are controlled by the RCC_APB1ENR register and The SPI1 and SPI4 are controlled by the RCC_APB2ENR register. See figures below.

31	30	29	28	27	26	25	24	23	22	21	20	19	18	17	16
Res.	Res.	DAC EN	PWR EN	CEC EN	CAN2 EN	CAN1 EN	FMPI2C1 EN	I2C3 EN	I2C2 EN	I2C1 EN	UART5 EN	UART4 EN	USART3 EN	USART2 EN	SPDIFRX EN
		rw	rw	rw	rw	rw	rw	rw	rw	rw	rw	rw	rw	rw	rw

15	14	13	12	11	10	9	8	7	6	5	4	3	2	1	0
SPI3 EN	SPI2 EN	Res.	Res.	WWDG EN	Res.	Res.	TIM14 EN	TIM13 EN	TIM12 EN	TIM7 EN	TIM6 EN	TIM5 EN	TIM4 EN	TIM3 EN	TIM2 EN
rw	rw			rw			rw	rw	rw	rw	rw	rw	rw	rw	rw

Bit 15 **SPI3EN:** SPI3 clock enable

This bit is set and cleared by software.

0: SPI3 clock disabled

Bit 14 **SPI2EN:** SPI2 clock enable

This bit is set and cleared by software.

0: SPI2 clock disabled

1: SPI2 clock enabled 1: SPI3 clock enabled

Figure 8-7: RCC APB1 peripheral clock enable register (RCC_APB1ENR)

31	30	29	28	27	26	25	24	23	22	21	20	19	18	17	16
Res.	Res.	Res.	Res.	Res.	Res.	Res.	Res.	SAI2 EN	SAI1 EN	Res.	Res.	Res.	TIM11 EN	TIM10 EN	TIM9 EN
								rw	rw				rw	rw	rw

15	14	13	12	11	10	9	8	7	6	5	4	3	2	1	0
Res.	SYSCFG EN	SPI4 EN	SPI1 EN	SDIO EN	ADC3 EN	ADC2 EN	ADC1 EN	Res.	Res.	USART6 EN	USART1 EN	Res.	Res.	TIM8 EN	TIM1 EN
	rw	rw	rw	rw	rw	rw	rw			rw	rw			rw	rw

Bit 13 **SPI4EN:** SPI4 clock enable

This bit is set and cleared by software.

0: SPI4 clock disabled

1: SPI4 clock enabled

Bit 12 **SPI1EN:** SPI1 clock enable

This bit is set and cleared by software.

0: SPI1 clock disabled

1: SPI1 clock enabled

Figure 8-8: RCC APB2 peripheral clock enable register (RCC_APB2ENR)

The SPI Control Registers

The SPI_CR1 (Control 1) and CR2 (Control 2) registers set the SPI configurations. See Figures 8-9 and 8-10. They describe the function of each bit for these registers. Although the conventional SPI uses only 8-bit data, the SPI module allows transfer of data for 16 bits too, as shown in by DFF (Data Frame Format) CR1 register. The SPI module in STM32F4xx supports both the Motorola and the TI protocols. The default is Motorola and we will leave it at that since it is the most common one.

15	14	13	12	11	10	9	8	7	6	5	4	3	2	1	0
BIDI MODE	BIDI OE	CRC EN	CRC NEXT	DFF	RX ONLY	SSM	SSI	LSB FIRST	SPE	BR [2:0]			MSTR	CPOL	CPHA
rw	rw	rw	rw	rw	rw	rw	rw	rw	rw	rw	rw	rw	rw	rw	rw

Bit 13 **CRCEN:** Hardware CRC calculation enable
> 0: CRC calculation disabled
> 1: CRC calculation enabled

Bit 12 **CRCNEXT:** CRC transfer next
> 0: Data phase (no CRC phase)
> 1: Next transfer is CRC (CRC phase). See STM32F4xx Ref. Manual

Bit 11 **DFF:** Data frame format
> 0: 8-bit data frame format is selected for transmission/reception
> 1: 16-bit data frame format is selected for transmission/reception

Bit 6 **SPE:** SPI enable
> 0: Peripheral disabled
> 1: Peripheral enabled

Bits 5:3 **BR[2:0]:** Baud rate control
> 000: fPCLK/2
> 001: fPCLK/4
> 010: fPCLK/8
> 011: fPCLK/16

> 100: fPCLK/32
> 101: fPCLK/64
> 110: fPCLK/128
> 111: fPCLK/256

Bit 2 **MSTR:** Master selection
> 0: Slave configuration
> 1: Master configuration

Bit1 **CPOL:** Clock polarity
> 0: CK to 0 when idle
> 1: CK to 1 when idle

Bit 0 **CPHA:** Clock phase
> 0: The first clock transition is the first data capture edge
> 1: The second clock transition is the first data capture edge

Figure 8-9: SPI Control 1 (SPI_CR1) Register in STM32F4xx

15	14	13	12	11	10	9	8	7	6	5	4	3	2	1	0
Res.	Res.	Res.	Res.	Res.	Res.	Res.	Res.	TXEIE	RXNEIE	ERRIE	FRF	Res.	SSOE	TXDMAEN	RXDMAEN
								rw	rw	rw	rw		rw	rw	rw

Bit 7 **TXEIE:** Tx buffer empty interrupt enable
> 0: TXE interrupt masked
> 1: TXE interrupt not masked. Used to generate an interrupt request when the TXE flag is set.

Bit 6 **RXNEIE:** RX buffer not empty interrupt enable

    0: RXNE interrupt masked

    1: RXNE interrupt not masked. Used to generate an interrupt request when the RXNE flag is set.

Bit 5 **ERRIE:** Error interrupt enable

    This bit controls the generation of an interrupt when an error condition occurs (OVR, CRCERR, MODF, FRE in SPI mode, and UDR, OVR, FRE in I^2S mode).

    0: Error interrupt is masked

    1: Error interrupt is enabled

Bit 4 **FRF:** Frame format

    0: SPI Motorola mode

    1: SPI TI mode

Figure 8-10: SPI_CR2 (Contolr 2) Registers in STM32F4xx

When SPE is set (SPE=1), the SPI module is enabled.

Clock Polarity and Clock Phase

As discussed in Section 8.1, we need to choose clock polarity and clock phase that agree with the devices connected to the SPI. In the STM32F4xx, the clock polarity is determined by CPOL bit and the clock phase is determined by CPHA bit both in the SPI_CR1 register.

Master or Slave

The SPI Module inside the STM32F4xx chip can be a master or a slave. See Figures 8-11A and 8-11B. A master is a device that generates the clock and drives the SCLK pin. A slave is a device that uses the SCK pin as the SPI clock. We use MSTR (Master Selection) bit in SPI Control register 1 (SPI_CR1) to designate the SPI Module in the STM32F4xx chip as an SPI master or an SPI slave. Each module is independent of others. Some of them may be configured as masters and the others as slaves.

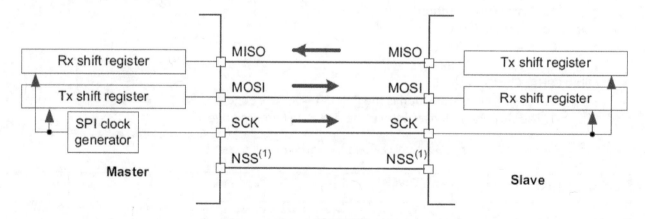

Figure 8-11A: Using STM32F4xx SPI module as Master

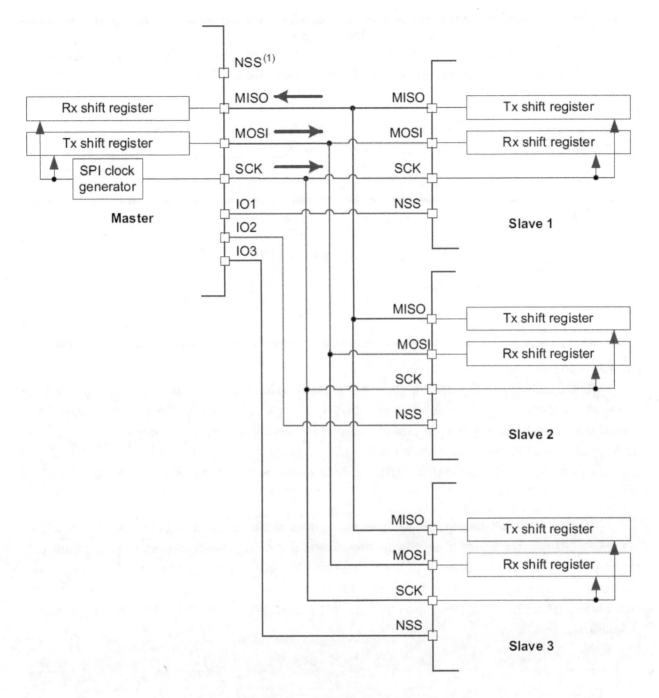

Figure 8-11B: Using STM32F4xx SPI module as Master

Setting Bit Rate

Like some other peripherals, the SPI clock is derived from the APBx clock which comes from SYSCLK through AHB and APBx prescalers. In SPI module, the BR bits in the SPI_CR1 register are used to set the clock rate. See Examples 8-1 and 8-2.

Example 8-1

Assume the SYSCLK clock frequency of 16MHz is fed to SPI module. Find the values for the BR (baud rate) bits of the SPI_CR1 register for the bit rate of (a) 1M, (b) 500K, and (c) 62,500.

Solution

(a) 16 MHz / 1MHz = 16, then we use 011 (in binary) for BR bits in SPI_CR1 register.

(b) 16 MHz / 500KHz = 32, then we use 100 for BR bits in SPI_CR1 register.

(c) 16 MHz / 62,500 = 256, then we use 111 for BR bits in SPI_CR1 register.

Example 8-2

In a given STM32F4xx trainer board, The BR bits are set to 110 (binary) and the SYSCLK is 16MHz. What is the baud rate for the SPI?

Solution:

16MHz / 128 = 125KHz

Data Register

The transmit data register and the receive data register share the same address and the same name in the programs. The data is written into the SPI_DR register for transmission and the received data is read from the SPI_DR register. The transmit register is double buffered, meaning there is a transmit data register in addition to the transmit shift register. When a byte of data is written to the SPI_DR register, it will be loaded into the shift register and makes the transmit data register empty to be ready to accept another byte of data.

Notice in the SPI_DR register, we have the options of 8-bit or 16-bit data frame size. The DFF bit in the SPI_CR1 register is used to set the data frame size of 8 or 16. In 8-bit data size selection, the data must be placed into the lower 8-bits of the register and the rest of the register is unused. In the receive mode, the received data is held in the lower 8-bit of the register. Also notice, data can be shifted out either MSB-first or LSB-first depending on the value of the LSBFIRST bit in the SPI_CR1 Register. The default is MSB-first.

15	14	13	12	11	10	9	8	7	6	5	4	3	2	1	0
							DR[15:0]								
rw	rw	rw	rw	rw	rw	rw	rw	rw	rw	rw	rw	rw	rw	rw	rw

Bits 15:0 **DR[15:0]:** Data register
Data received or to be transmitted.
The data register is split into 2 buffers - one for writing (Transmit Buffer) and another one for reading (Receive buffer). A write to the data register will write into the Tx buffer and a read from the data register will return the value held in the Rx buffer.

Figure 8-12: SPI_DR (Data) register

SPI Status Flag Register

In master mode, we can monitor the TXE (Transmit buffer empty) flag in the SPI_SR (Status) register to see whether the transmit data register is empty and can accept another byte of data for transmission. When the first byte of data is written to the SPI_DR register, it is transferred to the shift register immediately and the data register remains empty and the TXE flag stays set. When another byte of data is written to the Data register while the shift register is occupied, the TXE is cleared.

When data is loaded into the receive buffer register from the shift register, the RXNE (Receive buffer not empty) bit of SPI_SR register flag is set. The software must poll the RXNE flag or set up the RXNE interrupt to read the SPI_DR register as soon as possible to avoid the loss of data. See Figure 8-13 and Table 8-4.

15	14	13	12	11	10	9	8	7	6	5	4	3	2	1	0
Res.	Res.	Res.	Res.	Res.	Res.	Res.	FRE	BSY	OVR	MODF	CRC ERR	UDR	CHSIDE	TXE	RXNE
							r	r	r	r	rc_w0	r	r	r	r

Figure 8-13: SPI_SR (Status) Register

Bits	Name	Function	Description
1	TXE: Transmit buffer empty	Data Register Empty	The bit is 1 when the transmit data is empty and can accept another byte of data.
0	RXNE: Receive buffer not empty	Receive Complete	The bit is 1 when there is new data in the receive buffer registers. It is cleared when data are read.

Table 8-4: SPI_SR (Status) Register

Configuring GPIO for SPI

In using SPI, we must also configure the GPIO pins to allow the connection of SPI module signals to the external pins of the device. The input/output pin multiplexing has two levels. The SPI I/O functions are mapped to the four pins using function multiplexing. They are mapped according to Table 8-5. The mapping of input pins and output pins are independent of each other so that the data out pin may be mapped to the same pin as the input pin, effectively creates a local loop-around path for testing while the output data can still be monitored at the pin.

Not all the pins need to be configured. For example, if the program only writes to the slave device and never reads it, the MISO pin is not used. The slave select pin is designated for hardware slave select. If software slave select is used, any available GPIO output pin can be used for slave select. Because the use of hardware slave select of STM32F devices is rather limited, we will only use software slave select.

For the pin selection, we first must use GPIOx_MODER to select the alternate function. After that, we use GPIOx_AFRL to select AF4 or AF5 from Table 8-5 depending on which pin we use.

Port		AF0	AF1	AF2	AF3	AF4	AF5	AF6	AF7
		SYS	TIM1/2	TIM3/4/5	TIM8/9/10/11/CEC	I2C1/2/3/4/CEC	SPI1/2/3/4	SPI2/3/4/SAI1	SPI2/3/USART1/2/3/UART5/SPDIFRX
Port A	PA0	-	TIM2_CH1/TIM2_ETR	TIM5_CH1	TIM8_ETR	-	-	-	USART2_CTS
	PA1	-	TIM2_CH2	TIM5_CH2	-	-	-	-	USART2_RTS
	PA2	-	TIM2_CH3	TIM5_CH3	TIM9_CH1	-	-	-	USART2_TX
	PA3	-	TIM2_CH4	TIM5_CH4	TIM9_CH2	-	-	SAI1_FS_A	USART2_RX
	PA4	-	-	-	-	-	SPI1_NSS/I2S1_WS	SPI3_NSS/I2S3_WS	USART2_CK
	PA5	-	TIM2_CH1/TIM2_ETR	-	TIM8_CH1N	-	SPI1_SCK/I2S1_CK	-	-
	PA6	-	TIM1_BKIN	TIM3_CH1	TIM8_BKIN	-	SPI1_MISO	I2S2_MCK	-
	PA7	-	TIM1_CH1N	TIM3_CH2	TIM8_CH1N	-	SPI1_MOSI/I2S1_SD		-
	PA8	MCO1	TIM1_CH1	-	-	I2C3_SCL	-	-	USART1_CK
	PA9	-	TIM1_CH2	-	-	I2C3_SMBA	SPI2_SCK/I2S2_CK	SAI1_SD_B	USART1_TX
	PA10	-	TIM1_CH3	-	-	-	-	-	USART1_RX
	PA11	-	TIM1_CH4	-	-	-	-	-	USART1_CTS
	PA12	-	TIM1_ETR	-	-	-	-	-	USART1_RTS
	PA13	JTMS-SWDIO	-	-	-	-	-	-	-
	PA14	JTCK-SWCLK	-	-	-	-	-	-	-
	PA15	JTDI	TIM2_CH1/TIM2_ETR	-	-	HDMI_CEC	SPI1_NSS/I2S1_WS	SPI3_NSS/I2S3_WS	-

Table 8-5: Alternate pin Function multiplexing for STM32F446RE (See Appendix B for complete list)

31	30	29	28	27	26	25	24	23	22	21	20	19	18	17	16
MODER15[1:0]		MODER14[1:0]		MODER13[1:0]		MODER12[1:0]		MODER11[1:0]		MODER10[1:0]		MODER9[1:0]		MODER8[1:0]	
rw	rw	rw	rw	rw	rw	rw	rw	rw	rw	rw	rw	rw	rw	rw	rw
15	14	13	12	11	10	9	8	7	6	5	4	3	2	1	0
MODER7[1:0]		MODER6[1:0]		MODER5[1:0]		MODER4[1:0]		MODER3[1:0]		MODER2[1:0]		MODER1[1:0]		MODER0[1:0]	
rw	rw	rw	rw	rw	rw	rw	rw	rw	rw	rw	rw	rw	rw	rw	rw

Bits 2y:2y+1 **MODERy[1:0]:** Port x configuration bits (y = 0..15)

These bits are written by software to configure the I/O direction mode.

00: Input (reset state)

01: General purpose output mode

10: Alternate function mode

11: Analog mode

Figure 8-14A: GPIOx_MODER

31	30	29	28	27	26	25	24	23	22	21	20	19	18	17	16
AFRL7[3:0]				AFRL6[3:0]				AFRL5[3:0]				AFRL4[3:0]			
rw	rw	rw	rw	rw	rw	rw	rw	rw	rw	rw	rw	rw	rw	rw	rw
15	14	13	12	11	10	9	8	7	6	5	4	3	2	1	0
AFRL3[3:0]				AFRL2[3:0]				AFRL1[3:0]				AFRL0[3:0]			
rw	rw	rw	rw	rw	rw	rw	rw	rw	rw	rw	rw	rw	rw	rw	rw

Bits 31:0 **AFRLy:** Alternate function selection for port x bit y (y = 0..7)

These bits are written by software to configure alternate function I/Os

AFRLy selection:

0000: AF0	1000: AF8
0001: AF1	1001: AF9
0010: AF2	1010: AF10
0011: AF3	1011: AF11
0100: AF4	1100: AF12
0101: AF5	1101: AF13
0110: AF6	1110: AF14
0111: AF7	1111: AF15

Figure 8-14B: GPIOx_AFRL Register

Transmitting data using software controlled slave select

The hardware slave select signal of STM32F devices is asserted when the SPI module is enabled and de-asserted when the SPI module is disabled. This does not work with many peripheral slave devices that require the trailing edge of the slave select for the data transfer to take effect. The peripheral transmission slave select is only available in STM32F7 family devices. So we will only discuss software controlled slave select here. Besides, there are several advantages of using software controlled slave select.

Using software to control slave select allows us to share one SPI module with multiple slave devices in parallel. Each slave has a separate slave select signal. Only when its slave select is enabled, the clock and data will affect the slave. The other advantage of software controlled slave select is that several bytes of data may be transmitted in one transaction, which may be necessary for some slave devices as we will see in next section.

For software controlled slave select, the program needs to assert the slave select signal first before writing data to the Data register to initiate a transmission. After all the bytes in a transmission are written, the program needs to wait until the Busy flag (BSY bit 7) is set in SPI_SR (status register) before taking away the slave select. Slave select signal is usually low active but not always so.

Here are the steps to configure an SPI to transmit a byte of data for STM32F4xx using software controlled slave select.

1) Enable the SPI clock at RCC_APBxENR register
2) Enable the GPIOx clock at RCC_AHB1ENR register
3) Configure the port pins for SPI by GPIOx_MODER and GPIOx_AFRy registers
4) Configure a port pin for Slave Select by GPIOx_MODER register
5) Configure SPI_CR1 register to select data bit ordering, clock polarity, clock phase, Baud rate, SPI master mode, data frame size, and others.
6) Clear or leave SPI_CR2 in default
7) Enable the SPI by setting SPE (SPI enable) bit of SPI_CR1 register
8) Monitor the TXE (Transfer buffer Empty) flag bit of the SPI_SR (status) register until the transmit data register is empty
9) Assert slave select pin
10) Write data to SPI_DR (data) register to be transmitted
11) Wait until BSY flag is cleared in SPI_SR then deassert slave select
10) To transmit another character, go to step 8

See figure below for signal connections.

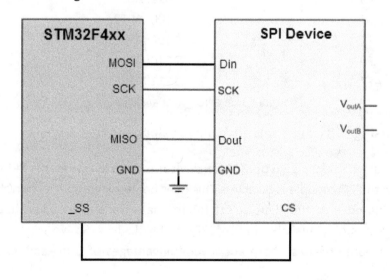

```c
/* p8_1.c: Using SPI1 to send A to Z characters
 *
 * SPI1 is configured as master with software slave select.
 * Clock rate is set to 1 MHz. Polarity/Phase are 0, 0
 *
 * PA7  MOSI
 * PA5  SCK
 * PA4  SS
 *
 * This program was tested with Keil uVision v5.24a with DFP v2.11.0
 */

#include "stm32f4xx.h"

void delayMs(int n);
void SPI1_init(void);
void SPI1_write(unsigned char data);

int main(void) {
    char c;

    SPI1_init();

    while(1) {
        for (c = 'A'; c <= 'Z'; c++) {
            SPI1_write(c);          /* write the letter through SPI1 */
            delayMs(100);
        }
    }
}

/* enable SPI1 and associated GPIO pins */
void SPI1_init(void) {
    RCC->AHB1ENR |= 1;              /* enable GPIOA clock */
    RCC->APB2ENR |= 0x1000;         /* enable SPI1 clock */

    /* PORTA 5, 7 for SPI1 MOSI and SCLK */
    GPIOA->MODER &= ~0x0000CC00;    /* clear pin mode */
    GPIOA->MODER |=  0x00008800;    /* set pin alternate mode */
    GPIOA->AFR[0] &= ~0xF0F00000;   /* clear alt mode */
    GPIOA->AFR[0] |=  0x50500000;   /* set alt mode SPI1 */

    /* PORTA4 as GPIO output for SPI slave select */
    GPIOA->MODER &= ~0x00000300;    /* clear pin mode */
    GPIOA->MODER |=  0x00000100;    /* set pin output mode */

    SPI1->CR1 = 0x31C;              /* set the Baud rate, 8-bit data frame */
    SPI1->CR2 = 0;
    SPI1->CR1 |= 0x40;              /* enable SPI1 module */
}

/* This function enables slave select, writes one byte to SPI1,
   wait for transmission complete and deassert slave select. */
void SPI1_write(unsigned char data) {
    while (!(SPI1->SR & 2)) {}      /* wait until Transfer buffer Empty */
```

```
        GPIOA->BSRR = 0x00100000;        /* assert slave select */
        SPI1->DR = data;                 /* write data */
        while (SPI1->SR & 0x80) {}       /* wait for transmission done */
        GPIOA->BSRR = 0x00000010;        /* deassert slave select */
}

/* 16 MHz SYSCLK */
void delayMs(int n) {
    int i;
    for (; n > 0; n--)
        for (i = 0; i < 3195; i++) ;
}
```

Review Questions

1. True or false. SPI Master shares a clock with SPI device.
2. True or false. SPI module can also be used as USART too.
3. In SPI, which signal is used to enable a slave device?
4. In STM32F4xx, which register is used to enable the SPI module?
5. In STM32F4xx, which register is used to set the master mode?

Section 8.3: LTC1661 SPI DAC

Sending Control/Data to LTC1661 in 8-bit Mode

In Chapter 7, we examined the DAC concepts. In this section, we show an SPI-based DAC and its interfacing to STM32F4xx Arm MCU. LTC1661 is a 10-bit SPI serial DAC from Linear Technology. It has two separate output channels, named A and B, as shown in Figure 8-15.

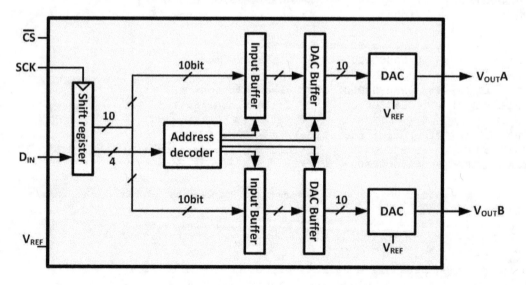

Figure 8-15: LTC1661 Internal Block Diagram

The relation between the input number and the output voltage is as follows:

$$VOUT = \frac{(VREF \times DIN)}{1024}$$

The LTC1661 is controlled by sending 16 bits of data through SPI. As shown in Figure 8-16, the 16-bit data is made of 3 parts: control code (4 bits), data (10 bits), and 2 padded bits. The control codes are used to control the internal parts of the LTC1661.

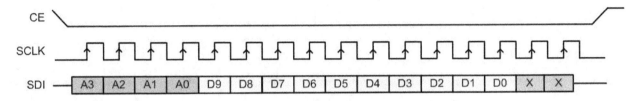

Figure 8-16: Sending a Packet of Data to LTC166x

As shown in Figure 8-15, each DAC is double buffered to provide a simultaneous update. To do so, we load input buffers with proper values in two transactions and then load the DAC buffers from the input buffers simultaneously. Table 8-6 shows the list of available control codes. To decrease power consumption, the DAC has a sleep mode, as well. We can switch between sleep and awake modes using proper control code.

A3 A2 A1 A0	Interrupt Register	DAC Register	Power Down Status	Comments
0 0 0 0	No Change	No Update	No Change	No operation. power-down status unchanged
0 0 0 1	Load DAC A	No Update	No Change	Load input register A with data. DAC outputs unchanged. power-down Status unchanged
0 0 1 0	Load DAC B	No Update	No Change	Load input register B with data. DAC outputs unchanged. power-down status unchanged
0 0 1 1	-	-	-	Reserved
0 1 0 0	-	-	-	Reserved
0 1 0 1	-	-	-	Reserved
0 1 1 0	-	-	-	Reserved
0 1 1 1	-	-	-	Reserved
1 0 0 0	No Change	Update Outputs	Wake	Load both DAC Regs with existing contents of input Regs. Outputs update. Part wakes up
1 0 0 1	Load DAC A	Update Outputs	Wake	Load input Reg A. Load DAC Regs with new contents of input Reg A and existing contents of Reg B. Outputs update.
1 0 1 0	Load DAC B	Update Outputs	Wake	Load input Reg B. Load DAC Regs with existing contentsof input Reg A and new contents of Reg B. Outputs update
1 0 1 1	-	-	-	Reserved
1 1 0 0	-	-	-	Reserved

1 1 0 1	No Change	No Update	Wake	Part wakes up. Input and DAC Regs unchanged. DAC outputs reflect existing contents of DAC Regs
1 1 1 0	No Change	No Update	Sleep	Part goes to sleep. Input and DAC Regs unchanged. DAC outputs set to high impedance state
1 1 1 1	Load ADCs A, B with same 10-bit code	Update Outputs	Wake	Load both input Regs. Load both DAC Regs with new contents of input Regs. Outputs update. Part wakes up

Table 8-6: LTC1661 DAC Control Functions

See Examples 8-4 and 8-5.

Example 8-4

Assuming that V_{REF} = 3.3 V, find the result of sending the following packets to LTC1661:

a) 0001 0001 0000 0000 binary   (0x1100)
b) 1010 1000 1111 1100 binary   (0xA8FC)

Solution:

a) In 0001 0001 0000 0000, control code is 0001. As a result, it loads data = 0001 0000 00 (decimal 64) to the input buffer register for channel A. Note the output is not updated with this control code. The output will be updated after a control code of 1000 is sent. Therefore V_{OUTA} = V_{REF} * D_{IN}/ 1024 = 3.3 * 64 / 1024 = 0.206V.

b) In 1010 1000 1111 1100, the control code is 1010. As a result it loads data 1000 1111 11 (decimal 575) to the input buffer register of channel B and also updates the output. Therefore, V_{OUTB} = V_{REF} * D_{IN} / 1024 = 3.3 * 575 / 1024 = 1.853V.

Example 8-5

Assuming that V_{REF}= 3.3 V, find the packets that should be sent to LTC1661 to:

a) send out 0.5V from channel A
b) send out 1.0V from channel B
c) send out 0.5V and 1.0V from channels A and B, simultaneously

Solution:

a) V_{OUTA} = V_{REF}× D_{IN} / 1024
    0.5V = 3.3 × D_{IN} / 1024
    D_{IN} = 155 (binary 0010 0110 11).

We send 1001 0010 0110 1100 binary (0x926C) since control code 9 loads input buffer register of channel A and updates the channel output.

b) $V_{OUTB} = V_{REF} \times D_{IN} / 1024$

$1.0V = 3.3 \times D_{IN} / 1024$

$D_{IN} = 310$ (binary 0100 1101 10)

We send 1010 0100 1101 1000 binary (0xA4D8) since control code 1010 loads input buffer register of channel B and updates the channel output.

c) In order to change the outputs simultaneously, we need to load the input buffer register for channel A without updating the output first then load the input buffer register for channel B and update the outputs at the same time.

First, we load channel A input buffer register using control code 0001 0010 0110 1100 binary (0x126C). Note it is the same code as (*Part a*) without the most significant bit set.

Then, we load channel B input buffer register, and update the outputs using control code 1010 0100 1101 1000 binary (0xA4D8)

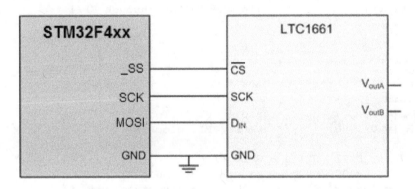

Figure 8-17: Connecting LTC1661 to the STM32F4xx

In the following program, we demonstrate a program to generate a sawtooth waveform using LTC1661 via SPI. The LTC1661 expects the chip select to stay low for the duration of the whole 16-bit transmission, so we use the software controlled slave select and use a GPIO pin PA4 as the chip select signal. From the timing diagram (shown earlier), we see the clock is idling low and the low to high transition (the leading edge) of the clock latches the data bit, so the clock polarity is set to 0 and the clock phase is 0 (SPI Mode 0).

The loop count 'i' of the for-loop is counting from 0 to 1023 and the values are sent to LTC1661 DAC. For each transmission of the value, first the chip select is asserted, the command 9 (write to register A and update the analog output) with the most significant four bits (i >> 6) are sent first, then the least significant six bits padded with two 0s ((i << 2) & 0xFF) are sent. The program waits for the transmission to complete before removing the chip select.

```
/* p8_2.c: Using SPI1 to generate a sawtooth waveform on LTC1661
 *
 * SPI1 is configured as master with software slave select.
 * Clock rate is set to 1 MHz. Polarity/Phase are 0, 0
 *
 * PA7   MOSI
 * PA5   SCK
 * PA4   SS
 *
 * This program was tested with Keil uVision v5.24a with DFP v2.11.0
 */

#include "stm32f4xx.h"

void SPI1_init(void);
void DAC_write(short data);

int main(void) {
    short i;

    SPI1_init();

    while(1) {
        for (i = 0; i < 1024; i++) {
            DAC_write(i);        /* write the letter through SPI1 */
        }
    }
}

/* enable SPI1 and associated GPIO pins */
void SPI1_init(void) {
    RCC->AHB1ENR |= 1;           /* enable GPIOA clock */
    RCC->APB2ENR |= 0x1000;      /* enable SPI1 clock */

    /* PORTA 5, 7 for SPI1 MOSI and SCLK */
    GPIOA->MODER &= ~0x0000CC00;    /* clear pin mode */
    GPIOA->MODER |=  0x00008800;    /* set pin alternate mode */
    GPIOA->AFR[0] &= ~0xF0F00000;   /* clear alt mode */
    GPIOA->AFR[0] |=  0x50500000;   /* set alt mode SPI1 */

    /* PORTA4 as GPIO output for SPI slave select */
    GPIOA->MODER &= ~0x00000300;    /* clear pin mode */
    GPIOA->MODER |=  0x00000100;    /* set pin output mode */

    SPI1->CR1 = 0x31C;              /* set the Baud rate, 8-bit data frame */
    SPI1->CR2 = 0;
    SPI1->CR1 |= 0x40;              /* enable SPI1 module */
}

/* This function enables slave select, writes one byte to SPI1,
   wait for transmit complete and deassert slave select. */
void DAC_write(short data) {
    data &= 0x03FF;                 /* make sure data is 10-bit */
    while (!(SPI1->SR & 2)) {}      /* wait until Transfer buffer Empty */
    GPIOA->BSRR = 0x00100000;       /* deassert slave select */
```

254

```
        SPI1->DR = 0x90 | (data >> 6);    /* write command and upper 4 bits of data */
        while (!(SPI1->SR & 2)) {}        /* wait until Transfer buffer Empty */
        SPI1->DR = (data << 2) & 0xFF;
        while (SPI1->SR & 0x80) {}        /* wait for transmission done */
        GPIOA->BSRR = 0x00000010;         /* assert slave select */
}
```

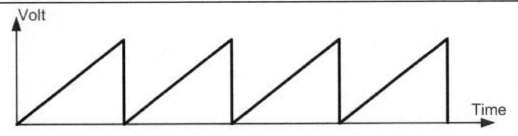

Figure 8-18: The Generated Sawtooth waveform

Sending Control/Data to LTC1661 in 16-bit Mode

In the earlier discussion, we mentioned that the DFF bit in SPI_CR1 register may be used to select 8-bit data frame format or 16-bit data frame format. Since LTC1661 requires a 16-bit transaction, it is natural to use the 16-bit data frame format. The program below uses 16-bit data frame format to perform the task as the previous program 8-2. You will see the code that sends data through SPI is simpler and more efficient.

```
Program 8-3: Generating a sawtooth waveform at LTC1661 DAC through SPI in 16-bit mode

/* p8_3.c: Using SPI1 to generate a sawtooth waveform on LTC1661
 *
 * SPI1 is configured as master with software slave select.
 * Clock rate is set to 1 MHz. Polarity/Phase are 0, 0.
 * This program is similar to p8_2 except the data frame size
 * is set to 16-bit.
 *
 * PA7   MOSI
 * PA5   SCK
 * PA4   SS
 *
 * This program was tested with Keil uVision v5.24a with DFP v2.11.0
 */

#include "stm32f4xx.h"

void SPI1_init(void);
void DAC_write(short data);

int main(void) {
    short i;

    SPI1_init();

    while(1) {
        for (i = 0; i < 1024; i++) {
```

```
            DAC_write(i);        /* write the letter through SPI1 */
        }
    }
}

/* enable SPI1 and associated GPIO pins */
void SPI1_init(void) {
    RCC->AHB1ENR |= 1;           /* enable GPIOA clock */
    RCC->APB2ENR |= 0x1000;      /* enable SPI1 clock */

    /* PORTA 5, 7 for SPI1 MOSI and SCLK */
    GPIOA->MODER &= ~0x0000CC00;     /* clear pin mode */
    GPIOA->MODER |=  0x00008800;     /* set pin alternate mode */
    GPIOA->AFR[0] &= ~0xF0F00000;    /* clear alt mode */
    GPIOA->AFR[0] |=  0x50500000;    /* set alt mode SPI1 */

    /* PORTA4 as GPIO output for SPI slave select */
    GPIOA->MODER &= ~0x00000300;     /* clear pin mode */
    GPIOA->MODER |=  0x00000100;     /* set pin output mode */

    SPI1->CR1 = 0xB1C;               /* set the Baud rate, 16-bit data frame */
    SPI1->CR2 = 0;
    SPI1->CR1 |= 0x40;               /* enable SPI1 module */
}

/* This function enables slave select, writes one byte to SPI1,
   wait for transmit complete and deassert slave select. */
void DAC_write(short data) {
    while (!(SPI1->SR & 2)) {}       /* wait until Transfer buffer Empty */
    GPIOA->BSRR = 0x00100000;        /* deassert slave select */
    SPI1->DR = 0x9000 | ((data << 2) & 0x0FFF);  /* write command and data */
    while (SPI1->SR & 0x80) {}       /* wait for transmission done */
    GPIOA->BSRR = 0x00000010;        /* assert slave select */
}
```

Now you may be wondering if using 16-bit data frame format is simpler and more efficient, why would we want to use the 8-bit format? The answer lies in the portability. Because 8-bit SPI is common to all the devices from all the manufacturer, the code written for 8-bit format can be easily ported to a different device. If you want to reuse the 16-bit program in a device that does not support the 16-bit format, the changes to the program will be larger.

Review Questions

1. True or false. LTC1661 is an ADC.
2. True or false. LTC1661 is a 10-bit DAC.
3. True or false. There are 4 output channels in the LTC1661.

Answers to Review Questions

Section 8.1

1. False
2. True

Section 8.2

1. True
2. False
3. Slave Select (SS)
4. SPIx_CR1
5. SPIx_CR1

Section 8.3

1. False
2. True
3. False, it has only two analog output channels

Chapter 9: I2C Protocol and RTC Interfacing

This chapter covers I2C bus interfacing and programming. Section 9.1 examines the I2C bus protocol. Section 9.2 shows the inner working of I2C module in STM32F4xx Arm devices. The DS1337 RTC and its I2C interfacing and programming are covered in Section 9.3.

Section 9.1: I2C Bus Protocol

The IIC (Inter-Integrated Circuit) is a bus interface connection incorporated into many devices such as sensors, RTC, and EEPROM. The IIC is also referred to as I2C, I^2C, or I square C in many technical literatures. In this section, we examine the signals of the I2C bus and focus on I2C terminology and protocols.

I2C Bus

The I2C bus was originally started by Philips, but in recent years has become a widely used standard adopted by many semiconductor companies. I2C is ideal to attach low-speed peripherals to a motherboard or embedded system or anywhere that a reliable communication over a short distance is required. As we will see in this chapter, I2C provides a connection-oriented communication with acknowledgement. I2C devices use only 2 pins for data transfer, instead of the 8 or more pins used in traditional parallel buses. These two signals are called SCL (Serial Clock) which synchronizes the data transfer between two chips, and SDA (Serial Data). The reduction of communication pins reduces the package size and power consumption drastically, making them ideal for many applications in which space is a major concern. These two pins, SDA, and SCK, make the I2C a 2-wire interface. In some application notes, I2C is referred to as Two-Wire Serial Interface (TWI).

I2C line electrical characteristics

I2C devices use only 2 bidirectional open-drain pins for data communication. To implement I2C, a 4.7k ohm pull-up resistor for each of bus lines is needed (see Figure 9-1). This implements a wired-AND which is needed to implement I2C protocols. It means that if one or more devices pull the line to low (zero) level, the line state is zero. The level of the line will be 1 only if none of the devices pull the line to low level.

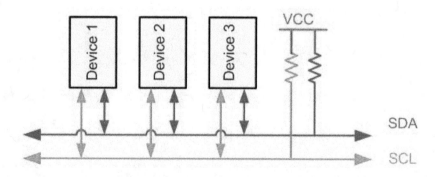

Figure 9-1: I2C Bus Characteristics

I2C Nodes

In I2C protocol, more than 100 devices can share an I2C bus. Each of these devices is called a *node*. In I2C terminology, each node can operate as either master or slave. Master is a device that generates the

Clock for the system, it also initiates and terminates a transmission. Slave is a node that receives the clock and is addressed by the master. In I2C, both master and slave can receive or transmit data. So there are 4 modes of operation for each node. They are: master transmitter, master receiver, slave transmitter and slave receiver. Notice that each node can have more than one mode of operation at different times but it has only one mode of operation at any given time. See Example 9-1

Example 9-1

Give an example to show how a device (node) can use more than one mode of operation.

Solution:

If you connect a microcontroller to an EEPROM with I2C, the microcontroller does master transmit operation to write to EEPROM and master receive operation to read from EEPROM

In next sections, you will see that a node can do the operations of master and slave at a different time.

Bit Format

I2C is a synchronous serial protocol; each data bit transferred on the SDA line is synchronized by a high to low pulse of the clock on SCL line. According to I2C protocols, the data line cannot change when the clock line is high, it can change only when the clock line is low. See Figure 9-2. STOP and START condition are the only exceptions to this rule.

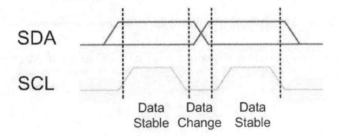

Figure 9-2: I2C Bit Format

START and STOP conditions

As we mentioned before, I2C is a connection-oriented communication protocol, it means that each transmission is initiated by a START condition and is terminated by STOP condition. Between the START and STOP, a connection is established between the master and the slave. Remember that the START and STOP conditions are generated by the master.

STOP and START conditions must be distinguished from bits of address or data and that is why they do not obey the bit format rule that we mentioned before.

START and STOP conditions are generated by keeping the level of the SCL line to high and then changing the level of the SDA line. START condition is generated by a high-to-low change in SDA line when SCL is high. STOP condition is generated by a low-to-high change in SDA line when SCL is high. See Figure 9-3.

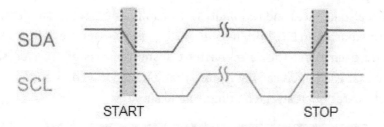

Figure 9-3: START and STOP Conditions

The bus is considered busy between each pair of START and STOP conditions and no other master tries to take control of the bus when it is busy. If a master, which has the control of the bus, wishes to initiate a new transfer and does not want to release the bus before starting the new transfer, it issues a new START condition between a pair of START and STOP condition. It is called REPEATED START condition or simply RESTART condition. See Figure 9-4.

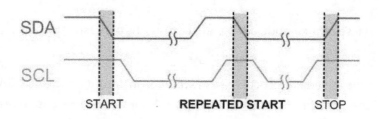

Figure 9-4: REPEATED START Condition

Example 9-2 shows why REPEATED START condition is necessary.

Example 9-2

Give an example to show when a master must use REPEATED START condition. What will happen if the master does not use it?

Solution:

If you connect two microcontrollers (uA and uB) and an EEPROM with I2C, and the uA wants to display the sum of the contents at address 0x34 and 0x35 of EEPROM, it has to use REPEATED START condition. Let's see what may happen if the uA does not use REPEATED START condition. uA transmit a START condition, reads the content of address 0x34 of EEPROM and transmit a STOP condition to release the bus. Before uA reads the contents of address 0x35, the uB seize the bus and change the contents of address 0x34 and 0x35 of EEPROM. Then uA reads the content of address 0x35, adds it to last content of address 0x34 and display the result to LCD. The result on the LCD is neither the sum of old values of address 0x34 and 0x35 nor the sum of the new values of address 0x34 and 0x35 of EEPROM!

Message format in I2C

In I2C, each address or data to be transmitted must be framed in 9 bit long. The first 8 bits are put on SDA line by the transmitter and the 9th bit is the acknowledgment by the receiver or it may be NACK (negative acknowledge). Notice that the clock is always generated by the master, regardless of it being transmitter or receiver. To allow acknowledge, the transmitter release the SDA line during the 9th clock so the receiver can pull the SDA line low to indicate an ACK. If the receiver doesn't pull the SDA line low, it is considered as NACK. See Figure 9-5.

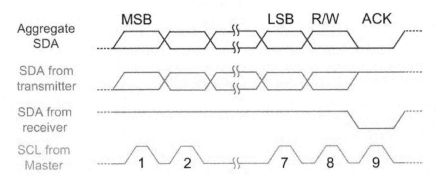

Figure 9-5: Byte Format in I2C

In I2C, each byte may contain either address or data. Also, notice that: **START condition + slave address byte + one or more data byte + STOP condition** together form a complete data transfer. Next, we will study slave address and data byte formats and how to combine them to make a complete transmission.

Address Byte Format

Like any other bytes, all address bytes transmitted on the I2C bus are nine bits long. It consists of seven address bits, one READ/WRITE control bit, and an acknowledge bit. (See Figure 9-6)

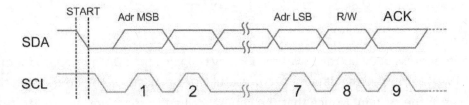

Figure 9-6: Address Byte Format in I2C

Slave address bits are used to address a specific slave device on the bus. Seven bit address let the master to address maximum of 128 slaves on the bus. Although address 0000 000 is reserved for general call and all address of the format 1111 xxx are reserved for many devices. There are 8 more reserved addresses. That means 111 (128-1-8-8) devices can share an I2C bus. In I2C bus the MSB of the address is transmitted first. The I2C bus also supports 10-bit address where the address is split into two frames at the beginning of the transmission. For the rest of the discussion, we will focus on 7 bit address only.

The 8th bit in the address byte is READ/WRITE control bit. If this bit is high, the master will read the next byte from the slave, otherwise, the master will write the next byte on the bus to the slave. When a slave detects its address on the bus, it knows that it is being addressed and it should acknowledge in the ninth clock cycle by pulling SDA to low. If the addressed slave is not ready or for any reason does not want to respond to the master, it should leave the SDA line high in the 9th clock cycle. It is considered as NACK. In case of NACK, the master can transmit a STOP condition to terminate the transmission, or a REPEATED START condition to initiate a new transmission.

Example 9-3 shows how a master says that it wants to write to a slave.

Example 9-3

Show how a master initiates a write to a slave with address 1001101?

Solution:

The following actions are performed by the master:
1) The master put a high to low pulse on SDA while SCL is high to generate a start condition to start the transmission
2) The master transmits 1001101 0 into the bus. The first seven bits (1001101) indicates the slave address and the 8th bit (0) indicate write operation and the master will write the next byte (data) to the slave.

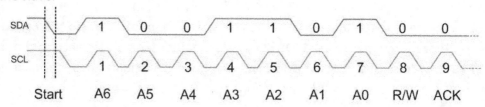

An address byte consisting of a slave address and a READ is called SLA+R while an address byte consisting of a slave address and a WRITE is called SLA+W.

As we mentioned before, address 0000 000 is reserved for a general call. It means that when a master transmits address 0000 000 all slaves respond by changing the SDA line to zero for one clock cycle for an ACK and wait to receive the data byte. It is useful when a master wants to transmit the same data byte to all slaves in the system. Notice that the general call address cannot be used to read data from slaves because no more than one slave is able to write to the bus at a given time. Also, not all the devices respond to a general call.

Data Byte Format

Like other bytes, data bytes are 9 bits long too. The first 8 bits are a byte of data to be transmitted and the 9th bit, is for ACK. If the receiver has received the last byte of data and does not wish to receive more data, it may signal a NACK by leaving the SDA line high. The master should terminate the transmission with a STOP after a NACK appears. In data bytes, like address bytes, MSB is transmitted first.

Combining Address and Data Bytes into a Transmission

In I2C, normally, a transmission is started by a START condition, followed by an address byte (SLA+R/W), one or more data bytes and finished by a STOP condition. Figure 9-7 shows a typical data transmission. Try to understand each element in the figure. (See Example 9-4)

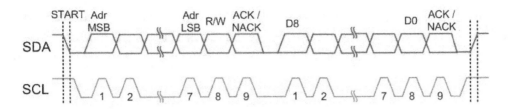

Figure 9-7: Typical Data Transmission

Example 9-4

Show how a master writes data value 1111 0000 to a slave with an address 1001 101?

Solution:

The following actions are performed by the master:

1) The master puts a high to low transition on SDA while SCL is high to generate a START condition to start the transmission

2) The master transmits 1001 101 0 on the bus. The first seven bits (1001 101) indicate the slave address and the 8th bit (0) indicates a write operation and says that the master will write the next byte (data) to the slave.

3) The slave pulls the SDA line low at the 9th clock pulse to signal an ACK to say that it is ready to receive data

4) After receiving the ACK, the master will transmit the data byte (1111 0000) on the SDA line. (MSB first)

5) When the slave device receives the data, it leaves the SDA line high to signal NACK and inform the master that the slave received the last data byte and does not need any more data

6) After receiving the NACK, the master will know that no more data should be transmitted. The master changes the SDA line from low to high when the SCL line is high to transmit a STOP condition and then releases the bus.

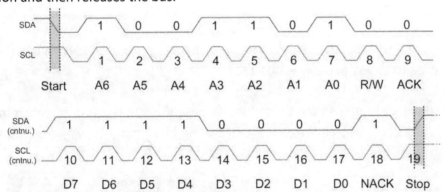

Clock stretching

One of the features of the I2C protocol is clock stretching. It is used by a slow slave device to synchronize with the master. If an addressed slave device is not ready to process more data it will stretch the clock by holding the clock line (SCL) low after receiving (or sending) a bit of data so the master will not be able to raise the clock line (because devices are wire-ANDed) and will wait until the slave releases the SCL line to show it is ready for the next bit. See Figure 9-8. Clock stretching can be used to slow down the clock for each bit or it can be used to temporarily halt the clock at the end of a byte while the receiver is processing the data.

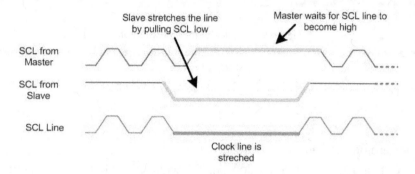

Figure 9-8: Clock Stretching

Arbitration

I2C protocol supports multi-master bus system. It doesn't mean that more than one master can use the bus at the same time. Each master waits for the current transmission to finish and then start to use the bus. But it is possible that two or more masters initiate a transmission at about the same time. In this case, the arbitration happens.

Each master has to check the level of the bus and compare it with the levels it is driving; if it doesn't match, that master has lost the arbitration and will switch to slave mode. In the case of arbitration, the winning master will continue the transmission. Notice that neither the bus is corrupted nor the data is lost. See Example 9-5

Example 9-5

If two master A and B start at about the same time, what happens if master A wants to write to slave 0010 000 and master B wants to write to slave 0001 111?

Solution:

Master A will lose the arbitration in the third clock because the SDA line is different from the output of master A at the third clock. Master A switches to slave mode and stops driving the bus after losing the arbitration.

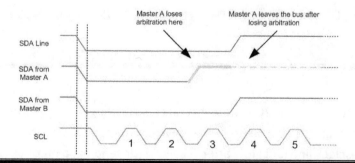

Multi-byte burst write

Burst mode writing is an effective means of loading data into consecutive memory locations. It is supported in I2C, SPI, and many other serial protocols. In burst mode, we provide the address of the first memory location, followed by the data for that location. From then on, consecutive bytes are written to consecutive memory locations. In this mode, the I2C device internally increments the address location as long as STOP condition is not detected. The following steps are used to send (write) multiple bytes of data in burst mode for I2C devices.

1. The master generates a START condition.
2. The master transmits the slave address followed by a zero bit (for write).
3. The master transmits the memory address of the first location.
4. The master transmits the data to the first memory location and from then on, the master simply provides consecutive bytes of data to be placed in consecutive memory locations in the slave.
5. The master generates a STOP condition.

Figure 9-9 shows how to write 0x05, 0x16, and 0x0B to 3 consecutive locations starting from location 00001111 of slave 1111000.

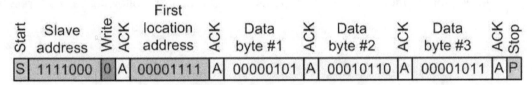

Figure 9-9: Multi-byte Burst Write

Multi-byte burst read

Burst mode reading is an effective means of bringing out the contents of consecutive memory locations. In burst mode, we provide the address of the first memory location only. From then on, contents are brought out from consecutive memory locations. In this mode, the I2C device internally increments the address location as long as STOP condition is not detected. The following steps are used to get (read) multiple bytes of data using burst mode for I2C devices.

1. The master generates a START condition.
2. The master transmits the slave address followed by a zero bit (for writing the memory address).
3. The master transmits the memory address of the first memory location.
4. The master generates a RESTART condition to switch the bus direction from write to read.
5. The master transmits the slave address followed by a one bit (for read).
6. The master clocks the bus 8 times and the slave device provides the data for the first location.
7. The master provides an ACK.
8. The master reads the consecutive locations and provides an ACK for each byte.
9. The master gives a NACK for the last byte received to signal the slave that the read is complete.
10. The master generates a STOP condition.

Figure 9-10 shows how to read three consecutive locations starting from location 00001111 of slave number 1111000.

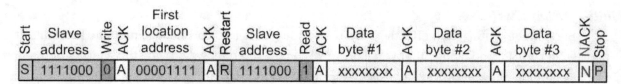

Start	Slave address	Write	ACK	First location address	ACK	Restart	Slave address	Read	ACK	Data byte #1	ACK	Data byte #2	ACK	Data byte #3	NACK	Stop
S	1111000	0	A	00001111	A	R	1111000	1	A	xxxxxxxx	A	xxxxxxxx	A	xxxxxxxx	N	P

Figure 9-10: Multi-byte Burst Read

Review Questions

1. True or false. I2C protocol is ideal for short distance.
2. How many bits are there in a frame? Which bit is for acknowledgement?
3. True or false. START and STOP conditions are generated when the SDA is high.
4. What is the name of the procedure a slow slave device uses to synchronize with a fast master?
5. True or false. After arbitration of two masters, both of them must start transmission from beginning.

Section 9.2: I2C Programming in STM32F4xx Arm

The STM32F4xx chip comes with several on-chip I2C modules. In this section, we examine the registers and features of I2C module. The I2C modules are located at the following base addresses:

I2C Module	Base Address
I2C1	0x4000 5400 - 0x4000 57FF
I2C2	0x4000 5800 - 0x4000 5BFF
I2C3	0x4000 5C00 - 0x4000 5FFF

Table 9-1: I2C Module Base Address for STM32F4xx

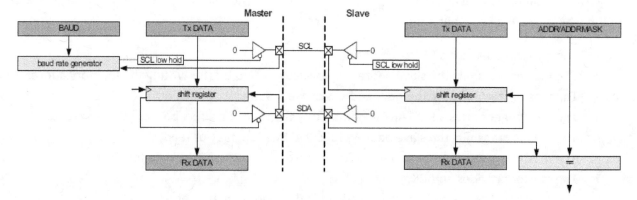

Figure 9-11: I2C Master Slave connection

Enabling clock to I2C

Just like other peripherals we must enable the clock to the I2C modules before we can use it. This is done with RCC APB1 peripheral clock enable register (RCC_APB1ENR). See Figure 9-12:

31	30	29	28	27	26	25	24	23	22	21	20	19	18	17	16
Res	Res	DAC EN	PWR EN	CEC EN	CAN2 EN	CAN1 EN	FMPI2C1 EN	I2C3 EN	I2C2 EN	I2C1 EN	UART5 EN	UART4 EN	USART3 EN	USART2 EN	SPDIFRX EN
		rw	rw	rw	rw	rw	rw	rw	rw	rw	rw	rw	rw	rw	rw

15	14	13	12	11	10	9	8	7	6	5	4	3	2	1	0
SPI3 EN	SPI2 EN	Res	Res	WWDG EN	Res	Res	TIM14 EN	TIM13 EN	TIM12 EN	TIM7 EN	TIM6 EN	TIM5 EN	TIM4 EN	TIM3 EN	TIM2 EN
rw	rw			rw			rw	rw	rw	rw	rw	rw	rw	rw	rw

Bit 23 **I2C3EN:** I2C3 clock enable

This bit is set and cleared by software.

0: I2C3 clock disabled

1: I2C3 clock enabled

Bit 22 **I2C2EN:** I2C2 clock enable

This bit is set and cleared by software.

0: I2C2 clock disabled

1: I2C2 clock enabled

Bit 21 **I2C1EN:** I2C1 clock enable

This bit is set and cleared by software.

0: I2C1 clock disabled

1: I2C1 clock enabled

Figure 9-12: RCC APB1 peripheral clock enable register (RCC_APB1ENR) to enable clock to I2C

I2C Registers

To program the I2C module, we need to examine the registers associated with it. Table 9-2 shows some of the registers. Notice that I2C and SPI are called synchronous since a single clock is used to synchronize the data transfer between the STM32F4xx and I2C (or SPI) devices. Recall from Chapter 4 that there was no such a clock for asynchronous USART. USART used only TxD and RxD and common ground between the Arm and other devices.

Register Name	Register Function	Register Address
I2C_CR1	Control 1	0x0000
I2C_CR2	Control 2	0x0004
I2C_DR	Data	0x0010
I2C_SR1	Status 1	0x0014
I2C_SR2	Status 2	0x0018
I2C_CCR	Clock Control	0x001C
I2C_TRISE	SCL Rising Time	0x0020

Table 9-2: Some I2C Registers in STM32F4xx

Configuring the I2C Module

Both I2C_CR1 (Control 1) and I2C_CR2 (Control 2) registers are used to configure the I2C. See figures below.

15	14	13	12	11	10	9	8	7	6	5	4	3	2	1	0
SW RST	Res	ALERT	PEC	POS	ACK	STOP	START	NO STRET CH	ENGC	ENPEC	ENARP	SMB TYPE	Res	SM BUS	PE
rw		rw	rw	rw	rw	rw	rw	rw	rw	rw	rw	rw		rw	rw

Bit 15 **SWRST**: Software reset

When set, the I2C is under reset state. Before resetting this bit, make sure the I2C lines are released and the bus is free.

0: I2C Peripheral not under reset

1: I2C Peripheral under reset state

Bit 10 **ACK**: Acknowledge enable

This bit is set and cleared by software and cleared by hardware when PE=0.

0: No acknowledge returned

1: Acknowledge returned after a byte is received (matched address or data)

Bit 9 **STOP**: Stop generation

The bit is set and cleared by software, cleared by hardware when a Stop condition is detected, set by hardware when a timeout error is detected.

In Master Mode:

0: No Stop generation.

1: Stop generation after the current byte transfer or after the current Start condition is sent.

In Slave mode:

0: No Stop generation.

1: Release the SCL and SDA lines after the current byte transfer.

Bit 8 **START**: Start generation

This bit is set and cleared by software and cleared by hardware when start is sent or PE=0.

In Master Mode:

0: No Start generation

1: Repeated start generation

In Slave mode:

0: No Start generation

1: Start generation when the bus is free

Bit 0 **PE**: Peripheral enable

0: Peripheral disable

1: Peripheral enable

Figure 9-13A: I2C_CR1 (Control 1) Register

15	14	13	12	11	10	9	8	7	6	5	4	3	2	1	0
Res	Res	Res	LAST	DMA EN	ITBUF EN	ITEVT EN	ITERR EN	Res	Res			FREQ[5:0]			
			rw	rw	rw	rw	rw			rw	rw	rw	rw	rw	rw

Bits 5:0 **FREQ[5:0]**: Peripheral clock frequency

> The FREQ bits must be configured with the APB clock frequency value (I2C peripheral
> connected to APB). The FREQ field is used by the peripheral to generate data setup and
> hold times compliant with the I2C specifications. The minimum allowed frequency is 2
> MHz,
> the maximum frequency is limited by the maximum APB frequency (42 MHz) and cannot
> exceed 50 MHz (peripheral intrinsic maximum limit).
> 0b000000: Not allowed
> 0b000001: Not allowed
> 0b000010: 2 MHz
>
> ...
>
> 0b110010: 50 MHz
> Higher than 0b101010: Not allowed

Figure 9-13B: I2C_CR2 (Control 2) Register

Master or Slave

The I2C Module is in slave mode when it is enabled by writing a '1' to the PE (Peripheral Enable) bit of I2C_CR1 (Control 1) register. When the software writes a '1' to the START bit of I2C_CR1 register, a start condition is generated on the I2C bus and the I2C module becomes the master. The I2C module stays as the master until it issues a STOP condition or the bus arbitration failed then it returns to slave mode. When the I2C module is in master mode, it is responsible to generate the bus clock signal.

Bus *Clock Speed*

Because the I2C bus is an open-drain bus, the I2C module has limited control over the clock speed. The I2C module controls how much time it holds the clock signal low and how long it leaves the clock signal high before driving it low again. Because of the clock stretching mentioned in the previous section, slave is allowed to stretch the clock by keeping the signal low longer, the period of SCL may also vary from cycle to cycle. The rise time of the signal depends on the pull-up resistor value and the stray capacitance of the circuit. On the other hand, for a synchronous communication, the precision of the clock frequency is usually not important because all the devices are driven by the same clock.

In the STM32F4xx I2C module, the I2C module supports both standard mode (Sm) of 100KHz and Fast mode (Fm) of 400KHz. There are three registers involved in configuring the I2C bus clock. Standard mode or fast mode is selected by F/S bit of the I2C Clock control register (I2C_CCR). See the Figure 9-14. Note that The I2C_CCR register can be configured only when the I2C is disabled, which is done by setting the PE (Peripheral Enable) bit to '0' in the I2C_CR1 register.

15	14	13	12	11	10	9	8	7	6	5	4	3	2	1	0
F/S	DUTY	Res	Res	CCR[11:0]											
rw	rw			rw	rw	rw	rw	rw	rw	rw	rw	rw	rw	rw	rw

Bit 15 **F/S:** I2C master mode selection

    0: Sm mode I2C

    1: Fm mode I2C

Bit 14 **DUTY:** Fm mode duty cycle

    0: Fm mode t_{low}/t_{high} = 2

    1: Fm mode t_{low}/t_{high} = 16/9 (see CCR)

Bits 13:12 Reserved, must be kept at reset value

Bits 11:0 **CCR[11:0]:** Clock control register in Fm/Sm mode (Master mode)

    Controls the SCL clock in master mode.

    Sm mode or SMBus:

    Thigh = CCR * T_{PCLK1}

    Tlow = CCR * T_{PCLK1}

Figure 9-14: I2C Clock Control register (I2C_CCR)

The I2C clock is derived from the APB peripheral clock which is the system clock (SYSCLK) going through AHB and APB prescaler just like other peripherals such as USART, SPI, ADC and so on. We have used the default 16 MHz as SYSCLK and also 16 MHz APB clock so far in this book. The low-time and the high-time of the SCL are specified in the CCR bits of the I2C_CCR register. They are the period of APB clock multiplied by the value of CCR bits.

The value of the FREQ bits of the I2C_CR2 register should match the APB clock frequency in MHz. The minimum APB frequency is 2MHz and the maximum is 50MHz as shown in Table 9-3.

FREQ[5:0] in binary	Allowed Freq
000000	Not allowed
000001	Not allowed
000010	2 MHz (minimum acceptable for Standard mode)
000011	3 MHz
000100	4 MHz (minimum acceptable for Fast mode)
000101	5 MHz
000110	6 MHz
000111	7 MHz
001000	8 MHz
...	
...	
010000	16 MHz
...	
...	
110010	50 MHz
Higher than 0b100100: Not allowed	

Table 9-3: I2C Frequency Selection in I2C_CR2 Register

Example 9-6

Assume the SYSCLK of 16MHz is fed into I2C, find the value of I2C_CR2 register if we do not use interrupt or DMA?

Solution:

From Table 9-3, we see FREQ = 1000 for 16MHz. That means I2C_CR2 is 0000 0000 0001 0000 = 0x10 since we are not enabling any of the interrupt or DMA features of the I2C.

Example 9-7A

Find the value of I2C_CR2 and I2C_CRR for I2C standard mode of 100 KHz with clock frequency of 8MHz. Leave the interrupt and DMA bits 0.

Solution:

From Table 9-3, we see FREQ = 01000(in binary) for 8 MHz. That means I2C_CR2 is 0000 0000 0000 1000 = 0x08 since we are not enabling any of the interrupt or DMA features of the I2C.

The period of the APB bus is

T_{PCLK1} = 1 / 8 MHz = 125 ns.

The period of 100 KHz is

1 / 100 KHz = 10,000 ns for period.

Half of the period is in T_{high} and half of the period is in T_{low}.

Half of 10,000 ns = 5000ns

5000 ns / 125 ns = 40 = 0x28 therefore we need to place 0x28 in the CCR bits. That means I2C_CCR=0000 0000 0010 1000 = 0x28

Example 9-7B

Repeat the last example using 16MHz for APB clock.

Solution:

From Table 9-3, we see FREQ = 10000 (in binary) for 16 MHz. That means I2C_CR2 is 0000 0000 0001 0000=0x10.

T_{PCLK1} = 1 / 16 MHz = 62.5 ns.

1 / 100KHz = 10,000ns for period.

Half of 10,000 ns = 5000 ns.

5000 ns / 62.5 ns = 80 = 0x50 therefore we need to place 0x50 in CCR bits. That means I2C_CCR = 0000 0000 0101 0000 = 0x50

The I2C_TRISE register is used for the maximum duration of the rise time of the I2C clock to keep a stable SCL frequency. In Sm mode, the maximum allowed SCL rise time by the specification is 1000 ns.

In the earlier example for the I2C_CR2 register, the value of FREQ[5:0] = 16 for 16 MHz which gives T_{PCLK1} = 62.5 ns. That means, TRISE[5:0] of this register bits must be programmed with 17 since 1000 ns / 62.5 ns = 16 + 1.

271

15	14	13	12	11	10	9	8	7	6	5	4	3	2	1	0
Res	Res	Res	Res	Res	Res	Res	Res	Res	Res	\multicolumn{6}{c}{TRISE[5:0]}					
										rw	rw	rw	rw	rw	rw

Bits 15:6 Reserved, must be kept at reset value

Bits 5:0 **TRISE[5:0]**: Maximum rise time in Fm/Sm mode (Master mode)

These bits should provide the maximum duration of the SCL feedback loop in master mode. The purpose is to keep a stable SCL frequency whatever the SCL rising edge duration.

These bits must be programmed with the maximum SCL rise time given in the I2C bus specification, incremented by 1.

Figure 9-15: I2C TRISE register (I2C_TRISE)

Transmit and Receive Data (I2C_DR) Register

In transmit mode, we place a byte of address or data in I2C_DR register for transmission. During continuous transmission, when the Data register empty flag (TxE) of the I2C_SR1 register is set, the data should be written into the data register. This is a 16-bit register but only the lowest 8 bits are used.

In receive mode, the received data is placed in I2C_DR register. Reading this register gets the last byte of received data. During continuous transmission, when the Data register not empty the flag RxNE of the I2C_SR1 register is set, the data should be read as soon as possible.

15	14	13	12	11	10	9	8	7	6	5	4	3	2	1	0
Res	Res	Res	Res	Res	Res	Res	Res	\multicolumn{8}{c}{DR[7:0]}							
								rw	rw	rw	rw	rw	rw	rw	rw

Bits 7:0 **DR[7:0]** 8-bit data register

Byte received or to be transmitted to the bus.

− Transmitter mode: Byte transmission starts automatically when a byte is written in the DR register. A continuous transmit stream can be maintained if the next data to be transmitted is put in DR once the transmission is started (TxE=1)

− Receiver mode: Received byte is copied into DR (RxNE=1). A continuous transmit Stream can be maintained if DR is read before the next data byte is received (RxNE=1).

Figure 9-16: I2C_DR (Data Register) for Transmit/Receive Buffer Register

I2C Status Register 1 (I2C_SR1)

The Status Register (I2C_SR1) contains many flags indicating the events that need attention. These flags are important to the operations of the I2C module.

The TxE (Data register empty for transmitter) indicates that I2C_DR data register is empty and ready to accept another byte of data.

The RxNE (Data register not empty for receiver) is set when a byte is successfully received in master read mode. This indicates that Data register is full and the I2C module has a byte of data to be picked up by the CPU. In other words, this flag is set when an I2C master has received a byte successfully. This flag is cleared when we read a byte from Data Register to be saved before it is lost by next incoming I2C receive.

15	14	13	12	11	10	9	8	7	6	5	4	3	2	1	0
SMB ALERT	TIMEO UT	Res.	PEC ERR	OVR	AF	ARLO	BERR	TxE	RxNE	Res.	STOPF	ADD10	BTF	ADDR	SB
rc_w0	rc_w0		rc_w0	rc_w0	rc_w0	rc_w0	rc_w0	r	r		r	r	r	r	r

Figure 9-17: : I2C Status Register 1 (I2C_SR1)

Bits	Field	Description
7	TxE	Data register empty (transmitter) This is set when the transmit data register is empty and a byte of data can be written into the data register 0: Data register not empty 1: Data register empty
6	RxNE	Data register not empty (receiver) This is set when a byte is received in receive mode 0: Data register empty 1: Data register not empty
2	BTF	Byte transfer finished In transmit mode, it is set when all the data are transmitted. The program should wait until this bit is set before issuing a stop condition. In receive mode, it is set when a byte of data is received. The program should wait until this bit is set before reading from the data register. 0: data byte transfer not done 1: data byte transfer succeeded

Table 9-4: I2C Status Register 1(I2C_SR1) Bit Description

Configuring GPIO for I2C

In using I2C, we must configure the GPIO pins to allow the connections of the SCL and SDA signals to two GPIO pins of the device. In this regard, it is similar to other peripherals. To assign GPIO pins to I2C module, the GPIOx_AFRL register is used to set the alternative pin option of AF4 as shown in Table 9-6.

Pin	Function
PB6	I2C1_SCL
PB7	I2C1_SDA
PB8	I2C1_SCL
PB9	I2C1_SDA
PB10	I2C2_SCL
PB11	I2C2_SDA
PA8	I2C3_SCL
PC9	I2C3_SDA

Table 9-5: I2C pins in STM32F4xx (See Appendix B full listing)

273

Port		AF0	AF1	AF2	AF3	AF4	AF5	AF6	AF7
		SYS	TIM1/2	TIM3/4/5	TIM8/9/ 10/11/ CEC	I2C1/2/3 /4/CEC	SPI1/2/3/ 4	SPI2/3/4/ SAI1	SPI2/3/ USART1/ 2/3/UART 5/SPDIFR X
Port B	PB0	-	TIM1_CH2N	TIM3_CH3	TIM8_ CH2N̄	-	-	-	SPI3_MOS I/ I2S3_SD
	PB1	-	TIM1_CH3N	TIM3_CH4	TIM8_ CH3N̄	-	-	-	-
	PB2	-	TIM2_CH4	-	-	-	-	SAI1_ SD_Ā	SPI3_MOS I/ I2S3_SD
	PB3	JTDO/ TRACES WO	TIM2_CH2	-	-	I2C2_ SDA	SPI1_SCK /I2S1_CK	SPI3_SCK / I2S3_CK	-
	PB4	NJTRST	-	TIM3_CH1	-	I2C3_ SDA	SPI1_MISO	SPI3_ MISŌ	SPI2_NSS/ I2S2_WS
	PB5	-	-	TIM3_CH2	-	I2C1_ SMBĀ	SPI1_MOSI /I2S1_SD	SPI3_ MOSI/ I2S3_SD	-
	PB6	-	-	TIM4_CH1	HDMI_ CEC	I2C1_ SCL	-	-	USART1_ TX
	PB7	-	-	TIM4_CH2	-	I2C1_ SDA	-	-	USART1_ RX
	PB8	-	TIM2_CH1/ TIM2_ETR	TIM4_CH3	TIM10_ CH1	I2C1_ SCL	-	-	-
	PB9	-	TIM2_ CH2	TIM4_CH4	TIM11_ CH1	I2C1_ SDA	SPI2_NSS/ I2S2_WS	SAI1_ FS_B̄	-
	PB10	-	TIM2_CH3	-	-	I2C2_ SCL	SPI2_SCK/ I2S2_CK	SAI1_ SCK_Ā	USART3_ TX
	PB11	-	TIM2_CH4	-	-	I2C2_ SDA	-	-	USART3_ RX
	PB12	-	TIM1_BKIN	-	-	I2C2_ SMBA	SPI2_NSS/ I2S2_WS	SAI1_ SCK_B̄	USART3_ CK
	PB13	-	TIM1_CH1N	-	-	-	SPI2_SCK/ I2S2_CK	-	USART3_ CTS
	PB14	-	TIM1_CH2N	-	TIM8_ CH2N̄	-	SPI2_MISO	-	USART3_ RTS
	PB15	RTC_ REFIN	TIM1_CH3N	-	TIM8_ CH3N̄	-	SPI2_MOSI /I2S2_SD	-	-

Table 9-6: Alternative pin function multiplexing (See Appendix B for full List)

31	30	29	28	27	26	25	24	23	22	21	20	19	18	17	16
MODER15[1:0]		MODER14[1:0]		MODER13[1:0]		MODER12[1:0]		MODER11[1:0]		MODER10[1:0]		MODER9[1:0]		MODER8[1:0]	
rw	rw	rw	rw	rw	rw	rw	rw	rw	rw	rw	rw	rw	rw	rw	rw
15	14	13	12	11	10	9	8	7	6	5	4	3	2	1	0
MODER7[1:0]		MODER6[1:0]		MODER5[1:0]		MODER4[1:0]		MODER3[1:0]		MODER2[1:0]		MODER1[1:0]		MODER0[1:0]	
rw	rw	rw	rw	rw	rw	rw	rw	rw	rw	rw	rw	rw	rw	rw	rw

Bits 2y:2y+1 **MODERy[1:0]:** Port x configuration bits (y = 0..15)

These bits are written by software to configure the I/O direction mode.

00: Input (reset state)

01: General purpose output mode

10: Alternate function mode

11: Analog mode

Figure 9-18: GPIOx_MODER Register Options

31	30	29	28	27	26	25	24	23	22	21	20	19	18	17	16
AFRL7[3:0]				AFRL6[3:0]				AFRL5[3:0]				AFRL4[3:0]			
rw	rw	rw	rw	rw	rw	rw	rw	rw	rw	rw	rw	rw	rw	rw	rw
15	14	13	12	11	10	9	8	7	6	5	4	3	2	1	0
AFRL3[3:0]				AFRL2[3:0]				AFRL1[3:0]				AFRL0[3:0]			
rw	rw	rw	rw	rw	rw	rw	rw	rw	rw	rw	rw	rw	rw	rw	rw

Bits 31:0 **AFRLy:** Alternate function selection for port x bit y (y = 0..7)

These bits are written by software to configure alternate function I/Os

AFRLy selection:

0000: AF0	1000: AF8
0001: AF1	1001: AF9
0010: AF2	1010: AF10
0011: AF3	1011: AF11
0100: AF4	1100: AF12
0101: AF5	1101: AF13
0110: AF6	1110: AF14
0111: AF7	1111: AF15

Figure 9-19: AFRL Register

Configuring I2C for master data transmission

Here are the steps to configure the I2C for master data transmission and receiving. The sample programs are in the next section using DS1337 as the slave device.

1. Enable the clock to GPIOB that has the I2C I/O pins
2. Enable the clock to I2C using the RCC_APB1ENR register.
3. Configure the port pins for I2C by with GPIOx_MODER and GPIOx_AFRL registers
4. Configure the port pins for I2C to be open-drain output with pull-up resistors
5. Reset the I2C using bit 15 of I2C_CR1
6. Configure I2C_CR1 and I2C_CR2 registers to select I2C master mode
7. Set the SCL frequency using I2C_CCR register
8. Configure the maximum rise time of I2C SCL using I2C_TRISE register
9. Enable the I2C by setting PE=1 bit of I2C_CR2 register

Send a byte of data to a slave device

Most of the I2C slave devices have a set of registers. Writing a byte of data to a specific register requires that the register address is written first before the data. So a single byte data write to the device incurs three writes from the I2C master to the slave device: a) the slave address, b) the register address, and c) the data. There are many I2C EEPROM/Flash devices that require the same procedure. The memory address is sent to the device after the slave address before writing the data to the memory. Most of them support sequential access that is after the first access, the next access without restart will go to the next location. The sequential access helps improve the throughput of the I2C bus. We will demonstrate the sequential access in Program 9-3, 9-4 of next section.

1. Monitor the BUSY bit of I2C_SR2 (Status 2) register until the bus is idle
2. Write to START bit (bit 8) of I2C_CR1 (Control 1) register to generate a START condition on the bus
3. Wait until the START condition is complete, the SB bit (bit 0) of I2C_SR1 register is set
4. Write the slave address with the R/W bit (bit 0) cleared (for a write) to I2C_DR (Data Register), this will transmit the slave address
5. Wait until ADDR bit (bit 1) of I2C_SR1 register is set signaling that the slave address is sent
6. Read I2C_SR1 and I2C_SR2 to clear the ADDR bit
7. Wait until TxE bit of I2C_SR1 register is set signaling that the transmit data register is empty
8. Write the register/memory address to I2C_DR register
9. Wait until TxE bit of I2C_SR1 register is set signaling that the transmit data register is empty
10. Write the data to I2C_DR register
11. Wait until BTF (Byte Transfer Finished) bit of I2C_SR1 register is set signaling that the data is sent
12. Write to STOP bit (bit 9) of I2C_CR1 register to generate a STOP condition on the bus

The procedure listed above is a simplified version. In real-world application, the error bits of the I2C_SR1 register should be checked after each byte is sent to make sure there was no bus collision and the slave responded with an acknowledge.

Read a byte of data from a slave device

Reading a byte of data from the slave requires two parts: write the register/memory address and read the data. For the first part, the slave address is transmitted with the R/W bit cleared (for a write) then followed by the register/memory address. At this point, the I2C bus is in master write to slave direction. To read the data from the slave, the bus direction needs to be reversed. The way to change the bus direction is to issue a RESTART condition then transmit the slave address with the R/W bit set (for a read). The master will clock the SCL eight times for the slave to reply with the 8-bit data. Then the master should send a NACK to let the slave know that the transaction is over before generate a STOP condition to relinquish the bus.

1. Monitor the BUSY bit of I2C_SR2 (Status 2) register until the bus is idle
2. Write to START bit (bit 8) of I2C_CR1 (Control 1) register to generate a START condition on the bus
3. Wait until the START condition is complete, the SB bit (bit 0) of I2C_SR1 register is set
4. Write the slave address with the R/W bit (bit 0) cleared (for a write) to I2C_DR (Data Register), this will transmit the slave address
5. Wait until ADDR bit (bit 1) of I2C_SR1 register is set signaling that the slave address is sent
6. Read I2C_SR1 and I2C_SR2 to clear the ADDR bit
7. Wait until TxE bit of I2C_SR1 register is set signaling that the transmit data register is empty
8. Write the register/memory address to I2C_DR register
9. Wait until TxE bit of I2C_SR1 register is set signaling that the transmit data register is empty
10. Write to START bit (bit 8) of I2C_CR1 (Control 1) register to generate a RESTART condition
11. Wait until the RESTART condition is complete, the SB bit (bit 0) of I2C_SR1 register is set
12. Write the slave address with the R/W bit (bit 0) set (for a read) to I2C_DR (Data Register), this will transmit the slave address with read
13. Wait until ADDR bit (bit 1) of I2C_SR1 register is set signaling that the slave address is sent
14. Clear ACK bit (bit 10) of I2C_CR1 register, preparing to return a NACK
15. Read I2C_SR1 and I2C_SR2 to clear the ADDR bit
16. Write to STOP bit (bit 9) of I2C_CR1 register to generate a STOP condition on the bus
17. Wait until RxNE bit of I2C_SR1 register is set signaling that the receive data register is not empty
18. Read I2C_DR register to retrieve the data

Review Questions

1. True or false. The I2C module in STM32F4xx can be used as SPI too, but not at the same time.
2. True or false. The I2C module in STM32F4xx can be used as USART at the same time.
3. True or false. There is no CS (chip select) pin in I2C.
4. In STM32F4xx, which register is used to select I2C mode of master and slave?
5. In STM32F4xx, which register is used to set the I2C baud rate?

Section 9.3: DS1337 RTC Interfacing and Programming

The real-time clock (RTC) is a common device that provides time and date information for many applications. Systems such as the PC come with such a chip on the motherboard. It provides the hour, minute, and second, in addition to year, month, and day to the operating system. Many RTC chips use an external battery, which keeps the time and date even when the power of the system is turned off. The DS1337 is an RTC with an I2C bus interface. In this section, we will develop the programs for the DS1337 RTC. The DS1337 is used as the replacement for popular DS1307 to be used with a 3.3V logic interface.

Next, we describe the pins of the DS1337. See Figure 9-20.

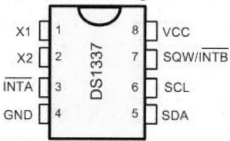

Figure 9-20: DS1337 Pins

Pinout of DS1337

X1–X2

These are pins that connect the DS1337 to an external crystal oscillator as the clock source to the chip. We must use a 32.768 kHz quartz crystal. The precision of the clock depends on the quality of this crystal oscillator.

VCC

Pin 8 is used as the voltage supply to the chip. The voltage source can be between 1.3 V to 5.5 V. When Vcc is above 1.3 V, the DS1337 starts working and keeps the time. But the I2C interface is disabled unless the Vcc is above 1.8 V.

Vcc can be connected to an external battery, thereby providing the power source to the chip when the external supply voltage is not available.

GND

Pin 4 is the ground.

SDA (Serial Data)

Pin 5 is the SDA pin and must be connected to the SDA line of the I2C bus.

SCL (Serial Clock)

Pin 6 is the SCL pin and must be connected to the SCL line of the I2C bus.

INTA# (Interrupt A)

The DS1337 has two AlArms: AlArm 1 and AlArm 2. If the alArm 1 is enabled, the INTA pin is asserted when the current time and date matches the values of AlArm 1 registers.

SWQ/INTB

Pin 7 is an output pin providing 1 kHz, 4 kHz, 8 kHz, or 32 kHz frequency if enabled. This pin needs an external pull-up resistor to generate the output signal because it has an open-drain driver. The pin can be used as the output for INTB, as well. For more information, see the DS1337 datasheet.

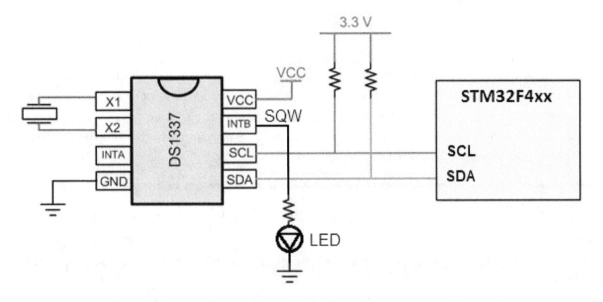

Figure 9-21: STM32F4xx Connections to RTC

DS1337 Registers

Address map of the DS1337

The DS1337 has a total of 15 bytes of address space with addresses 00–0FH. The first seven locations, 00–06, are set aside for RTC values of time, date, and year. Locations 07H-0DH are for Alarm 1 and Alarm 2 registers. The next bytes are used for control and status registers. Table 9-7 shows the address map of the DS1337. Next, we study the control register, and time and date access in DS1337.

Address	Bit7	Bit6	Bit5	Bit4	Bit3	Bit2	Bit1	Bit0	Function	Range
00H	0	10 Seconds			Seconds				Seconds	00-59
01H	0	10 Minutes			Minutes				Minutes	00-59
02H	0	12/24	10 hour PM/AM	10hour	Hours				Hours	1-12 0-23
03H	0	0	0	0	0	Day			Day	0-7
04H	0	0	10 Date		Date				Date	01-31
05H	Century	0	0	10Mnt	Month				Month Century	1-12+ Century
06H	10 Year				Year				Year	00-99
07H	A1M1	10 Seconds			Seconds				Alarm 1 Seconds	00-59
08H	A1M2	10 Minutes			Minutes				Alarm 1 Minutes	00-59
09H	A1M3	12/24	AM/PM 10 Hour	10 Hour	Hour				Alarm 1 Hours	1-12 00-23
0AH	A1M4	DY/DT	10 Date		Day				Alarm 1 Day	1-7
					Date				Alarm 1 Date	01-31
0BH	A2M2	10 Minutes			Minutes				Alarm 2 Minutes	00-59
0CH	A2M3	12/24	AM/PM		Hour				Alarm 2 Hours	

Address			10 Hour	10 Hour						1-12 / 00-23
0DH	A2M4	DY/DT	10 Date			Day			Alarm 2 Day	1-7
						Date			Alarm 2 Date	01-31
0EH	EOSC	0	0	RS2	RS1	INTCN	A2IE	A1IE	Control	-
0FH	OSF	0	0	0	0	0	A2F	A1F	Status	-

Table 9-7: DS1337 Address Map

Time and date address locations and modes

The byte addresses 0–6 are for time and date, as shown in Table 9-7. The DS1337 provides data in BCD format. Notice the data range for the hour mode. We can select 12-hour or 24-hour mode with bit 6 of Hours register at location 02. When bit 6 is 1, the 12-hour mode is selected, and when bit 6 = 0, it provides us with the 24-hour mode. In the 12-hour mode, bit 5 indicates whether it is AM or PM. If bit 5 = 0, it is AM; and if bit 5 = 1, it is PM. See Example 9-8.

Example 9-8

What value should be placed at location 02 to set the hour to (a) 21, (b) 11AM, (c) 12 PM.

Solution:

(a) For 24-hour mode, we have D6 = 0. Therefore, we place 0010 0001 (or 0x21) at location 02, which is 21 in BCD.

(b) For 12-hour mode, we have D6 = 1. Also, we have D5 = 0 for AM. Therefore, we place 0101 0001 at location 02, which is 51 in BCD.

(c) For 12-hour mode, we have D6 = 1. Also, we have D5 = 1 for PM. Therefore, we place 0111 0010 at location 02, which is 72 in BCD.

The DS1337 control register

As shown in Table 9-7, the control register has an address of 0EH. In the DS1337 control register, the bits control the function of the SQW/INTB and INTA pins. Figure 9-22 shows the simplified diagram for SQW/INTB pin.

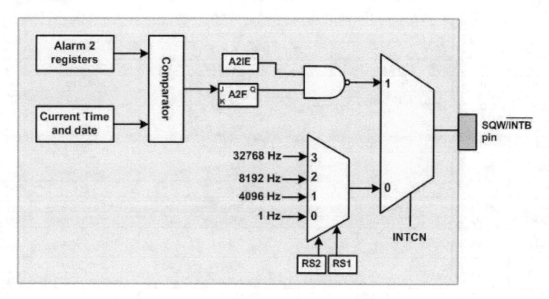

Figure 9-22: Simplified Structure of SQW/INTB Pin

The SQW/INTB pin can be used as a square wave generator or an interrupt generator. When the INTCN bit of control register is 0, the pin works as a square wave generator. Using the RS2 and RS1 bits, the frequency of the generated wave is chosen. RS2-RS1 (rate select) bits select the output frequency of the generated wave according to Table 9-8.

RS2	RS1	Output Frequency
0	0	1 Hz
0	1	4.096 kHz
1	0	8.192 kHz
1	1	32.768 kHz

Table 9-8: RS bits

When INTCN = 1, the SQW/INTB works as an interrupt generator. Locations 0BH-0DH of DS1337 memory are related to Alarm 2. The contents of the Alarm 2 registers are compared with the values current time and date (locations 00H-06H). When the current date and time matches the alarm 2 values, the A2F flag of the status register (location 0FH) goes high. If the A2IE (AlArm2 Interrupt Enable) bit of the control register is set, the INTB becomes 0. The pin remains 0 until the A2F flag is cleared by software. To clear the A2F flag, write a 0 to it.

It can make an interrupt every minute, hour, day, or date. The bit 7 of alarm registers are mask registers. If it is 0, the value of the register is compared with the timekeeping registers; otherwise, it is masked. Table 9-9 shows how to make interrupts every minute, hour, day, or date.

DY/DT	A2M4	A2M3	A2M2	AlArm Rate
X	1	1	1	Alarm once per minute
X	1	1	0	Alarm when minutes match
X	1	0	0	Alarm when hours and minutes match
0	0	0	0	Alarm when date, hours, and minutes match
1	0	0	0	Alarm when day, hours, and minutes match

Table 9-9: AlArm 2 Register Mask Bits

The bit 7 of the control register is EOSC (Enable Oscillator) bit. This bit is active low. If it is 0, the oscillator works. By default, the oscillator is powered-up active.

Register pointer

In DS1337, there is a register pointer that specifies the byte that will be accessed in the next read or write command. The first read or write operation sets the value of the pointer. After each read or write operation, the content of the register pointer is automatically incremented to point to the next location. This is useful in multi-byte read or write. When it points to location 0x0F, in the next read/write it rolls over to 0.

Writing to DS1337

To set the value of the register pointer and write one or more bytes of data to DS1337, you can use the following steps:

1. To access the DS1337 for a write operation, after sending a START condition, you should transmit the address of DS1337 (1101 000) followed by 0 to indicate a write operation.
2. The first byte of data in the write operation will set the register pointer. For example, if you want to write to the control register you should send 0x07.
3. Check the acknowledgement bit to be sure that DS1337 responded.
4. If you want to write one or more bytes of data, you should transmit them one byte at a time and check the acknowledgement bit at the end of each byte sent. Remember that the register pointer is automatically incremented and you can simply transmit bytes of data to consecutive locations in a multi-byte burst write.
5. Transmit a STOP bit condition.

Reading from DS1337

Notice that before reading a byte, you should load the address of the byte to the register pointer by doing a write operation as mentioned before.

To read one or more bytes of data from the DS1337 you should do the following steps:

1. To access the DS1337 for a read operation, you need to set the register pointer first. After sending a START condition, you should transmit the address of DS1337 (1101 000) followed by 0 to indicate a write operation (writing the register pointer).
2. Check the acknowledgement bit to be sure that DS1337 responded.
3. The byte of data in the write operation will set the register pointer. For example, if you want to read from the control register you should send 0x07. Check the acknowledgement bit to be sure that DS1337 responded.
4. Now you need to change the bus direction from transmit to receive. Send a RESTART condition (a Repeated START), then transmit the address of DS1337 (1101 000) followed by 1 to indicate a read operation. Check the acknowledgement bit to be sure that DS1337 responded.
5. You can read one or more bytes of data. Remember that the register pointer inside the DS1337 indicates which location will be read. The register pointer is automatically incremented and you can receive consecutive bytes of data in a multi-byte burst read. After each byte of data is read, the master should reply with an ACK (keep the ACK bit in I2C_CR1 register set). After the last byte of data is read, a NACK should be sent to let the DS1337 know the transaction is over.
6. Transmit a STOP bit condition.

Setting the Square Wave Output of DS1337

Program 9-1 initializes the square wave output pin (SQW) with 1Hz using single-byte write operation. SQW pin is open-drain and needs a pull-up resistor. You may connect an LED to it. The pin is rated at 5.5V and 3mA.

The program generates a START condition then sends the slave address and write flag. Following that, the address of the control register (0x0E) and the byte with control bits are sent. The transaction is terminated with a STOP condition.

Program 9-1: I2C single byte write

```c
/* P9_1.c - I2C byte write to a DS1337
 *
 * This program initializes the I2C and sends a
 * command to the DS1337 to turn on the 1 Hz output.
 * 1 Hz output is an open-drain output. It needs a pull-up
 * to observe the signal.
 * No errors or acknowledgement are checked.
 *
 * The connections
 * I2C1_SCL - PB08
 * I2C1_SDA - PB09
 *
 * This program was tested with Keil uVision v5.24a with DFP v2.11.0
 */

#include "stm32f4xx.h"
#define SLAVE_ADDR 0x68     /* 1101 000.    DS1337 */

void delayMs(int n);

void I2C1_init(void);
int I2C1_byteWrite(char saddr, char maddr, char data);

int main(void)
{
    I2C1_init();

    I2C1_byteWrite(SLAVE_ADDR, 0x0E, 0);

    while(1)
    {
    }
}

void I2C1_init(void) {
    RCC->AHB1ENR |=  2;                     /* Enable GPIOB clock */
    RCC->APB1ENR |=  0x00200000;            /* Enable I2C1 clock */

    /* configure PB8, PB9 pins for I2C1 */
    GPIOB->AFR[1]   &= ~0x000000FF;         /* PB8, PB9 I2C1 SCL, SDA */
    GPIOB->AFR[1]   |=  0x00000044;
```

```
    GPIOB->MODER      &= ~0x000F0000;          /* PB8, PB9 use alternate function */
    GPIOB->MODER      |=  0x000A0000;
    GPIOB->OTYPER     |=  0x00000300;          /* output open-drain */
    GPIOB->PUPDR      &= ~0x000F0000;          /* with pull-ups */
    GPIOB->PUPDR      |=  0x00050000;

    I2C1->CR1         =   0x8000;              /* software reset I2C1 */
    I2C1->CR1         &= ~0x8000;              /* out of reset */
    I2C1->CR2         =   0x0010;              /* peripheral clock is 16 MHz */
    I2C1->CCR         =   80;                  /* standard mode, 100kHz clock */
    I2C1->TRISE       =   17;                  /* maximum rise time */
    I2C1->CR1         |=  0x0001;              /* enable I2C1 module */
}

/* this funtion writes a byte of data to the memory location maddr of
 * a device with I2C slave device address saddr.
 * For simplicity, no error checking or error report is done.
 */
int I2C1_byteWrite(char saddr, char maddr, char data) {
    volatile int tmp;

    while (I2C1->SR2 & 2);                     /* wait until bus not busy */

    I2C1->CR1 |=  0x100;                       /* generate start */
    while (!(I2C1->SR1 & 1));                  /* wait until start flag is set */

    I2C1->DR = saddr << 1;                     /* transmit slave address */
    while (!(I2C1->SR1 & 2));                  /* wait until addr flag is set */
    tmp = I2C1->SR2;                           /* clear addr flag */

    while (!(I2C1->SR1 & 0x80));               /* wait until data register empty */
    I2C1->DR = maddr;                          /* send memory address */

    while (!(I2C1->SR1 & 0x80));               /* wait until data register empty */
    I2C1->DR = data;                           /* transmit data */

    while (!(I2C1->SR1 & 4));                  /* wait until transfer finished */
    I2C1->CR1 |= 0x200;                        /* generate stop */

    return 0;
}
```

Reading the Second Counter of DS1337

Program 9-2 reads the second counter of the DS1337 using single byte read and write the least significant bit to the onboard LED. The LED should toggle every second.

After sending the slave address, the address of the second counter (0x00) with the write bit is sent then a RESTART with the same slave address with a read bit is send to change the bus direction to read from the slave. A NACK and a STOP condition are sent at the end of the transaction.

Program 9-2: I2C single byte read

```
/* P9_2.c - I2C byte read from a DS1337
 *
 * This program initializes the I2C and continuously reads
```

```
 * the register 0 of the DS1337.
 * Register 0 contains the second count. The clock is powered-up
 * enabled and the second count is incrementing. The bit 0 is
 * used to turn on and off the LED of the Nucleo board. The LED
 * should blink every second.
 * No errors or acknowledgement are checked.
 *
 * The connections
 * I2C1_SCL - PB08
 * I2C1_SDA - PB09
 *
 * This program was tested with Keil uVision v5.24a with DFP v2.11.0
 */

#include "stm32f4xx.h"
#define SLAVE_ADDR 0x68     /* 1101 000.    DS1337 */


void delayMs(int n);

void I2C1_init(void);
int I2C1_byteRead(char saddr, char maddr, char* data);
void delayMs(int n);

int main(void)
{
    char data;

    I2C1_init();

    /* configure PA5 for the green LED (LD2) */
    RCC->AHB1ENR |= 1;                  /* enable GPIOA clock */
    GPIOA->MODER &= ~0x00000C00;    /* clear pin mode */
    GPIOA->MODER |= 0x00000400;     /* set pin to output mode */

    while (1) {
        I2C1_byteRead(SLAVE_ADDR, 0, &data);
        if (data & 1)
            GPIOA->ODR |= 0x00000020;  /* turn on LED */
        else
            GPIOA->ODR &= ~0x00000020;  /* turn off LED */

        delayMs(10);
    }
}

void I2C1_init(void) {
    RCC->AHB1ENR |= 2;                          /* Enable GPIOB clock */
    RCC->APB1ENR |= 0x00200000;             /* Enable I2C1 clock */

    /* configure PB8, PB9 pins for I2C1 */
    GPIOB->AFR[1]    &= ~0x000000FF;            /* PB8, PB9 I2C1 SCL, SDA */
    GPIOB->AFR[1]    |= 0x00000044;
    GPIOB->MODER     &= ~0x000F0000;            /* PB8, PB9 use alternate function */
    GPIOB->MODER     |= 0x000A0000;
    GPIOB->OTYPER    |= 0x00000300;             /* output open-drain */
    GPIOB->PUPDR     &= ~0x000F0000;            /* with pull-ups */
    GPIOB->PUPDR     |= 0x00050000;
```

```c
    I2C1->CR1       =     0x8000;              /* software reset I2C1 */
    I2C1->CR1       &=  ~0x8000;              /* out of reset */
    I2C1->CR2       =     0x0010;              /* peripheral clock is 16 MHz */
    I2C1->CCR       =     80;                  /* standard mode, 100kHz clock */
    I2C1->TRISE     =     17;                  /* maximum rise time */
    I2C1->CR1       |=    0x0001;              /* enable I2C1 module */
}


/* this funtion reads a byte of data from the memory location
 * maddr of a device with I2C slave device address saddr.
 * For simplicity, no error checking or error report is done.
 */
int I2C1_byteRead(char saddr, char maddr, char* data) {
    volatile int tmp;

    while (I2C1->SR2 & 2);                     /* wait until bus not busy */

    I2C1->CR1 |=  0x100;                       /* generate start */
    while (!(I2C1->SR1 & 1));                  /* wait until start flag is set */

    I2C1->DR = saddr << 1;                     /* transmit slave address + Write */
    while (!(I2C1->SR1 & 2));                  /* wait until addr flag is set */
    tmp = I2C1->SR2;                           /* clear addr flag */

    while (!(I2C1->SR1 & 0x80));               /* wait until data register empty */
    I2C1->DR = maddr;                          /* send memory address */

    while (!(I2C1->SR1 & 0x80));               /* wait until data register empty */

    I2C1->CR1 |= 0x100;                        /* generate restart */
    while (!(I2C1->SR1 & 1));                  /* wait until start flag is set */
    I2C1->DR = saddr << 1 | 1;                 /* transmit slave address + Read */

    while (!(I2C1->SR1 & 2));                  /* wait until addr flag is set */
    I2C1->CR1 &= ~0x400;                       /* Disable Acknowledge */
    tmp = I2C1->SR2;                           /* clear addr flag */

    I2C1->CR1 |= 0x200;                        /* generate stop after data received */

    while (!(I2C1->SR1 & 0x40));               /* Wait until RXNE flag is set */
    *data++ = I2C1->DR;                        /* Read data from DR */

    return 0;
}


/* 16 MHz SYSCLK */
void delayMs(int n) {
    int i;
    for (; n > 0; n--)
        for (i = 0; i < 3195; i++) ;
}
```

Setting the date/time of DS1337 using burst write

Program 9-3 shows how to setup the DS1337 RTC chip. It uses multi-byte burst mode for writing the time, day (of the week), date, month, and year, which occupy the first seven registers of the device.

The program first set the register address to 0 and writes the first register. The register address pointer automatically incremented to point to the next register and the subsequent write goes to the next register. A STOP condition is generated after the last byte of data is transmitted. For simplicity, this code does not check for error conditions nor the acknowledgment.

```
Program 9-3: Setting the date/time/year of DS1337 using burst write

/* P9_3.c - I2C burst write to a DS1337
 *
 * This program initializes the I2C and write the
 * initialization data to a DS1337.
 * No errors or acknowledgement are checked.
 *
 * The connections
 * I2C1_SCL - PB08
 * I2C1_SDA - PB09
 *
 * This program was tested with Keil uVision v5.24a with DFP v2.11.0
 */

#include "stm32f4xx.h"
#define SLAVE_ADDR 0x68     /* 1101 000.    DS1337 */

void delayMs(int n);

void I2C1_init(void);
void I2C1_burstWrite(char saddr, char maddr, int n, char* data);

int main(void)
{
    /*                          00    01    02    03    04    05    06 */
    char timeDateToSet[15] = {0x55, 0x58, 0x10, 0x03, 0x26, 0x09, 0x17, 0};
                                /* 2017 September 26, Tuesday, 10:58:55 */
    I2C1_init();
    I2C1_burstWrite(SLAVE_ADDR, 0, 7, timeDateToSet);

    while (1) {
    }
}

void I2C1_init(void) {
    RCC->AHB1ENR  |= 2;                         /* Enable GPIOB clock */
    RCC->APB1ENR  |= 0x00200000;            /* Enable I2C1 clock */

    /* configure PB8, PB9 pins for I2C1 */
    GPIOB->AFR[1]   &= ~0x000000FF;             /* PB8, PB9 I2C1 SCL, SDA */
    GPIOB->AFR[1]   |= 0x00000044;
    GPIOB->MODER    &= ~0x000F0000;             /* PB8, PB9 use alternate function */
    GPIOB->MODER    |= 0x000A0000;
    GPIOB->OTYPER   |= 0x00000300;              /* output open-drain */
    GPIOB->PUPDR    &= ~0x000F0000;             /* with pull-ups */
    GPIOB->PUPDR    |= 0x00050000;

    I2C1->CR1       = 0x8000;                   /* software reset I2C1 */
    I2C1->CR1       &= ~0x8000;                 /* out of reset */
```

```
    I2C1->CR2        =    0x0010;              /* peripheral clock is 16 MHz */
    I2C1->CCR        =    80;                  /* standard mode, 100kHz clock */
    I2C1->TRISE      =    17;                  /* maximum rise time */
    I2C1->CR1        |=   0x0001;              /* enable I2C1 module */
}

/* this funtion writes multiple bytes of data to the memory location maddr of
 * a device with I2C slave device address saddr.
 * For simplicity, no error checking or error report is done.
 */
void I2C1_burstWrite(char saddr, char maddr, int n, char* data) {
    int i;
    volatile int tmp;

    while (I2C1->SR2 & 2);                     /* wait until bus not busy */
    I2C1->CR1 &= ~0x800;                       /* disable POS */
    I2C1->CR1 |= 0x100;                        /* generate start */
    while (!(I2C1->SR1 & 1));                  /* wait until start flag is set */
    I2C1->DR = saddr << 1;                     /* transmit slave address */
    while (!(I2C1->SR1 & 2));                  /* wait until addr flag is set */
    tmp = I2C1->SR2;                           /* clear addr flag */
    while (!(I2C1->SR1 & 0x80));               /* wait until data register empty */
    I2C1->DR = maddr;                          /* send memory address */

    /* write all the data */
    for (i = 0; i < n; i++) {
        while (!(I2C1->SR1 & 0x80));           /* wait until data register empty */
        I2C1->DR = *data++;                    /* transmit memory address */
    }

    while (!(I2C1->SR1 & 4));                  /* wait until transfer finished */
    I2C1->CR1 |= 0x200;                        /* generate stop */
}
```

Reading the date/time of DS1337 using burst read

Program 9-4 shows how to read the date, time and year from DS1337 using multi-byte burst mode for reading. As you can see in the program, the register pointer is set to 0 and then you can use multi-byte burst read to read the values of the second, minute, hour, day, date, month and year in the consecutive locations. After the reception of the last byte, a NACK and a STOP condition is sent at the end. For simplicity, this code does not check for error conditions nor acknowledgment.

Program 9-4: Reading date/time/year of DS1337 using burst read

```
/* P9_4.c - I2C burst read from a DS1337
 *
 * This program initializes the I2C and continuously
 * reads all the time registers of the DS1337 using burst reads.
 * Register 0 contains the second count. The clock is powered-up
 * enabled and the second count is incrementing. The bit 0 is
 * used to turn on and off the LED of the Nucleo board. The LED
 * should blink every second.
 * No errors or acknowledgement are checked.
 *
 * The connections
 * I2C1_SCL - PB08
```

```c
 * I2C1_SDA - PB09
 *
 * This program was tested with Keil uVision v5.24a with DFP v2.11.0
 */

#include "stm32f4xx.h"
#define SLAVE_ADDR 0x68      /* 1101 000.    DS1337 */

void delayMs(int n);

void I2C1_init(void);
void I2C1_burstRead(char saddr, char maddr, int n, char* data);
void delayMs(int n);

int main(void)
{
    char timeDateReadback[15];

    I2C1_init();

    /* configure PA5 for the green LED (LD2) */
    RCC->AHB1ENR |= 1;                  /* enable GPIOA clock */
    GPIOA->MODER &= ~0x00000C00;    /* clear pin mode */
    GPIOA->MODER |= 0x00000400;     /* set pin to output mode */

    while (1) {
        I2C1_burstRead(SLAVE_ADDR, 0, 7, timeDateReadback);
        if (timeDateReadback[0] & 1)
            GPIOA->ODR |= 0x00000020;  /* turn on LED */
        else
            GPIOA->ODR &= ~0x00000020;  /* turn off LED */

        delayMs(10);
    }
}

void I2C1_init(void) {
    RCC->AHB1ENR |= 2;                  /* Enable GPIOB clock */
    RCC->APB1ENR |= 0x00200000;        /* Enable I2C1 clock */

    /* configure PB8, PB9 pins for I2C1 */
    GPIOB->AFR[1]   &= ~0x000000FF;        /* PB8, PB9 I2C1 SCL, SDA */
    GPIOB->AFR[1]   |= 0x00000044;
    GPIOB->MODER    &= ~0x000F0000;        /* PB8, PB9 use alternate function */
    GPIOB->MODER    |= 0x000A0000;
    GPIOB->OTYPER   |= 0x00000300;        /* output open-drain */
    GPIOB->PUPDR    &= ~0x000F0000;        /* with pull-ups */
    GPIOB->PUPDR    |= 0x00050000;

    I2C1->CR1       = 0x8000;             /* software reset I2C1 */
    I2C1->CR1       &= ~0x8000;            /* out of reset */
    I2C1->CR2       = 0x0010;             /* peripheral clock is 16 MHz */
    I2C1->CCR       = 80;                 /* standard mode, 100kHz clock */
    I2C1->TRISE     = 17;                 /* maximum rise time */
    I2C1->CR1       |= 0x0001;            /* enable I2C1 module */
}
```

```c
/* this funtion reads multiple bytes of data from the memory location
 * maddr of a device with I2C slave device address saddr.
 * For simplicity, no error checking or error report is done.
 */
void I2C1_burstRead(char saddr, char maddr, int n, char* data) {
    volatile int tmp;

    while (I2C1->SR2 & 2);                  /* wait until bus not busy */
    I2C1->CR1 &= ~0x800;                    /* disable POS */
    I2C1->CR1 |= 0x100;                     /* generate start */
    while (!(I2C1->SR1 & 1));               /* wait until start flag is set */
    I2C1->DR = saddr << 1;                  /* transmit slave address + Write */
    while (!(I2C1->SR1 & 2));               /* wait until addr flag is set */
    tmp = I2C1->SR2;                        /* clear addr flag */
    while (!(I2C1->SR1 & 0x80));            /* wait until transmitter empty */
    I2C1->DR = maddr;                       /* send memory address */
    while (!(I2C1->SR1 & 0x80));            /* wait until transmitter empty */

    I2C1->CR1 |= 0x100;                     /* generate restart */
    while (!(I2C1->SR1 & 1));               /* wait until start flag is set */
    I2C1->DR = saddr << 1 | 1;              /* transmit slave address + Read */
    while (!(I2C1->SR1 & 2));               /* wait until addr flag is set */
    tmp = I2C1->SR2;                        /* clear addr flag */
    I2C1->CR1 |= 0x0400;                    /* Enable Acknowledge */

    while(n > 0U)
    {
        /* One byte left */
        if(n == 1U)
        {
            I2C1->CR1 &= ~(0x400);          /* Disable Acknowledge */
            I2C1->CR1 |= 0x200;             /* Generate Stop */
            while (!(I2C1->SR1 & 0x40));    /* Wait for RXNE flag set */
            *data++ = I2C1->DR;             /* Read data from DR */
            break;
        }
        else
        {
            while (!(I2C1->SR1 & 0x40));    /* Wait until RXNE flag is set */
            (*data++) = I2C1->DR;           /* Read data from DR */
            n--;
        }
    }
}
/* 16 MHz SYSCLK */
void delayMs(int n) {
    int i;
    for (; n > 0; n--)
        for (i = 0; i < 3195; i++) ;
}
```

Review Questions

1. How many bytes in the DS1337 are set aside for the time, date, and year?

    (a) 7 bytes

    (b) 8 bytes

    (c) 56 bytes

(d) 64 bytes

2. True or false. The DS1337 has a single pin for data.

3. Which pin of the DS1337 is used for clock in I2C connection?

4. True or false. The value of the EOSC (enable oscillator) bit is zero at power-up time.

5. What is the address location for the control register?

   (a) 0x07

   (b) 0x08

   (c) 0x56

   (d) 0x64

Answers to Review Questions

Section 9-1

1. True

2. 9, the 9th bit is for acknowledge

3. False, START and STOP conditions are generated when the SCL is high.

4. Clock stretching.

5. False, the master who won the arbitration will continue.

Section 9-2

1. False

2. False

3. True

4. START and STOP bits of CR1 register. When the I2C module successfully generates a start condition, it becomes the bus master. When the I2C module generates a stop condition, it falls back to be a bus slave.

5. I2C_CR2 and I2C_CCR

Section 9-3

1. (a)

2. True

3. SCL

4. False

5. (a)

Chapter 10: Relay, Optoisolator, and Stepper Motor Interfacing

Microcontrollers are widely used in motor control. We also use relays and optoisolators in motor control. This chapter discusses motor control and shows Arm interfacing with relays, optoisolators, and stepper motors.

Section 10.1: Relays and Optoisolators

This section begins with an overview of the basic operations of electromechanical relays, solid-state relays, reed switches, and optoisolators. Then we describe how to interface them to the Arm. We use the C language programs to demonstrate their control.

Electromechanical relays

A *relay* is an electrically controllable switch widely used in industrial controls, automobiles, and appliances. It allows the isolation of two separate sections of a system with two different voltage sources. For example, a +5 V system can be isolated from a 120 V system by placing a relay between them. One such relay is called an *electromechanical* (or *electromagnetic*) *relay* (EMR) as shown in Figure 10-1. The EMRs have three components: the coil, spring, and contacts.

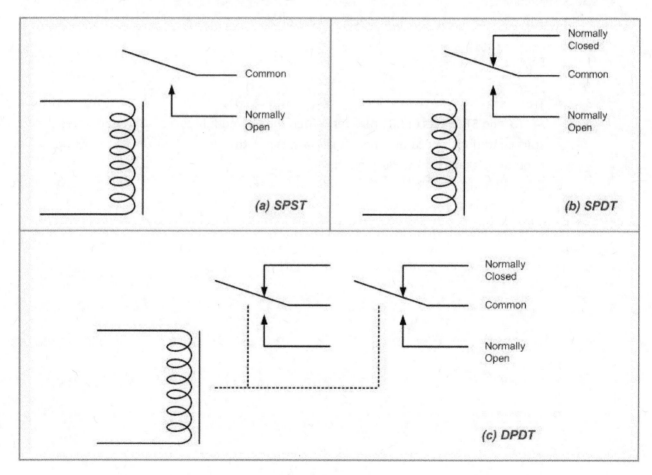

Figure 10-1: Relay Diagrams

In Figure 10-1, a digital +5 V on the left side can control a 12 V motor on the right side without any physical contact between them. When current flows through the coil, a magnetic field is created around the coil (the coil is energized), which causes the Armature to be attracted to the coil. The Armature's contact acts like a switch and closes or opens the circuit. When the coil is not energized, a spring pulls the Armature to its normal state of open or closed. In the block diagram for electromechanical relays (EMR) we do not show the spring, but it does exist internally. There are all types of relays for all kinds of applications. In choosing a relay the following characteristics need to be considered:

1. The contacts can be normally open (NO) or normally closed (NC). In the NC type, the contacts are closed when the coil is not energized. In the NO type, the contacts are open when the coil is unenergized.
2. There can be one or more contacts. For example, we can have SPST (single pole, single throw), SPDT (single pole, double throw), and DPDT (double pole, double throw) relays.
3. The voltage and current needed to energize the coil. The voltage can vary from a few volts to 50 volts, while the current can be from a few mA to 20 mA. The relay has a minimum voltage, below which the coil will not be energized. This minimum voltage is called the "pull-in" voltage. In the datasheets for relays we might not see current, but rather coil resistance. The V/R will give you the pull-in current. For example, if the coil voltage is 5 V, and the coil resistance is 500 ohms, we need a minimum of 10 mA (5 V/500 ohms = 10 mA) pull-in current.
4. The maximum DC/AC voltage and current that can be handled by the contacts. This is in the range of a few volts to hundreds of volts, while the current can be from a few amps to 40 A or more, depending on the relay. Notice the difference between this voltage/current specification and the voltage/current needed for energizing the coil. The fact that one can use such a small amount of voltage/current on one side to handle a large amount of voltage/current on the other side is what makes relays so widely used in industrial controls. Examine Table 10-1 for some relay characteristics.

Part No.	Contact Form	Coil Volts	Coil Ohms	Contact Volts	Current
106462CP	SPST-NO	5 VDC	500	100 VDC	0.5 A
138430CP	SPST-NO	5 VDC	500	100 VDC	0.5 A
106471CP	SPST-NO	12 VDC	1000	100 VDC	0.5 A
138448CP	SPST-NO	12 VDC	1000	100 VDC	0.5 A
129875CP	DPDT	5 VDC	62.5	30 VDC	1 A

Table 10-1: Selected DIP Relay Characteristics (www.Jameco.com)

Driving a relay

Digital systems and microcontroller pins lack sufficient current to drive the relay. While the relay's coil needs around 10 mA to be energized, the microcontroller's pin can provide a maximum of 8 mA current. For this reason, we place a driver, such as the ULN2803, or a transistor between the microcontroller and the relay as shown in Figure 10-2. In the circuit, we can turn the lamp on and off by setting and clearing the PA10.

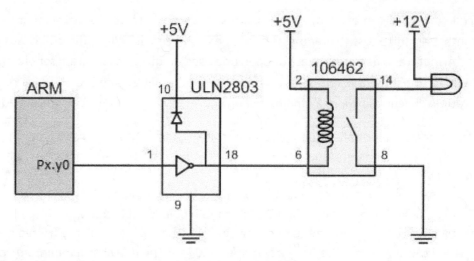

Figure 10-2: Arm Connection to Relay

Program 10-1 turns the lamp shown in Figure 10-2 on and off by energizing and de-energizing the relay every second.

Program 10-1 Turning relay on and off

```
/* p10_1.c Relay control
*
* This program turns the relay connected to PA5 on and off every second.
*
* This program was tested with Keil uVision v5.23 with DFP v2.11.0.
*/

#include "stm32f4xx.h"

void delayMs(int n);

int main(void) {
    RCC->AHB1ENR |=  1;                 /* enable GPIOA clock */
    GPIOA->MODER &= ~0x00000C00;     /* clear pin mode */
    GPIOA->MODER |=  0x00000400;     /* set pin to output mode */

    while(1) {
        GPIOA->BSRR = 0x00000020;    /* turn on output */
        delayMs(500);
        GPIOA->BSRR = 0x00200000;    /* turn off output */
        delayMs(500);
    }
}

/* 16 MHz SYSCLK */
void delayMs(int n) {
    int i;
    for (; n > 0; n--)
        for (i = 0; i < 3195; i++) ;
}
```

Solid-state relay

Another widely used relay is the solid-state relay. See Table 10-2.

294

Part No.	Contact Style	Control Volts	Contact Volts	Contact Current
143058CP	SPST	4-32 VDC	240 VAC	3 A
139053CP	SPST	3-32 VDC	240 VAC	25 A
162341CP	SPST	3-32 VDC	240 VAC	10 A
172591CP	SPST	3-32 VDC	60 VAC	2 A
175222CP	SPST	3-32 VDC	60 VAC	4 A
176647CP	SPST	3-32 VDC	120 VAC	5 A

Table 10-2: Selected Solid-State Relay Characteristics (www.Jameco.com)

In this relay, there is no coil, spring, or mechanical contact switch. The entire relay is made out of semiconductor materials. Because no mechanical parts are involved in solid-state relays, their switching response time is much faster than that of electromechanical relays. Another advantage of the solid-state relay is its greater life expectancy. The life cycle for the electromechanical relay can vary from a few hundred thousand to a few million operations. Wear and tear on the contact points can cause the relay to malfunction after a while. Solid-state relays, however, have no such limitations. Extremely low input current and small packaging make solid-state relays ideal for microcontroller and logic control switching. They are widely used in controlling pumps, solenoids, alArms, and other power applications. Some solid-state relays have a phase control option, which is ideal for motor-speed control and light-dimming applications. Figure 10-3 shows control of a fan using a solid-state relay (SSR).

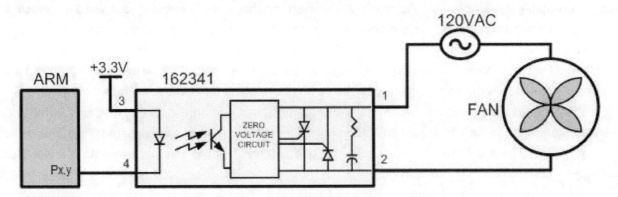

Figure 10-3: Arm Connection to a Solid-State Relay

Reed switch

Another popular switch is the reed switch. When the reed switch is placed in a magnetic field, the contact is closed. When the magnetic field is removed, the contact is forced open by its spring. See Figure 10-4. The reed switch is ideal for moist and marine environments where it can be submerged in fuel or water. Reed switches are also widely used in dirty and dusty atmospheres because they are tightly sealed.

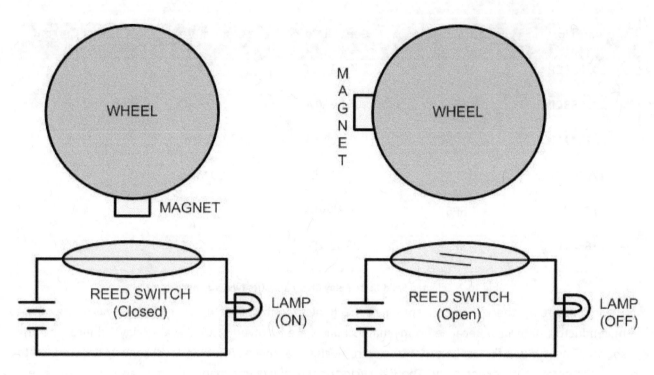

Figure 10-4: Reed Switch and Magnet Combination

Optoisolator

In some applications, we use an optoisolator (also called optocoupler) to isolate two parts of a system. An example is driving a motor. Motors can produce what is called *back EMF*, a high-voltage spike produced by a sudden change of current as indicated in the formula V = Ldi/dt. In situations such as printed circuit board design, we can reduce the effect of this unwanted voltage spike (called *ground bounce*) by using decoupling capacitors (see Appendix A). In systems that have inductors (coil winding), such as motors, a decoupling capacitor or a diode will not do the job. In such cases we use optoisolators. An optoisolator has an LED (light-emitting diode) transmitter and a photosensor receiver, separated from each other by a gap. When current flows through the diode, it transmits a signal light across the gap and the receiver produces the same signal with the same phase but a different current and amplitude. See Figure 10-5. Optoisolators are also widely used in communication equipment such as modems. This device allows a computer to be connected to a telephone line without risk of damage from high voltage of telephone line. The gap between the transmitter and receiver of optoisolators prevents the electrical voltage surge from reaching the system.

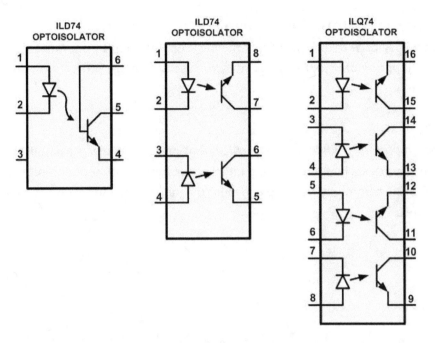

Figure 10-5: Optoisolator Package Examples

Interfacing an optoisolator

The optoisolator comes in a small IC package with four or more pins. There are also packages that contain more than one optoisolator. When placing an optoisolator between two circuits, we must use two separate voltage sources, one for each side, as shown in Figure 10-6. Unlike relays, no drivers need to be placed between the microcontroller/digital output and the optoisolators.

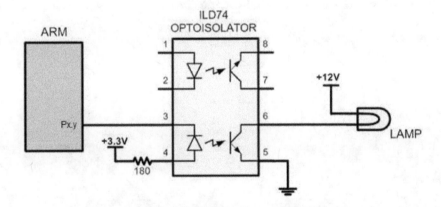

Figure 10-6: Controlling a Lamp via an Optoisolator

Review Questions

1. Give one application where would you use a relay.
2. Why do we place a driver between the microcontroller and the relay?
3. What is an NC relay?
4. Why are relays that use coils called electromechanical relays?
5. What is the advantage of a solid-state relay over EMR?
6. What is the advantage of an optoisolator over an EMR?

Section 10.2: Stepper Motor Interfacing

This section begins with an overview of the basic operation of stepper motors. Then we describe how to interface a stepper motor to the Arm. Finally, we use C language programs to demonstrate control of the rotation of stepper motor.

Stepper motors

A *stepper motor* is a widely used device that translates electrical pulses into mechanical movement. In applications such as dot matrix printers and robotics, the stepper motor is used for position control. Stepper motors commonly have a permanent magnet *rotor* (also called the *shaft*) surrounded by a stator (see Figure 10-7).

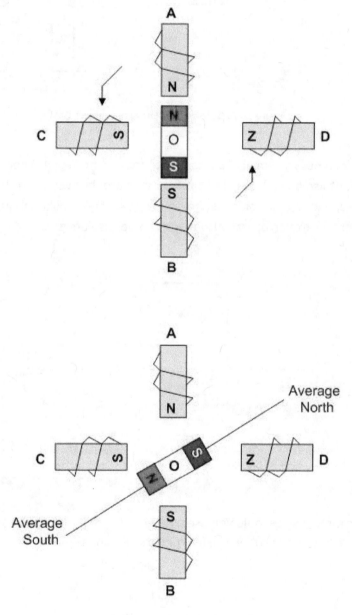

Figure 10-7: Rotor Alignment

There are also steppers called *variable reluctance stepper motors* that do not have a permanent magnet rotor. The most common stepper motors have four stator windings that are paired with a center-tapped common as shown in Figure 10-8.

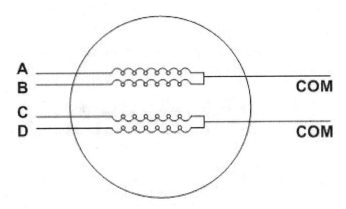

Figure 10-8: Stator Winding Configuration

This type of stepper motor is commonly referred to as a four-phase or unipolar stepper motor. The center tap allows a change of current direction in each of two coils when a winding is grounded, thereby resulting in a polarity change of the stator. Notice that while a conventional motor shaft runs freely, the stepper motor shaft moves in a fixed repeatable increment, which allows it to move to a precise position. This repeatable fixed movement is possible as a result of basic magnetic theory where poles of the same polarity repel and opposite poles attract. The direction of the rotation is dictated by the stator poles. The stator poles are determined by the current sent through the wire coils. As the direction of the current is changed, the polarity is also changed causing the reverse motion of the rotor. The stepper motor discussed here has a total of six leads: four leads representing the four stator windings and two commons for the center-tapped leads. As the sequence of power is applied to each stator winding, the rotor will rotate. There are several widely used sequences, each of which has a different degree of precision. Table 10-3 shows a two-phase, four-step stepping sequence.

	Step #	Winding A	Winding B	Winding C	Winding D	Counter Clockwise
Clockwise	1	1	0	0	1	
⬇	2	1	1	0	0	⬆
	3	0	1	1	0	
	4	0	0	1	1	

Table 10-3: Normal Four-Step Sequence

Note that although we can start with any of the sequences in Table 10-3, once we start, we must continue in the proper order. For example, if we start with step 3 (0110), we must continue in the sequence of steps 4, 1, 2, and so on.

Step angle

How much movement is associated with a single step? This depends on the internal construction of the motor, in particular, the number of teeth on the stator and the rotor. The step angle is the minimum degree of rotation associated with a single step. Various motors have different step angles. Table 10-4 shows some step angles for various motors. In Table 10-4, notice the term steps per revolution. This is the total number of steps needed to rotate one complete rotation or 360 degrees (e.g., 180 steps × 2 degrees = 360).

Step Angle	Step per Revolution
0.72	500
1.8	200
2.0	180
2.5	144
5.0	72
7.5	48
15	24

Table 10-4: Stepper Motor Step Angles

It must be noted that perhaps contrary to one's initial impression, a stepper motor does not need more terminal leads for the stator to achieve smaller steps. All the stepper motors discussed in this section have four leads for the stator winding and two COM wires for the center tap. Although some manufacturers set aside only one lead for the common signal instead of two, they always have four leads for the stators. See Example 10-1. Next, we discuss some associated terminology in order to understand the stepper motor further.

Example 10-1

Describe the Arm connection to the stepper motor of Figure 10-9 and code a program to rotate it continuously.

Solution:

The following steps show the Arm connection to the stepper motor and its programming:

1. Use an ohmmeter to measure the resistance of the leads. This should identify which COM leads are connected to which winding leads.
2. The common wire(s) are connected to the positive side of the motor's power supply. In many motors, +5 V is sufficient.

3. The four leads of the stator winding are controlled by four bits of the Arm port (PB0–PB3). Because the microcontroller lacks sufficient current to drive the stepper motor windings, we must use a driver such as the ULN2003 (or ULN2803) to energize the stator. Instead of the ULN2003, we could have used transistors as drivers, as shown in Figure 10-11. However, notice that if transistors are used as drivers, we must also use diodes to take care of inductive current generated when the coil is turned off. One reason that using the ULN2003 is preferable to the use of transistors as drivers is that the ULN2003 has an internal diode to take care of back EMF.

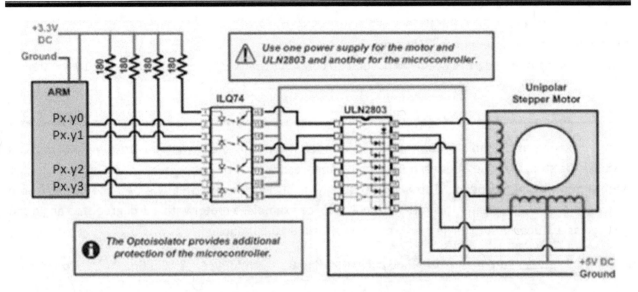

Figure 10-9: Arm Connection to Stepper Motor

Steps per second and RPM relation

The relation between RPM (revolutions per minute), steps per revolution, and steps per second is as follows.

$$Step\ per\ second = \frac{RPM \times Steps\ per\ revolution}{60}$$

The 4-step sequence and number of teeth on rotor

The switching sequence shown earlier in Table 10-3 is called the 4-step switching sequence because after four steps the same two windings will be "ON". How much movement is associated with these four steps? Therefore, in a stepper motor with 200 steps per revolution, the rotor has 50 teeth because 4 × 50 = 200 steps are needed to complete one revolution. This leads to the conclusion that the minimum step angle is always a function of the number of teeth on the rotor. In other words, the smaller the step angle, the more teeth the rotor has. See Example 10-2.

Example 10-2

Give the number of times the four-step sequence in Table 10-3 must be applied to a stepper motor to make an 80-degree move if the motor has a 2-degree step angle.

Solution:

A motor with a 2-degree step angle has the following characteristics:

Step angle: 2 degrees
Steps per revolution: 180
Number of rotor teeth: 45
Movement per 4-step sequence: 8 degrees

To move the rotor 80 degrees, we need to send 10 consecutive 4-step sequences, because 10 × 4 steps × 2 degrees = 80 degrees.

Looking at Example 10-2, one might wonder what happens if we want to move 45 degrees because the steps are 2 degrees each. To provide finer resolutions, all stepper motors allow what is called an 8-step switching sequence. The 8-step sequence is also called half-stepping because in the 8-step sequence each step is half of the normal step angle. For example, a motor with a 2-degree step angle can be used as a 1-degree step angle if the sequence of Table 10-5 is applied.

	Step #	Winding A	Winding B	Winding C	Winding D	Counter Clockwise
Clockwise	1	1	0	0	1	
	2	1	0	0	0	
	3	1	1	0	0	
	4	0	1	0	0	
	5	0	1	1	0	
	6	0	0	1	0	
	7	0	0	1	1	
	8	0	0	0	1	

Table 10-5: Half-Step 8-Step Sequence

Motor speed

The motor speed, measured in steps per second (steps/s), is a function of the switching rate. Notice in Example 10-1 that by changing the length of the time delay loop, we can achieve various rotation speeds.

Holding torque

The following is a definition of holding torque: "With the motor shaft at standstill or zero rpm condition, the amount of torque, from an external source, required to break away the shaft from its holding position. This is measured with rated voltage and current applied to the motor." The unit of torque is ounce-inch (or kg-cm).

Wave drive 4-step sequence

In addition to the 8-step and the 4-step sequences discussed earlier, there is another sequence called the *wave drive 4-step sequence*. It is shown in Table 10-6.

Clockwise	Step #	Winding A	Winding B	Winding C	Winding D	Counter Clockwise
	1	1	0	0	0	
	2	0	1	0	0	
	3	0	0	1	0	
	4	0	0	0	1	

Table 10-6: Wave Drive 4-Step Sequence

Notice that the 8-step sequence of Table 10-5 is simply the combination of the wave drive 4-step and normal 4-step normal sequences shown in Tables 10-6 and 10-3, respectively. Experimenting with the wave drive 4-step sequence is left to the reader.

Unipolar versus bipolar stepper motor interface

There are three common types of stepper motor interfacing: universal, unipolar, and bipolar. They can be identified by the number of connections to the motor. A universal stepper motor has eight, while the unipolar has six and the bipolar has four. The universal stepper motor can be configured for all three modes, while the unipolar can be either unipolar or bipolar. Obviously the bipolar cannot be configured for a universal nor unipolar mode. Table 10-7 shows selected stepper motor characteristics.

Part No.	Step Angle	Drive System	Volts	Phase Resistance	Current
151861CP	7.5	unipolar	5 V	9 ohms	550 mA
171601CP	3.6	unipolar	7 V	20 ohms	350 mA
164056CP	7.5	bipolar	5 V	6 ohms	800 mA

Table 10-7: Selected Stepper Motor Characteristics (www.Jameco.com)

Figure 10-10 shows the basic internal connections of all three types of configurations.

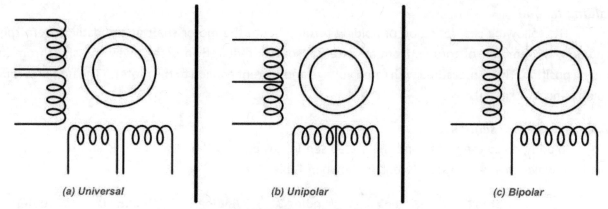

(a) Universal   (b) Unipolar   (c) Bipolar

Figure 10-10: Common Stepper Motor Types

Unipolar stepper motors can be controlled using the basic interfacing shown in Figure 10-11, whereas the bipolar stepper requires H-Bridge circuitry. Bipolar stepper motors require a higher operational current than the unipolar; the advantage of this is a higher holding torque.

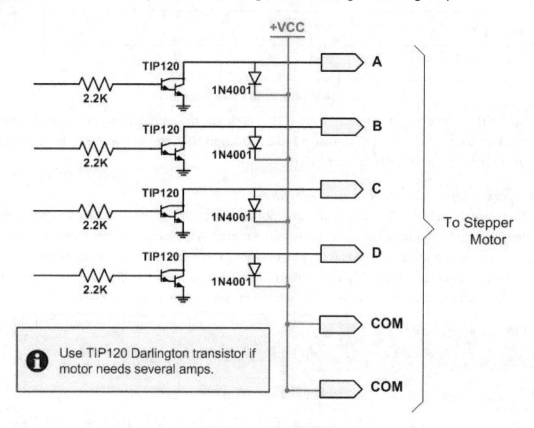

Figure 10-11: Using Transistors for Stepper Motor Driver

Using transistors as drivers

Figure 10-11 shows an interface to a unipolar stepper motor using transistors. Diodes are used to reduce the back EMF spike created when the coils are energized and de-energized, similar to the electromechanical relays discussed earlier. TIP transistors can be used to supply higher current to the motor. Table 10-8 lists the common industrial Darlington transistors. These transistors can accommodate higher voltages and currents.

304

NPN	PNP	V$_{CEO}$ (volts)	I$_c$ (amps)	hfe (common)
TIP110	TIP115	60	2	1000
TIP111	TIP116	80	2	1000
TIP112	TIP117	100	2	1000
TIP120	TIP125	60	5	1000
TIP121	TIP126	80	5	1000
TIP122	TIP127	100	5	1000
TIP140	TIP145	60	10	1000
TIP141	TIP146	80	10	1000
TIP142	TIP147	100	10	1000

Table 10-8: Darlington Transistor Listing

Controlling stepper motor via optoisolator

In the first section of this chapter, we examined the optoisolator and its use. Optoisolators are widely used to isolate the stepper motor's EMF voltage and keep it from damaging the digital/microcontroller system. This is shown in Figure 10-12.

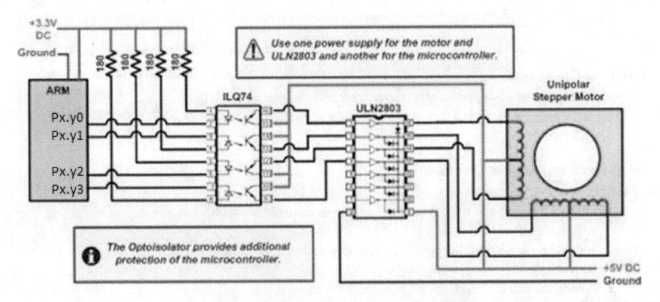

Figure 10-12: Controlling Stepper Motor via Optoisolator

See Program 10-2.

```
/* p10_2.c Stepper motor control
 *
 * This program controls a unipolar stepper motor using PTA7, 6, 5, 4.
 *
 * This program was tested with Keil uVision v5.23 with DFP v2.11.0.
 */
#include "stm32f4xx.h"

void delayMs(int n);
int main(void) {
    const char steps[ ] = {0x90, 0x30, 0x60, 0xC0};
    int i;

    /* PTA7, 6, 5, 4 for motor control */
    RCC->AHB1ENR |= 1;                  /* enable GPIOA clock */
    GPIOA->MODER &= ~0x0000FF00;     /* clear pin mode */
    GPIOA->MODER |= 0x00005500;      /* set pins to output mode */

    for (;;) {
        GPIOA->ODR = steps[i++ & 3];    /* set the output pattern */
        delayMs(100);
    }
}
/* 16 MHz SYSCLK */
void delayMs(int n) {
    int i;
    for (; n > 0; n--)
        for (i = 0; i < 3195; i++) ;
}
```

Review Questions

1. Give the 4-step sequence of a stepper motor if we start with 0110.
2. A stepper motor with a step angle of 5 degrees has _____ steps per revolution.
3. Why do we put a driver between the microcontroller and the stepper motor?

Answers to Review Questions

Section 10.1

1. With a relay we can use a 5 V digital system to control 12 V–120 V devices such as horns and appliances.
2. Because microcontroller/digital outputs lack sufficient current to energize the relay, we need a driver.
3. When the coil is not energized, the contact is closed.
4. When current flows through the coil, a magnetic field is created around the coil, which causes the Armature to be attracted to the coil.
5. It is faster and needs less current to get energized.
6. It is smaller and can be connected to the microcontroller directly without a driver.

Section 10.2

1. 1100, 0110, 0011, 1001 for clockwise; and 1001, 0011, 0110, 1100 for counterclockwise
2. 72

3. The microcontroller pins do not provide sufficient current to drive the stepper motor.

Chapter 11: PWM and DC Motor Control

This chapter discusses the topic of PWM (pulse width modulation) and shows Arm interfacing with DC motors. The characteristics of DC motors are discussed along with their interfacing to the Arm. We use C programming examples to create PWM pulses.

Section 11.1: DC Motor Interfacing and PWM

This section begins with an overview of the basic operation of the DC motors. Then we describe how to interface a DC motor to the Arm. Finally, we use C language programs to demonstrate the concept of pulse width modulation (PWM) and show how to control the speed and direction of a DC motor.

DC motors

A direct current (DC) motor is a widely used device that translates electrical current into mechanical movement. In the DC motor, we have only + and − leads. Connecting them to a DC voltage source moves the motor in one direction. By reversing the polarity, the DC motor will rotate in the opposite direction. One can easily experiment with the DC motor. While a stepper motor moves in discrete steps of 1 to 15 degrees, the DC motor moves continuously. In a stepper motor, if we know the starting position we can easily count the number of steps the motor has moved and calculated the final position of the motor. This is not possible in a DC motor. The maximum speed of a DC motor is indicated in RPM and is given in the data sheet. The DC motor has two types of RPM: no-load and loaded. The manufacturer's data sheet gives the no-load RPM. The no-load RPM can be from a few thousand to tens of thousands. The RPM is reduced when moving a load and it decreases as the load is increased. For example, a drill turning a screw has a much lower RPM speed than when it is in the no-load situation. DC motors also have voltage and current ratings. The nominal voltage is the voltage for that motor under normal conditions and can be from 1 to 150 V, depending on the motor. As we increase the voltage, the RPM goes up. The current rating is the current consumption when the nominal voltage is applied with no load and can be from 25 mA to a few amps. As the load increases, the RPM is decreased, unless the current or voltage provided to the motor is increased, which in turn increases the torque. With a fixed voltage, as the load increases, the current (power) consumption of a DC motor is increased. If we overload the motor it will stall, and that can damage the motor due to the heat generated by high current consumption.

Unidirectional control

Figure 11-1 shows the DC motor clockwise (CW) and counterclockwise (CCW) rotations.

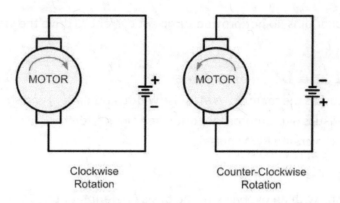

Clockwise
Rotation

Counter-Clockwise
Rotation

Figure 11-1: DC Motor Rotation (Permanent Magnet Field)

See Table 11-1 for selected DC motors.

Part No.	Nominal Volts	Volt Range	Current	RPM	Torque
154915CP	3 V	1.5–3 V	0.070 A	5,200	4.0 g-cm
154923CP	3 V	1.5–3 V	0.240 A	16,000	8.3 g-cm
177498CP	4.5 V	3–14 V	0.150 A	10,300	33.3 g-cm
181411CP	5 V	3–14 V	0.470 A	10,000	18.8 g-cm

Table 11-1: Selected DC Motor Characteristics (http://www.Jameco.com)

Bidirectional control

With the help of relays, transistor circuit or some specially designed chips we can change the direction of the DC motor rotation. Figures 11-2 through 11-4 show the basic concepts of the H-Bridge control of DC motors.

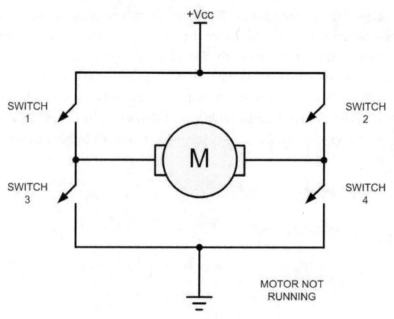

Figure 11-2: H-Bridge Motor Configuration

Figure 11-2 shows the connection of an H-Bridge using simple switches. All the switches are open, which does not allow the motor to turn.

Figure 11-3 shows the switch configuration for turning the motor in one direction. When switches 1 and 4 are closed, current is allowed to pass through the motor.

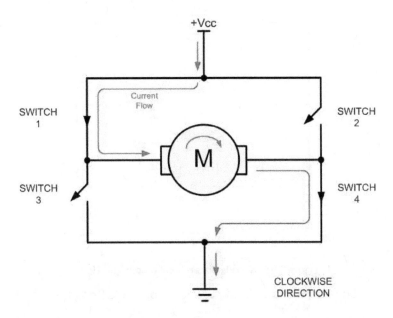

Figure 11-3: H-Bridge Motor Clockwise Configuration

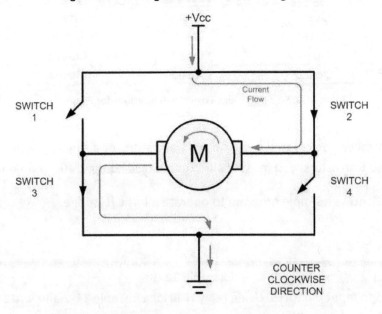

Figure 11-4: H-Bridge Motor Counterclockwise Configuration

Figure 11-4 shows the switch configuration for turning the motor in the opposite direction from the configuration of Figure 11-3. When switches 2 and 3 are closed, current is allowed to pass through the motor.

Figure 11-5 shows an invalid configuration. Current flows directly to ground, creating a short circuit. The same effect occurs when switches 1 and 3 are closed or switches 2 and 4 are closed.

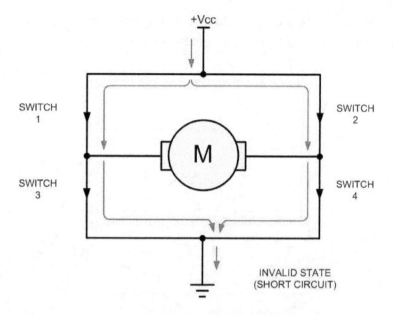

Figure 11-5: H-Bridge in an Invalid Configuration

Table 11-2 shows some of the logic configurations for the H-Bridge design.

Motor Operation	SW1	SW2	SW3	SW4
Off	Open	Open	Open	Open
Clockwise	Closed	Open	Open	Closed
Counterclockwise	Open	Closed	Closed	Open
Invalid	Closed	Closed	Closed	Closed

Table 11-2: Some H-Bridge Logic Configurations for Figure 11-2

H-Bridge control can be created using relays, transistors, or a single IC solution such as the L298. When using relays and transistors, you must ensure that invalid configurations do not occur.

Example 11-1 shows a simple program to operate a basic H-Bridge.

Example 11-1

A switch is connected to input pin PA15. Using relay H-Bridge in Table 11-2 and write the proper program to control the motor direction by the switch:

(a) If PA15 = 1, the DC motor moves clockwise.

(b) If PA15 = 0, the DC motor moves counterclockwise.

Solution 1 (Using SPST Relays):

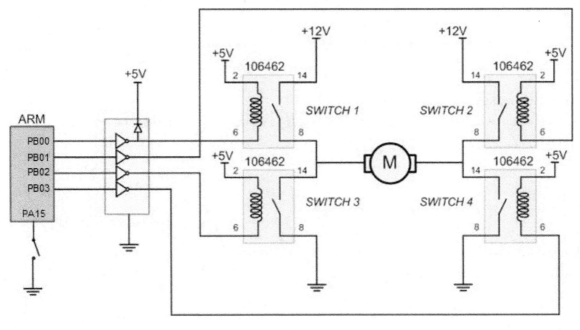

```c
#include "stm32f4xx.h"

void delayMs(int n);

int main(void) {
    /* PA15 for input */
    RCC->AHB1ENR |= 1;              /* enable GPIOA clock */
    GPIOA->MODER &= ~0xC0000000;    /* clear pin mode */
    GPIOA->MODER &= ~0xC0000000;    /* set pins to input mode */
    GPIOA->PUPDR &= ~0x80000000;    /* enable pull-up resistor of input pin */
    GPIOA->PUPDR |=  0x40000000;

    /* PB3, 2, 1, 0 for motor control output */
    RCC->AHB1ENR |= 2;              /* enable GPIOB clock */
    GPIOB->MODER &= ~0x000000FF;    /* clear pin mode */
    GPIOB->MODER |=  0x00000055;    /* set pins to output mode */

    for (;;) {
        if (GPIOA->IDR & 0x8000) {      /* if PA15 is high */
            GPIOB->BSRR = 0x000F0000;   /* open all switches */
            delayMs(100);               /* wait 0.1 second */
            GPIOB->BSRR = 0x00000009;   /* close SW1 & SW4 */
            while((GPIOA->IDR & 0x8000) != 0);   /* wait till switch closes */
        } else {                        /* if switch is closed */
            GPIOB->BSRR = 0x000F0000;   /* open all switches */
            delayMs(100);               /* wait 0.1 second */
            GPIOB->BSRR = 0x00000006;   /* close SW2 & SW3 */
            while((GPIOA->IDR & 0x8000) == 0);   /* wait till switch opens */
        }
    }
}

/* 16 MHz SYSCLK */
void delayMs(int n) {
```

```
        int i;
        for (; n > 0; n--)
            for (i = 0; i < 3195; i++) ;
}
```

Solution 2 (Using SPDT Relays):

The H-bridge can also be made using two SPDT relays as shown in the following figure.

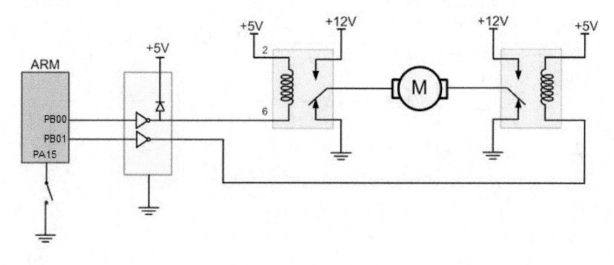

```
#include "stm32f4xx.h"

void delayMs(int n);

int main(void) {
    /* PA15 for input */
    RCC->AHB1ENR |= 1;                /* enable GPIOA clock */
    GPIOA->MODER &= ~0xC0000000;      /* clear pin mode */
    GPIOA->MODER &= ~0xC0000000;      /* set pins to input mode */
    GPIOA->PUPDR &= ~0x80000000;      /* enable pull-up resistor of input pin */
    GPIOA->PUPDR |= 0x40000000;

    /* PB3, 2, 1, 0 for motor control output */
    RCC->AHB1ENR |= 2;                /* enable GPIOB clock */
    GPIOB->MODER &= ~0x0000000F;      /* clear pin mode */
    GPIOB->MODER |= 0x00000005;       /* set pins to output mode */

    for (;;) {
        if (GPIOA->IDR & 0x8000) {        /* if PA15 is high */
            GPIOB->BSRR = 0x00030000;     /* open all switches */
            delayMs(100);                 /* wait 0.1 second */
            GPIOB->BSRR = 0x00000001;     /* close SW1 */
            while((GPIOA->IDR & 0x8000) != 0);  /* wait till switch closes */
        } else {                          /* if switch is closed */
            GPIOB->BSRR = 0x00030000;     /* open all switches */
            delayMs(100);                 /* wait 0.1 second */
            GPIOB->BSRR = 0x00000002;     /* close SW2 */
            while((GPIOA->IDR & 0x8000) == 0);  /* wait till switch opens */
        }
    }
}
```

```
/* 16 MHz SYSCLK */
void delayMs(int n) {
    int i;
    for (; n > 0; n--)
        for (i = 0; i < 3195; i++) ;
}
```

Figure 11-6 shows the connection of the L298N to the microcontroller. Be aware that the L298N will generate heat during operation. For a sustained operation of the motor, use a heat sink.

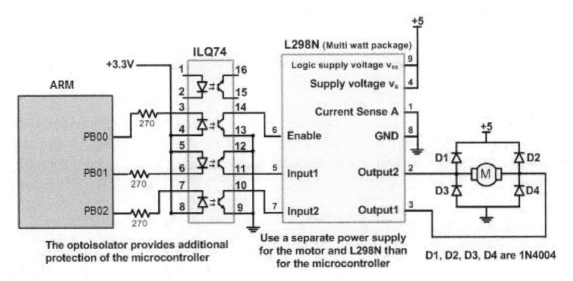

Figure 11-6: Bidirectional Motor Control Using an L298 Chip

Pulse width modulation (PWM)

The speed of the motor depends on three factors: (a) load, (b) voltage, and (c) current. For a given fixed load we can maintain a steady speed by using a method called pulse width modulation (PWM). By changing (modulating) the width of the pulse applied to the DC motor we can increase or decrease the amount of power provided to the motor, thereby increasing or decreasing the motor speed. Notice that, although the voltage has a fixed amplitude, it has a variable duty cycle. That means the wider the pulse, the higher the speed. PWM is so widely used in DC motor control that many microcontrollers come with an on-chip PWM circuitry. In such microcontrollers, all we have to do is load the proper registers with the values of the high and low portions of the desired pulse and the rest is taken care of by the microcontroller. This allows the microcontroller to do other things. For microcontrollers without on-chip PWM circuitry, we must create the various duty cycle pulses using software, which prevents the microcontroller from doing other things. The ability to control the speed of the DC motor using PWM is one reason that DC motors are preferable over AC motors. AC motor speed is dictated by the AC frequency of the voltage applied to the motor and the frequency is generally fixed. As a result, we cannot control the speed of the AC motor when the load is increased. As will be shown later, we can also change the DC motor's direction and torque. See Figure 11-7 for PWM comparisons.

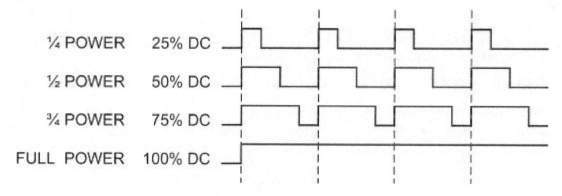

Figure 11-7: Pulse Width Modulation Comparison

DC motor control with optoisolator

The optoisolator is indispensable in many motor control applications. Figures 11-8 and 11-9 show the connections to a simple DC motor using a bipolar and a MOSFET transistor. Notice that the microcontroller is protected from EMI created by motor brushes by using an optoisolator and a separate power supply.

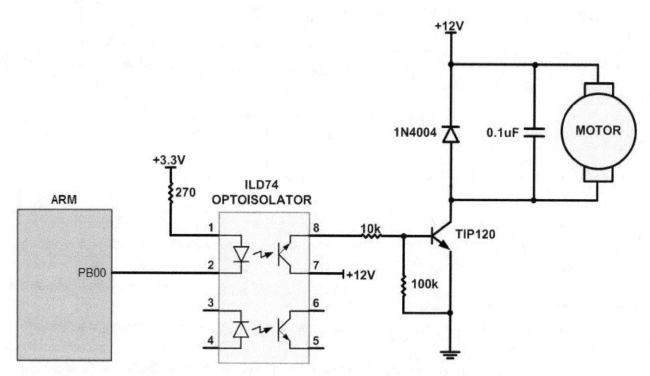

Figure 11-8: DC Motor Connection Using a Darlington Transistor

Figures 11-8 and 11-9 show optoisolators for single directional motor control and the same principle should be used for most motor applications. Separating the power supplies of the motor and logic will reduce the possibility of damage to the control circuit. Figure 11-8 shows the connection of a bipolar transistor to a motor. Protection of the control circuit is provided by the optoisolator. The motor

314

and the microcontroller use separate power supplies. The separation of power supplies also allows the use of high-voltage motors. Notice that we use a decoupling capacitor across the motor; this helps reduce the EMI created by the motor. The motor is switched on by clearing bit PTD0.

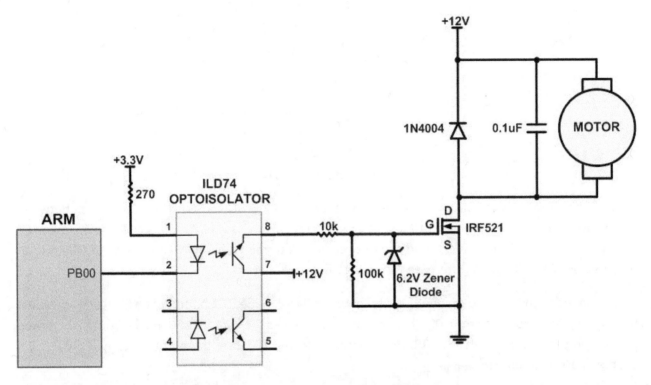

Figure 11-9: DC Motor Connection Using a MOSFET Transistor

Figure 11-9 shows the connection of a MOSFET transistor. The optoisolator protects the microcontroller from EMI. The Zener diode is required for the transistor to reduce gate voltage below the rated maximum value.

Review Questions

1. True or false. The permanent magnet field DC motor has only two leads for + and − voltages.
2. True or false. As with a stepper motor, one can control the exact angle of a DC motor's move.
3. Why do we put a driver between the microcontroller and the DC motor?
4. How do we change a DC motor's rotation direction?
5. What is stall in a DC motor?
6. The RPM rating given for the DC motor is for _____ (no-load, loaded).

Section 11.2: Programming PWM in STM Arm

Generate PWM with Timer

In STM Arm, the PWM (Pulse Width Modulation) is incorporated into the Timers. We demonstrated the use of timers to generate waveform outputs with fixed 50% duty cycle in Chapter 5.

The Timer/Counters can operate as PWM with various duty cycles. The PWM option is chosen by OCxM bits of the TIMx_CCMRx register.

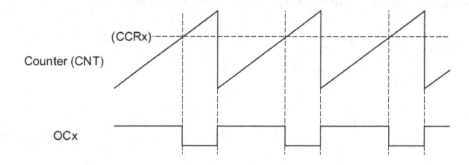

Figure 11-10: PWM Mode

The OCxM bits can be set as mode 1 (110) or mode 2 (111) for PWM. The difference between these two options is the way the output starts as active or inactive state. For the PWM, the frequency is determined by TIMxARR register value and duty cycle is determined by the value of TIMx_CCRx (for 16-bit mode or 32-bit timers) register. See Figure 11-10.

In program 11-1, the channel 1 is configured as PWM mode. The output of Ch1 is turned on when the counter starts counting from 0. When the counter matches the content of CCR1, Ch1 output is turned off. When the counter matches ARR, the counter is cleared to 0 and the output is turned on and the counter starts counting up again.

Program 11-1 uses TIM2 to generate 60 Hz and 33.3% duty cycle output. Program 11-1 is similar to Program 5-8 (in Chapter 5) except the PWM operation is used. TIM2 is configured as 32-bit up-counter in PWM mode. The top count is the value of TIM2_ARR, which determines the period of the waveform. The pulse width is determined by the value of TIM2_CCR1. The PWM output is on channel 1 PA5 pin connected to LED. You can also use an oscilloscope on PA5 pin of the STM32F446 Nucleo board to observe the waveform. Notice the SYSCLK 16MHz is divided by 10 using the TIM2_PSC which gives us timer/counter value of 1.6MHz. This is divided by 26,667 (1.6MHz/26,667=60Hz) using TIM2_ARR to get the PWM frequency of 60Hz. Now, the pulse width is CCRx/APR= 8,889/26,667=33%.

Program 11-1: Using 32-bit TIM2 for PWM Output

```
/* p11_1.c Using TIM2 for PWM Output
 *
 * This program configures TIM2 with prescaler divides by 10
 * so that the timer counter is counting at 1.6 MHz.
 * ARR register is loaded with 26666 and CCR1 is loaded with 8888.
 * The channel 1 is configured as PWM mode. The output of Ch1 is
 * turned on when the counter starts counting from 0. When the
 * counter matches the content of CCR1, Ch1 output is turned off.
 * When the counter matches ARR, the counter is cleared to 0 and
 * the output is turned on and the counter starts counting up again.
 * The LED will be on for 8889/26667 = 30% of the time.
 * The output pin of TIM2 Ch1 is PA5 and the alternate function
 * of PA5 should be set to AF1.
```

```
 *
 * This program was tested with Keil uVision v5.24a with DFP v2.11.0
 */

#include "stm32f4xx.h"

int main(void) {
    RCC->AHB1ENR |= 1;                      /* enable GPIOA clock */

    GPIOA->AFR[0] |= 0x00100000;            /* PA5 pin for tim2 */
    GPIOA->MODER &= ~0x00000C00;
    GPIOA->MODER |=  0x00000800;

    /* setup TIM2 */
    RCC->APB1ENR |= 1;                      /* enable TIM2 clock */
    TIM2->PSC = 10 - 1;                     /* divided by 10 */
    TIM2->ARR = 26667 - 1;                  /* divided by 26667 */
    TIM2->CNT = 0;
    TIM2->CCMR1 = 0x0060;                   /* PWM mode */
    TIM2->CCER = 1;                         /* enable PWM Ch1 */
    TIM2->CCR1 = 8889 - 1;                  /* pulse width 1/3 of the period */
    TIM2->CR1 = 1;                          /* enable timer */

    while(1) {
    }
}
```

PWM with 16-bit TIM8

The TIM2 is 32-bit timer and we saw how it is used for PWM. Now, we can use the 16-bit timer such as TIM8 for PWM. The 16-bit timer registers have the same name as TIM2 except they are 16-bit instead of 32-bit. In some case the registers might the same name but the contents of these register are different. For example, TIM8_CCER bits are different from TIM2_CCER register as shown in Figure 11-11 For 16-bit TIM8 channels have complementary output. The CHx and CHxn are complement of each other. The Program 11-2 is similar to Program 11-1 except it uses 16-bit TIM8. Notice the use of CH1 and its complement CH1N output. Also notice on order to enable the output we use TIM8_BDTR register.

15	14	13	12	11	10	9	8	7	6	5	4	3	2	1	0
Res	Res	CC4P	CC4E	CC3NP	CC3NE	CC3P	CC3E	CC2NP	CC2NE	CC2P	CC2E	CC1NP	CC1NE	CC1P	CC1E
		rw	rw	rw	rw	rw	rw	rw	rw	rw	rw	rw	rw	rw	rw

Bits 15:14 Reserved, must be kept at reset value.

Bit 13 **CC4P**: Capture/Compare 4 output polarity

refer to CC1P description

Bit 12 **CC4E**: Capture/Compare 4 output enable

refer to CC1E description

Bit 11 **CC3NP**: Capture/Compare 3 complementary output polarity

refer to CC1NP description

Bit 10 **CC3NE**: Capture/Compare 3 complementary output enable

refer to CC1NE description

Bit 9 **CC3P**: Capture/Compare 3 output polarity

refer to CC1P description

Bit 8 **CC3E**: Capture/Compare 3 output enable

refer to CC1E description

Bit 7 **CC2NP**: Capture/Compare 2 complementary output polarity

refer to CC1NP description

Bit 6 **CC2NE**: Capture/Compare 2 complementary output enable

refer to CC1NE description

Bit 5 **CC2P**: Capture/Compare 2 output polarity

refer to CC1P description

Bit 4 **CC2E**: Capture/Compare 2 output enable

refer to CC1E description

Bit 3 **CC1NP**: Capture/Compare 1 complementary output polarity

CC1 channel configured as output:

0: OC1N active high.

1: OC1N active low.

CC1 channel configured as input:

This bit is used in conjunction with CC1P to define the polarity of TI1FP1 and TI2FP1. Refer to CC1P description.

in TIMx_BDTR register) and CC1S="00" (the channel is configured in output).

Bit 2 **CC1NE**: Capture/Compare 1 complementary output enable

0: Off - OC1N is not active. OC1N level is then function of MOE, OSSI, OSSR, OIS1, OIS1N and CC1E bits.

1: On - OC1N signal is output on the corresponding output pin depending on MOE, OSSI, OSSR, OIS1, OIS1N and CC1E bits.

Bit 1 **CC1P**: Capture/Compare 1 output polarity

CC1 channel configured as output:

0: OC1 active high

1: OC1 active low

CC1 channel configured as input:

CC1NP/CC1P bits select the active polarity of TI1FP1 and TI2FP1 for trigger or capture operations.

00: non-inverted/rising edge

01: inverted/falling edge

10: reserved, do not use this configuration.

11: non-inverted/both edges

Bit 0 **CC1E**: Capture/Compare 1 output enable

CC1 channel configured as output:

0: Off - OC1 is not active. OC1 level is then function of MOE, OSSI, OSSR, OIS1, OIS1N and CC1NE bits.

1: On - OC1 signal is output on the corresponding output pin depending on MOE, OSSI, OSSR, OIS1, OIS1N and CC1NE bits.

CC1 channel configured as input:

This bit determines if a capture of the counter value can actually be done into the input capture/compare register 1 (TIMx_CCR1) or not.

0: Capture disabled.

1: Capture enabled.

Figure 11-11: TIM8_CCER

15	14	13	12	11	10	9	8	7	6	5	4	3	2	1	0
MOE	AOE	BKP	BKE	OSSR	OSSI	LOCK[1:0]		DTG[7:0]							
rw	rw	rw	rw	rw	rw	rw	rw	rw	rw	rw	rw	rw	rw	rw	rw

Bit 15 **MOE**: Main output enable

This bit is cleared asynchronously by hardware as soon as the break input is active. It is set by software or automatically depending on the AOE bit. It is acting only on the channels which are configured in output.

0: OC and OCN outputs are disabled or forced to idle state.

1: OC and OCN outputs are enabled if their respective enable bits are set (CCxE, CCxNE in TIMx_CCER register).

Figure 11-12: TIM8_BDTR

Program 11-2: Using 16-bit TIM8 for Simple PWM Output

```c
/* p11_2.c Using TIM8 for PWM Output
 *
 * This program configures TIM8 with prescaler divides by 10
 * so that the timer counter is counting at 1.6 MHz.
 * ARR register is loaded with 26666 and CCR1 is loaded with 8888.
 * The channel 1 is configured as PWM mode. The output of Ch1N is
 * turned on when the counter starts counting from 0. When the
 * counter matches the content of CCR1, Ch1N output is turned off.
 * When the counter matches ARR, the counter is cleared to 0 and
 * the output is turned on and the counter starts counting up again.
 * The LED will be on for 8889/26667 = 30% of the time.
 * The output pin of TIM8 Ch1N is PA5 and the alternate function
 * of PA5 should be set to AF1.
 *
 * This program is similar to p11_1.c except:
 * 1. Each PWM output channel (Chx) has a complementary output (ChxN)
 *    and we are using the Ch1N output.
 * 2. The output needs to be enabled at TIM8_BDTR register.
 *
 * This program was tested with Keil uVision v5.24a with DFP v2.11.0
 */

#include "stm32f4xx.h"

int main(void) {
    RCC->AHB1ENR |= 1;              /* enable GPIOA clock */

    GPIOA->AFR[0] |= 0x00300000;   /* PA5 pin for TIM8 */
    GPIOA->MODER &= ~0x00000C00;
```

```
        GPIOA->MODER |=  0x00000800;

        /* setup TIM8 */
        RCC->APB2ENR |= 2;                  /* enable TIM8 clock */
        TIM8->PSC = 10 - 1;                 /* divided by 10 */
        TIM8->ARR = 26667 - 1;              /* divided by 26667 */
        TIM8->CNT = 0;
        TIM8->CCMR1 = 0x0060;               /* PWM mode */
        TIM8->CCER = 4;                     /* enable PWM Ch1N */
        TIM8->CCR1 = 8889 - 1;              /* pulse width 1/3 of the period */
        TIM8->BDTR |= 0x8000;               /* enable output */
        TIM8->CR1 = 1;                      /* enable timer */

        while(1) {
        }
}
```

Program 11-3 is based on Program 11-2 but in the infinite loop, the value of CCRx is incremented by 10% every 50ms. The increasing CCRx value lengthens the duty cycle and increases the LED light intensity when the output is connected to the LED on the STM32F4xx Nucleo board.

Program 11-3: Use PWM to control LED intensity

```
/* p11_3.c Variable duty cycle PWM to control LED intensity
 *
 * This program is the same as p11_2.c except the pulse width is
 * started with a small value and incremented by 10% every 50 ms
 * in the infinite loop. The change of duty cycle will modulate
 * the intensity of the LED.
 *
 * This program was tested with Keil uVision v5.24a with DFP v2.11.0
 */

#include "stm32f4xx.h"

void delayMs(int n);

int main(void) {
    RCC->AHB1ENR |= 1;                  /* enable GPIOA clock */

    GPIOA->AFR[0] |= 0x00300000;        /* PA5 pin for TIM8 */
    GPIOA->MODER &= ~0x00000C00;
    GPIOA->MODER |=  0x00000800;

    /* setup TIM8 */
    RCC->APB2ENR |= 2;                  /* enable TIM8 clock */
    TIM8->PSC = 10 - 1;                 /* divided by 10 */
    TIM8->ARR = 26667 - 1;              /* divided by 26667 */
    TIM8->CNT = 0;
    TIM8->CCMR1 = 0x0068;               /* PWM mode */
    TIM8->CCER = 4;                     /* enable PWM Ch1N */
    TIM8->CCR1 = 90;                    /* pulse width */
    TIM8->BDTR |= 0x8000;               /* enable output */
    TIM8->CR1 = 1;                      /* enable timer */

    while(1) {
```

```
        TIM8->CCR1 = TIM8->CCR1 * 110 / 100;
        if (TIM8->CCR1 > 26666)
            TIM8->CCR1 = 90;
        delayMs(50);
    }
}

/* 16 MHz SYSCLK */
void delayMs(int n) {
    int i;
    for (; n > 0; n--)
        for (i = 0; i < 3195; i++) ;
}
```

Program 11-4 uses the prescaler to divide the clock by 16,000 for counter clock. This slows enough that the duty cycle changes can be observed with naked eyes.

Program 11-4: Based on Program 11-3 but slow down the PWM frequency so that the duty cycle change can be observed with naked eyes

```
/* p11_4.c Variable duty cycle PWM to control LED on duration
 *
 * This program is the same as p11_3.c except the frequency is much
 * slower so that the change of the duration when the LED is on
 * can be observed by naked eyes.
 *
 * This program was tested with Keil uVision v5.24a with DFP v2.11.0
 */

#include "stm32f4xx.h"

void delayMs(int n);

int main(void) {
    RCC->AHB1ENR |= 1;                /* enable GPIOA clock */

    GPIOA->AFR[0] |= 0x00300000;      /* PA5 pin for TIM8 */
    GPIOA->MODER &= ~0x00000C00;
    GPIOA->MODER |=  0x00000800;

    /* setup TIM8 */
    RCC->APB2ENR |= 2;                /* enable TIM8 clock */
    TIM8->PSC = 16000 - 1;            /* divided by 16000 */
    TIM8->ARR = 1000 - 1;             /* divided by 1000 */
    TIM8->CNT = 0;
    TIM8->CCMR1 = 0x0068;             /* PWM mode */
    TIM8->CCER = 4;                   /* enable PWM Ch1N */
    TIM8->CCR1 = 10;                  /* pulse width */
    TIM8->BDTR |= 0x8000;             /* enable output */
    TIM8->CR1 = 1;                    /* enable timer */

    while(1) {
        TIM8->CCR1 = TIM8->CCR1 * 110 / 100;
        if (TIM8->CCR1 > 1000)
```

```
            TIM8->CCR1 = 10;
        delayMs(400);
    }
}

/* 16 MHz SYSCLK */
void delayMs(int n) {
    int i;
    for (; n > 0; n--)
        for (i = 0; i < 3195; i++) ;
}
```

Edge-aligned and Centered-aligned PWM

For the PWM we can use center-aligned or edge-aligned. In the edge-aligned, the output starts high for duration of duty cycle and then goes Low for the rest of the period. In the centered-aligned the high is moved to center. The Program 11-5 shows how to create edge-aligned and centered-aligned PWM.

Program 11-5: Comparison between edge-aligned and center-aligned PWM

```
/* p11_5.c Comparison between edge-aligned and center-aligned PWM
 *
 * In this program, TIM8 Ch1 is configured as center-aligned PWM with
 * output on PC6 pin and TIM2 Ch1 is configured as edge-aligned PWM
 * with output on PA5 pin for comparison.
 *
 * You will find two differences between these two PWM generation:
 * 1. For edge-aligned PWM, the counter counts from 0 to the value
 *     of ARR then it takes one clock cycle to reset to 0. So to
 *     count 1000 clock cycles, the ARR should be loaded with 999.
 *     For center-aligned PWM, the counter counts up from 0 to the
 *     value of ARR then immediately counts down back to 0. So to
 *     count 1000 clock cycles, the ARR should be loaded with 1000.
 * 2. For edge-aligned PWM, each output cycle the counter counts
 *     from 0 to the value of ARR. For center-aligned PWM, each
 *     output cycle, the counter counts from 0 up to the value of
 *     ARR then back down to 0. For the same value of ARR, the
 *     center-aligned PWM takes twice as long as edge-aligned PWM
 *     to complete an output cycle.
 *
 * This program was tested with Keil uVision v5.24a with DFP v2.11.0
 */

#include "stm32f4xx.h"

void TIM8_center_aligned(void);
void TIM2_edge_aligned(void);

int main(void) {
    TIM8_center_aligned();
    TIM2_edge_aligned();

    while(1) {
```

```
        }
}

void TIM8_center_aligned(void) {
    RCC->AHB1ENR |= 4;                  /* enable GPIOC clock */

    GPIOC->AFR[0] |= 0x03000000;        /* PC6 pin for tim8 Ch1 */
    GPIOC->MODER &= ~0x00003000;
    GPIOC->MODER |=  0x00002000;

    /* setup TIM8 */
    RCC->APB2ENR |= 2;                  /* enable TIM8 clock */
    TIM8->PSC = 16 - 1;                 /* divided by 16 */
    TIM8->ARR = 1000;                   /* divided by 1000 */
    TIM8->CNT = 0;
    TIM8->CCMR1 = 0x0060;               /* PWM mode */
    TIM8->CCER = 1;                     /* enable PWM Ch1 */
    TIM8->CCR1 = 300 - 1;               /* pulse width 300 */
    TIM8->BDTR |= 0x8000;               /* enable output */
    TIM8->CR1 = 0x21;                   /* center-aligned, enable timer */
}

void TIM2_edge_aligned(void) {
    RCC->AHB1ENR |= 1;                  /* enable GPIOA clock */

    GPIOA->AFR[0] |= 0x00100000;        /* PA5 pin for tim2 */
    GPIOA->MODER &= ~0x00000C00;
    GPIOA->MODER |=  0x00000800;

    /* setup TIM2 */
    RCC->APB1ENR |= 1;                  /* enable TIM2 clock */
    TIM2->PSC = 16 - 1;                 /* divided by 16 */
    TIM2->ARR = 1000 - 1;               /* divided by 1000 */
    TIM2->CNT = 0;
    TIM2->CCMR1 = 0x0060;               /* PWM mode */
    TIM2->CCER = 1;                     /* enable PWM Ch1 */
    TIM2->CCR1 = 300 - 1;               /* pulse width 300 */
    TIM2->CR1 = 1;                      /* edge-aligned enable timer */
}
```

Dead-time Generation (Case Study)

One application of center-aligned PWM is to generate outputs with dead-time. Recall in the first section of this chapter, when we switched the direction of the H-bridge circuit, we opened all switches and delayed for a period of time. That is dead-time, a period of time when all switches are open to avoid the possibility of overlapping time when both switches on the same leg of the H-bridge are on which will cause a short circuit. The same problem exists with transistor circuits because transistors are faster to turn on and slower to turn off. If we turn one on and the other off, there will be a short period of time that both transistors are on.

To generate dead-time, we use two center-aligned channels on the PWM module. One of the channels has a positive pulse and the other negative pulse. Assuming the circuit is active high, now we have one channel centered at the time when the timer counter reaches the value in BDTR register and the other channel centered at the time when the timer counter reaches 0 so they are 180 degrees out of phase. For each channel we program them to have less than 50% duty cycle, therefore, dead times are created between the two channels. See Figure 11-13.

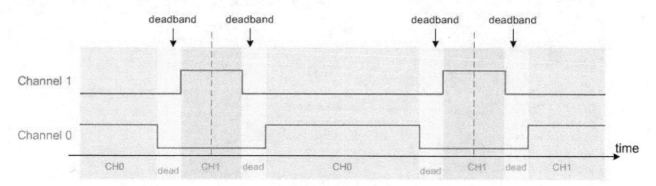

Figure 11-13: Dead band

Program 11-6: Dead-time Generation with TIM8 PWM

```
/* p11_6.c Dead time creation with TIM8 PWM
 *
 * In this program, TIM8 Ch1 and Ch1N are configured as complementary
 * outputs of the center-aligned PWM. The output of Ch1 is PC6 and
 * the output of Ch1N is PA5.
 * To exaggerate the dead time, the dead time clock is set to four
 * times the timer counter clock in TIM8_CR1 and the dead time value
 * is set to maximum in TIM8_BDTR.
 *
 * This program was tested with Keil uVision v5.24a with DFP v2.11.0
 */
#include "stm32f4xx.h"

int main(void) {
    RCC->AHB1ENR |= 5;                  /* enable GPIOA clock */

    GPIOC->AFR[0] |= 0x03000000;        /* set pin for tim8 Ch1 */
    GPIOC->MODER &= ~0x00003000;
    GPIOC->MODER |=  0x00002000;

    GPIOA->AFR[0] |= 0x00300000;        /* set pin for tim8 Ch1N */
    GPIOA->MODER &= ~0x00000C00;
    GPIOA->MODER |=  0x00000800;

    /* setup TIM8 */
    RCC->APB2ENR |= 2;                  /* enable TIM8 clock */
    TIM8->PSC = 16 - 1;                 /* divided by 16 */
    TIM8->ARR = 1000;                   /* divided by 1000 */
    TIM8->CNT = 0;
    TIM8->CCMR1 = 0x0060;
    TIM8->CCER = 5;                     /* enable PWM Ch1, Ch1N */
    TIM8->CCR1 = 500 - 1;              /* pulse width 500 */
    TIM8->BDTR |= 0x80FF;              /* enable output, set max dead time */
```

```
    TIM8->CR1 = 0x221;                /* slow DT clock, center-aligned, enable timer */

    while(1) {
    }
}
```

Review Questions

1. We use _____register to set the PWM output Frequency.
2. We use _____register to set the PWM output pulse width.
3. True or false. OCxM bits are used to generate PWM waves.
4. True or false. Center-Aligned PWM is generated by the counter counting both up and down.

Answers to Review Questions

Section 11.1

1. True
2. False
3. Because microcontroller/digital outputs lack sufficient current to drive the DC motor.
4. By reversing the polarity of voltages connected to the motor leads
5. The DC motor is stalled if the load is beyond what it can handle.
6. No-load

Section 11.2

1. TIMxARR
2. TIMxCCRx
3. True
4. True

Chapter 12: Programming Graphic LCD

Chapter 3 used the character LCD. In this chapter, we examine the graphic LCDs and show some programming examples, although an entire book can be dedicated to graphic LCD and its programming. Section 12.1 covers some basic concepts of graphic LCDs. In Section 12.2, we give some programming examples of graphic LCD.

Section 12.1: Graphic LCDs

The screen of graphic LCDs is made of pixels. The pictures and the texts are created using pixels and the programmers have control over each and every individual pixel. See Figures 12-1 and 12-2.

Figure 12-1: A picture on a Mono-color LCD

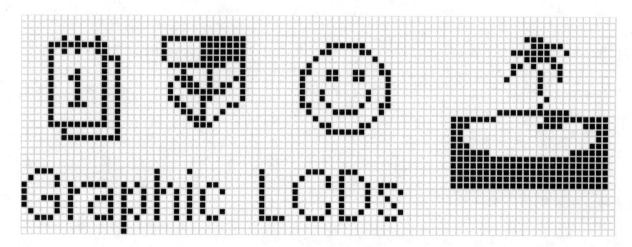

Figure 12-2: A Zoomed Picture on a Mono-color LCD

The graphic LCDs can be mono-colored (monochorme) or colored. In mono-colored LCDs each pixel can be on or off or different shades of gray; in contrast in colored LCDs each pixel can have different colors. In fact, the colored pixels can display red, green, and blue; using the 3 primary color lights they make different colors.

Some LCD Characteristics

Resolution

The total number of pixels (dots) per screen is a major factor in assessing an LCD and is shown below:

$$Resolution = Pixels\ per\ line \times number\ of\ lines$$

For example, when the resolution of an LCD is 720 × 350, there are 720 pixels per line and 350 lines per screen, giving a total of 252,000 pixels. The total number of pixels per screen is determined by the size of the pixel and how far apart the pixels are spaced. For this reason, one must look at what is called the *dot pitch* in LCD specifications.

Dot pitch

Dot pitch is the distance between adjacent pixels (dots) and is given in millimeters. For example, a dot pitch of 0.31 means that the distance between pixels is 0.31 mm. Consequently, the smaller the size of the pixel itself and the smaller the space between them, the higher the total number of pixels and the better the resolution. Dot pitch varies from 0.6 inch in some low-resolution LCDs to 0.2 inch in higher-resolution LCDs. Figure 12-3 shows Dot Pitch and Dot Size parameters.

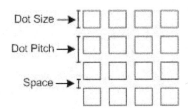

Figure 12-3: Dot Pitch and Dot Size

The specifications of a sample mono-colored LCD are shown in Figure 12-4.

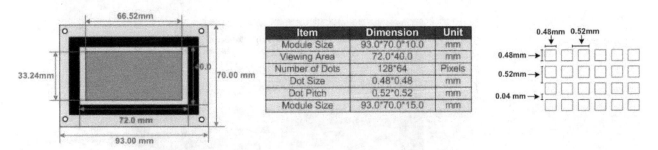

Item	Dimension	Unit
Module Size	93.0*70.0*10.0	mm
Viewing Area	72.0*40.0	mm
Number of Dots	128*64	Pixels
Dot Size	0.48*0.48	mm
Dot Pitch	0.52*0.52	mm
Module Size	93.0*70.0*15.0	mm

Figure 12-4: Mechanical specifications of a GDM12864 128x64 LCD

In some LCD specifications, it is given in terms of the number of dots per square inch, which is the same way it is given for laser printers, for example, 300 DPI (dots per inch).

Dot pitch and LCD size

LCDs, like televisions, are advertised according to their diagonal size. For example, a 14-inch monitor means that its diagonal measurement is 14 inches. There is a relation between the number of horizontal and vertical pixels, the dot pitch, and the diagonal size of the image on the screen. The diagonal size of the image must always be less than the LCD's diagonal size. The following simple equation can be used to relate these three factors to the diagonal measurement. It is derived from the Pythagorean Theorem:

$$(\text{image diagonal size})^2 = (\text{number of horizontal pixels} \times \text{dot pitch})^2$$

$$+ (\text{number of vertical pixels} \times \text{dot pitch})^2$$

Since the dot pitch is in millimeters, the size given by the equation above would be in mm, so it must be multiplied by 0.039 to get the size of the monitor in inches. See Example 12-1.

Example 12-1

A manufacturer has advertised a 14-inch monitor of 1024 × 768 resolution with a dot pitch of 0.28. Calculate the diagonal size of the image on the screen. It must be less than 14 inches.

Solution:

The calculation is as follows:
(image diagonal size)^2 = (number of horizontal pixels × dot pitch)^2 + (number of vertical pixels × dot pitch)^2

(diagonal size)^2 = (1024 × 0.28 mm)^2 + (768 × 0.28 mm)^2 = 358.4 mm
diagonal size (inches) = 358.4 mm × 0.039 inch per mm = 13.98 inches
In the LCD the diagonal size of the image area is 13.98 inches while the diagonal size of the viewing area is 14 inches.

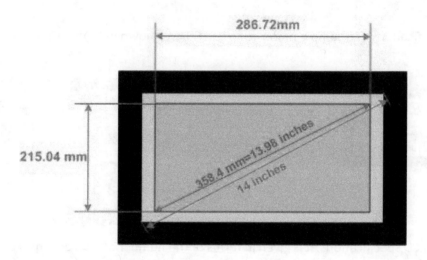

Displaying on the graphic LCDs

To display a picture on the screen, a distinct color must be shown on each pixel of the LCD. To do so, there is a display memory (frame buffer) that retrieves the attributes (colors) of the entire pixels of the screen and there is an LCD controller which displays the contents of the frame buffer memory on the LCD. See Figure 12-5.

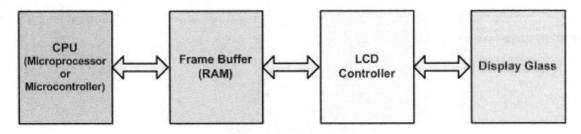

Figure 12-5: The Relationship between CPU and LCD

Graphic LCDs might come with or without frame buffer and the LCD controller. In cases that the LCD does not have frame buffer memory or controller they must be provided externally. Some new microcontrollers have the LCD controllers internally which can directly drive the LCDs. To display a picture on the screen the microcontroller writes it to the frame buffer memory.

Since the attributes (colors) of the entire pixels are stored in the frame buffer memory, the higher the number of pixels and colors options, the larger the amount of memory is needed to store them. In other words, the memory requirement goes up as the resolution and the number of supported colors go up. The number of colors displayed at one time is always 2^n where n is the number of bits set aside for the color. For example, when 4 bits are assigned to the color of the pixel, this allows 16 combinations of colors to be displayed at one time because $2^4 = 16$. The number of bits used for a pixel color is called color depth or bits per pixel (BPP). See Table 12-1.

BPP	Colors
1	on or off (monochrome)
2	4
4	16
8	256
16	65,536
24	16,777,216

Table 12-1: BPP (bit per pixel) vs. color

In Table 12-1, notice that in a monochrome LCD a single bit is assigned for the color of the pixel and it is for "on" or "off".

Mixing RGB (Red, Green, Blue) colors

We can get other colors by mixing the three primary colors of Red, Green, and Blue. The intensity (proportion) of the colors mixed can also affect the color we get. In many high-end graphics systems, an 8-bit value is used to represent the intensity. Its value can be between 0 and 255 (0 to 0xFF) representing high intensity (255) and zero intensity. See Table 12-2. Using three primary colors and intensity, we can make many colors we want. See Figure 12-6.

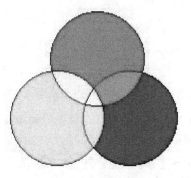

Figure 12-6: Making New Light Colors by Mixing the 3 Primary Light Colors

I	R	G	B	Color
0	0	0	0	Black
0	0	0	1	Blue
0	0	1	0	Green
0	0	1	1	Cyan
0	1	0	0	Red
0	1	0	1	Magenta
0	1	1	0	Brown
0	1	1	1	Light Gray
1	0	0	0	Dark Gray
1	0	0	1	Light blue
1	0	1	0	Light green
1	0	1	1	Light cyan
1	1	0	0	Light red
1	1	0	1	Light Magenta
1	1	1	0	Yellow
1	1	1	1	White

Table 12-2: The 16 Possible Colors

Example 12-2

In a certain graphic LCD, a maximum of 256 colors can be displayed at one time. How many bits are set aside for the color of the pixels?

Solution:

To display 256 colors at once, we must have 8 bits set for color since $2^8 = 256$.

LCD Buffer memory size and color

In discussing the graphics, we need to clarify the relationship between pixel resolution, the number of colors supported, and the amount of frame buffer RAM needed to store them. There are two facts associated with every pixel on the screen:

1. The location of the pixel
2. The attributes: color and intensity

These two facts must be stored in the frame buffer RAM. The higher the number of pixels and colors options, the larger the amount of memory that is needed to store them. In other words, the memory requirement goes up as the resolution and the number of colors supported goes up. As we just mentioned, the number of colors displayed at one time is always 2^n where n is the number of bits set aside for the color. For example, when 4 bits are assigned to the color of the pixel, this allows 16 combinations of colors to be displayed at one time because $2^4 = 16$. The commonly used graphics resolutions are 176 x 144 (QCIF), 352x288 (CIF), 320x240 (QVGA), 480x272 (WQVGA), 640x480 (VGA) and 800x480 (WVGA). You may find the definitions of these abbreviations on the Internet.

We use the following formula to calculate the minimum frame buffer memory requirement for a graphic LCD:

$$Buffer\ memory\ size\ (in\ byte) = \frac{Horizontal\ Pixels\ \times Vertical\ Pixels\ \times color\ BPP}{8}$$

Example 12-3 shows how to calculate the memory need for various resolutions and color depth.

Example 12-3

Find the frame buffer RAM needed for (a) 176x144 with 4 BPP and (b) 640x480 resolution with 256 colors.

Solution:

331

(a) For this resolution, there are a total of 25,344 pixels (176 columns × 144 rows = 25,344). With 4 bits for the color of each pixel, we need a total of (25,344 × 4)/8= 16,672 bytes of frame buffer RAM. These 4 bits give rise to 16 colors.

(b) For this resolution, there is a total of 640 × 480=307200 pixels. With 256 colors, we need 8 bits for the color of each pixel. Now, total of (640 × 480 × 8) / 8 = 307200 bytes of frame buffer RAM needed.

In VGA, 640 x 480 resolution with support for 256 colors displayed at one time requires a minimum of 640 × 480 × 8 = 2,457,600 bits =307,200 bytes of memory, but due to the memory organization used, the amount of memory used is higher.

Storing pixels in the memory of mono-color LCDs

In mono-colored LCDs, each pixel can be on or off. Therefore, 1 bit can preserve the state of 1 pixel and a byte preserves 8 adjacent pixels. In some LCDs, e.g. GDM12864A and PCD8544, pixels are stored vertically in the bytes, as shown in Figure 12-7, while in some other LCDs, e.g. T6963, the pixels are stored horizontally.

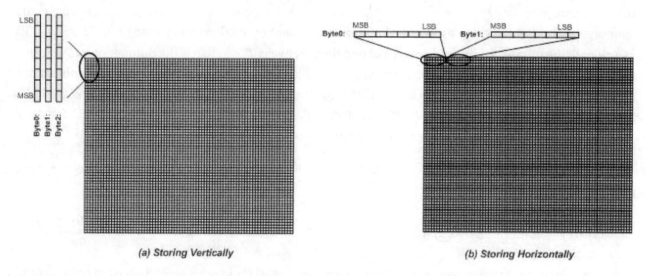

(a) Storing Vertically   (b) Storing Horizontally

Figure 12-7: Storing Data in the LCD Memory of Mono-colored LCDs

Review Questions

1. As the number of pixels goes up, the size of display memory _____ (increases, decreases).
2. If a total of 24 bits is set aside for color, how many colors are available?
3. Calculate the total video memory needed for 1024 × 768 resolution with 16 colors displayed at the same time.
4. With BPP of 16, we get _____colors.

Section 12.2: Displaying Texts on Graphic LCDs

As shown in Figure 12-8 each character can be made by putting pixels next to each other.

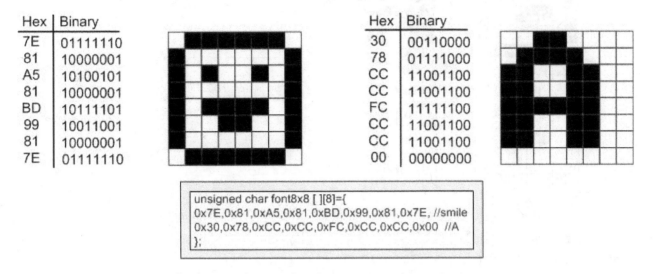

Hex	Binary
7E	01111110
81	10000001
A5	10100101
81	10000001
BD	10111101
99	10011001
81	10000001
7E	01111110

Hex	Binary
30	00110000
78	01111000
CC	11001100
CC	11001100
FC	11111100
CC	11001100
CC	11001100
00	00000000

```
unsigned char font8x8 [ ][8]={
0x7E,0x81,0xA5,0x81,0xBD,0x99,0x81,0x7E, //smile
0x30,0x78,0xCC,0xCC,0xFC,0xCC,0xCC,0x00  //A
};
```

Figure 12-8: Pixel Patterns of Characters Happy Face and Letter A

To display characters on the screen, we must have the pixel patterns of the entire characters. Whenever we want to display a character on the screen we copy its pixel pattern into the display memory. See Figure 12-9.

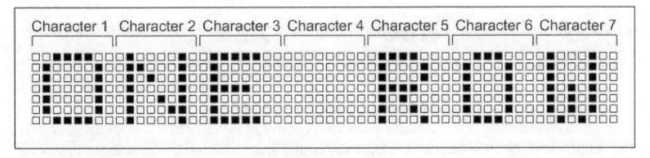

Figure 12-9: A Sample Text

The pixel patterns are stored in an array in the same way that they should be stored in the LCD memory. This means that for horizontal LCDs the bits are stored horizontally and for vertical LCDs the pixels are stored vertically. Figure 12-8 shows the way patterns are stored for horizontal LCDs. In Figure 12-10 the same patterns are stored for vertical LCDs.

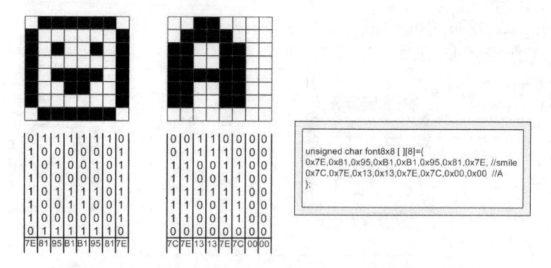

Figure 12-10: Pixel Patterns of Happy Face and Character A and its font for Vertical LCD

To get better-looking characters, the font resolution must be increased, which translates to more pixels horizontally and vertically. See Figure 12-11.

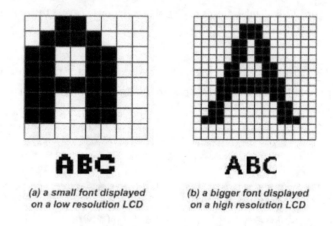

(a) a small font displayed
on a low resolution LCD

(b) a bigger font displayed
on a high resolution LCD

Figure 12-11: A Bigger Font vs. a Smaller Font

See Program 12-1. A lookup table of the pixel patterns of the characters is made using an array. The GLCD_putchar function accesses the lookup array to display characters on the LCD. The connection between the PCD8544 LCD and the microcontroller is shown in Figure 12-12. For more information about the PCD8544 see its datasheet on the Web.

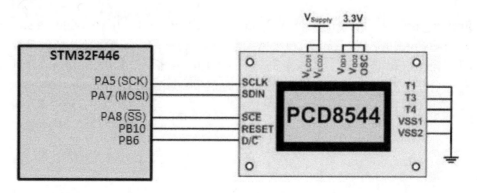

Figure 12-12: The PCD8544 LCD connection to the STM32F446 Nucleo

```
/* P12_1.c: PCD8544 (Nokia5110) GLCD via SPI with STM32F446
 *
 * Letters A,B,C are written on the display.
 *
 * The connections
 * GLCD      Arduino          STM32F446
 * 1 RST     D6     reset      PB10
 * 2 CE      D7     chip select PA8
 * 3 DC      D10    reg select  PB6
 * 4 DIN     D11    SPI MOSI    PA7
 * 5 CLK     D13    SPI SCK     PA5
 * 6 VCC
 * 7 LIGHT
 * 8 GND
 *
 * This program was tested with Keil uVision v5.24a with DFP v2.11.0
 */

#include "stm32f4xx.h"

/* define the pixel size of display */
#define GLCD_WIDTH  84
#define GLCD_HEIGHT 48

void GLCD_setCursor(unsigned char x, unsigned char y);
void GLCD_clear(void);
void GLCD_init(void);
void GLCD_data_write(unsigned char data);
void GLCD_command_write(unsigned char data);
void GLCD_putchar(int c);
void SPI_init(void);
void SPI_write(unsigned char data);

/* sample font table */
const char font_table[][6] = {
    {0x7e, 0x11, 0x11, 0x11, 0x7e, 0},   /* A */
    {0x7f, 0x49, 0x49, 0x49, 0x36, 0},   /* B */
    {0x3e, 0x41, 0x41, 0x41, 0x22, 0}    /* C */
};

int main(void) {
    GLCD_init();        /* initialize the GLCD controller */
    GLCD_clear();       /* clear display and home the cursor */

    GLCD_putchar(0);    /* display letter A */
    GLCD_putchar(1);    /* display letter B */
    GLCD_putchar(2);    /* display letter C */

    while(1) {
    }
}

void GLCD_putchar(int c) {
    int i;
    for (i = 0; i < 6; i++)
```

335

```c
        GLCD_data_write(font_table[c][i]);
}

void GLCD_setCursor(unsigned char x, unsigned char y) {
    GLCD_command_write(0x80 | x);   /* column */
    GLCD_command_write(0x40 | y);   /* bank (8 pixel rows per bank) */
}


/* clears the GLCD by writing zeros to the entire screen */
void GLCD_clear(void) {
    int32_t index;
    for (index = 0 ; index < (GLCD_WIDTH * GLCD_HEIGHT / 8) ; index++)
        GLCD_data_write(0x00);

    GLCD_setCursor(0, 0); /* return to the home position */
}


/* send the initialization commands to PCD8544 GLCD controller */
void GLCD_init(void) {
    SPI_init();

    /* PORTB 6, 10 as GPIO output for GLCD DC and RESET */
    RCC->AHB1ENR |= 2;                  /* enable GPIOB clock */
    GPIOB->MODER &= ~0x00303000;        /* clear pin mode */
    GPIOB->MODER |=  0x00101000;        /* set pin output mode */

    /* hardware reset of GLCD controller */
    GPIOB->BSRR = 0x04000000;           /* assert RESET */
    GPIOB->BSRR = 0x00000400;           /* deassert RESET */

    GLCD_command_write(0x21);           /* set extended command mode */
    GLCD_command_write(0xB8);           /* set LCD Vop for contrast */
    GLCD_command_write(0x04);           /* set temp coefficient */
    GLCD_command_write(0x14);           /* set LCD bias mode 1:48 */
    GLCD_command_write(0x20);           /* set normal command mode */
    GLCD_command_write(0x0C);           /* set display normal mode */
}

/* write to GLCD controller data register */
void GLCD_data_write(unsigned char data) {
    GPIOB->BSRR = 0x00000040;           /* select data register */
    SPI_write(data);                    /* send data via SPI */
}

/* write to GLCD controller command register */
void GLCD_command_write(unsigned char data) {
    GPIOB->BSRR = 0x00400000;           /* select command register */
    SPI_write(data);                    /* send data via SPI */
}

void SPI_init(void) {
    RCC->AHB1ENR |= 1;                  /* enable GPIOA clock */
    RCC->APB2ENR |= 0x1000;             /* enable SPI1 clock */

    /* PORTA 5, 7 for SPI1 MOSI and SCLK */
    GPIOA->MODER &= ~0x0000CC00;        /* clear pin mode */
    GPIOA->MODER |=  0x00008800;        /* set pin alternate mode */
```

```
    GPIOA->AFR[0] &= ~0xF0F00000;   /* clear alt mode */
    GPIOA->AFR[0] |=  0x50500000;   /* set alt mode SPI1 */

    /* PORTA 8 as GPIO output for SPI slave select */
    GPIOA->MODER &= ~0x00030000;    /* clear pin mode */
    GPIOA->MODER |=  0x00010000;    /* set pin output mode */

    SPI1->CR1 = 0x31C;
    SPI1->CR2 = 0;
    SPI1->CR1 |= 0x40;              /* enable SPI1 module */
}

void SPI_write(unsigned char data) {
    GPIOA->BSRR = 0x01000000;       /* assert slave select */
    while (!(SPI1->SR & 2)) {}      /* wait until transfer buffer Empty */
    SPI1->DR = data;                /* write command and upper 4 bits of data */
    while (SPI1->SR & 0x80) {}      /* wait for transmission done */
    GPIOA->BSRR = 0x00000100;       /* deassert slave select */
}
```

Review Questions

1. True or false. The same font table can be used for vertical and horizontal LCDs.
2. True or false. To display a character on the LCD, its pixel pattern should be copied onto the LCD display memory.

Answers to Review Questions

Section 12-1:

1. increases
2. 2^{24} = 16.7 million
3. $1024 \times 768 \times 4$ = 3,145,728 bits = 384K bytes, but it uses 512 KB due to bit planes.
4. 2^{16} = 65,536

Section 12-2:

1. False

2. True

Chapter 13: DMA Programming

This chapter examines the concept of DMA (Direct Memory Address) and shows how to program it. The DMA in Arm microcontrollers are implemented differently by various vendors and can be very complex. This chapter is simply an introduction.

Section 13.1: Concept of DMA

In computers, there is often a need to transfer a large number of bytes of data between memory and peripherals such as disk drives. In such cases, using the microprocessor to transfer the data is too slow since the data first must be fetched into the CPU and then sent to its destination. In addition, the process of fetching and decoding the instructions that move the data themselves adds to the overhead. For this reason, in most computers and microcontrollers there is a DMAC (direct memory access controller), whose function is to bypass the CPU and provide a direct connection between peripherals and memory, thus transferring the data as fast as possible.

One problem with using DMA is that there is only one set of buses (one set of each bus: data bus, address bus, control bus) in a given computer and no bus can serve two masters at the same time. The buses can be used either by the main CPU or the DMAC (DMA Controller). Since the CPU has primary control over the buses, it must give permission to DMAC to use them. How is this done? The answer is that any time the DMAC needs to use the buses to transfer data, it sends a signal called HOLD to the CPU and the CPU will respond by sending back the signal HLDA (hold acknowledge) to indicate to the DMAC that it can go ahead and use the buses. While the DMAC is using the buses to transfer data, the CPU is staying away from the buses, and conversely, when the CPU is using the bus, the DMA is sitting idle. After DMAC finishes transferring the data, it will make HOLD go low and then the CPU will regain control over the buses. See Figure 13-1.

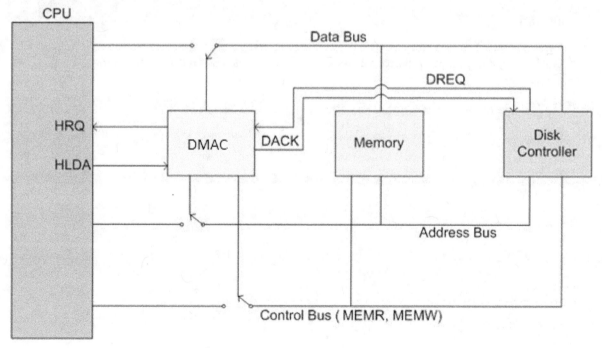

Figure 13- 1: DMA Usage of System Bus

For example, if the DMAC is to transfer a block of data from memory to an I/O device such as a disk controller, it must know the address of the beginning of the data block (address of the first byte of data) and the number of bytes (count) it needs to transfer. Then it will go through the following steps:

1. The peripheral device (such as the disk controller) will request the service of DMA by pulling DREQ (DMA request) high.
2. The DMAC will put a high on its HRQ (hold request), signaling the CPU through its HOLD pin that it needs to use the buses.
3. The CPU will finish the present bus cycle and respond to the DMAC request by putting high on its HLDA (hold acknowledge), thus telling the DMAC that it can go ahead and use the buses to perform its task. HOLD must remain active high as long as DMAC is performing its task.
4. DMAC will activate DACK (DMA acknowledge), which tells the peripheral device that it will start to transfer the data.
5. DMAC starts to transfer the data from memory to the peripheral by putting the address of the first byte of the block on the address bus and activating MEMR, thereby reading the byte from memory onto the data bus; it then changes the address to be the peripheral data register and activates MEMW to write the data to the peripheral. Then DMAC decrements the counter and increments the address pointer and repeats this process until the count reaches zero and the task is finished.
6. After the DMA has finished its job, it will deactivate HRQ, signaling the CPU that it can regain control over its buses.

This above discussion indicates that DMAC can only transfer data; unlike the CPU, it cannot decode and execute instructions. One could look at the DMAC as a kind of CPU without the instruction decoder/executer logic circuitry. For the DMAC to be able to transfer data it is equipped with the address bus, data bus, and control bus signals.

The handshaking signals between the peripheral and the DMAC or the signals between the DMAC and the CPU are described here for clarification of the operations. Their activities are transparent to the programmer. As you will see in the programming examples later, once the DMAC is properly configured and enabled, the DMA request, acknowledgment and the bus request, acknowledgment are all handled by the hardware without the intervention of the software.

In this example of a disk controller, it has a large data buffer for DMA to fill in one operation. For other peripherals such as UART or ADC, as we will see later, the data is usually transferred in one or two bytes at a time. Instead of granting the DMAC the exclusive use of the bus for the transfer of the data block, the CPU will allow the DMAC to take over the bus only when the CPU is not using it. This way, the DMA impact on the CPU performance can be reduced even further.

DMA in Microcontrollers

As we mentioned, DMA (Direct Memory Access) is a method of allowing peripherals to gain access to the memory without involving the CPU. This is usually accomplished by adding a DMA controller and a memory bus arbiter to the system that transfers data between memory and peripherals over the same data bus CPU reads/writes the memory. In the microcontroller such as Arm, the software configures the

DMA controller by setting up the source address, the destination address, the data width, and the amount of data to transfer. The software also configures the DMA controller and the peripheral for the event that triggers the data transfer. Since the idea of DMA is to reduce the involvement of CPU in the data transfer, interrupt is usually used to notify the completion of the data transfer.

The main reason of performing DMA is to free up the CPU to do other tasks while the peripherals are moving data in and out of the memory. In this chapter, we will be using UART and ADC data transmission to illustrate how DMA works.

Consider if we need to transmit a 2 Kbyte of data through a UART at 9600 Baud. Using a polling method, the CPU will be waiting for the UART transmit data register to be available before reading a byte of the data from the memory and writing it to the UART transmit data register. For the duration of transmitting the 2 Kbyte data, the CPU is completely occupied without doing any other tasks. At 9600 Baud, this will take a little longer than two seconds to transmit 2 Kbyte of data. For these two seconds, the system cannot perform other tasks.

In Chapter 6, we introduced the interrupt. Using interrupt, the CPU will be able to perform other tasks while transmitting data. When the UART transmit data register becomes empty, it generates an interrupt to the CPU. The CPU halts the current task, saves the current CPU registers on the stack then executes the interrupt handler. The interrupt handler reads a byte of data from memory and writes it to the UART transmit data register. The CPU restores the registers from the stack and resumes the task that was interrupted. All these CPU operations incurred just to move one byte of data. With 16 MHz of the system clock, it takes a couple of microseconds of CPU time to send a byte of data to the UART. For two Kbyte of data, it takes several milliseconds of the CPU time. From the performance perspective, it is several magnitudes better than using polling but we can do even better with DMA.

With DMA in Arm, the software needs to configure the DMA controller by setting the beginning address of the data in memory in the source address register, the UART transmit register address in the destination register, and the number of bytes to transmit in data count register. The software then sets the UART to trigger the DMA transfer when the UART transmit data register is empty. From here on, the DMA controller will run on its own without involving the CPU until all the bytes are sent. When the UART transmit data register becomes empty, it notifies the DMA controller. The DMA controller requests the memory data bus from the bus arbiter. When it is granted the data bus, it reads the data from the memory using the source address register and writes the data to the UART transmit data register. The DMA controller will increment the source address register to point to the next byte of data and decrement the data count register to see whether all the data were sent. When the data count register reaches zero, the DMA controller generates transfer complete interrupt to let the CPU know that all the data were sent. All the DMA operations until the transfer complete interrupt, do not involve the CPU and the CPU may perform other tasks without being interrupted.

Review Questions
1. True or false. When the DMA is working, the CPU is not using the bus.
2. True or false. When the CPU is using the bus, the DMA is sitting idle.

3. True or false. No bus can serve two masters at the same time.

Section 13.2: DMA Programming in STM32

The STM32F446RE microcontroller has two DMA controllers. See Figure 13-2. Each DMA controller has eight DMA Streams. Together, they have 16 streams that may perform DMA operations independently. Each DMA stream has eight channels. The associations of peripherals to DMA channels/streams are hardwired and can be seen in Tables 13-1 and 13-2.

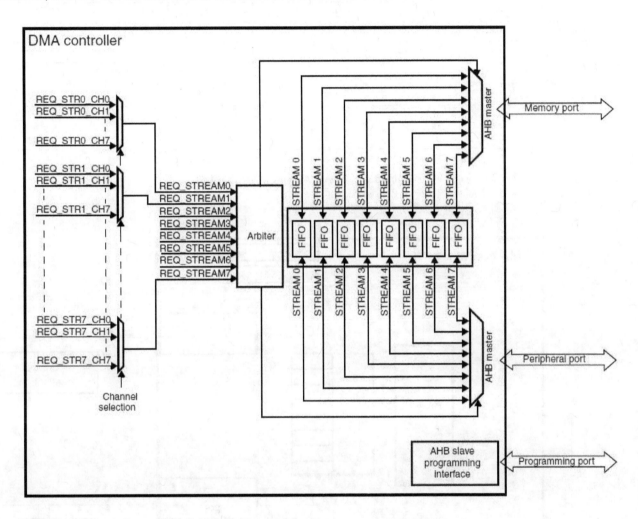

Figure 13- 2: DMA Block Diagram in STM32F4xx

Peripheral requests	Stream 0	Stream 1	Stream 2	Stream 3	Stream 4	Stream 5	Stream 6	Stream 7
Channel 0	ADC1	SAI1_A	TIM8_CH1 TIM8_CH2 TIM8_CH3	SAI1_A	ADC1	SAI1_B	TIM1_CH1 TIM1_CH2 TIM1_CH3	SAI2_B
Channel 1	-	DCMI	ADC2	ADC2	SAI1_B	-	-	DCMI
Channel 2	ADC3	ADC3	-	-	-	-	-	-
Channel 3	SPI1_RX	-	SPI1_RX	SPI1_TX	SAI2_A	SPI1_TX	SAI2_B	QUADSPI
Channel 4	SPI4_RX	SPI4_TX	USART1_RX	SDIO		USART1_RX	SDIO	USART1_TX
Channel 5	-	USART6_RX	USART6_RX	SPI4_RX	SPI4_TX	-	USART6_TX	USART6_TX
Channel 6	TIM1_TRIG	TIM1_CH1	TIM1_CH2	TIM1_CH1	TIM1_CH4 TIM1_TRIG TIM1_COM	TIM1_UP	TIM1_CH3	-
Channel 7	-	TIM8_UP	TIM8_CH1	TIM8_CH2	TIM8_CH3	-	-	TIM8_CH4 TIM8_TRIG TIM8_COM

Table 13- 1: DMA1 Mapping in STM32F4xx

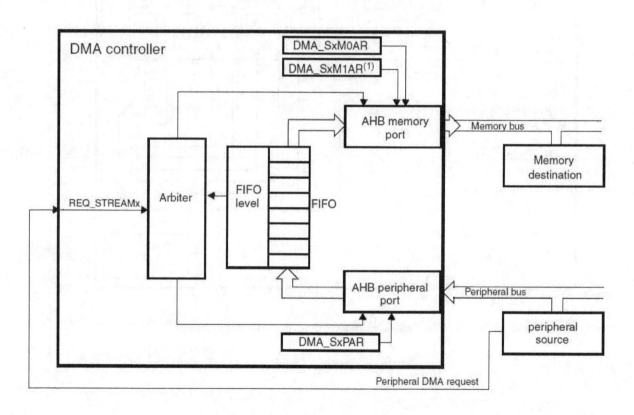

Figure 13-3: Peripheral-to-memory mode

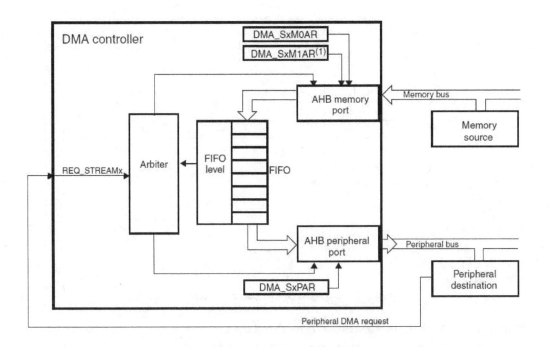

Figure 13-4: Memory-to-peripheral mode

Peripheral requests	Stream 0	Stream 1	Stream 2	Stream 3	Stream 4	Stream 5	Stream 6	Stream 7
Channel 0	SPI3_RX	SPDIFRX_DT	SPI3_RX	SPI2_RX	SPI2_TX	SPI3_TX	SPDIFRX_CS	SPI3_TX
Channel 1	I2C1_RX	I2C3_RX	TIM7_UP	-	TIM7_UP	I2C1_RX	I2C1_TX	I2C1_TX
Channel 2	TIM4_CH1	-	FMPI2C1_RX	TIM4_CH2	-	FMPI2C1_RX	TIM4_UP	TIM4_CH3
Channel 3	-	TIM2_UP TIM2_CH3	I2C3_RX	-	I2C3_TX	TIM2_CH1	TIM2_CH2 TIM2_CH4	TIM2_UP TIM2_CH4
Channel 4	UART5_RX	USART3_RX	UART4_RX	USART3_TX	UART4_TX	USART2_RX	USART2_TX	UART5_TX
Channel 5	-	-	TIM3_CH4 TIM3_UP	-	TIM3_CH1 TIM3_TRIG	TIM3_CH2	-	TIM3_CH3
Channel 6	TIM5_CH3 TIM5_UP	TIM5_CH4 TIM5_TRIG	TIM5_CH1	TIM5_CH4 TIM5_TRIG	TIM5_CH2	-	TIM5_UP	-
Channel 7	-	TIM6_UP	I2C2_RX	I2C2_RX	USART3_TX	DAC1	DAC2	I2C2_TX

Table 13- 2: DMA2 Mapping in STM32F4xx

Each stream has six registers and also shares with other streams for interrupt status bits and interrupt flag clear bits in four registers.

DMA Clock Enable

As we have seen before, we use RCC_AHB1ENR register to enable the clock. See DMA1EN (bit21) in figure below.

31	30	29	28	27	26	25	24	23	22	21	20	19	18	17	16
Res.	OTGHS ULPIEN	OTGHS EN	Res.	Res.	Res.	Res.	Res.	Res.	DMA2 EN	DMA1 EN	Res.	Res.	BKP SRAMEN	Res.	Res.
	rw	rw							rw	rw			rw		

15	14	13	12	11	10	9	8	7	6	5	4	3	2	1	0
Res.	Res.	Res.	CRC EN	Res.	Res.	Res.	Res.	GPIOH EN	GPIOG EN	GPIOF EN	GPIOE EN	GPIOD EN	GPIOC EN	GPIOB EN	GPIOA EN
			rw					rw	rw	rw	rw	rw	rw	rw	rw

Bit 22 **DMA2EN:** DMA2 clock enable

This bit is set and cleared by software.

0: DMA2 clock disabled

1: DMA2 clock enabled

Bit 21 **DMA1EN:** DMA1 clock enable

This bit is set and cleared by software.

0: DMA1 clock disabled

1: DMA1 clock enabled

Figure 13- 5: RCC_AHB1ENR Register to Enable DMA Clock

DMA Stream Configuration Register (DMA_SxCR)

This is one of the most important registers in the DMA operation. See Figure 13-6. We examine the bits and show the program in choosing them.

31	30	29	28	27	26	25	24	23	22	21	20	19	18	17	16
Res.	Res.	Res.	Res.	CHSEL[2:0]			MBURST [1:0]		PBURST[1:0]		Res.	CT	DBM	PL[1:0]	
				rw	rw	rw	rw	rw	rw	rw		rw	rw	rw	rw

15	14	13	12	11	10	9	8	7	6	5	4	3	2	1	0
PINCOS	MSIZE[1:0]		PSIZE[1:0]		MINC	PINC	CIRC	DIR[1:0]		PFCTRL	TCIE	HTIE	TEIE	DMEIE	EN
rw	rw	rw	rw	rw	rw	rw	rw	rw	rw	rw	rw	rw	rw	rw	rw

Bits 31:28 Reserved, must be kept at reset value.

Bits 27:25 **CHSEL[2:0]:** channel selection

These bits are set and cleared by software.

000: channel 0 selected

001: channel 1 selected

010: channel 2 selected

011: channel 3 selected

100: channel 4 selected

101: channel 5 selected

110: channel 6 selected

111: channel 7 selected

These bits are protected and can be written only if EN is '0'.

Bits 24:23 **MBURST[1:0]:** memory burst transfer configuration

These bits are set and cleared by software.

00: single transfer

01: INCR4 (incremental burst of 4 beats)

10: INCR8 (incremental burst of 8 beats)

11: INCR16 (incremental burst of 16 beats)

These bits are protected and can be written only if EN is '0'.

In direct mode, these bits are forced to 0x0 by hardware as soon as bit EN= '1'.

Bits 22:21 **PBURST[1:0]:** peripheral burst transfer configuration

These bits are set and cleared by software.

00: single transfer
01: INCR4 (incremental burst of 4 beats)
10: INCR8 (incremental burst of 8 beats)
11: INCR16 (incremental burst of 16 beats)
These bits are protected and can be written only if EN is '0'.
In direct mode, these bits are forced to 0x0 by hardware.

Bit 20 Reserved, must be kept at reset value.

Bit 19 **CT**: current target (only in double-buffer mode)
This bit is set and cleared by hardware. It can also be written by software.
0: current target memory is Memory 0 (addressed by the DMA_SxM0AR pointer)
1: current target memory is Memory 1 (addressed by the DMA_SxM1AR pointer)
This bit can be written only if EN is '0' to indicate the target memory area of the first transfer.
Once the stream is enabled, this bit operates as a status flag indicating which memory area
is the current target.

Bit 18 **DBM**: double-buffer mode
This bit is set and cleared by software.
0: no buffer switching at the end of transfer
1: memory target switched at the end of the DMA transfer
This bit is protected and can be written only if EN is '0'.

Bits 17:16 **PL[1:0]**: priority level
These bits are set and cleared by software.
00: low
01: medium
10: high
11: very high
These bits are protected and can be written only if EN is '0'.

Bit 15 **PINCOS**: peripheral increment offset size
This bit is set and cleared by software
0: The offset size for the peripheral address calculation is linked to the PSIZE
1: The offset size for the peripheral address calculation is fixed to 4 (32-bit alignment).
This bit has no meaning if bit PINC = '0'.
This bit is protected and can be written only if EN = '0'.
This bit is forced low by hardware when the stream is enabled (bit EN = '1') if the direct mode
is selected or if PBURST are different from "00".

Bits 14:13 **MSIZE[1:0]**: memory data size
These bits are set and cleared by software.
00: byte (8-bit)
01: half-word (16-bit)
10: word (32-bit)
11: reserved
These bits are protected and can be written only if EN is '0'.
In direct mode, MSIZE is forced by hardware to the same value as PSIZE as soon as
bit EN = '1'.

Bits 12:11 **PSIZE[1:0]**: peripheral data size
These bits are set and cleared by software.
00: byte (8-bit)
01: half-word (16-bit)
10: word (32-bit)
11: reserved
These bits are protected and can be written only if EN is '0'.

Bit 10 **MINC**: memory increment mode
This bit is set and cleared by software.

0: memory address pointer is fixed

1: memory address pointer is incremented after each data transfer (increment is done according to MSIZE)

This bit is protected and can be written only if EN is '0'.

Bit 9 **PINC**: peripheral increment mode

This bit is set and cleared by software.

0: peripheral address pointer is fixed

1: peripheral address pointer is incremented after each data transfer (increment is done according to PSIZE)

This bit is protected and can be written only if EN is '0'.

Bit 8 **CIRC**: circular mode

This bit is set and cleared by software and can be cleared by hardware.

0: circular mode disabled

1: circular mode enabled

When the peripheral is the flow controller (bit PFCTRL = 1) and the stream is enabled (bit EN = 1), then this bit is automatically forced by hardware to 0.

It is automatically forced by hardware to 1 if the DBM bit is set, as soon as the stream is enabled (bit EN ='1').

Bits 7:6 **DIR[1:0]**: data transfer direction

These bits are set and cleared by software.

00: peripheral-to-memory

01: memory-to-peripheral

10: memory-to-memory

11: reserved

These bits are protected and can be written only if EN is '0'.

Bit 5 **PFCTRL**: peripheral flow controller

This bit is set and cleared by software.

0: DMA is the flow controller

1: The peripheral is the flow controller

This bit is protected and can be written only if EN is '0'.

When the memory-to-memory mode is selected (bits DIR[1:0]=10), then this bit is automatically forced to 0 by hardware.

Bit 4 **TCIE**: transfer complete interrupt enable

This bit is set and cleared by software.

0: TC interrupt disabled

1: TC interrupt enabled

Bit 3 **HTIE**: half transfer interrupt enable

This bit is set and cleared by software.

0: HT interrupt disabled

1: HT interrupt enabled

Bit 2 **TEIE**: transfer error interrupt enable

This bit is set and cleared by software.

0: TE interrupt disabled

1: TE interrupt enabled

Bit 1 **DMEIE**: direct mode error interrupt enable

This bit is set and cleared by software.

0: DME interrupt disabled

1: DME interrupt enabled

Bit 0 **EN**: stream enable / flag stream ready when read low

This bit is set and cleared by software.

0: stream disabled

1: stream enabled

This bit may be cleared by hardware:
– on a DMA end of transfer (stream ready to be configured)
– if a transfer error occurs on the AHB master buses
– when the FIFO threshold on memory AHB port is not compatible with the size of the burst
When this bit is read as 0, the software is allowed to program the configuration and FIFO bits registers. It is forbidden to write these registers when the EN bit is read as 1.

Figure 13- 6: DMA Stream x Configuration Register (DMA_SxCR, x = 0..7)

Channel selection

For each stream, only one channel is active at a time. The channels of a stream are selected by bits CHSEL[2:0] in DMA_SxCR register.

Direction

The DMA controller may transfer data from memory to peripheral, peripheral to memory, or from memory to memory. See the DIR bits in DMA_SxCR register.

Double buffered

The DMA controller allows two buffers associated with a stream. This way, the CPU may be operating on the data in one buffer while the DMA controller is transferring data to the other. The DBM bit enables the double buffer mode. The CT bit tells which buffer is used by the DMA controller at that time. See DMA_SxCR register.

Address increment

Both memory address registers and peripheral address register may be automatically incremented after each data transfer. This allows the DMA controller to send or receive a block of memory without the intervention of CPU. The address increment is enabled by MINC bit and PINC bit. See DMA_SxCR register.

Data transfer size

Each data transfer may be 8-bit, 16-bit, or 32-bit in size. They are determined by MSIZE field and PSIZE field. See DMA_SxCR register.

Interrupt enables

There are four possible interrupts from a DMA stream: Transfer complete, Half transfer complete, Transfer error and Direct mode error. They are enabled by TCIE, HTIE, TEIE, and DMEIE bits respectively. See DMA_SxCR register.

DMA stream enable

The DMA stream is enabled by setting the EN bit. Before configuring the DMA stream, the stream should be disabled by writing a 0 to the EN bit and wait until the EN bit is read back as 0. See DMA_SxCR register.

DMA Stream Number of Data Register (DMA_SxNDTR)

The Number of Data Register should be written with the number of transfers desired. After each data transfer, the number is decremented. When the number reaches zero, the transfer is complete. The number of data items to transfer can be from 0 and goes up to 65535. See figure below.

31	30	29	28	27	26	25	24	23	22	21	20	19	18	17	16
Res.	Res.	Res.	Res.	Res.	Res.	Res.	Res.	Res.	Res.	Res.	Res.	Res.	Res.	Res.	Res.

15	14	13	12	11	10	9	8	7	6	5	4	3	2	1	0
						NDT[15:0]									
rw	rw	rw	rw	rw	rw	rw	rw	rw	rw	rw	rw	rw	rw	rw	rw

Bits 31:16 Reserved, must be kept at reset value.

Bits 15:0 **NDT[15:0]**: number of data items to transfer (0 up to 65535)

This register can be written only when the stream is disabled. When the stream is enabled, this register is read-only, indicating the remaining data items to be transmitted. This register decrements after each DMA transfer.

Once the transfer is completed, this register can either stay at zero (when the stream is in normal mode) or be reloaded automatically with the previously programmed value in the following cases:

– when the stream is configured in circular mode.

– when the stream is enabled again by setting EN bit to '1'.

If the value of this register is zero, no transaction can be served even if the stream is enabled.

Figure 13- 7: DMA Stream x Number of Data Register (DMA_SxNDTR, x = 0..7)

DMA Stream Peripheral Address Register (DMA_SxPAR)

This register holds the address of the peripheral. The data is written to the location specified by this register during memory-to-peripheral transfer and read from during peripheral-to-memory transfer. See (DMA_SxPAR) register below.

31	30	29	28	27	26	25	24	23	22	21	20	19	18	17	16
							PAR[31:16]								
rw	rw	rw	rw	rw	rw	rw	rw	rw	rw	rw	rw	rw	rw	rw	rw

15	14	13	12	11	10	9	8	7	6	5	4	3	2	1	0
							PAR[15:0]								
rw	rw	rw	rw	rw	rw	rw	rw	rw	rw	rw	rw	rw	rw	rw	rw

Bits 31:0 **PAR[31:0]**: peripheral address

Base address of the peripheral data register from/to which the data is read/written.

These bits are write-protected and can be written only when bit EN = '0' in the DMA_SxCR register.

Figure 13- 8: DMA Stream x Peripheral Address Register (DMA_SxPAR, x = 0..7)

DMA Stream Memory 0 Address Register (DMA_SxM0AR)

This register holds the address of the data buffer in memory. The data is written to the location specified by this register during peripheral-to-memory transfer and read from during memory-to-peripheral transfer. See DMA_SxM0AR register below.

31	30	29	28	27	26	25	24	23	22	21	20	19	18	17	16
							M0A[31:16]								
rw	rw	rw	rw	rw	rw	rw	rw	rw	rw	rw	rw	rw	rw	rw	rw
15	14	13	12	11	10	9	8	7	6	5	4	3	2	1	0
							M0A[15:0]								
rw	rw	rw	rw	rw	rw	rw	rw	rw	rw	rw	rw	rw	rw	rw	rw

Bits 31:0 **M0A[31:0]**: memory 0 address

Base address of memory area 0 from/to which the data is read/written.

These bits are write-protected. They can be written only if:

– the stream is disabled (bit EN= '0' in the DMA_SxCR register) or

– the stream is enabled (EN='1' in DMA_SxCR register) and bit CT = '1' in the DMA_SxCR register (in double-buffer mode).

Figure 13- 9: DMA Stream x Memory 0 Address Register (DMA_SxM0AR, x = 0..7)

DMA Stream Memory 1 Address Register (DMA_SxM1AR)

This register is used only when double buffer mode is enabled. It is used the same way as the previous register when buffer 1 is currently used. See DMA_SxM1AR register below.

31	30	29	28	27	26	25	24	23	22	21	20	19	18	17	16
							M1A[31:16]								
rw	rw	rw	rw	rw	rw	rw	rw	rw	rw	rw	rw	rw	rw	rw	rw
15	14	13	12	11	10	9	8	7	6	5	4	3	2	1	0
							M1A[15:0]								
rw	rw	rw	rw	rw	rw	rw	rw	rw	rw	rw	rw	rw	rw	rw	rw

Bits 31:0 **M1A[31:0]**: memory 1 address (used in case of double-buffer mode)

Base address of memory area 1 from/to which the data is read/written.

This register is used only for the double-buffer mode.

These bits are write-protected. They can be written only if:

– the stream is disabled (bit EN= '0' in the DMA_SxCR register) or

– the stream is enabled (EN='1' in DMA_SxCR register) and bit CT = '0' in the DMA_SxCR register.

Figure 13- 10: DMA Stream x Memory 1 Address Register (DMA_SxM1AR, x = 0..7)

DMA Stream FIFO Register (DMA_SxFCR)

Each DMA stream has a FIFO (First-in-first-out buffer) associated with it to improve the performance. This register is used to configure the FIFO. See DMA_SxFCR register below.

31	30	29	28	27	26	25	24	23	22	21	20	19	18	17	16
Res.	Res.	Res.	Res.	Res.	Res.	Res.	Res.	Res.	Res.	Res.	Res.	Res.	Res.	Res.	Res.
15	14	13	12	11	10	9	8	7	6	5	4	3	2	1	0
Res.	Res.	Res.	Res.	Res.	Res.	Res.	Res.	FEIE	Res.	FS[2:0]			DMDIS	FTH[1:0]	
								rw		r	r	r	rw	rw	rw

Bits 31:8 Reserved, must be kept at reset value.

Bit 7 **FEIE**: FIFO error interrupt enable

This bit is set and cleared by software.

0: FE interrupt disabled

1: FE interrupt enabled

Bit 6 Reserved, must be kept at reset value.

Bits 5:3 **FS[2:0]**: FIFO status

These bits are read-only.

000: 0 < fifo_level < 1/4

001: 1/4 ≤ fifo_level < 1/2

010: 1/2 ≤ fifo_level < 3/4

011: 3/4 ≤ fifo_level < full

100: FIFO is empty

101: FIFO is full

others: no meaning

These bits are not relevant in the direct mode (DMDIS bit is zero).

Bit 2 **DMDIS**: direct mode disable

This bit is set and cleared by software. It can be set by hardware.

0: direct mode enabled

1: direct mode disabled

This bit is protected and can be written only if EN is '0'.

This bit is set by hardware if the memory-to-memory mode is selected (DIR bit in DMA_SxCR are "10") and the EN bit in the DMA_SxCR register is '1' because the direct mode is not allowed in the memory-to-memory configuration.

Bits 1:0 **FTH[1:0]**: FIFO threshold selection

These bits are set and cleared by software.

00: 1/4 full FIFO

01: 1/2 full FIFO

10: 3/4 full FIFO

11: full FIFO

These bits are not used in the direct mode when the DMIS value is zero.

These bits are protected and can be written only if EN is '0'.

Figure 13- 11: DMA Stream x FIFO Control Register (DMA_SxFCR, x = 0..7)

DMA Use of Interrupt

The two registers of DMA_HISR and DMA_HIFCR allow us to use DMA with interrupts. See figures below.

31	30	29	28	27	26	25	24	23	22	21	20	19	18	17	16
Res.	Res.	Res.	Res.	TCIF7	HTIF7	TEIF7	DMEIF7	Res.	FEIF7	TCIF6	HTIF6	TEIF6	DMEIF6	Res.	FEIF6
				r	r	r	r		r	r	r	r	r		r
15	14	13	12	11	10	9	8	7	6	5	4	3	2	1	0
Res.	Res.	Res.	Res.	TCIF5	HTIF5	TEIF5	DMEIF5	Res.	FEIF5	TCIF4	HTIF4	TEIF4	DMEIF4	Res.	FEIF4
				r	r	r	r		r	r	r	r	r		r

Bits 31:28, 15:12 Reserved, must be kept at reset value.

Bits 27, 21, 11, 5 **TCIFx**: stream x transfer complete interrupt flag (x = 7..4)

This bit is set by hardware. It is cleared by software writing 1 to the corresponding bit in the DMA_HIFCR register.

0: no transfer complete event on stream x

1: atransfer complete event occurred on stream x

Bits 26, 20, 10, 4 **HTIFx**: stream x half transfer interrupt flag (x = 7..4)
  This bit is set by hardware. It is cleared by software writing 1 to the corresponding bit in the DMA_HIFCR register.
  0: no half transfer event on stream x
  1: a half transfer event occurred on stream x
Bits 25, 19, 9, 3 **TEIFx**: stream x transfer error interrupt flag (x = 7..4)
  This bit is set by hardware. It is cleared by software writing 1 to the corresponding bit in the DMA_HIFCR register.
  0: no transfer error on stream x
  1: a transfer error occurred on stream x
Bits 24, 18, 8, 2 **DMEIFx**: stream x direct mode error interrupt flag (x = 7..4)
  This bit is set by hardware. It is cleared by software writing 1 to the corresponding bit in the DMA_HIFCR register.
  0: no direct mode error on stream x
  1: a direct mode error occurred on stream x
Bits 23, 17, 7, 1 Reserved, must be kept at reset value.
Bits 22, 16, 6, 0 **FEIFx**: stream x FIFO error interrupt flag (x = 7..4)
  This bit is set by hardware. It is cleared by software writing 1 to the corresponding bit in the DMA_HIFCR register.
  0: no FIFO error event on stream x
  1: a FIFO error event occurred on stream x

Figure 13-12: DMA High Interrupt Status Register (DMA_HISR)

31	30	29	28	27	26	25	24	23	22	21	20	19	18	17	16
Res.	Res.	Res.	Res.	CTCIF7	CHTIF7	CTEIF7	CDMEIF7	Res.	CFEIF7	CTCIF6	CHTIF6	CTEIF6	CDMEIF6	Res.	CFEIF6
				w	w	w	w		w	w	w	w	w		w

15	14	13	12	11	10	9	8	7	6	5	4	3	2	1	0
Res.	Res.	Res.	Res.	CTCIF5	CHTIF5	CTEIF5	CDMEIF5	Res.	CFEIF5	CTCIF4	CHTIF4	CTEIF4	CDMEIF4	Res.	CFEIF4
				w	w	w	w		w	w	w	w	w		w

Bits 31:28, 15:12 Reserved, must be kept at reset value.
Bits 27, 21, 11, 5 **CTCIFx**: stream x clear transfer complete interrupt flag (x = 7..4)
  Writing 1 to this bit clears the corresponding TCIFx flag in the DMA_HISR register.
Bits 26, 20, 10, 4 **CHTIFx**: stream x clear half transfer interrupt flag (x = 7..4)
  Writing 1 to this bit clears the corresponding HTIFx flag in the DMA_HISR register.
Bits 25, 19, 9, 3 **CTEIFx**: stream x clear transfer error interrupt flag (x = 7..4)
  Writing 1 to this bit clears the corresponding TEIFx flag in the DMA_HISR register.

Bits 24, 18, 8, 2 **CDMEIFx**: stream x clear direct mode error interrupt flag (x = 7..4)
  Writing 1 to this bit clears the corresponding DMEIFx flag in the DMA_HISR register.
Bits 23, 17, 7, 1 Reserved, must be kept at reset value.
Bits 22, 16, 6, 0 **CFEIFx**: stream x clear FIFO error interrupt flag (x = 7..4)
  Writing 1 to this bit clears the corresponding CFEIFx flag in the DMA_HISR register.

Figure 13-13: DMA High Interrupt Flag Clear Register (DMA_HIFCR)

DMA Use of UART

We have not used any DMA option in all the UART2 examples we have done so far. The DMA option of the UART is selected by the DMAT (DMA transmitter) and DMAR (DMA receiver) bits in USART_CR3 register. See figure below.

31	30	29	28	27	26	25	24	23	22	21	20	19	18	17	16
Res.	Res.	Res.	Res.	Res.	Res.	Res.	Res.	Res.	Res.	Res.	Res.	Res.	Res.	Res.	Res.

15	14	13	12	11	10	9	8	7	6	5	4	3	2	1	0
Res.	Res.	Res.	Res.	ONEBIT	CTSIE	CTSE	RTSE	DMAT	DMAR	SCEN	NACK	HDSEL	IRLP	IREN	EIE
				rw	rw	rw	rw	rw	rw	rw	rw	rw	rw	rw	rw

Bit 7 **DMAT**: DMA enable transmitter
This bit is set/reset by software
1: DMA mode is enabled for transmission.
0: DMA mode is disabled for transmission.

Bit 6 **DMAR**: DMA enable receiver
This bit is set/reset by software
1: DMA mode is enabled for reception
0: DMA mode is disabled for reception

Figure 13-14: USART Control Register 3 (USART_CR3)

An Example of DMA Memory to USART2 Transmitter

In this example, we are going to configure the DMA controller to transfer data from memory to USART2 Transmitter. USART2 is chosen because it is connected to the virtual COM port of the ST-Link USB connection of the NucleoF446 board. The transmit output will be available without additional hardware.

From Table 13-1 in this chapter, we can see USART2_TX is connected to Channel 4 of Stream 6 of DMA1.

The USART2 is initialized the same as in chapter 4. In addition, the transfer complete interrupt is enabled. The DMA1 controller is initialized by enabling the clock in RCC_AHB1ENR and the interrupt is enabled in NVIC. Table 6-7 of interrupt chapter (Chapter 6) shows the IRQ 17 is assigned to DMA1 Stream6 global interrupt.

Steps to configure a DMA stream
1. The DMA stream must be disabled before modifying the configuration. It is disabled by writing a 0 to the EN bit of the Stream Control register then wait for the EN bit to read back as 0.
2. The interrupt flags should be cleared.
3. The Peripheral Address Register is loaded with the address of USART2 Transmit Data Register.
4. The Memory 0 Address Register is loaded with the starting address of the data buffer.
5. The Number of Data Register is loaded with the byte count of the data buffer.
6. The channel select field is set to the desired channel (in this case, channel 4).
7. Set the data size (in this example, 8-bit), memory address increment, peripheral address no increment, and direction (memory-to-peripheral).
8. Enable transfer complete interrupt and error interrupts.
9. Disable FIFO.
10. Enable DMA Stream.
11. Clear UART transmit complete interrupt flag by writing a 0 to it.
12. Enable USART2 DMA transmit by setting DMAT bit of Control Register 3.

Once the USART2 DMAT bit is set, the data transfer starts immediately. When the data transfer is complete, both DMA interrupt and USART2 interrupt will occur. In practice, you may only need to handle one interrupt. In that case, the DMA interrupt may be the more desirable one because it also covers the DMA data transfer error interrupts. In the example program below, we left a placeholder for error handling in the DMA interrupt handler. The USART2 interrupt handler sets a flag for the main function to know that the data transfer has completed.

Program 13-1: Send a string to USART2 by DMA

```c
/* p13_1.c Send a string to USART2 by DMA
 *
 * USART2 transmit is on DMA1 Stream6 Channel 4.
 * See Reference manual Table 28 RM0390 July 2017.
 *
 * USART2 Tx signal is connected to pin PA0. To see the output of USART2
 * on a PC, you need to use a USB-serial module. Connect the Rx pin of
 * the module to the PA0 pin of the STM32F446 Nucleo board. Make sure
 * the USB-serial module you use has a 3.3V interface.
 *
 * By default, the system clock is running at 16 MHz.
 * The UART is configured for 9600 Baud.
 * PA0 - USART2 TX (AF8)
 *
 * This program was tested with Keil uVision v5.24a with DFP v2.11.0
 */
#include "stm32F4xx.h"

void USART2_init(void);
void DMA1_init(void);
void DMA1_Stream6_setup(unsigned int src, unsigned int dst, int len);

int done = 1;

int main (void) {
    char alphabets[] = "abcdefghijklmnopqrstuvwxyz";
    char message[80];
    int i;
    int size = sizeof(alphabets);

    USART2_init();
    DMA1_init();

    while (1) {
        /* prepare the message for transfer */
        for (i = 0; i < size; i++)
            message[i] = alphabets[i];

        /* send the message out by USART2 using DMA */
        while (done == 0) {}    /* wait until DMA data transfer is done */
        done = 0;               /* clear done flag */
        DMA1_Stream6_setup((unsigned int)message, (unsigned int)&USART2->DR, size);
    }
}
/*  Initialize UART pins, Baudrate
    The USART2 is configured to send output to pin PA2 at 9600 Baud.
 */
void USART2_init (void) {
    RCC->AHB1ENR |= 1;          /* enable GPIOA clock */
    RCC->APB1ENR |= 0x20000;    /* enable USART2 clock */

    /* Configure PA2 for USART2_TX */
```

```
    GPIOA->AFR[0] &= ~0x0F00;
    GPIOA->AFR[0] |=  0x0700;    /* alt7 for USART2 */
    GPIOA->MODER  &= ~0x0030;
    GPIOA->MODER  |=  0x0020;    /* enable alternate function for PA2 */

    USART2->BRR = 0x0683;        /* 9600 baud @ 16 MHz */
    USART2->CR1 = 0x0008;        /* enable Tx, 8-bit data */
    USART2->CR2 = 0x0000;        /* 1 stop bit */
    USART2->CR3 = 0x0000;        /* no flow control */
    USART2->CR1 |= 0x2000;       /* enable USART2 */

    USART2->SR = ~0x40;          /* clear TC flag */
    USART2->CR1 |= 0x0040;       /* enable transmit complete interrupt */

    NVIC_EnableIRQ(USART2_IRQn);     /* USART2 interrupt enable at NVIC */
}


/*   Initialize DMA1 controller
 *   DMA1 controller's clock is enabled and also the DMA interrupt is
 *   enabled in NVIC.
 */
void DMA1_init(void) {
    RCC->AHB1ENR |= 0x00200000;      /* DMA controller clock enable */
    DMA1->HIFCR = 0x003F0000;        /* clear all interrupt flags of Stream 6 */
    NVIC_EnableIRQ(DMA1_Stream6_IRQn);  /* DMA interrupt enable at NVIC */
}


/*   Set up a DMA transfer for USART2
 *   The USART2 is connected to DMA1 Stream 6. This function sets up the
 *   peripheral register address, memory address, number of transfers,
 *   data size, transfer direction, and DMA interrupts are enabled.
 *   At the end, the DMA controller is enabled and the USART2 transmit
 *   DMA is enabled.
 */
void DMA1_Stream6_setup(unsigned int src, unsigned int dst, int len) {
    DMA1_Stream6->CR &= ~1;          /* disable DMA1 Stream 6 */
    while (DMA1_Stream6->CR & 1) {}  /* wait until DMA1 Stream 6 is disabled */
    DMA1->HIFCR = 0x003F0000;        /* clear all interrupt flags of Stream 6 */
    DMA1_Stream6->PAR = dst;
    DMA1_Stream6->M0AR = src;
    DMA1_Stream6->NDTR = len;
    DMA1_Stream6->CR = 0x08000000;   /* USART2_TX on DMA1 Stream6 Channel 4 */
    DMA1_Stream6->CR |= 0x00000440;  /* data size byte, mem incr, mem-to-peripheral */
    DMA1_Stream6->CR |= 0x16;        /* enable interrupts DMA_IT_TC | DMA_IT_TE |
DMA_IT_DME */
    DMA1_Stream6->FCR  = 0;          /* direct mode, no FIFO */
    DMA1_Stream6->CR |= 1;           /* enable DMA1 Stream 6 */

    USART2->SR &= ~0x0040;           /* clear UART transmit complete interrupt flag */
    USART2->CR3 |= 0x80;             /* enable USART2 transmitter DMA */
}


/*   DMA1 Stream6 interrupt handler
     This function handles the interrupts from DMA1 controller Stream6. The error
interrupts
     have a placeholder for error handling code. If the interrupt is from DMA data
```

```
                transfer complete, the DMA controller is disabled, the interrupt flags are
                cleared.
     */
    void DMA1_Stream6_IRQHandler(void)
    {
        if (DMA1->HISR & 0x000C0000)      /* if an error occurred */
            while(1) {}                    /* substitute this by error handling */
        DMA1->HIFCR = 0x003F0000;         /* clear all interrupt flags of Stream 6 */
        DMA1_Stream6->CR &= ~0x10;        /* disable DMA1 Stream 6 TCIE */
    }


    /*  USART2 interrupt handler
     *  USART2 transmit complete interrupt is used to set the done flag to signal
     *  the other part of the program that the data transfer is done.
     */
    void USART2_IRQHandler(void)
    {
        USART2->SR &= ~0x0040;            /* clear transmit complete interrupt flag */
        done = 1;                          /* set the done flag */
```

An Example of DMA from ADC Peripheral to Memory

In this example, the ADC is triggered periodically by a timer (TIM2 Ch2). The conversion results are stored in a buffer in the memory by DMA. When the buffer is full, a transfer complete interrupt is generated by the DMA controller to notify the program. Once it is set up, until the interrupt acknowledgment, all these activities are done without the involvement of the CPU.

This is very useful for data acquisition. Typically, the double buffered mode will be used so that while the ADC data is transferred into one buffer, the CPU can be processing the previous data in the other buffer. But for simplicity, we used only a single buffer. When the buffer is full, the TIM2, ADC, and DMA are stopped while the CPU is processing the data and send them out through USART2.

Program 13-2: Acquire data from ADC by DMA

```
/* p13_2.c Acquire data from ADC by DMA
 *
 * The program sets up the timer TIM2 channel 2 to trigger ADC1 to
 * convert the analog input channel 0. The output of the ADC1 is transferred
 * to the buffer in memory by DMA. Once the buffer if full, the DMA is
 * stopped. That data are converted to decimal ASCII numbers and sent
 * to USART2 to be displayed on the console.
 *
 * A global variable, done, is used by the DMA transfer complete interrupt
 * handler to signal the other part of the program that a buffer full of
 * data conversion is done.
 *
 * This program was tested with Keil uVision v5.24a with DFP v2.11.0
 */

#include "stm32f4xx.h"
#include "stdio.h"

#define ADCBUFSIZE 64

void USART2_init (void);      /* Initialize UART pins, Baudrate */
```

```c
void DMA2_init(void);            /* Initialize DMA2 controller */
void DMA2_Stream0_setup(unsigned int src, unsigned int dst, int len); /* set up a DMA
transfer for ADC1 */
void TIM2_init(void);            /* initialize TIM2 */
void ADC1_init(void);            /* setup ADC */

int done = 1;
char adcbuf[ADCBUFSIZE];      /* buffer to receive DMA data transfers from ADC
conversion results */
char uartbuf[ADCBUFSIZE * 5];    /* buffer to hold ASCII numbers for display */

int main(void) {
    int i;
    char* p;

    USART2_init();
    DMA2_init();
    TIM2_init();
    ADC1_init();

    while(1) {
        done = 0;                   /* clear done flag */
        /* start a DMA of ADC data transfer */
        DMA2_Stream0_setup((uint32_t)adcbuf, (uint32_t)&(ADC1->DR), ADCBUFSIZE);
        while (done == 0) {}     /* wait for ADC DMA transfer complete */

        /* convert the ADC data into decimal ASCII numbers for display */
        p = uartbuf;
        for (i = 0; i < ADCBUFSIZE; i++) {
            sprintf(p, "%3d ", adcbuf[i]);
            p += 4;
        }

        /* send the ADC numbers through USART2 to the console terminal */
        for (i = 0; i < p - uartbuf; i++)
        {
            while (!(USART2->SR & 0x40))   {}
            USART2->DR = uartbuf[i];
        }
    }
}

/*  Initialize ADC
    ADC1 is configured to do 8-bit data conversion and triggered by
    the rising edge of timer TIM2 channel 2 output.
 */
void ADC1_init(void) {
    RCC->AHB1ENR |=  1;                 /* enable GPIOA clock */
    GPIOA->MODER |=  3;                 /* PA0 analog */
    RCC->APB2ENR |= 0x0100;            /* enable ADC1 clock */
    ADC1->CR1 = 0x2000000;             /* 8-bit conversion */
    ADC1->CR2 = 0x13000000;            /* exten rising edge, extsel 3 = tim2.2 */
    ADC1->CR2 |= 0x400;                /* enable setting EOC bit after each conversion */
    ADC1->CR2 |= 1;                    /* enable ADC1 */
}

/*  Initialize TIM2
```

```
         Timer TIM2 channel 2 is configured to generate PWM at 1 kHz. The output of
      the timer signal is used to trigger ADC conversion.
   */
void TIM2_init(void) {
     RCC->AHB1ENR |=  2;                  /* enable GPIOB clock */
     GPIOB->MODER |=  0x80;               /* PB3 timer2.2 out */
     GPIOB->AFR[0] |= 0x1000;             /* set pin for timer output mode */
     RCC->APB1ENR |= 1;                   /* enable TIM2 clock */
     TIM2->PSC = 160 - 1;                 /* divided by 160 */
     TIM2->ARR = 100 - 1;                 /* divided by 100, sample at 1 kHz */
     TIM2->CNT = 0;
     TIM2->CCMR1 = 0x6800;                /* pwm1 mode,  preload enable */
     TIM2->CCER = 0x10;                   /* ch2 enable */
     TIM2->CCR2 = 50 - 1;
}


/*  Initialize DMA2 controller
 *  DMA2 controller's clock is enabled and also the DMA interrupt is
 *  enabled in NVIC.
 */
void DMA2_init(void) {
     RCC->AHB1ENR |= 0x00400000;        /* DMA2 controller clock enable */
     DMA2->HIFCR = 0x003F;              /* clear all interrupt flags of Stream 0 */
     NVIC_EnableIRQ(DMA2_Stream0_IRQn);  /* DMA interrupt enable at NVIC */
}


/*  Set up a DMA transfer for ADC
 *  The ADC1 is connected to DMA2 Stream 0. This function sets up the
 *  peripheral register address, memory address, number of transfers,
 *  data size, transfer direction, and DMA interrupts are enabled.
 *  At the end, the DMA controller is enabled, the ADC conversion
 *  complete is used to trigger DMA data transfer, and the timer
 *  used to trigger ADC is enabled.
 */
void DMA2_Stream0_setup(unsigned int src, unsigned int dst, int len) {
     DMA2_Stream0->CR &= ~1;          /* disable DMA2 Stream 0 */
     while (DMA2_Stream0->CR & 1) {} /* wait until DMA2 Stream 0 is disabled */
     DMA2->HIFCR = 0x003F;            /* clear all interrupt flags of Stream 0 */
     DMA2_Stream0->PAR = dst;
     DMA2_Stream0->M0AR = src;
     DMA2_Stream0->NDTR = len;
     DMA2_Stream0->CR = 0x00000000;  /* ADC1_0 on DMA2 Stream0 Channel 0 */
     DMA2_Stream0->CR |= 0x00000400; /* data size byte, mem incr, peripheral-to-mem */
     DMA2_Stream0->CR |= 0x16;       /* enable interrupts DMA_IT_TC | DMA_IT_TE |
DMA_IT_DME */
     DMA2_Stream0->FCR = 0;          /* direct mode, no FIFO */
     DMA2_Stream0->CR |= 1;          /* enable DMA2 Stream 0 */

     ADC1->CR2 |= 0x0100;            /* enable ADC conversion complete DMA data
transfer */
     TIM2->CR1 = 1;                  /* enable timer2 */
}



/*  DMA2 Stream0 interrupt handler
    This function handles the interrupts from DMA2 controller Stream0. The error
interrupts
```

```
    have a placeholder for error handling code. If the interrupt is from DMA data
    transfer complete, the DMA controller is disabled, the interrupt flags are
    cleared, the ADC conversion complete DMA trigger is turned off and the timer
    that triggers ADC conversion is turned off too.
 */
void DMA2_Stream0_IRQHandler(void)
{
    if (DMA2->HISR & 0x000C)        /* if an error occurred */
        while(1) {}                 /* substitute this by error handling */

    DMA2_Stream0->CR = 0;           /* disable DMA2 Stream 0 */
    DMA2->LIFCR = 0x003F;           /* clear DMA2 interrupt flags */
    ADC1->CR2 &= ~0x0100;           /* disable ADC conversion complete DMA */
    TIM2->CR1 &= ~1;                /* disable timer2 */

    done = 1;
}


/*  Initialize UART pins, Baudrate
    The USART2 is configured to send output to pin PA2 at 9600 Baud.
    This is used to display the ADC conversion results on the console terminal.
 */
void USART2_init (void) {
    RCC->AHB1ENR |= 1;              /* enable GPIOA clock */
    RCC->APB1ENR |= 0x20000;        /* enable USART2 clock */

    /* Configure PA2 for USART2_TX */
    GPIOA->AFR[0] &= ~0x0F00;
    GPIOA->AFR[0] |=  0x0700;       /* alt7 for USART2 */
    GPIOA->MODER  &= ~0x0030;
    GPIOA->MODER  |=  0x0020;       /* enable alternate function for PA2 */

    USART2->BRR = 0x0683;           /* 9600 baud @ 16 MHz */
    USART2->CR1 = 0x0008;           /* enable Tx, 8-bit data */
    USART2->CR2 = 0x0000;           /* 1 stop bit */
    USART2->CR3 = 0x0000;           /* no flow control */
    USART2->CR1 |= 0x2000;          /* enable USART2 */
```

Review Questions

1. True or false. STM32F4xx Arm has 2 DMA Controllers.
2. In STM32F4xx Arm, how many streams can we have?
3. True or false. STM32F4xx can do only memory-to memory data transfer using DMA.
4. In STM32F4xx Arm, what is the maximum number of data that can be transferred using DMA?
5. In STM32F4xx Arm, why do we use byte size data when we use DMA to UART2 data transfer?

Answer to Review Questions

Section 13.1: Concept of DMA

1. True
2. True

3. True

Section 13.2: DMA Programming in STM32

1. True
2. 6
3. False
4. 65535
5. Because UART2 can only accept byte size data. Although DMA can transfer/receive 4 bytes at a time

Appendix A: IC Interfacing, System Design, and Failure Analysis

See our website:

https://www.NicerLand.com/

Appendix B: Pin Alternate Function for STM Arm STM32F446RE LQFP64 Package

The following pages show Alternate Pin Functions Table for STM32F446RE chip. Please check the alternate pin function for your device in the STM32F4xx datasheet. Notice that your device might be different from STM32F446RE.

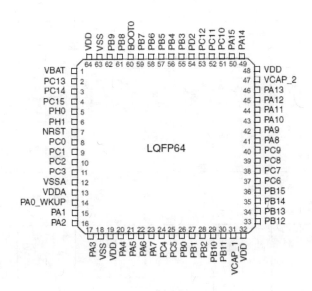

Figure B – 1: STM32F4xx LQFP 64 pinout used in Nucleo-F446RE board

Port A

Port	SYS	TIM1/2	TIM3/4/5	TIM8/9/10/11/CEC	I2C1/2/3/4/CEC	SPI1/2/3/4	SPI2/3/4/SAI1	SPI2/3/USART1/2/3/UART5/SPDIFRX	SAI/USART6/UART4/5/SPDIFRX	CAN1/2/TIM12/13/14/QUADSPI	SAI2/QUADSPI/OTG2_HS/OTG1_FS	OTG1_FS	FMC/SDIO/OTG2_FS	DCMI	-	SYS
	AF0	AF1	AF2	AF3	AF4	AF5	AF6	AF7	AF8	AF9	AF10	AF11	AF12	AF13	AF14	AF15
PA0	-	TIM2_CH1/TIM2_ETR	TIM5_CH1	TIM8_ETR	-	-	-	USART2_CTS	UART4_TX	-	-	-	-	-	-	EVENTOUT
PA1	-	TIM2_CH2	TIM5_CH2	-	-	-	-	USART2_RTS	UART4_RX	QUADSPI_BK1_IO3	SAI2_MCLK_B	-	-	-	-	EVENTOUT
PA2	-	TIM2_CH3	TIM5_CH3	TIM9_CH1	-	-	-	USART2_TX	SAI2_SCK_B	-	-	-	-	-	-	EVENTOUT
PA3	-	TIM2_CH4	TIM5_CH4	TIM9_CH2	-	-	SAI1_FS_A	USART2_RX	-	-	OTG_HS_ULPI_D0	-	-	-	-	EVENTOUT
PA4	-	-	-	-	-	SPI1_NSS/I2S1_WS	SPI3_NSS/I2S3_WS	USART2_CK	-	-	-	-	OTG_HS_SOF	DCMI_HSYNC	-	EVENTOUT
PA5	-	TIM2_CH1/TIM2_ETR	-	TIM8_CH1N	-	SPI1_SCK/I2S1_CK	-	-	-	-	OTG_HS_ULPI_CK	-	-	-	-	EVENTOUT
PA6	-	TIM1_BKIN	TIM3_CH1	TIM8_BKIN	-	SPI1_MISO	I2S2_MCK	-	-	TIM13_CH1	-	-	-	DCMI_PIXCLK	-	EVENTOUT
PA7	-	TIM1_CH1N	TIM3_CH2	TIM8_CH1N	-	SPI1_MOSI/I2S1_SD	-	-	-	TIM14_CH1	-	-	FMC_SDNWE	-	-	EVENTOUT
PA8	MCO1	TIM1_CH1	-	-	I2C3_SCL	-	-	USART1_CK	-	-	OTG_FS_SOF	-	-	-	-	EVENTOUT
PA9	-	TIM1_CH2	-	-	I2C3_SMBA	SPI2_SCK/I2S2_CK	SAI1_SD_B	USART1_TX	-	-	-	-	-	DCMI_D0	-	EVENTOUT
PA10	-	TIM1_CH3	-	-	-	-	-	USART1_RX	-	-	OTG_FS_ID	-	-	DCMI_D1	-	EVENTOUT
PA11	-	TIM1_CH4	-	-	-	-	-	USART1_CTS	-	CAN1_RX	OTG_FS_DM	-	-	-	-	EVENTOUT
PA12	-	TIM1_ETR	-	-	-	-	-	USART1_RTS	SAI2_FS_B	CAN1_TX	OTG_FS_DP	-	-	-	-	EVENTOUT
PA13	JTMS-SWDIO	-	-	-	-	-	-	-	-	-	-	-	-	-	-	EVENTOUT
PA14	JTCK-SWCLK	-	-	-	-	-	-	-	-	-	-	-	-	-	-	EVENTOUT
PA15	JTDI	TIM2_CH1/TIM2_ETR	-	-	HDMI_CEC	SPI1_NSS/I2S1_WS	SPI3_NSS/I2S3_WS	-	UART4_RTS	-	-	-	-	-	-	EVENTOUT

Port	AF0 SYS	AF1 TIM1/2	AF2 TIM3/4/5	AF3 TIM8/9/10/11/CEC	AF4 I2C1/2/3/CEC	AF5 SPI1/2/3/4	AF6 SPI2/3/4/SAI1	AF7 SPI2/3/USART1/2/3/UART4/5/SPDIFRX	AF8 SAI/USART6/UART4/5/SPDIFRX	AF9 CAN1/2/TIM12/13/14/QUADSPI	AF10 SAI2/QUADSPI/OTG2_HS/OTG1_FS	AF11 OTG1_FS	AF12 FMC/SDIO/OTG2_FS	AF13 DCMI	AF14 -	AF15 SYS
PB15	RTC_REFIN	TIM1_CH3N	-	TIM8_CH3N	-	SPI2_MOSI/I2S2_SD	-	-	-	TIM12_CH2	-	-	OTG_HS_DP	-	-	EVENT_OUT
PB14	-	TIM1_CH2N	-	TIM8_CH2N	-	SPI2_MISO	-	USART3_RTS	-	TIM12_CH1	-	-	OTG_HS_DM	-	-	EVENT_OUT
PB13	-	TIM1_CH1N	-	-	-	SPI2_SCK/I2S2_CK	SAI1_SCK_B	USART3_CTS	-	CAN2_TX	OTG_HS_ULPI_D6	-	-	-	-	EVENT_OUT
PB12	-	TIM1_BKIN	-	-	I2C2_SMBA	SPI2_NSS/I2S2_WS	-	USART3_CK	-	CAN2_RX	OTG_HS_ULPI_D5	-	OTG_HS_ID	-	-	EVENT_OUT
PB11	-	TIM2_CH4	-	-	I2C2_SDA	-	-	USART3_RX	-	-	OTG_HS_ULPI_D4	-	-	-	-	EVENT_OUT
PB10	-	TIM2_CH3	-	-	I2C2_SCL	SPI2_SCK/I2S2_CK	SAI1_SCK_A	USART3_TX	-	-	OTG_HS_ULPI_D3	-	-	-	-	EVENT_OUT
PB9	-	-	TIM4_CH4	TIM11_CH1	I2C1_SDA	SPI2_NSS/I2S2_WS	SAI1_FS_B	-	-	CAN1_TX	-	-	SDIO_D5	DCMI_D7	-	EVENT_OUT
PB8	-	-	TIM4_CH3	TIM10_CH1	I2C1_SCL	-	-	-	-	CAN1_RX	-	-	SDIO_D4	DCMI_D6	-	EVENT_OUT
PB7	-	-	TIM4_CH2	-	I2C1_SDA	-	-	USART1_RX	SPDIF_RX0	-	-	-	FMC_NL	DCMI_VSYNC	-	EVENT_OUT
PB6	-	-	TIM4_CH1	HDMI_CEC	I2C1_SCL	-	-	USART1_TX	-	CAN2_TX	QUADSPI_BK1_NCS	-	FMC_SDNE1	DCMI_D5	-	EVENT_OUT
PB5	-	-	TIM3_CH2	-	I2C1_SMBA	SPI1_MOSI/I2S1_SD	SPI3_MOSI/I2S3_SD	-	-	CAN2_RX	OTG_HS_ULPI_D7	-	FMC_SDCKE1	DCMI_D10	-	EVENT_OUT
PB4	NJTRST	-	TIM3_CH1	-	I2C3_SDA	SPI1_MISO	SPI3_MISO	-	-	-	SAI2_SD_A	-	-	-	-	EVENT_OUT
PB3	JTDO/TRACESWO	TIM2_CH2/TIM2_ETR	-	-	I2C2_SDA	SPI1_SCK/I2S1_CK	SPI3_SCK/I2S3_CK	-	-	-	-	-	-	-	-	EVENT_OUT
PB2	-	-	-	-	-	-	-	SPI3_MOSI/I2S3_SD	-	QUADSPI_CLK	-	-	-	-	-	EVENT_OUT
PB1	-	TIM1_CH3N	TIM3_CH4	TIM8_CH3N	-	-	-	-	-	-	OTG_HS_ULPI_D2	-	-	-	-	EVENT_OUT
PB0	-	TIM1_CH2N	TIM3_CH3	TIM8_CH2N	-	-	-	-	-	-	OTG_HS_ULPI_D1	-	-	-	-	EVENT_OUT

Port B

Port	AF0	AF1	AF2	AF3	AF4	AF5	AF6	AF7	AF8	AF9	AF10	AF11	AF12	AF13	AF14	AF15
	SYS	TIM1/2	TIM3/4/5	TIM8/9/10/11/CEC	I2C1/2/3/4/CEC	SPI1/2/3/4	SPI2/3/4/I2S/SAI1	SPI2/3/USART1/2/3/UART4/5/SPDIFRX	SAI/USART6/UART4/5/SPDIFRX	CAN1/2/TIM12/13/14/QUADSPI	SAI2/QUADSPI/OTG2_HS/OTG1_FS	OTG1_FS	FMC/SDIO/OTG2_FS	DCMI	-	SYS
PC0	-	-	-	-	-	-	SAI1_MCLK_B	-	-	-	OTG_HS_ULPI_STP	-	FMC_SDNWE	-	-	EVENT OUT
PC1	-	-	-	-	-	-	SAI1_SD_A	SPI2_MOSI/I2S2_SD	-	-	-	-	-	-	-	EVENT OUT
PC2	-	-	-	-	-	SPI2_MISO	-	-	-	-	OTG_HS_ULPI_DIR	-	FMC_SDNE0	-	-	EVENT OUT
PC3	-	-	-	-	-	SPI2_MOSI/I2S2_SD	-	-	-	-	OTG_HS_ULPI_NXT	-	FMC_SDCKE0	-	-	EVENT OUT
PC4	-	-	-	-	-	I2S1_MCK	-	-	SPDIFRX_IN2	-	-	-	-	-	-	EVENT OUT
PC5	-	-	-	-	-	-	-	USART3_RX	SPDIFRX_IN3	-	-	-	-	-	-	EVENT OUT
PC6	-	-	TIM3_CH1	TIM8_CH1	FMPI2C1_SCL	I2S2_MCK	-	-	USART6_TX	-	-	-	SDIO_D6	DCMI_D0	-	EVENT OUT
PC7	-	-	TIM3_CH2	TIM8_CH2	FMPI2C1_SDA	SPI2_SCK/I2S2_CK	I2S3_MCK	SPDIFRX_IN1	USART6_RX	-	-	-	SDIO_D7	DCMI_D1	-	EVENT OUT
PC8	TRACE D0	-	TIM3_CH3	TIM8_CH3	-	-	-	UART5_RTS	USART6_CK	-	-	-	SDIO_D0	DCMI_D2	-	EVENT OUT
PC9	MCO2	-	TIM3_CH4	TIM8_CH4	I2C3_SDA	I2S_CKIN	-	UART5_CTS	-	QUADSPI_BK1_IO0	-	-	SDIO_D1	DCMI_D3	-	EVENT OUT
PC10	-	-	-	-	-	-	SPI3_SCK/I2S3_CK	USART3_TX	UART4_TX	QUADSPI_BK1_IO1	-	-	SDIO_D2	DCMI_D8	-	EVENT OUT
PC11	-	-	-	-	-	-	SPI3_MISO	USART3_RX	UART4_RX	QUADSPI_BK2_NCS	-	-	SDIO_D3	DCMI_D4	-	EVENT OUT
PC12	-	-	-	-	I2C2_SDA	-	SPI3_MOSI/I2S3_SD	USART3_CK	UART5_TX	-	-	-	SDIO_CK	DCMI_D9	-	EVENT OUT
PC13	-	-	-	-	-	-	-	-	-	-	-	-	-	-	-	EVENT OUT
PC14	-	-	-	-	-	-	-	-	-	-	-	-	-	-	-	EVENT OUT
PC15	-	-	-	-	-	-	-	-	-	-	-	-	-	-	-	EVENT OUT

Port C

Port	AF0	AF1	AF2	AF3	AF4	AF5	AF6	AF7	AF8	AF9	AF10	AF11	AF12	AF13	AF14	AF15
	SYS	TIM1/2	TIM3/4/5	TIM8/9/10/11/CEC	I2C1/2/3/4/CEC	SPI1/2/3/4	SPI2/3/4/SAI1	SPI2/3/USART1/2/3/UART5/SPDIFRX	SAI/USART6/UART4/5/SPDIFRX	CAN1/2 TIM12/13/14/QUADSPI	SAI2/QUADSPI/OTG2_HS/OTG1_FS	OTG1_FS	FMC/SDIO/OTG2_FS	DCMI	-	SYS

Port H		AF0	AF1	AF2	AF3	AF4	AF5	AF6	AF7	AF8	AF9	AF10	AF11	AF12	AF13	AF14	AF15
Port H	PH0	-	-	-	-	-	-	-	-	-	-	-	-	-	-	-	EVENT OUT
	PH1	-	-	-	-	-	-	-	-	-	-	-	-	-	-	-	EVENT OUT

Table B - 1: STM32F446RE Alternative Functions (AF0-AF15) Pin Selection

31	30	29	28	27	26	25	24	23	22	21	20	19	18	17	16
MODER15[1:0]		MODER14[1:0]		MODER13[1:0]		MODER12[1:0]		MODER11[1:0]		MODER10[1:0]		MODER9[1:0]		MODER8[1:0]	
rw	rw	rw	rw	rw	rw	rw	rw	rw	rw	rw	rw	rw	rw	rw	rw

15	14	13	12	11	10	9	8	7	6	5	4	3	2	1	0
MODER7[1:0]		MODER6[1:0]		MODER5[1:0]		MODER4[1:0]		MODER3[1:0]		MODER2[1:0]		MODER1[1:0]		MODER0[1:0]	
rw	rw	rw	rw	rw	rw	rw	rw	rw	rw	rw	rw	rw	rw	rw	rw

Bits 2y:2y+1 **MODERy[1:0]:** Port x configuration bits (y = 0..15)

These bits are written by software to configure the I/O direction mode.

00: Input (reset state)

01: General purpose output mode

10: Alternate function mode

11: Analog mode

Figure B - 2: GPIOx_MODER (GPIO Mode) for Direction Register (x=A, B, C,..)

31	30	29	28	27	26	25	24	23	22	21	20	19	18	17	16
AFRL7[3:0]				AFRL6[3:0]				AFRL5[3:0]				AFRL4[3:0]			
rw	rw	rw	rw	rw	rw	rw	rw	rw	rw	rw	rw	rw	rw	rw	rw

15	14	13	12	11	10	9	8	7	6	5	4	3	2	1	0
AFRL3[3:0]				AFRL2[3:0]				AFRL1[3:0]				AFRL0[3:0]			
rw	rw	rw	rw	rw	rw	rw	rw	rw	rw	rw	rw	rw	rw	rw	rw

Bits 31:0 **AFRLy:** Alternate function selection for port x bit y (y = 0..7)

These bits are written by software to configure alternate function I/Os

AFRLy selection:

0000: AF0   1000: AF8

0001: AF1   1001: AF9

0010: AF2   1010: AF10

0011: AF3   1011: AF11

0100: AF4   1100: AF12

0101: AF5   1101: AF13

0110: AF6   1110: AF14

0111: AF7   1111: AF15

Figure B - 3: GPIOx_AFRL (GPIOx Alternate Function Low) register to select alternate pin functions

31	30	29	28	27	26	25	24	23	22	21	20	19	18	17	16
AFRH15[3:0]				AFRH14[3:0]				AFRH13[3:0]				AFRH12[3:0]			
rw	rw	rw	rw	rw	rw	rw	rw	rw	rw	rw	rw	rw	rw	rw	rw

15	14	13	12	11	10	9	8	7	6	5	4	3	2	1	0
AFRH11[3:0]				AFRH10[3:0]				AFRH9[3:0]				AFRH8[3:0]			
rw	rw	rw	rw	rw	rw	rw	rw	rw	rw	rw	rw	rw	rw	rw	rw

Bits 31:0 **AFRHy:** Alternate function selection for port x bit y (y = 8..15)

These bits are written by software to configure alternate function I/Os

AFRHy selection:

0000: AF0	1000: AF8
0001: AF1	1001: AF9
0010: AF2	1010: AF10
0011: AF3	1011: AF11
0100: AF4	1100: AF12
0101: AF5	1101: AF13
0110: AF6	1110: AF14
0111: AF7	1111: AF15

Figure B - 4: GPIOx_AFRH (GPIOx Alternate Function High) register to select alternate pin functions 269 -8.4.10

Appendix C: STM32F4xx Clock and SYSCLK

Although clock circuits of the devices in the STM32F4xx family are very similar, they all have a different maximal frequency for each clock. In this appendix, all the clock frequencies are based on the STM32F466 devices. Please consult the datasheet and the reference manual for other devices.

There are two possible clock sources for the system clock of a STM32F4xx device. One is an on-chip RC circuit oscillator. The other is from an external crystal oscillator or ceramic resonator. The RC oscillator comes with the device without the need of additional components but it is not very accurate nor stable. In using a crystal oscillator, we can get very accurate clock source but it requires additional component like the crystal or the resonator.

In STM32F4xx Arm, the SYSCLK (system clock) is the clock that runs the CPU and most of the peripherals such as ADC, Timer, USART, and so on. The SYSCLK comes from the internal clock source or the external clock source directly or through the Phase Lock Loop (PLL). They are:

1. HSI (High Speed Internal) RC oscillator clock.

2. HSE (High Speed External) oscillator clock using a crystal value of 4 MHz to 26 MHz.

3. One of the outputs of the PLL circuit.

There are also two low-speed clock sources of LSI (low speed internal) and LSE (low speed external). By external, it means the clock source comes from an external device such as a crystal oscillator or a signal generator. But these two clock sources are used for Real Time Clock and Watch Dog Timer only.

First, we will examine the high-speed clock sources. The low-speed clock sources are reviewed later.

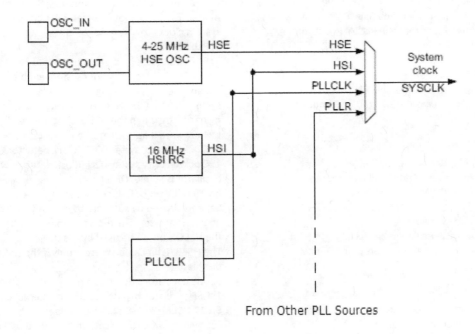

Figure C-1: STM32F466RE Clock Sources

When not in use, these clock sources can be switched off independently to reduce the power consumption.

HSI Clock and SYSCLK

The HSI clock signal is generated from an internal 16 MHz RC oscillator. It can be used directly as a system clock or used as PLL input. The HSI RC oscillator has the advantage of providing a clock source at low cost (no external components required). It has a faster startup time than the HSE oscillator. The HSI frequency is not as accurate or stable as a crystal oscillator or a ceramic resonator. But it has an advantage that when the device is powered up or reset, the HIS is always present and has a known default frequency of 16MHz.

The HIS oscillator can be turned on or off by the HSION bit (bit 0) of the RCC_CR (Reset and Clock Control - Control Register). After turning on the HSI oscillator, it is necessary to wait until HSIRDY bit (bit 1) is set before switching to use HSI.

The HSION and HSIRDY bits are shown in Figure C-2 ().

31	30	29	28	27	26	25	24	23	22	21	20	19	18	17	16
Res	Res	PLLSAI RDY	PLLSAI ON	PLLI2S RDY	PLLI2S ON	PLL RDY	PLL ON	Res	Res	Res	Res	CSS ON	HSE BYP	HSE RDY	HSE ON
		r	rw	r	rw	r	rw					rw	rw	r	rw

15	14	13	12	11	10	9	8	7	6	5	4	3	2	1	0
HSICAL[7:0]								HSITRIM[4:0]					Res	HSI RDY	HSI ON
r	r	r	r	r	r	r	r	rw	rw	rw	rw	rw		r	rw

Bits 31:28 Reserved, must be kept at reset value.

Bit 29 PLLSAIRDY: PLLSAI clock ready flag

Set by hardware to indicate that the PLLSAI is locked.

0: PLLSAI unlocked

1: PLLSAI locked

Bit 28 PLLSAION: PLLSAI enable

Set and cleared by software to enable PLLSAI.

Cleared by hardware when entering Stop or Standby mode.

0: PLLSAI OFF

1: PLLSAI ON

Bit 27 PLLI2SRDY: PLLI2S clock ready flag

Set by hardware to indicate that the PLLI2S is locked.

0: PLLI2S unlocked

1: PLLI2S locked

Bit 26 PLLI2SON: PLLI2S enable

Set and cleared by software to enable PLLI2S.

Cleared by hardware when entering Stop or Standby mode.

0: PLLI2S OFF

1: PLLI2S ON

Bit 25 PLLRDY: Main PLL (PLL) clock ready flag

Set by hardware to indicate that PLL is locked.

0: PLL unlocked

1: PLL locked

Bit 24 PLLON: Main PLL (PLL) enable

Set and cleared by software to enable PLL.

Cleared by hardware when entering Stop or Standby mode. This bit cannot be reset if PLL clock is used as the system clock.

0: PLL OFF

1: Bits 23:20 Reserved, must be kept at reset value.

Bit 19 CSSON: Clock security system enable

Set and cleared by software to enable the clock security system. When CSSON is set, the clock detector is enabled by hardware when the HSE oscillator is ready, and disabled by hardware if an oscillator failure is detected.

0: Clock security system OFF (Clock detector OFF)

1: Clock security system ON (Clock detector ON if HSE oscillator is stable, OFF if not)

Bit 18 HSEBYP: HSE clock bypass

Set and cleared by software to bypass the oscillator with an external clock. The external clock must be enabled with the HSEON bit, to be used by the device.

The HSEBYP bit can be written only if the HSE oscillator is disabled.

0: HSE oscillator not bypassed

1: HSE oscillator bypassed with an external clock

Bit 17 HSERDY: HSE clock ready flag

Set by hardware to indicate that the HSE oscillator is stable. After the HSEON bit is cleared, HSERDY goes low after 6 HSE oscillator clock cycles.

0: HSE oscillator not ready

1: HSE oscillator ready

Bit 16 **HSEON**: HSE clock enable
Set and cleared by software.
Cleared by hardware to stop the HSE oscillator when entering Stop or Standby mode. This bit cannot be reset if the HSE oscillator is used directly or indirectly as the system clock.
0: HSE oscillator OFF
1: HSE oscillator ON
Bits 15:8 HSICAL[7:0]: Internal high-speed clock calibration
These bits are initialized automatically at startup.
Bits 7:3 HSITRIM[4:0]: Internal high-speed clock trimming
These bits provide an additional user-programmable trimming value that is added to the HSICAL[7:0] bits. It can be programmed to adjust to variations in voltage and temperature that influence the frequency of the internal HSI RC.

Bit 2 Reserved, must be kept at reset value.
Bit 1 HSIRDY: Internal high-speed clock ready flag
Set by hardware to indicate that the HSI oscillator is stable. After the HSION bit is cleared,
HSIRDY goes low after 6 HSI clock cycles.
0: HSI oscillator not ready
1: HSI oscillator ready
Bit 0 HSION: Internal high-speed clock enable
Set and cleared by software.
Set by hardware to force the HSI oscillator ON when leaving the Stop or Standby mode or in case of a failure of the HSE oscillator used directly or indirectly as the system clock. This bit cannot be cleared if the HSI is used directly or indirectly as the system clock.
0: HSI oscillator OFF
1: HSI oscillator ON PLL ON

Figure C-2: RCC_CR (RCC Control Register) for Enabling Clock Sources

From Figure C-2, you see the reset value is 0x83. The lower 2 bits are 11 (HSION=1, HSIRDY=1) meaning the RC 16MHz HSI is the source of the clock for the system upon Power-on Reset. The HSIRDY bit indicates that the HSI oscillator is stable and ready to be used. We can switch the default clock source of HSI to External clock source of HSE or PLL, as we will see later.

SYSCLK and Peripheral Clocks

The CPU and peripheral bus clocks are derived from the System Clock (SYSCLK). Figure C-3 shows several prescalers to configure the AHB clock, the high-speed APB (APB2) and the low-speed APB (APB1) domains. Each peripheral clock can be enabled independently. Notice from Figures C-3, the SYSCLK goes first through the AHB prescaler. The lowest value for the AHB prescaler can divide by is 1 and the highest is 512. The HPRE bits (bit 7 – bit 4) of RCC_CFGR register dictate the AHB prescaler value. The output of the AHB prescaler is the HCLK that goes to the CPU core, memory, and the DMA. In an STM32F466, the highest frequency HCLK will run is 180 MHz.

The APB1 peripheral clock is the HCLK divided by the APB1 Prescaler. The APB1 Prescaler is determined by the PPRE1 bits (bit 12 – bit 10) of RCC_CFGR. It can divide the HCLK by 1, 2, 4, 8, or 16. The highest frequency the APB1 peripherals will run is 45 MHz but the timers on APB1 bus runs at twice the frequency of other APB1 peripherals and has the highest frequency of 90 MHz.

The APB2 peripheral clock is the HCLK divided by the APB2 Prescaler. The APB2 Prescaler is determined by the PPRE2 bits (bit 15 – bit 13) of RCC_CFGR. It can divide the HCLK by 1, 2, 4, 8, or 16. The highest frequency the APB2 peripherals will run is 90 MHz but the timers on APB2 bus runs at twice the frequency of other APB2 peripherals and has the highest frequency of 180 MHz.

The default values after power-on reset for all these prescaler is no division.

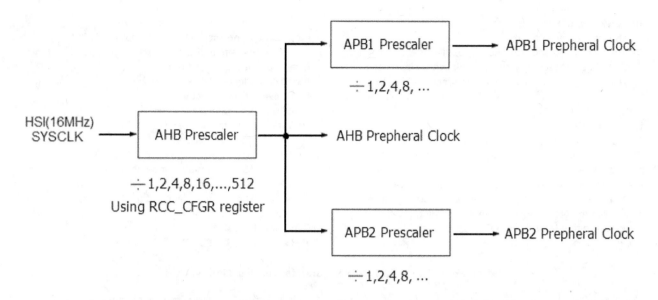

Figure C-3: Clock Generation for peripherals to CPU and peripherals

31	30	29	28	27	26	25	24	23	22	21	20	19	18	17	16
MCO2[1:0]		MCO2 PRE[2:0]			MCO1 PRE[2:0]			Res	MCO1		RTCPRE[4:0]				
rw		rw	rw	rw	rw	rw	rw		rw		rw	rw	rw	rw	rw

15	14	13	12	11	10	9	8	7	6	5	4	3	2	1	0
PPRE2[2:0]			PPRE1[2:0]			Res	Res		HPRE[3:0]			SWS[1:0]		SW[1:0]	
rw	rw	rw	rw	rw	rw			rw	rw	rw	rw	r	r	rw	rw

Bits 31:30 **MCO2[1:0]:** Microcontroller clock output 2
Set and cleared by software. Clock source selection may
generate glitches on MCO2. It is highly recommended to
configure these bits only after reset before enabling the
external oscillators and the PLLs.
00: System clock (SYSCLK) selected
01: PLLI2S clock selected
10: HSE oscillator clock selected
11: PLL clock selected
Bits 27:29 **MCO2PRE:** MCO2 prescaler
Set and cleared by software to configure the prescaler of
the MCO2. Modification of this prescaler may generate
glitches on MCO2. It is highly recommended to change this
prescaler only after reset before enabling the external
oscillators and the PLLs.
0xx: no division
100: division by 2
101: division by 3
110: division by 4
111: division by 5
Bits 24:26 **MCO1PRE:** MCO1 prescaler
Set and cleared by software to configure the prescaler of
the MCO1. Modification of this prescaler may generate
glitches on MCO1. It is highly recommended to change this
prescaler only after reset before enabling the external
oscillators and the PLL.
0xx: no division
100: division by 2
101: division by 3
110: division by 4

111: division by 5
Bit 23 Reserved, must be kept at reset value.
Bits 22:21 **MCO1:** Microcontroller clock output 1
Set and cleared by software. Clock source selection may
generate glitches on MCO1. It is highly recommended to
configure these bits only after reset before enabling the
external oscillators and PLL.
00: HSI clock selected
01: LSE oscillator selected
10: HSE oscillator clock selected
11: PLL clock selected

Bits 20:16 **RTCPRE:** HSE division factor for RTC clock
Set and cleared by software to divide the HSE clock input
clock to generate a 1 MHz clock for RTC.
Caution: The software has to set these bits correctly to
ensure that the clock supplied to the
RTC is 1 MHz. These bits must be configured if needed
before selecting the RTC clock source.
00000: no clock
00001: no clock
00010: HSE/2
00011: HSE/3
00100: HSE/4
...
11110: HSE/30
11111: HSE/31
Bits 15:13 **PPRE2:** APB high-speed prescaler (APB2)

Set and cleared by software to control APB high-speed clock division factor.

Caution: The software has to set these bits correctly not to exceed 90 MHz on this domain.

The clocks are divided with the new prescaler factor from 1 to 16 AHB cycles after PPRE2 write.

0xx: AHB clock not divided
100: AHB clock divided by 2
101: AHB clock divided by 4
110: AHB clock divided by 8
111: AHB clock divided by 16

Bits 12:10 **PPRE1:** APB Low speed prescaler (APB1)

Set and cleared by software to control APB low-speed clock division factor.

Caution: The software has to set these bits correctly not to exceed 45 MHz on this domain.

The clocks are divided with the new prescaler factor from 1 to 16 AHB cycles after PPRE1 write.

0xx: AHB clock not divided
100: AHB clock divided by 2
101: AHB clock divided by 4
110: AHB clock divided by 8
111: AHB clock divided by 16

Bits 9:8 Reserved, must be kept at reset value.

Bits 7:4 **HPRE:** AHB prescaler

Set and cleared by software to control AHB clock division factor.

Caution: The clocks are divided with the new prescaler factor from 1 to 16 AHB cycles after HPRE write.

Caution: The AHB clock frequency must be at least 25 MHz when the Ethernet is used.

0xxx: system clock not divided
1000: system clock divided by 2
1001: system clock divided by 4
1010: system clock divided by 8
1011: system clock divided by 16
1100: system clock divided by 64
1101: system clock divided by 128
1110: system clock divided by 256
1111: system clock divided by 512

Bits 3:2 **SWS[1:0]:** System clock switch status

Set and cleared by hardware to indicate which clock source is used as the system clock.

00: HSI oscillator used as the system clock
01: HSE oscillator used as the system clock
10: PLL used as the system clock
11: PLL_R used as the system clock

Bits 1:0 **SW[1:0]:** System clock switch

Set and cleared by software to select the system clock source.

Set by hardware to force the HSI selection when leaving the Stop or Standby mode or in case of failure of the HSE oscillator used directly or indirectly as the system clock.

00: HSI oscillator selected as system clock
01: HSE oscillator selected as system clock
10: PLL_P selected as system clock
11: PLL_R selected as system clock

Figure C-4: RCC_CFGR (Clock Configuration Register) Clock Select Register bit assignment

From Figure C-4, notice the lower 2 bits (SW) bit of the RCC clock configuration register (RCC_CFGR) can be used to switch the default clock source of HSI to External clock source of HSE or PLL.

HSE Clock and SYSCLK

In STM32F4xx Arm, the high-speed external clock signal (HSE) can be generated from two possible clock sources. They are:

1) HSE external active clock and

2) HSE external crystal/ceramic resonator.

When an external active clock is used, it is connected to the OSC_in pin and the OSC_out pin is left open. The HSEBYP and HSEON bits in RCC_CR (RCC clock control register) should be set. This way, the external clock becomes the HSE clock. In this mode, the HSE accepts external clock ranging from 1 MHz to 50 MHz.

When a passive crystal oscillator or a ceramic resonator is used, the HSE circuit can become an oscillator based on the external device. The external device is connected to the OSC_in and OSC_out pins. The HSEON bit in the RCC_CR should be set and the HSEBYP bit should be cleared. The HSE oscillator takes some time to start up and become stable. This is indicated by the HSERDY (HSE clock ready flag) bit in the RCC_CR. The software must wait until HSERDY is set before using HSE clock source. The HSE oscillator can support a frequency range of 4MHz to 26MHz.

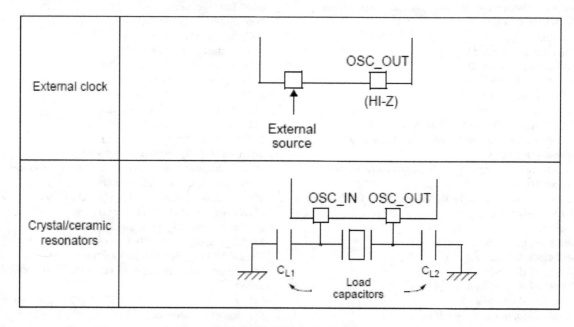

Figure C-5: HSE clock sources

A major advantage of HSE over the HSI is the fact that we can produce a very accurate clock rate for the SYSCLK clock and peripheral clocks. In some applications such as USB, the serial communication clock needs to be more accurate than what HSI can supply. The other advantage is it can go beyond 16MHz of HSI.

On the Nucleo-446RE board, the STLINK processor uses an external 8 MHz crystal oscillator for the HSE clock source. It produces the MCO (Microcontroller Clock Out, will be discussed later) that feeds into the target MCU as an external active clock on HSE. In this design, it only needs one crystal oscillator for two processors.

PLL Clock and SYSCLK

The Phase Lock Loop (PLL) is a circuit that may generate a wide range of frequency based on a single input frequency. The STM32F4xx device has a PLL circuit that may be used for the generation of the SYSCLK. This PLL circuit takes an input signal from either HSI or HSE. It has four dividers/multiplier M, N, P, and R that are pertaining to the SYSCLK. The values of M, N, P, and R are set in the RCC_PLLCFGR register. The SYSCLK takes one of the two outputs PLLCLK and PLLR from the PLL circuit.

For PLLCLK, the output frequency is the input frequency divided by M, multiplied by N then divided by P. M has the range of 2 to 63. N has the range of 50 to 432. P has the range of 2 to 8. Together they can produce large choices of SYSCLK frequencies.

For example, as on the Nucleo-446RE board, the external 8 MHz clock can be used as the HSE with bypass set. One combination of the PLL settings is M = 4, N = 180, and P = 2. This produces

$$8\ MHz\ /\ 4\ \times\ 180\ /\ 2\ =\ 180\ MHz$$

as the output PLLCLK. There are other combinations that may produce the same output frequency mathematically but not all the combinations are operable with the PLL circuit. The MCO is a valuable tool to verify the PLLCLK frequency and we will discuss that later.

The PLLR output is similar to PLLCLK except it uses M, N, and R to determine the frequency.

Like HSI and HSE, the PLL output takes time to become stable after it is enabled. The software must wait for the PLLRDY bit to become set before switching to use PLLCLK.

Although with PLL the SYSCLK may go as high as 180 MHz, the on-chip flash memory will not keep up with it without inserting wait states in flash access at higher clock rate. Wait states are inserted by configuring the FLASH_ACR register. The number of wait states needed depends on the SYSCLK rate and the voltage the device is running. The value can be found in the device's reference manual. It does not improve the performance of the device if the high clock rate CPU is waiting for the flash access all the time. So the caches and prefetch should be enabled when wait states are inserted. They can be accomplished at the FLASH_ACR register also.

LSI and LSE Clocks

In STM32F4xx Arm, we also have LSI (low speed internal) and LSE (low speed external) clock sources in addition to HSI, HSE and PLL.

The LSI is an RC-based low-power clock source with a clock frequency of around 32 kHz. This allows the system to keep running in Stop and Standby mode to save power without losing any information.

The LSE clock is intended to generate a clock from a 32.768 kHz external crystal or ceramic resonator. It is used to provide a low-power but highly accurate clock source to the real-time clock peripheral (RTC) for clock/calendar or other timing functions.

 It must be noted that there are separate pins for connection of crystal oscillator to generate the LSE frequency. They are called OSC32_in and OSC32_out. On the Nucleo-446RE board, the OSC32_in and OSC32_out pins are connected to a crystal oscillator of 32.768 KHz. To explore the LSI and LSE options further, see STM32F4xx reference manual and user manual of your board.

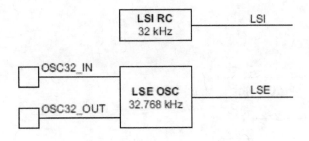

Figure C-6: LSI and LSE clock sources

Clocks Output Pins

The STM32F4xx gives us the option of connecting some of the clock signals of the clock circuit to one of the two pins. This is called Microcontroller Clock Output (MCO). There are two microcontroller clock output (MCO) pins, MCO1 and MCO2.

MCO1 (microcontroller clock output 1)

We can select one of the four clock signals for the MCO1 pin (PA8) with following options:

- HSI clock
- LSE clock
- HSE clock
- PLLCLK clock

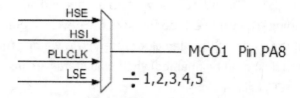

Figure C-7: MCO1 Clock Output Pin

The desired clock source is selected using the MCO1 (Microcontroller clock output 1) bits in the RCC clock configuration register (RCC_CFGR). The MCO1PRE bits of the same register allow prescaler divisions of 1, 2, 3, 4 and 5.

The output pin also needs to be configured for the selected signal to appear on the pin. PA8 must be configured to use Alternate Function 0 using GPIOA_MODER and GPIOA_AFRH registers. Most of the clock selections have very high frequencies. The output pin frequency needs to be set in GPIOA_OSPEEDR to match the clock frequency.

MCO2 (microcontroller clock output 2)

We can select one of the four clock signals for the MCO2 pin (PC9) with following options:

- SYSCLK clock
- PLLI2S clock
- HSE clock
- PLL clock

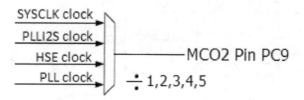

Figure C-8: MCO2 Clock Output Pin

The desired clock source is selected using the MCO2 bits in the RCC clock configuration register (RCC_CFGR). The MCO2PRE bits of the RCC_CFGR register allow prescaler divisions of 1, 2, 3, 4 and 5.

Again, the output pin PC9 needs to be configured to match the signal.

Sample Code for 180 MHz SYSCLK

The following sample program configures the MCU of the Nucleo-446RE to use the 8 MHz clock of the STLINK as the HSE clock source and the PLL output at 180 MHz. The SYSCLK is divided by 5 (36 MHz) and comes out on MCO1 pin (PA8)

```
/* Program to configure SYSCLK to 180 MHz using PLL
 * based on HSE with 8 MHz external clock
 *
 * Pin PA8 is used to monitor SYSCLK / 5 and should be 36 MHz.
 *
 * This program was tested with Keil uVision v5.24a with DFP v2.11.0
 */
#include "stm32f4xx.h"

int main(void) {
    /* set up to monitor clock on MCO1 pin */
    RCC->AHB1ENR |= 1;                  /* enable GPIOA clock */
    RCC->CFGR &= ~0x07E00000;
    RCC->CFGR |=  0x07600000;           /* MCO1 (PA8) = SYSCLK / 5 */
    GPIOA->MODER |= 0x00020000;
    GPIOA->AFR[1] &= ~3;
    GPIOA->OSPEEDR |= 3 << 8 * 2;       /* output high speed */

    RCC->CR &= ~0x000F0000;             /* set HSE_ON */
    RCC->CR |=  0x00010000;
    while(!(RCC->CR & 0x00020000)) {}  /* wait until HSE_RDY */

    RCC->CFGR &= ~0x00000003;    /* use HSI for system clock while configuring PLL */
    RCC->PLLCFGR = 0x00402D04;   /* configure PLL, SRC = HSE, P = 2, N = 180, M = 4 */
    RCC->CR |= 0x01000000;       /* turn on PLL */
    while(!(RCC->CR & 0x02000000)) {}  /* wait until PLL_RDY */

    FLASH->ACR = 0x0705;         /* insert 5 flash wait states and enable caches */
    RCC->CFGR &= ~0x000000F0;    /* AHB prescaler (HPRE) = 0 */
    RCC->CFGR |= 0x00000002;     /* use PLL for system clock */
    while((RCC->CFGR & 0x0C) != 0x08) {} /* wait until PLL ready for system clock */

    while(1) {
    }
}
```

Peripheral Enable Registers

To save power, the SYSCLK clocks to the peripherals are disabled upon power-on Reset. The clock to the peripheral must be enabled before attempting access to the peripheral registers of that module. The next few figures show these registers.

31	30	29	28	27	26	25	24	23	22	21	20	19	18	17	16
Res	OTGHS ULPIEN	OTGHS EN	Res	Res	Res	Res	Res	Res	DMA2 EN	DMA1 EN	Res	Res	BKP SRAMEN	Res	Res
	rw	rw							rw	rw			rw		

15	14	13	12	11	10	9	8	7	6	5	4	3	2	1	0
Res	Res	Res	CRC EN	Res	Res	Res	Res	GPIOH EN	GPIOG EN	GPIOF EN	GPIOE EN	GPIOD EN	GPIOC EN	GPIOB EN	GPIOA EN
			rw					rw	rw	rw	rw	rw	rw	rw	rw

Bit 31 Reserved, must be kept at reset value.
Bit 30 **OTGHSULPIEN:** USB OTG HSULPI clock enable
This bit is set and cleared by software.
0: USB OTG HS ULPI clock disabled
1: USB OTG HS ULPI clock enabled
Bit 29 **OTGHSEN:** USB OTG HS clock enable
This bit is set and cleared by software.
0: USB OTG HS clock disabled
1: USB OTG HS clock enabled
Bits 28:23 Reserved, must be kept at reset value.
Bit 22 **DMA2EN:** DMA2 clock enable
This bit is set and cleared by software.
0: DMA2 clock disabled
1: DMA2 clock enabled
Bit 21 **DMA1EN:** DMA1 clock enable
This bit is set and cleared by software.
0: DMA1 clock disabled
1: DMA1 clock enabled
Bits 20:19 Reserved, must be kept at reset value.
Bit 18 **BKPSRAMEN:** Backup SRAM interface clock enable
This bit is set and cleared by software.
0: Backup SRAM interface clock disabled
1: Backup SRAM interface clock enabled
Bits 17:13 Reserved, must be kept at reset value.
Bit 12 **CRCEN:** CRC clock enable
This bit is set and cleared by software.
0: CRC clock disabled
1: CRC clock enabled
Bits 11:8 Reserved, must be kept at reset value.

Bit 7 **GPIOHEN:** IO port H clock enable
This bit is set and cleared by software.

0: IO port H clock disabled
1: IO port H clock enabled
Bit 6 **GPIOGEN:** IO port G clock enable
This bit is set and cleared by software.
0: IO port G clock disabled
1: IO port G clock enabled
Bit 5 **GPIOFEN:** IO port F clock enable
This bit is set and cleared by software.
0: IO port F clock disabled
1: IO port F clock enabled
Bit 4 **GPIOEEN:** IO port E clock enable
This bit is set and cleared by software.
0: IO port E clock disabled
1: IO port E clock enabled
Bit 3 **GPIODEN:** IO port D clock enable
This bit is set and cleared by software.
0: IO port D clock disabled
1: IO port D clock enabled
Bit 2 **GPIOCEN:** IO port C clock enable
This bit is set and cleared by software.
0: IO port C clock disabled
1: IO port C clock enabled
Bit 1 **GPIOBEN:** IO port B clock enable
This bit is set and cleared by software.
0: IO port B clock disabled
1: IO port B clock enabled
Bit 0 **GPIOAEN:** IO port A clock enable
This bit is set and cleared by software.
0: IO port A clock disabled
1: IO port A clock enabled

Fig C-9: RCC AHB1 peripheral clock enable register

31	30	29	28	27	26	25	24	23	22	21	20	19	18	17	16
Res	Res	DAC EN	PWR EN	CEC EN	CAN2 EN	CAN1 EN	FMPI2C1 EN	I2C3 EN	I2C2 EN	I2C1 EN	UART5 EN	UART4 EN	USART3 EN	USART2 EN	SPDIFRX EN
		rw	rw	rw	rw	rw	rw	rw	rw	rw	rw	rw	rw	rw	rw

15	14	13	12	11	10	9	8	7	6	5	4	3	2	1	0
SPI3 EN	SPI2 EN	Res	Res	WWDG EN	Res	Res	TIM14 EN	TIM13 EN	TIM12 EN	TIM7 EN	TIM6 EN	TIM5 EN	TIM4 EN	TIM3 EN	TIM2 EN
rw	rw			rw			rw	rw	rw	rw	rw	rw	rw	rw	rw

Bits 31:30 Reserved, must be kept at reset value.
Bit 29 **DACEN:** DAC interface clock enable
This bit is set and cleared by software.

0: DAC interface clock disabled
1: DAC interface clock enable
Bit 28 **PWREN:** Power interface clock enable

This bit is set and cleared by software.
0: Power interface clock disabled
1: Power interface clock enable
Bit 27 **CECEN:** CEC interface clock enable
This bit is set and cleared by software.
0: CEC interface clock disabled
1: CEC interface clock enabled
Bit 26 **CAN2EN:** CAN 2 clock enable
This bit is set and cleared by software.
0: CAN 2 clock disabled
1: CAN 2 clock enabled
Bit 25 **CAN1EN:** CAN 1 clock enable
This bit is set and cleared by software.
0: CAN 1 clock disabled
1: CAN 1 clock enabled
Bit 24 **FMPI2C1EN:** FMPI2C1 clock enable
This bit is set and cleared by software.
0: FMPI2C1 clock disabled
1: FMPI2C1 clock enabled
Bit 23 **I2C3EN:** I2C3 clock enable
This bit is set and cleared by software.
0: I2C3 clock disabled
1: I2C3 clock enabled
Bit 22 **I2C2EN:** I2C2 clock enable
This bit is set and cleared by software.
0: I2C2 clock disabled
1: I2C2 clock enabled
Bit 21 **I2C1EN:** I2C1 clock enable
This bit is set and cleared by software.
0: I2C1 clock disabled
1: I2C1 clock enabled

Bit 20 **UART5EN:** UART5 clock enable
This bit is set and cleared by software.
0: UART5 clock disabled
1: UART5 clock enabled
Bit 19 **UART4EN:** UART4 clock enable
This bit is set and cleared by software.
0: UART4 clock disabled
1: UART4 clock enabled
Bit 18 **USART3EN:** USART3 clock enable
This bit is set and cleared by software.
0: USART3 clock disabled
1: USART3 clock enabled
Bit 17 **USART2EN:** USART2 clock enable
This bit is set and cleared by software.
0: USART2 clock disabled
1: USART2 clock enabled
Bit 16 **SPDIFRXEN:** SPDIF-Rx clock enable
This bit is set and cleared by software.
0: SPDIF-Rx clock disabled
1: SPDIF-Rx clock enabled
Bit 15 **SPI3EN:** SPI3 clock enable

This bit is set and cleared by software.
0: SPI3 clock disabled
1: SPI3 clock enabled
Bit 14 **SPI2EN:** SPI2 clock enable
This bit is set and cleared by software.
0: SPI2 clock disabled
1: SPI2 clock enabled
Bits 13:12 Reserved, must be kept at reset value.
Bit 11 **WWDGEN:** Window watchdog clock enable
This bit is set and cleared by software.
0: Window watchdog clock disabled
1: Window watchdog clock enabled
Bits 10:9 Reserved, must be kept at reset value.
Bit 8 **TIM14EN:** TIM14 clock enable
This bit is set and cleared by software.
0: TIM14 clock disabled
1: TIM14 clock enabled
Bit 7 **TIM13EN:** TIM13 clock enable
This bit is set and cleared by software.
0: TIM13 clock disabled
1: TIM13 clock enabled
Bit 6 **TIM12EN:** TIM12 clock enable
This bit is set and cleared by software.
0: TIM12 clock disabled
1: TIM12 clock enabled

Bit 5 **TIM7EN:** TIM7 clock enable
This bit is set and cleared by software.
0: TIM7 clock disabled
1: TIM7 clock enabled
Bit 4 **TIM6EN:** TIM6 clock enable
This bit is set and cleared by software.
0: TIM6 clock disabled
1: TIM6 clock enabled
Bit 3 **TIM5EN:** TIM5 clock enable
This bit is set and cleared by software.
0: TIM5 clock disabled
1: TIM5 clock enabled
Bit 2 **TIM4EN:** TIM4 clock enable
This bit is set and cleared by software.
0: TIM4 clock disabled
1: TIM4 clock enabled
Bit 1 **TIM3EN:** TIM3 clock enable
This bit is set and cleared by software.
0: TIM3 clock disabled
1: TIM3 clock enabled
Bit 0 **TIM2EN:** TIM2 clock enable
This bit is set and cleared by software.
0: TIM2 clock disabled
1: TIM2 clock enabled

Fig C-10: RCC APB1 peripheral clock enable register

31	30	29	28	27	26	25	24	23	22	21	20	19	18	17	16
Res.	Res.	Res.	Res.	Res.	Res.	Res.	Res.	SAI2 EN	SAI1 EN	Res.	Res.	Res.	TIM11 EN	TIM10 EN	TIM9 EN
								rw	rw				rw	rw	rw

15	14	13	12	11	10	9	8	7	6	5	4	3	2	1	0
Res.	SYSCFG EN	SPI4 EN	SPI1 EN	SDIO EN	ADC3 EN	ADC2 EN	ADC1 EN		Res.	USART6 EN	USART1 EN		Res.	TIM8 EN	TIM1 EN
	rw	rw	rw	rw	rw	rw	rw			rw	rw			rw	rw

Bits 31:24 Reserved, must be kept at reset value.
Bit 23 **SAI2EN:** SAI2 clock enable
This bit is set and cleared by software.
0: SAI2 clock disabled
1: SAI2 clock enabled
Bit 22 **SAI1EN:** SAI1 clock enable
This bit is set and cleared by software.
0: SAI1 clock disabled
1: SAI1 clock enabled
Bits 21:19 Reserved, must be kept at reset value.
Bit 18 **TIM11EN:** TIM11 clock enable
This bit is set and cleared by software.
0: TIM11 clock disabled
1: TIM11 clock enabled
Bit 17 **TIM10EN:** TIM10 clock enable
This bit is set and cleared by software.
0: TIM10 clock disabled
1: TIM10 clock enabled
Bit 16 **TIM9EN:** TIM9 clock enable
This bit is set and cleared by software.
0: TIM9 clock disabled
1 Bit 15 Reserved, must be kept at reset value.
Bit 14 **SYSCFGEN:** System configuration controller clock enable
This bit is set and cleared by software.
0: System configuration controller clock disabled
1: System configuration controller clock enabled
Bit 13 **SPI4EN:** SPI4 clock enable
This bit is set and cleared by software.
0: SPI4 clock disabled
1: SPI4 clock enabled
Bit 12 **SPI1EN:** SPI1 clock enable
This bit is set and cleared by software.
0: SPI1 clock disabled
1: SPI1 clock enabled

Bit 11 **SDIOEN:** SDIO clock enable
This bit is set and cleared by software.
0: SDIO module clock disabled
1: SDIO module clock enabled
Bit 10 **ADC3EN:** ADC3 clock enable
This bit is set and cleared by software.
0: ADC3 clock disabled
1: Bit 9 **ADC2EN:** ADC2 clock enable
This bit is set and cleared by software.
0: ADC2 clock disabled
1: ADC2 clock disabled
Bit 8 **ADC1EN:** ADC1 clock enable
This bit is set and cleared by software.
0: ADC1 clock disabled
1: ADC1 clock disabled
Bits 7:6 Reserved, must be kept at reset value.
Bit 5 **USART6EN:** USART6 clock enable
This bit is set and cleared by software.
0: USART6 clock disabled
1: USART6 clock enabled
Bit 4 **USART1EN:** USART1 clock enable
This bit is set and cleared by software.
0: USART1 clock disabled
1: USART1 clock enabled
Bits 3:2 Reserved, must be kept at reset value.
Bit 1 **TIM8EN:** TIM8 clock enable
This bit is set and cleared by software.
0: TIM8 clock disabled
1: TIM8 clock enabled
Bit 0 **TIM1EN:** TIM1 clock enable
This bit is set and cleared by software.
0: TIM1 clock disabled
1: TIM1 clock enabled ADC3 clock disabled: TIM9 clock enabled

Fig C-11: RCC APB2 peripheral clock enable register

www.ingramcontent.com/pod-product-compliance
Lightning Source LLC
LaVergne TN
LVHW060134070326
832902LV00018B/2791